# AN INTIMATE WAR

MIKE MARTIN

# An Intimate War

*An Oral History of the*
*Helmand Conflict, 1978–2012*

HURST & COMPANY, LONDON

First published in the United Kingdom in 2014 by
C. Hurst & Co. (Publishers) Ltd.,
41 Great Russell Street, London, WC1B 3PL
© Mike Martin, 2014
All rights reserved.

A Cataloguing-in-Publication data record for this book
is available from the British Library.

ISBN: 9781849043366 (hardback)

www.hurstpublishers.com

This book is printed using paper from registered sustainable
and managed sources.

*For Chloe*

# CONTENTS

# CONTENTS

CONTENTS

# LIST OF FIGURES AND MAPS

## Figures

## Maps

# LIST OF FIGURES AND MAPS

# PREFACE

## AN INTRODUCTION TO HELMAND PROVINCE, AFGHANISTAN

Helmand is the largest of the Afghan provinces, comprising 9% of the national area. It is situated in the southwest of the country and shares its southern border with the Pakistani province of Baluchistan. The northern tip of Helmand stretches up into the central mountain range of the country, the Hindu Kush. It is a long way from Kabul, both physically and mentally. Ringed by deserts, and with a small strip of cultivated land running north–south along a river of the same name, it suffers extremes of climate with, as the locals say, sixty days of heat and sixty nights of cold (minus twenty degrees to plus fifty degrees centigrade).

Historically, the main town in Helmand has been Gereshk, perched on the main crossing point of the river; it was seen as the last line of defence for the much more important Kandahar, to the east. For this reason the Imperial British campaigned in Helmand during the 1800s. The road from Gereshk to Kandahar is part of a much longer axis between Iran and India, and is the route along which armies have travelled for centuries in attempts to control the region. The importance of Gereshk on that key military and trade route has given the Durrani Pushtun who populate Helmand power beyond that which the remoteness of their region would suggest.

The Helmand River contains 40 per cent of Afghanistan's surface water, but the province has an annual rainfall of less than four inches and only some 3 per cent of the land area is irrigated. Still an agricultural society, water is vital. The modern-day crop of choice is opium poppy: Helmand produces approximately 90 per cent of Afghanistan's opium, and poppy is one of the stated reasons for the British Helmand campaign of 2006–14.

Only fifty years old as a distinct political unit, the province was the scene of the largest engineering project that Afghanistan has ever seen: the Helmand Valley Project. The project brought large amounts of land into agriculture and settled over ten thousand non-indigenous families. Central Helmand, the project's focus and the focus of this book, was transformed beyond all recognition.

# ACKNOWLEDGEMENTS

This book could not have been completed, or even started, without vast amounts of help from a wide variety of people. First and foremost I would like to thank my long-suffering PhD supervisors, Professor Theo Farrell and Dr Alex Alderson, who regularly had to deal with my insistent cries for guidance during my doctoral research, upon which this book is partly based—without them, there would be no book.

*An Intimate War* began as a gut feeling during a meeting on a dusty helicopter pad in Helmand with a travelling academic, Theo. The fact that he took me on as a student that day, on the basis of an unconscious pitch, says a great deal about his vision. However, between that point in 2009 and starting the PhD in 2011 (and beyond), many people have supported me in shaping my ideas and helped me gain funding. Chief among these was Douglas Chalmers. But, listed alphabetically and without ranks, Alex Alderson, Newton Astbury, Richard Iron, Alisdair Johnson, Veronique Malone, Quentin Naylor, Mike Potter, Rich Roberts, Sir Bill Rollo and Kathryn Tomlinson were all exceptionally helpful in their comments and support. I am also grateful to the King's College London War Studies Department and the Royal Historical Society for small grants that enabled me to conduct my research trip to Kabul.

The funding for my research was due to the generosity and vision of Professor Sir Paul Newton: to him and to the British Army (who provided the funding), I am very grateful. At the same time, this book would not have been possible without the support of my Territorial Army regiment, the Royal Yeomanry. More broadly, my debt to the British military, and those contained within it, cannot be overstated. It will become clear to the reader that this book could be misconstrued as an implicit criticism of the military—that is not my intention. The situation in which thousands of British servicemen and women found themselves in southern Afghanistan was complex beyond measure. I wish for this book to be seen as a tribute to that complexity, rather than a kiss-and-tell exposé of incompetence (of which I would, in any case, take a share of the blame). I would be very happy if, in some small way, this book contributed to the debate over the British campaign in Helmand. For these reasons, I am jointly donating any royalties from sales to Combat Stress, a charity that supports British servicepersons' mental health, and the Afghan Appeal Fund, a charity that, among other things, builds schools in Afghanistan.

Once the research had actually begun, it would have been impossible to complete without the support of Alex Alderson, Douglas Chalmers and Patrick Sanders, who enabled me to be in the right places in Helmand and Kabul at the right times and with the right help. Others who were exceptionally kind in helping me explore Helmand include Aly Allum-Smith, Mick Aston, Sippi Azarbaijani-Moghaddam, James Bowder, Charlie Colbeck, Tom Copinger-Symes, John Goss, Jim Haggerty, Jonny Lloyd, Gerry McKay, Simon Puxley, Holly Pawsey, Bruce Radbourne, Tom Ross, Chris Sergeant, Anne Seton-Sykes, Alison Stephenson, Ty Volker and Royce Wiles. There were many, many more not included here for the sake of brevity, but they know who they are. The hundreds of random conversations I have had over the years, musing over Helmandi politics, have all guided me on this journey.

Being asked to read a manuscript such as this can be a deflating request to receive. My great thanks are due to those who offered their time in commenting on versions of the draft, including Mark Beautement, Martin Bayly, Andy Corcoran, Irene Dare, Christian Dennys, Deedee Derkson, Miranda Embleton-Smith, Jo Ensum, Claudio Franco, Antonio Giustozzi, Stuart Gordon, Jim Haggerty, Rob Johnson, David Mansfield, Rich Roberts, Emile Simpson and Ed Thompson. But the largest share of my thanks must go to my father, Peter Martin, who interrupted a very busy retirement to read the entire manuscript, several times. Finally, I would like to thank Sebastian Ballard, for his excellent rendering of my rather crude maps. All mistakes are, of course, mine alone.

However, the biggest debts of gratitude that I have are reserved for the Helmandis, and for Chloe. To the former for sitting, laughing,

## ACKNOWLEDGEMENTS

obsessing, explaining, scheming, hosting, conniving, dealing with and manipulating me over the years. You have taught me more about humanity than a thousand years of study. To the latter for unstintingly supporting me through the last four years, particularly when I have been either physically, or mentally, in Helmand.

# NOTE ON REFERENCING AND ENDNOTES

The 'boxes' that people are placed in are at the heart of this book. The two main types of personal classification that I have used—by tribe and jihadi party—are problematic. To aid future scholars, I have included these details in parentheses after a person's first occurrence in the text. This should be treated with some caution, as many of my interviewees habitually manipulated the labels that they applied to others and to themselves. I accept that in 'fixing' them in this book I am adding more weight to them than I should; however, I decided that the benefits of clarity outweigh the costs inherent in their arbitrariness. For example, if there are three Hamids then often the best way of differentiating between them is to indicate tribe or jihadi affiliation.

With regard to tribe, many in Helmand re-interpret tribal lineage in order to reflect the current political situation. 'Tribe' is both genealogical and political, and this 'untrue' depiction of 'history' is one way in which Helmandis explain the present. People change tribe.[1] In the text 'tribal hierarchy' is shown as tribe/sub-tribe/clan/sub-clan (for example, Barakzai/Nasratzai/Khanzai/Arabzai). Jihadi party is even more problematic. Several individuals depicted here changed jihadi party affiliation multiple times during the jihad, as well as working concurrently for the government. I indicate their contemporaneous party affiliation at that point in the text. I also accept that some government organisations—such as Khad—changed names several times. For simplicity, I have used the main name that Helmandis use for that organisation. Finally, I have gone against the usual practice of italicising foreign names in the text because of their ubiquity, instead reserving italics for emphasis.

**Endnotes:** Due to the variety of different sources used, I employ a shorthand system of interview and secondary source codes, detailed below. For interviewee descriptions see Appendix 1.

| | |
|---|---|
| Three-digit code beginning 0 (e.g. 001) | Anonymous interview of Helmandi notable. |
| Three-digit code beginning 1 (e.g. 101) | Anonymous interview of ISAF officer. |
| Three-digit code beginning 2 (e.g. 201) | Anonymous interview of Taliban commander. |
| Three-letter code or name (e.g. MMW) | On-the-record interview of senior Helmandi or Westerner. |
| Three-digit code with a 'G' (e.g. G102) | Refers to a Helmandi Guantanamo prisoner number. Source documentation and more details given in Appendix 6. |
| PersExp (e.g. PersExp, Bolan, 2008) | Refers to my personal experience. |
| WikiLeaks (e.g. WikiLeaks: '...' (5 June 2009) | From Wikileaks. Followed by cable subject and date. Archive available at http://cablegatesearch.net/ |
| Redacted | An interview conducted by me where I have withdrawn the code to protect the interviewee. |

*Shorthand system of interview and secondary source codes*

I wish to comment on my usage of punctuation. On many occasions in this book the reader will notice that an organisation appears in inverted commas thus: 'government' or 'Taliban'. This is to indicate that, in my analysis, this organisation's ideology is being used by an individual for his own personal reasons. Take the example of a village headman who applies to the government for permission to raise an official militia. He is in the 'government': not in any meaningful sense, and only so that he can defend his village from the 'Taliban' who are, in reality, members of a neighbouring village with whom they are feuding.

Finally, I have made great efforts to be accurate in my referencing; however, it is inevitable that I may have made mistakes. If you feel that you have not been adequately referenced then please let me know and I will endeavour to rectify any problems in future editions.

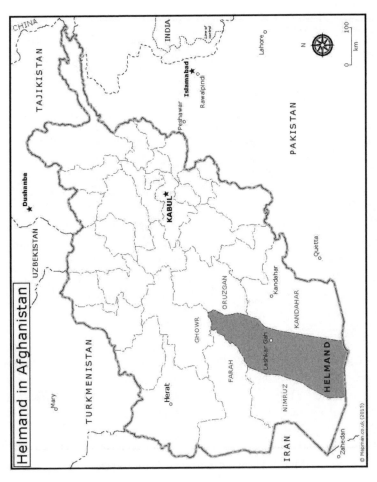

Map 1: Helmand in Afghanistan

Map 2: Helmand indicating district centres

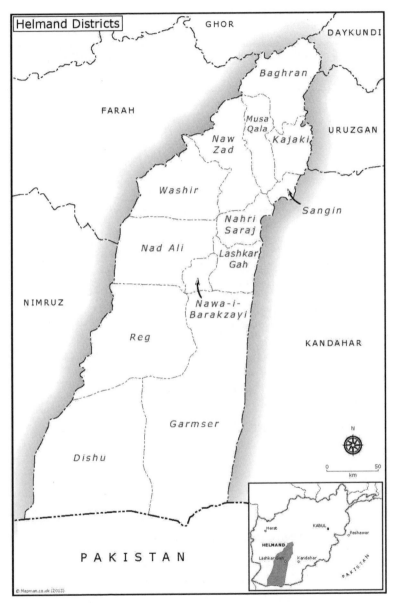

Map 3: Helmand districts

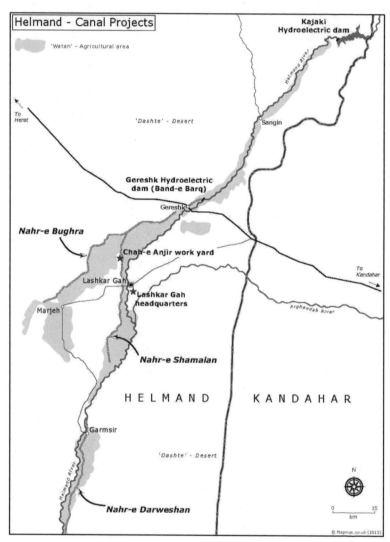

Map 4: Helmand—Canal projects

Map 5: Soviet-era defences

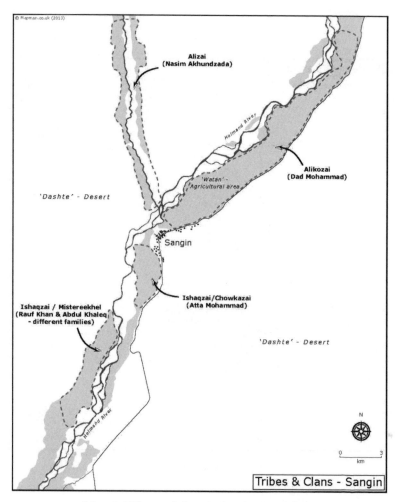

Map 6: Tribes and clans in Sangin (simplified)

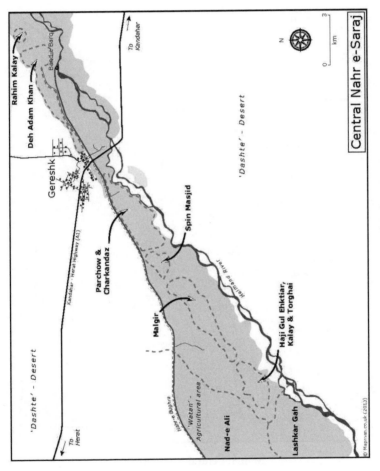

Map 7: Central Nahr-e Saraj

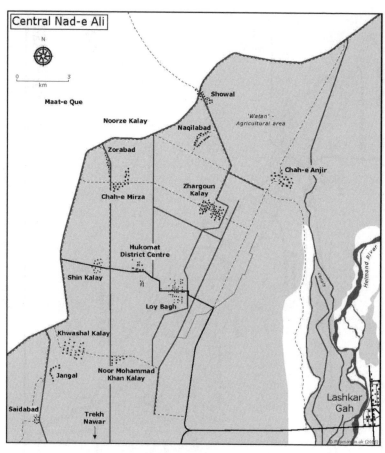

Map 8: Central Nad-e Ali

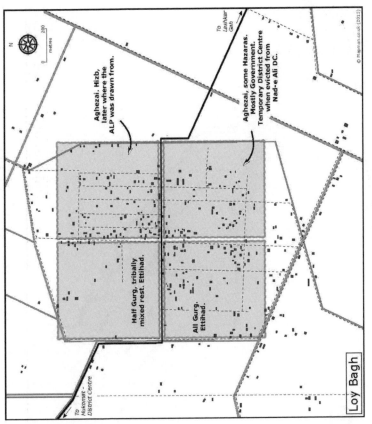

Map 9: Loy Bagh

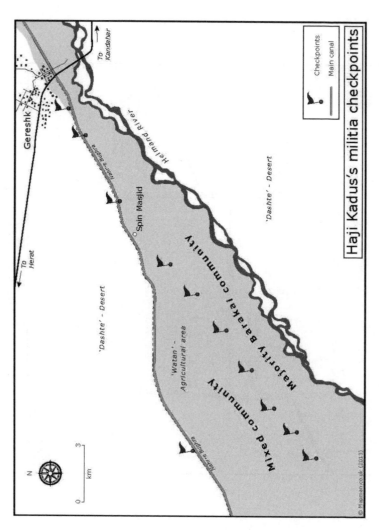

Map 10: Haji Kadus's militia checkpoints

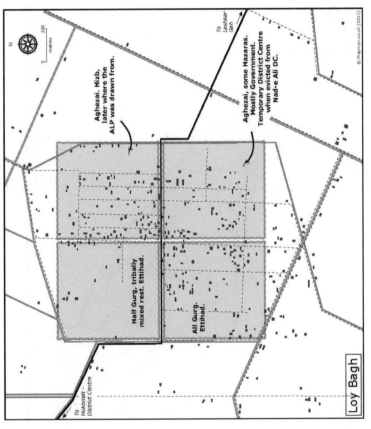

Map 9: Loy Bagh

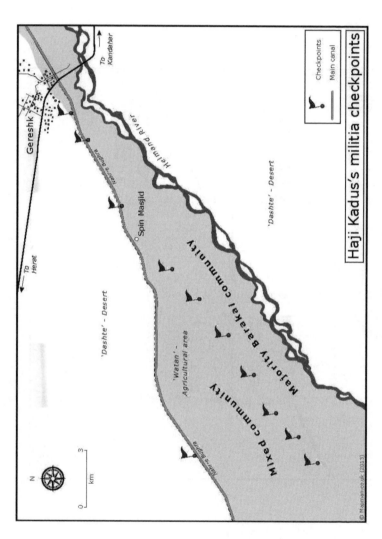

Map 10: Haji Kadus's militia checkpoints

# INTRODUCTION

The supreme, the most far-reaching act of judgement that a statesman and commander have to make is to establish ... the kind of war on which they are embarking, neither mistaking it, nor trying to turn it into, something that is alien to its nature. This is the first of all strategic questions and the most comprehensive.

Carl von Clausewitz[1]

> They place before them the Qur'an
> They read aloud from it
> But of their actions not a one
> Conforms with the Qur'an.

Khushal Khan Khattak[2]

*Nad-e Ali, Helmand, 2008*

'Where are the Taliban, Governor-Sahib?' I asked Habibullah, the recently appointed district governor of Nad-e Ali. He smiled at the innocence of my question and pointed at Shin Kalay, a village about two miles to the west of his battle-scarred district compound. 'They are all Taliban in Shin Kalay', he said, '*all Taliban*'. 'Very interesting, Governor' said the British colonel that I was advising at the time, 'I intend to do something about that tomorrow'.

At 3 a.m. the next morning I was awoken by gunfire. The lead elements of the British battle group, after sneaking their way towards Shin Kalay, had come under fire. The colonel appeared with his sleeping bag over his shoulder. We got into our vehicles and drove towards Shin Kalay.

A few hours later we were sipping tea in the mosque in Shin Kalay. The Taliban had put up a brief fight. The village elders were thanking us for liberating them from the yoke of Taliban oppression. 'They [the Taliban] even pulled our school down with a bulldozer', they said. To the British, this was a gift: a ready-made development project to demonstrate that the Afghan government (read: international money) would build where the Taliban destroyed. It seemed to fit with our narrative and it strongly supported our own self-view. We were liberators; saviours; we were the good guys.

But we did not understand what was going on. Some dynamics became clear fairly quickly. The 'Taliban' in the village were actually a tribal militia raised by the village elders to keep the district 'police' out: the 'police' had been raping village boys and stealing in recent months. It was unfortunate that the British had entered the village with twenty policemen in tow, but to us, we were there to operate in support of the Afghan government. Habibullah, it turned out, was from the same tribe as the police; the villagers from Shin Kalay a different tribe, and locked in a historical conflict with the first. Habibullah had been using *us* to get *his* police back into the village where they could tax the lucrative opium crop. This looked like a 'tribal' feud.

Delving a little deeper, and talking a little longer, it emerged that Habibullah had been to Nad-e Ali before. He had been the chief of police during the communist 1980s. The modern-day elders in Shin Kalay had been the jihadi commanders that he had fought then: in fact, they evicted him (and hence the government) from the district at the beginning of the 1990s. The next central government official to be appointed to Nad-e Ali was the same Habibullah, nearly two decades later. Now it began to look like a 'personal' fight.

What of the school? Once we understood that the Shin Kalay 'Taliban' were actually a self-defence militia, who were the 'Taliban' who had pulled the school down? Much, much later, and only after spending four years building relationships and trust with the elders of Shin Kalay, did I stumble on the truth: jealousy. One of the clans in the village had become so jealous of the prestige that the school had bestowed on another, upon whose land the school was built, that they had invited some 'Punjabis' to Shin Kalay to pull the school down. When the Taliban Quetta Shura (leadership in Pakistan) heard about this event, they sacked the Taliban governor for Nad-e Ali because he had not enforced their (at the time) pro-education policy. How do we define this fight?

The events depicted here are very far from the polarised narrative (that is, Afghan government with international help versus Taliban insurgents) that is often presented to explain the violence in Afghanistan. Suffice to say, the British had a very simplistic understanding of the conflict: an understanding that did not chime with how the Helmandis themselves saw the conflict. This book will explore how the Helmandis understand their own conflict, and how that understanding differs markedly from how outsiders, particularly interveners, have understood and interpreted the same conflict.

*Insurgency*

Insurgency is a pejorative term, one that is useful to governments in establishing their legitimacy or that of their allies and in defining their enemies. This book argues that the current Western[3] view of the Helmandi conflict as an insurgency is completely different from how Helmandis themselves perceive the conflict, and that previous eras of the same conflict have also been mischaracterised both in popular understanding and the scholarly literature. *An Intimate War* seeks to challenge tired Western clichés about this most individualistic of lands.[4]

The Helmandi conflict can be defined according to three periods, each relating to the different external actors involved in Afghanistan. The first period, from 1978 to 1992, encompasses Soviet influence; the second period, from 1992 to 2001, represents increasing and then dominant Pakistani influence; and the third period, from 2001 to the present, has been one of American, and to a much lesser degree European, influence. This book concludes that consecutive mischaracterisation across these three eras have exacerbated the Helmandi conflict: it has allowed the Helmandis to manipulate the foreigners. The first epigraph above demonstrates that this is not new thinking; however, in the context of the conflict in Afghanistan and Helmand, it certainly appears to be.

Many non-Helmandis currently view the violence in Helmand through the narrative adopted by the international community. According to this 'insurgency narrative' widely espoused by Western governments,[5] Western militaries fighting in Afghanistan,[6] Western[7]

3

and Afghan[8] media and a broad variety of scholarly works,[9] there is a legitimate Government of the Islamic Republic of Afghanistan (GIRoA), which is recognised and supported by the international community, but which is violently opposed by a movement of insurgents, called the Taliban, who have sanctuary in Quetta, Pakistan. From this perspective, the Taliban are religiously inspired insurgents who are opposed to the democratic rights and women's rights that the GIRoA embodies and promotes. This is all true and will not be refuted here.

But this 'insurgency narrative' of the Helmandi conflict does not fit with my own experiences in Helmand while serving as a British army officer. I went to Helmand several times (both in and out of uniform), with appropriate gaps between visits for study and reflection, and this analysis of the conflict seemed further from the events that I was observing and participating in each time I returned. As I witnessed the conflict, it appeared to be shaped and driven mainly by Helmandi individuals and their personal motivations. This book was born from my disquiet at that discordance.

In my view, the Taliban are not the main drivers of violent conflict in Helmand; earlier periods, including the Soviet and the civil war/ Taliban era (the Pakistani period described above), have been similarly misconstrued. In the current era, much of the violence in Helmand is mischaracterised as 'Taliban' insurgent violence when in fact it is not linked to the Taliban or the GIRoA, but is driven by dynamics between groups and individuals on the ground. The Helmandis themselves describe the conflict as 'pshe-pshe'. This literally translates as 'leg-leg', but refers to the different legs of a tribe or clan (the English term would be 'branch' [of a tribe]). Thus metaphorically, the phrase 'pshe-pshe' means group-on-group (warfare). This is a civil war.

Over the last four years in Helmand I have seen many foreigners struggle with the portrayal of the conflict as an 'insurgency'. The words 'Taliban' or 'government' would often be caveated by the speaker with 'but of course there are many different types of Taliban' or 'but government officials also smuggle drugs'.[10] This book is about the 'but'. It will show, for example, that the reason the 'policeman' is in the 'government' is to protect his other businesses. 'Government' is a temporary label and implies little presumption of genuine ideological affiliation. In the outsiders' world, however, once caveated, we would continue to use the words and concepts of 'government' and 'Taliban' as units of functional analysis around which strategy could be planned, or ideologies computed. We became victims of our own labels for the phenomena that we were observing because we had retreated to simple constructs that would support us in our attempts to plan, analyse and act. This meant that we often made the conflict worse, rather than better: this was usually as a result of Helmandis manipulating our ignorance. Conversely, during the Taliban era in Helmand (1994–2001; Chapter 3), I argue that detailed knowledge of the local political context enabled the Taliban to exert social control and calm the conflict.

However, this book stops short of asserting that the post-2001 Taliban do not exist. There is a movement, loosely organised around the leadership of the ousted Taliban government, based somewhere in Pakistan. Similarly, this book does not seek to question that there was a Soviet-backed government in Kabul, or several mujahidin parties based in Peshawar. But the fact that the Helmandi conflict has been continuing for thirty-five years—involving the same individuals, family networks and clan disputes (as documented here for the first time)—yet continues to be described as a succession of different conflicts, demonstrates that something is amiss with this commonly held understanding. To me, and I hope to the reader, this conflict is better described as a continuing civil war.

*Pushtun society at war*

Pushtun society can be succinctly described through a trinity of lenses—those of tribal power, state power and religious power (hereafter 'tribe', 'state' and 'mosque').[11] These power centres are represented at all levels of society. For example, within a village three of the most influential people will be the tribal leader (patriarch of a genealogy), the *mullah*, and the *malik* (government representative). Similarly, the tribesmen will ideally have access to three different types of dispute resolution: that of the tribal jirga governed under pushtunwali,[12] that of Islamic sharia or, for serious crimes, civil law, that is institutional justice offered by the state. The three power centres, or lenses, exist in equilibrium and exert different, and often competing, pulls on the individual tribesman.[13]

This equilibrium is an ideal. Scholars consistently emphasise that Afghanistan is experiencing great change, and the balance between the three power centres has been upset. This was commented on in 1970 by Leon Poullada,[14] as well as in the most recent era by Thomas

Barfield,[15] and the idea of flux is repeatedly mentioned in the literature (see the British sources discussing the tribal rebellion of the Alizai in Helmand in 1923[16] or the much better documented overthrow of Amanullah in 1929).[17] This appears to be a paradox: great change, yet a tripartite ideal dividing power that has had remarkable steadfastness over the years. The reality is one of constant flux: when scholars look at any particular era in detail they often observe and comment upon the struggle between tribe, state and mosque, yet, on a less detailed, chronological scale, one can see the movements in Pashtun society, either towards or away from, but always around, this balance.

Louis Dupree, when talking about the balance between tribe and state, described a process of fusion and fission as tribes (or other gene-alogical units) broke up or aggregated depending upon each one's particular military or political position within the society.[18] This context could be intrinsic to Pushtun society, perhaps driven by competition between lineages, or even cousins. Cousin warfare is exceptionally common among the Pushtun, so much so that the word for enmity is 'cousiness' (turborwali). This is mainly caused by a lack of primogeniture in Pushtun society such that patriarchal first cousins violently contest their grandfather's land inheritance.[19] Thus, the importance of land in Pushtun society cannot be overstated. Alternatively, the military context driving this fusion and fission could be external, caused by, perhaps, the invasion of a foreign enemy. At this, authors have commented that the 'tribes' are said to unite in the face of the outsider.[20] But there is a subtler process going on as well, one that is not often described: those internal fissures in Pashtun society are exacerbated by the presence of outsiders because the internal factions jockey for support from the outsiders in order to help them prosecute their local conflict, say, a land dispute with another clan.[21]

These are the processes of fusion and fission. External intervention exacerbates both of them. Tribes will unite, often under religious leadership, to fight wars and battles against an external enemy, but at the same time, some Pashtun factions will be nearer to the outsider than others, causing further disunity. These centrifugal and centripetal processes are often depicted in the same source,[22] making it difficult to define trends: the key difficulty is identifying whether a Pashtun leader (and the group that he currently leads) will react to an external intervener by aggregating with other Pashtun leaders (their differences temporarily buried) or by aggregating with the outsiders (to bring pressure to bear on his enemies within Pashtun society). I struggled with this problem repeatedly when serving in Helmand as a British officer. The balance between the two forces rests on the individual leader's personal history and his relationship with the wider societal context in which he lives, from village to nation state. And of course, that wider societal context changes as other Pashtun leaders make their own calculations and choices. These processes, and the difficulties of outsiders determining their true course, are writ large in this book.

The question arises of whether these power centres and processes can amalgamate in a long-term process of state building (here I am using the term 'state' in the sense of 'nation state' rather than 'government'). This has occurred in other countries through various means. England, for example, was detribalised over a millennium ago, and united church and state during the time of Henry VIII. The English monarch is still the 'Defender of the Faith'. In Afghanistan, there have been periods where a similar fusion has occurred, for instance, during Zahir Shah's reign in the twentieth century when the Mujaddidi family of religious leaders married into the royal lineage, enhancing stability; although if the two examples are not strictly comparable due to the non-unitary nature of Afghanistan's religious sphere in comparisonto the Church of England.[23]

Afghanistan is currently enduring processes of fusion and fission: tribal, religious and state.[24] This has been occurring since 1978, the starting point for this book, and has been partly caused by the multiple foreign interventions over the period and the resulting conflict(s). The violence is both an outcome of the dynamics and a cause: violence, itself, has a communicative property within the society. To counter this, there have been formal attempts over the last thirty-five years of conflict at 'rebalancing' Afghan and Pushtun society, some more sincere than others. Take, for example, the process of the national Loya Jirgas (big councils), which take place in Kabul every so often. Frequently used by Afghan rulers to legitimise their imposed decisions, the Loya Jirgas of 2002 appeared, at the time, to be the beginning of a period of equilibrium.[25] On a smaller scale, the three periods of Helmandi tribal rapprochement documented for the first time in this book point to a similar process; the most recent of these was in 2012 and is still continuing, the outcome yet undetermined.

Lastly, it is appropriate to discuss the concept of, and the processes surrounding, warlordism. Antonio Giustozzi sees this as part of the

process of state-building. His definition focuses on those military leaders who have risen to warlord status by exerting political power in the
areas that they control by dint of being the most powerful military
leader.[26] This is a very apt definition when one considers some of the
leaders in Helmand. These mini-states fulfil the role of the traditional
state in the tripartite equilibrium mentioned above, yet the leader may
originally have been a religious leader or a tribal leader—thus two of
the power centres may overlap. Authors sometimes treat the rise of
warlordism in Afghanistan as a new phenomenon,[27] when actually it is
an age-old process and merely represents the modern description of the
rise of new leaders—often using religious or tribal networks—into
positions of political, quasi-state power.

One example of this is the Alizai, the major tribe in northern
Helmand. There, Akhtur Khan (a religious leader) and Abu Bakr Khan
(a tribal leader), who led the Alizai against the British in the first and
second Anglo-Afghan wars respectively, rose to prominence and led the
Alizai, usurping the 'traditional' tribal leadership.[28] Neither, however,
was subsumed into or co-opted by the state, although arguably, as per
the above definition, they were warlords. And in the modern era Nasim
Akhundzada rose from clerical status to become primus inter pares in
the Alizai leadership in the 1980s.[29] His brothers, who inherited the
dynasty, became the provincial governors of Helmand. It is clear from
our definition that Nasim was a warlord, as were his brothers, even
though they had very different relationships with the state. More confusing is his nephew, Sher Mohammad, who, as shown in this book, is
part of the Afghan state as a senator, yet is simultaneously working
against them with the Taliban (Chapters 5 and 6). Yet, arguably, in
northern Helmand he is still a warlord, as a politico-military leader.
These examples will be explored further throughout the book.

In summary, this brief discussion of Pushtun society has outlined the
tribe, state and mosque tripartite equilibrium and the inherent processes of fusion and fission, much exacerbated by external interventions. The central importance of land has been emphasised and warlordism has been discussed in the context of state building. All of these
elements show us that Pushtun society dynamics (particularly rural
society dynamics, such as Helmand's) are remarkably resilient when
viewed over the long term.

*Research Methods: Interviews*

This book is primarily based on interviews with Helmandi district- and provincial-level leaders conducted in Pushtu in Helmand, Kabul and London Pushtu.[30] Using oral history techniques, this book aims to tell the Helmandi stories of the last thirty-five years. More broadly, this book is based upon nineteen months of participant observation in Helmand, both serving as a British army officer and as a researcher. These primary source materials have been blended with historically restructured secondary sources, that is, secondary sources which have been reappraised through the lens of the primary source material.

The genesis of this research rested on many things, but mostly on my previous military role in Helmand. There, I pioneered and developed the role of the cultural advisor for the British military.[31] This was something of a misnomer: the role of the job was not to advise on 'culture' per se, but to 'form relationships with Helmandi notables, and leverage those relationships for information gathering or influence'. In short, when developing the role I based it on the British political officers during the imperial era. To be clear, I am no apologist for empire; however, there were some elements of British rule that I consider were done well. The political officer, with extensive knowledge of local language and customs as well as deep (often solitary) immersion in the administered society, was one of those things.

Thus my extensive contacts with local Helmandi notables alongside deep knowledge from my previous work and contacts within the British army (to facilitate transport, for example, the logistics of conducting research in a warzone should not be underestimated) are what made this study possible. I recognise that these factors also present limitations to my work, but these were mitigated as far as possible by conducting interviews with Helmandi diasporas in London and Kabul (see below).

It is worth asking why the interviewees wished to speak with me and give me information when it might put them in danger. For many, it was that I had known them for three or four years, and in some cases interacted with them extensively. They knew me, and for many of them it was an interesting request to contribute to research about their home region. *They* were being requested to tell *me*, an outsider, the story of what has happened. Furthermore, interviews were beneficial to both parties. I often spoke as much about the British, ISAF (International

Security Assistance Force) and myself as they did about themselves: it was a trade.

However, there was a darker trade as well. Interviewees were often attempting to use me, either to help gain lucrative ISAF contracts, or perhaps to spread disinformation into the 'Western system'. This linked into my former identity where I worked as an advisor for the senior British commander in Helmand; my interviewees may have felt that I still had residual influence. In this raw environment, what better way to denounce your neighbour than to an unsuspecting academic?

To balance this unavoidable, yet not insubstantial, risk to my data validity, several steps were taken. For each interviewee, a detailed biography was recorded (from them and from others) in order to ascertain their predicted viewpoints on particular issues as they might describe them to a former British army officer, and taking into account what they might want from the interaction. I also recognise that there may have been a self-selection element within my interviewees, that is, they wanted to be interviewed by me to fulfil goals other than helping my research. Wherever possible and except where indicated in the text, events were verified by a minimum of two independent oral sources, preferably three (hence providing triangulation).[32] An iterative design allowed verification of facts and viewpoints in a continuous fashion.

There is an implicit balance to be struck in research of this sort. Prompting interviewees with certain questions may have guided them as to the answers that they thought I wanted to hear, whilst insufficient questions would have reduced their focus on relevant topics. Therefore, there was no predetermined question set beyond asking what happened, who was involved, why it happened and attempting to identify the perceptions and misperceptions surrounding an event, and how those may have fed into the event itself. As an iterative process, the chronology and question set expanded and improved such that some interviewees were re-interviewed as understanding developed. It is very hard to separate collection and analysis when interviewing.[33] Distinctions were made in my analysis between first- and second-hand knowledge as reported by the interviewees, as were reflections made by them about their own group as compared to competing groups.

The sample size was eighty-five anonymous interviews, of which seventy-one were conducted in Helmand, seven among the Helmandi diaspora in London and seven among Helmandis living in Kabul. A further eleven interviews were conducted with NATO officials to frame a small number of events.

INTRODUCTION

For ethical reasons,[34] namely that I was interviewing active partici-
pants in a conflict, the interviewees' identities are withheld and are represented by a three-digit code within the book. In a very few cases I
even had to redact the interview code, because linking the interviewee
description with the comment would make the interviewee's identity
clear. Appendix 1 lists the anonymous interviewee descriptions.
Assigned interviewee descriptions should be seen as a guide rather than
absolute categorisation. Everyone has multiple, overlapping identities,
and in Helmand they are often strongly juxtaposed. I discussed with
each interviewee the descriptions that they would use as their primary
identity within this history: they are included here simply as an aid to
reader understanding.

Interviewees were selected from my network of Helmandi contacts
and from other notables that they were willing to introduce me to.
This 'snowball sampling' was an especially useful technique when trying to study such a hidden and inaccessible population.[35] They were
chosen on the basis of having agency over their environment. The
majority were tribal leaders, jihadi commanders, religious leaders,
landowners, government and security officials or businessmen.

Interviewees were selected to give broad representation across tribal
groups, jihadi parties and positions with respect to the government
(although 'government' is a fluid concept in Helmand).[36] The iterative
snowball sampling allowed adjustment for this. The minimum age was
eighteen, and as the period from 1978 was focused on, many of the
interviewees were aged approximately fifty or over. Some worked
exceptionally closely with the individuals attacking British and Afghan
government forces including, in one case, a gentleman who facilitated
the supply of bomb components and coordinated attacks on British
patrols. These identity markers are withheld from the interview
descriptions in Appendix 1.

Almost all of the interviewees were men, by nature of Helmandi society, and where women were interviewed their sex is not disclosed for
purposes of anonymity. Interviewees were recognised as coming from a
vulnerable population, that is, potentially put at risk from being interviewed by me. However, these notables often communicate with coalition forces and international civilians. There was no element of coer-
cion or payment whatsoever (beyond refreshments). The approach used
was based on the principle of not putting anyone in danger. No interviews were discarded, although some were more useful than others.

The interviews were carried out over two trips to Helmand, one at the end of 2011 and one in the spring of 2012, as well as during a trip to Kabul in the summer of 2012. The diasporic interviews were carried out in London around the time of these visits. This deliberate peripatetic interview scheduling was to facilitate periods of reflection and refocusing between interviewing. Interviews in Helmand were conducted in ISAF or government locations, to enter which interviewees often had to pass some sort of security procedure. For that reason, the Kabul and London interview sets were added as control groups: these were carried out in the interviewees' homes.

Interviews conducted in London had a further distinguishing analytical perspective: in many cases these interviewees had split loyalties—both to Helmand and to Britain—leading to touching confusion over the words *us* and *we*. These aided me very much in separating perspectives. So too, the Kabul interviews: living freely in Kabul and being able to interview people on their own terms greatly helped my holistic understanding. These two different additional interview contexts, having the same target set of Helmandi notables, were deliberately chosen to provide contrasts to the Helmand-conducted interviews. For anonymity I do not say to which context the interviewee belonged. The interviews were all conducted in Pushtu, during which notes were taken; these notes were written up immediately after the interview. Interviews lasted between half-an-hour and five hours.

The interviewees that had not met me before would often begin describing the conflict in very general terms, and at times the social conventions governing conversations among the Pushtun make it difficult to ascertain 'hard facts'.[37] I sometimes found it necessary to inject some specific, localised and neutral knowledge—say, for example, identifying someone's brother in their story—in order to guide them to a greater level of detail. This, combined with a level of directness and honesty that they did not often experience from foreigners (a Pushtu-speaking foreigner is rare enough as it is), meant that a level of frankness usually ensued. I cannot overstate how important my previous in-depth knowledge was: one has to ask the right questions to get the right answers.

Other issues endemic to oral history with ill-educated populations were rife: not knowing their own ages, having idiosyncratic estimates of relative versus actual time, and distinguishing between different types of 'foreigner', for example. All required slight alterations to interview technique. Some interviewees were excellent for chronological structure, some for eyewitness detail, some for reflective perspectives and others for corroboration. This explains why some interviewees appear more than others in the endnotes. There was also a natural disinclination to talk about the Taliban. I was a foreigner, and the foreigners were fighting the Taliban. Readers will notice the Taliban-era section is slimmer on primary research than other periods. This is the reason why the interviews of Taliban commanders, discussed next, are so important.

By kind permission of Theo Farrell and Antonio Giustozzi I was given access to a set of fifty interviews conducted with Taliban commanders in Helmand and fifteen further interviews with Helmandi notables. I had some reservations over the use of these interviews as I had had no control over their commissioning or conduct. However, on balance, the interviews agree in style, tone and substance with my own interviews which, when combined with the rarity of interviews with active Taliban commanders, suggested I should utilise the data. Additionally, they offered a further 'control' group by virtue of being conducted by different interviewers.

Finally, I conducted a small number of on-the-record interviews with key Helmandi and Western personalities, in order to understand their thoughts and actions at the time of important events. Brief biographies of these on-the-record interviewees are included in Appendix 1.

### Caveats and limitations

This book might well be considered a pilot study for future work. I seek to use the Helmandi 'ecosystem' as an example to challenge the narratives surrounding the entire Afghan conflict. This book can only be the first step in such a gargantuan task. Furthermore, the limitations of conducting research in an illiterate society at war stretch academic credibility to the limit. However, at present, there are no other approaches that generate this quantity and quality of data.

What has made this research fascinating and frustrating in equal measure is the fact that at times it has felt like nothing more than catching snippets of rumours passing on the winds of Helmandi gossip. However, in Afghan society rumours are an established currency of political debate, and scholars now deliberately factor them into their analyses.[38] In illiterate societies, information is still mainly spread by word of mouth. This has only been augmented with the introduction of mobile phones, beginning in 2003.[39] Wherever possible, I have tried to explore these rumours and have attempted to corroborate them either with other interviewees or with secondary sources.

Ultimately, while I have striven to assuage any possible charges of orientalism, it is impossible, while engaged in the human sciences, to 'ignore or disclaim [my] involvement' in Helmand.[40] I first went there in 2008 as a British army officer, which is as far as can be from being neutral in the conflict. Furthermore, for many of the events in the 2008–12 section of the analysis I have relied upon my own direct participant-observation, albeit I have later tracked the same events in interviews. In areas where it appears that the British or the Americans have misstepped I, too, must accept my share of the blame: in some instances I was involved in formulating or implementing some of those policies. I was not above the fray, but I have done my utmost to detach myself and remain objective in this analysis. In addition, the benefit of my previous position was that I was able to juxtapose my participant viewpoint with ex post facto research of the same events.

This is not a complete history. It could never be. This is a selection of stories and events that I have been exposed to, and that I argue illuminate the overall dynamics in Helmand. For some events there exists such a multitude of explanations and stories that I have depicted the most significant views of an event and my assessment of how those perceptions have shaped subsequent events. Furthermore, with examples that I describe to be one way or the other, there will always be a counter-example. The analysis that I offer here, while the most nuanced to date, is still simplified by Helmandi standards. One of my closest Helmandi confidants teased me for knowing 'just one per cent' of what went on in Helmand, despite knowing 'a lot'.

This simplification also creates other imperfections in this work, for example there are certain positions that I have taken throughout the book on the balance of evidence. First, the overwhelming Helmandi feeling towards the British, or the Angrez (the Pushtu word for English), is antipathetic, and has been presented here as such.[41] Secondly, I argue it is inconceivable that Pakistan is not currently supporting the Taliban, as part of achieving 'strategic depth' vis-à-vis India.[42] Lastly, I maintain that there is comprehensive evidence demonstrating that Inter-Services Intelligence (ISI: Pakistan's main intelligence agency) is supplying arms, money and advice to the Taliban via the Taliban Quetta Shura.[43] The US has been aware of this since at least February 2005.[44] This is also the overwhelming Helmandi perception, including among Taliban commanders.[45]

## Structure

This chapter has presented an introduction to the Helmandi conflict and to the research that I conducted there. By way of further introduction, the next chapter (Chapter 1) presents a history of Helmand developed entirely from secondary sources covering the pre-1978 period. Readers, particularly those familiar with *A Brief History of Helmand*,[46] may wish to skip this and proceed to Chapter 2, where the oral history begins. Chapters 2 to 6 offer a historical analysis of the conflict from 1978 to 2012. Each of these chapters will begin with a depiction of the better-known, more official narratives of that era's events, against which the remainder of the chapter will be contrasted.

Chapter 2 offers the story of the conflict during the peak of Soviet influence in Helmand, from 1978 to 1989, tracing the narrative from several angles. Chapter 3 covers the period of rising and then dominant Pakistani influence, that is, 1989 to 2001. Chapters 4, 5 and 6 cover the era of dominant Western influence. Chapter 4 discusses the period before the British deployment to Helmand in 2006. Chapter 5 covers the era of British dominance in the province, that is, until mid-2009. Chapter 6 is thematic and discusses aspects of the counterinsurgency practised by British and American forces in Helmand from 2009 to 2012. It is in these three chapters that I present the clearest evidence for the difference between the Helmandi viewpoint and the dominant (Western) narratives about the conflict, and the fact that those differences in understanding allowed the Helmandis to manipulate the outsiders repeatedly. It is also where I am able to contrast my personal participant experiences, living the Western narrative, with the later, in-depth understanding provided by my research. The final chapter offers conclusions.

Thereafter, a glossary of terms, people, tribal diagrams, family trees and lists of Helmandi officials are appended, as well as an analysis of those Helmandis who have spent time in Guantanamo Bay prison camp, Cuba. Readers are advised to keep this to hand, as the history of Helmand is a complex one!

# 1

# PRE-1978 HELMANDI HISTORY

The River Helmand marks the furthest extent of the post-Mohammad Arab-Islamic expansion, with Bost (modern day Lashkar Gah) and Zamindawar (northern Helmand) being captured in 661.[1] This accounts for the modern-day Helmandi Pushtun sub-tribes who self-identify as 'Arabs'. They trace their descent to that invasion, and yet are fully incorporated into the Pushtun tribal structure, which one assumes arose beforehand. This early adoption of Islam has generated an exceptional degree of interwoveness between religion and culture, that is an enduring theme of Pushtun politics and identity. This feeds into the sense of superiority felt by the Pushtun, particularly those who inhabit the southwest of Afghanistan.[2] In Helmand, as elsewhere, it is very hard to separate religion and culture.

Helmand is trapped between Persia and India, but is much closer to Persia geographically and culturally. Thus historically, after Islam, Persia exerts the greatest external influence over Helmand. For example, Bost[3] was the Ghaznavid winter capital for approximately two centuries starting in 976. Their empire stretched from present day Iran to India, and this is the only time in recorded history that Helmand has been important in its own right as a major administrative centre. Originating in Persia, the Ghaznavids began a Persianisation of the area, a theme that was continued by the Ghorid and, later, the Safavid empires. The Ghorids, another Persian empire that ruled during the twelfth and thirteenth centuries, razed Bost in 1150. Rebuilt, Bost was finally destroyed by Genghis Khan in 1220.[4] Helmand then sank into obscurity and little is known about it until the rise of Kandahar and the Durrani and Ghilzai tribal federations, two and a half centuries later.

Kandahar marks the border between the Durrani and Ghilzai tribal federations, who represent two of the largest kinship units within the Pushtun. In 1468, the city declared itself an independent state[5] as it was fast becoming southwestern Afghanistan's politico-economic centre.[6] Prosperity prompted alternate invasions by the Moghul (Indian) and the Safavid (Persian) empires.[7] Although chronologically separated in their control of Kandahar, both empires had to manage the competition between the Durrani and Ghilzai groups, and often played them off against each other. That crucible is where the present-day mutual antipathy between the Durrani and Ghilzai was forged.

The Durrani federation, indigenous to Helmand, make their first recorded appearance as the Abdalis[8] when, in 1587, Saddo was chosen as their leader. His descendants form the Saddozai lineage that produced the monarchy in Afghanistan from 1747–1818 (the suffix 'zai' means 'son of').[9] The Abdalis probably lived in Zamindawar, on the Helmand River and around Kandahar.[10] The Alizai, a major tribe within the Durrani, are first definitively mentioned as a political unit in 1638. They are described as holding the balance of power when they agreed to support the Moghuls against the Safavids,[11] as previously they had attacked the Moghuls in Kandahar in 1556.[12] Balance-of-power politics is something that the Alizai have practiced repeatedly up to the modern era, as this book will detail.

The collapse of the Moghul and Safavid empires gave the Durrani and Ghilzai freedom from external influence. Thus, in 1722, Mirwais (a Hotak Ghilzai: Mullah Omar's[13] tribe) captured Kandahar from the Safavids. Previously the Ghilzai had driven the Durrani from Kandahar to Herat.[14] The Ghilzai triumph was short lived and in 1737 a Persian King, Nadir Shah, having defeated the Durrani in Herat in 1731 and, incorporated them into his army, captured Kandahar from the Ghilzai.[15] For their service, Nadir Shah granted the Durrani the lands they now occupy in modern Helmand and Kandahar, including the return of Ghilzai-occupied Durrani lands.[16] The Ghilzai were exiled to Tehran.[17] Previously the land had been held by a mixed peasant tenure, who then became client farmers of the Durrani khans (landowners), marking the birth of Durrani influence. In an instant, they went from being vassals of Nadir Shah to masters of their own vassals.[18]

The tribes were given land that was commensurate with their size, and with the condition of providing men for military service—'a horseman for every plough'.[19] This meant that, for example, the Alakozai had to give 850 horsemen annually and the Barakzai 907.[20] They were not taxed.[21] This balanced what the tribes received from the state with what they had to give. It was an elegant solution to the problem of independent groups who did not want to be part of a state.

When Nadir Shah was assassinated in 1747, Ahmad Shah Durrani, a Popalzai,[22] was crowned in Kandahar, his capital. At that time Helmand was called Pusht-e rud, which meant trans-river (the Helmand). Pusht-e rud had four districts: Zamindawar, Now Zad, Pusht-e rud and Garmsir. Nadir Shah redistributed his subjects' land, including returning some of the Ghilzai's Kandahar land[23] (see Appendix 4 for a tribal diagram). In this redistribution, the Alizai were re-legitimised in Zamindawar, in northern Helmand. The Noorzai received most of Garmsir as a defence against Baluch encroachment from the south;[24] the Barakzai received central Helmand (known as Pusht-e rud proper) and Now Zad, the fourth ancient district of Pusht-e rud, was split between the Noorzai and Ishaqzai.[25] The Alakozai received the Arghandab Valley in modern-day Kandahar province, although it is not known whether this included Sangin, or if that was only later occupied.[26]

The system was financed by plunder gained during foreign military service. Although Ahmad Shah increased the Durrani tax burden slightly, the Durrani were still largely exempt and he indulged them 'to almost a prodigal extent':[27] tax legislated and tax collected were not synonymous. He saw the Durrani tribes as a key part of his kingdom and, following Nadir Shah, bound them to his state with military service. As the amounts of land and number of horses demanded were appropriate to each other, the amount of plunder that they could physically carry home was also linked to the size of the tribe, its land holdings and the relative power of the groups.

Ahmad Shah's land grants and military service enshrined and enhanced Durrani tribal structures. Today, the Durrani exhibit a much more hierarchical (rutbavi) structure than the more egalitarian (quami) Ghilzai tribes.[28] In the quami system, power is swiftly passed from leader to leader based on personal attributes, but in a rutbavi system, power is less ephemeral than in a quami one, as it is consolidated in bloodlines. The reinforcing factor in this hierarchical kinship relationship is hereditary land ownership and the ensuing feudal client-patron system. Furthermore, the hereditary divisions of the clans and sub-clans exactly reflected the Durrani military groupings, so that kinsman fought alongside kinsman—each leader was in command of the men that he was patriarch of.[29] The importance of the land grants cannot be overestimated. Everything that has happened to land ownership in Helmand since then is seen as an aberration from the status quo that was established at that time.

With Ahmad Shah, the relative importance of the different tribes becomes clearer. Whereas under Nadir Shah positions of leadership had rotated between the different tribes,[30] Ahmad Shah established heredi-tary positions as a way of corresponding their power to their size: a de jure recognition of their de facto power. In this way the Barakzai, as the most powerful tribe, secured the understanding that they would always be ministers to the Popalzai crown,[31] as well as possession of the best land in Helmand, on the alluvial plains of four rivers (the area covered by the present-day areas of Babaji, Malgir and Spin Masjid). As loyal and important servants to the Popalzai,[32] it is not a coincidence that Gereshk, a strategic crossing point on the major fluvial barrier between Herat and Kandahar, is held by the Barakzai.

Ahmad Shah's death in 1772 signalled the zenith of Durrani power that they see as their birth right. Timur Shah,[33] his son, moved the cap-ital to Kabul and ceased the foreign expeditions that had characterised his father's reign.[34] The ensuing lack of plunder meant that Durrani taxes were increased at the very time that the tribes were receiving less. This caused much of the granted land to be traded, mortgaged or aban-doned,[35] weakening the link between land, tribe and state. The tribes also played both ends against the middle—the grantees would claim that the cultivators should be supplying the horsemen for the king and vice versa.[36] The ending of Nadir Shah's elegant solution to tribal insta-bility caused the empire to begin to collapse, a process that gathered momentum under Timur Shah's son, Zaman Shah.[37] This led to succes-sional struggles, which eventually allowed a Barakzai dynasty, led by Dost Mohammad,[38] to usurp the Popalzai throne in 1826.[39]

## The Barakzai, the Alizai and the British: Maiwand

The Barakzai ascension was of key importance for Helmand. The fact that there are relatively few Popalzai in Helmand meant that during the Popalzai monarchy the biggest Helmandi tribes were treated in a manner that was respectful of their perceived status. Suddenly, the king was not just a relative outsider, but was directly related to a Barakzai sub-tribe within Helmand (the Mohammadzai), and more distantly related to the whole of the Barakzai. Moreover, the Gereshk fort was a seat of the dynasty.[40] Relative equality of treatment for the tribes that had existed under the Popalzai dynasty ceased and the power of the Helmandi Barakzai began to increase vis-à-vis that of other tribes. The Alizai-Barakzai dynamic that still dominates Helmandi politics today was born.

To Dost Mohammad, Helmand was comprised of three areas. To the north, the Alizai of Zamindawar: a source of revenue. In the centre, the Barakzai of Gereshk: his distant relatives and a source of stability. And to the south, the Noorzai-led, but mixed and nomadic tribes of Garmsir: largely unimportant, as Garmsir was de facto independent during this time.[41] Accordingly, tax collection was gradually increased on non-Barakzai tribes in Helmand, particularly the Alizai.[42] Cruel Barakzai tax collectors were used; non-payment resulted in punitive expeditions being mounted into Zamindawar and Alizai clan chiefs being executed.[43] This reign of terror was brought to a close by the British intervention of 1839, which was an attempt to limit Russian influence by re-installing the previous Popalzai dynasty under Shah Shuja.

At the time of the British invasion both Kandahar and Gereshk were governed by brothers of Dost. Once Kandahar fell to the British in April, the governors fled to the family home in Gereshk[44] and a British brigade was dispatched in an abortive attempt to capture them.[45] The British occupied the royal fort in Gereshk for eight months before abandoning it due to sickness.[46] Once Shuja had been reinstalled in Kabul, the Durrani tribes attempted to get the old favours and titles that they had previously enjoyed reinstated.[47] Due to their geographical location and proclivity to instability, the Helmandi tribes put the monarch in a difficult position: he needed them to support him, but he also needed revenue from taxation. He reinstated their titles and delayed taxing them for a short period until his position was stronger. However, he kept the previous cruel Barakzai tax collectors in power and they restarted collection in 1840.[48]

The Alizai had come to look upon the Barakzai as their enemy after their viciousness in power.[49] The 'capture' of state legitimacy by a Helmandi group—the Mohammadzai, and more widely the Barakzai—

21

had meant that the influence of the state was exerted through the Barakzai. This upset the Alizai who were the targets of Barakzai predation. Becoming embroiled in the dynamic, the British may easily have been seen as potential friends by the Alizai; they had, after all, ousted the Barakzai. This was quickly overtaken by events that were sparked by the Alizai killing of a Barakzai revenue collector at Sarwan Qala in 1840.

Shortly after, and in the initial move in the Alizai-British relationship, a British force under Captain Farrington was dispatched from Kandahar to enforce collection. This settled any doubt in the Alizai mind about whose side the British were on.[50] It is not known whether the British were aware of the ramifications of the decision made by their Afghan partner Shah Shuja, but it is clear that they did not understand the causes of the ensuing rebellion, reflecting a lack of knowledge of the local dynamics.[51] The echoes are still reverberating in 2014. This was a political blunder leading to an open rebellion led by an Alizai leader called Akhtur Khan. He was able to manipulate the dispute to gain chieftainship of the Alizai. This gave him a pre-eminence that he had not previously possessed.[52]

After some skirmishing, the British sent a force to Zamindawar to talk to Akhtur Khan and secure his submission. They agreed to remove the revenue collection officers in return for the dispersal of his 1,300 followers.[53] This agreement broke down, and by May 1841 Akhtur Khan was at Gereshk with three thousand men. This swelled to an estimated six thousand when the British retook Gereshk at the beginning of June.[54] From there, punitive expeditions were launched from Barakzai territory into Alizai Zamindawar.[55] Eventually, the rebellion defeated, Akhtur Khan fled to Herat and the British retired to Kandahar. It appeared that they had managed to restore a perceived monopoly of violence.

Later on in the same year there was a general uprising across Afghanistan sparked by the murder of Alexander Burnes, the British political officer in Kabul. Therefore it was felt that Gereshk should be held, in the interests of the defence of Kandahar from Herat, which was at that time unfriendly to the British. Accordingly, proxy Barakzai horsemen were sent to Gereshk in November. Despite numerous Alizai attempts, the British-backed Barakzai held onto Gereshk until August 1842, largely because their Barakzai kinsmen surrounding the fort kept them supplied under the noses of the enemy.[56] With Dost Mohammad re-enthroned by tribal jirga,[57] the British evacuated the detachment to Kandahar, before leaving Afghanistan.

Dost's second reign[58] faced continued fiscal problems. This caused him to seek in 1857 the first British subsidy in order to fight Russian influence in Herat.[59] The subsidy marked an important point in Afghan and Helmandi history. Whilst previously rulers had distributed external resources across the kinship groups in Helmand, as seen in Ahmad Shah's distribution of plunder, this particular subsidy was not distributed equitably—it was used to strengthen some groups (the Barakzai) against others. Broadly speaking, patronage flowing through a system brings stability,[60] but only to groups who receive that patronage (the in-groups); to other groups (the out-groups) it reinforces divisions.

The fact that it was an external power that granted the subsidy was also important. It reinforced the idea in Helmandi minds that they could trade stability for cash; today, development funds arguably fulfil exactly the same role. It also very clearly emphasised the role of a leader in Helmandi society—that of accumulating resources externally and distributing them internally. This, of course, is inherently unstable as the leaders are accountable to the external sponsor and not the people. Thus, the ruler no longer has to rely on the tribes for revenue or service, arms can be purchased extra-territorially, and Helmandis know that they are able to gain resources from the state in return for stability. The subsidy hastened the decline of the relationship between the ruler and certain tribes, something that, in Afghanistan, has accelerated with time's progression.

The subsidy was meant to protect British interests from Russian influence. It had the additional effect of ranging Kandahar, Kabul and Britain against Herat, Persia and Russia. Gereshk and the Helmand River were the dividing line. Because Gereshk was still held by the Barakzai monarchy, the other Helmandi tribes were placed in a key balance-of-power role. When Dost died in 1862 the British withdrew the subsidy. This plunged southern Afghanistan into anarchy with a war of succession between two of his sons.[61] The Helmandi tribes fought as hired mercenaries[62] on one side (Sher Ali's) which helped swing the struggle towards a victory for Sher Ali after a 'severe' battle at Gereshk in 1868.[63]

Recognising his debt, Sher Ali did not attempt the previous scale of tax collection,[64] meaning that the Alizai did not rise up against him during his reign, even though they had the chance.[65] He reduced the allowances to the Barakzai khans.[66] These measures restored the natural balance of Helmandi politics. Sher Ali also recognised that Helmand was de facto powerful by making the four districts of Pusht-e rud the administrative charge of the newly created Farah province.[67] Previously, the modern day areas of Farah and Helmand had been part of Herat and Kandahar provinces, and Pusht-e rud (Helmand) was part of Kandahar. Detaching Pusht-e rud from Kandahar was an attempt to move it out of Kandahar's orbit and strengthen the link to Kabul (essentially an attempt to enable the monarch to influence Helmand without going through a relative in Kandahar). This demonstrated its strategic importance to the monarchy, in terms of location and the balance-of-power role that it had previously played. It is no different today.

In November 1878, British forces again invaded Afghanistan over fears of Russian influence. Kandahar was occupied, as was Gereshk, albeit briefly. The Alizai mobilised fifteen hundred men and attacked the British as they were withdrawing from Gereshk in February 1879.[68] The Alizai memories of the 1840s were still strong. Shortly after the withdrawal, Sher Ali died a natural death and the country dissolved into his relatives' fiefdoms, with the British controlling Kandahar and a Barakzai leader, Abdur Rahman, controlling Kabul.[69] The British had relearnt that a deployment of their own troops to Gereshk had unsatisfactory consequences and stirred local opposition.[70] Thus, attempting to defend Kandahar from Ayub Khan, Sher Ali's son based in Herat, the British sent a proxy Barakzai force, under Kandahar's governor, to occupy Gereshk as a forward defence.

Ayub began gathering forces to take Kandahar. His appeal to the Helmandis was based on evicting infidels and on the loot of British gold in Kandahar, but little encouragement was needed.[71] By October 1879, three or four thousand Alizai from Zamindawar and a smaller force of Noorzai from Now Zad had joined him.[72] Abu Bakr, an Alizai, was their leader.[73] Nervous, the British became unsure of 'their' proxy Barakzai, even though they had been loyal up to this point, and they reinforced them with a British detachment under General Burrowes.[74] Nonetheless, as the British occupied Gereshk in July 1880, the governor's Barakzai troops mutinied, joining the Alizai and Noorzai in Zamindawar.[75] This showed a rare confluence of Barakzai and Alizai interests, only possible in the face of an external enemy. It demonstrates very well how segmentary kinship solidarity can work in

Pushtun society—although the Barakzai and the Alizai were only distantly related, the British were more distantly related still.

The British withdrew to Khushk-e Nakhud.[76] Ayub and the, mostly Alizai, tribesmen followed and utterly defeated the British at Maiwand[77] on 27 July 1880. Tribesmen harassed the retreating British all the way to Kandahar, but were slow to press their advantage and take the city, as they were arguing over plunder.[78] The Alizai soon returned to Zamindawar, leaving Ayub to be defeated later by the British, well before he was able to capture Kandahar.[79] The alliances that Ayub had constructed for his winning army only lasted for the defeat of the British, and not a second beyond. Ayub needed to take Kandahar as a stepping-stone to controlling Afghanistan. However, the Alizai, and to a lesser degree the Barakzai, simply wished to get their own back on the British. This was achieved admirably by the battle of Maiwand where they helped defeat a 'Western' army in the field—something that has never been forgotten in Helmand. Having served its purpose, the alliance then split up. The dynamic of alliances forming and collapsing was to reach fever pitch during the mujahidin era a hundred years later (Chapters 2 and 3). The British had failed to understand that dynamic and left, handing a fractured Afghanistan and a subsidy to the Barakzai Abdur Rahman, who at that point only controlled Kabul.

Abdur Rahman, perhaps more than any other Afghan leader, understood the utility and application of violence. With this understanding and a judicious use of the British subsidy, he contributed, perhaps more than any other Afghan leader, to the formation of the Afghan state.[80] He used the subsidy in part as an incentive and in part as a way of buying the means to enforce a monopoly of violence: a professional army. With this, Abu Bakr was beaten and exiled, and the Alizai brought to heel. Such was the ferocity of Abdur Rahman's approach that the Alizai began paying tax.[81] The Ishaqzai and the Noorzai also suffered. A combination of positive inducements and force moved them from the lands granted by Nadir Shah on the Helmand River to the northwest of Afghanistan to populate the border region of Turkestan. It was a disaster and many returned, only able to retrieve scattered, less productive land holdings elsewhere in Helmand.[82]

The exodus directly impacted the power dynamic in Helmand as it took away the currency of that power (land) for some of the tribes. It is the foundation of the Ishaqzai, and to a lesser degree the Noorzai, disenfranchisement from government that has continued to the present day. They saw it as a fall from their position under Ahmad Shah. As a result, the Noorzai occupied marginal land in Helmand until the late twentieth century and the Ishaqzai still remain scattered across Helmand. These policies, weakening the non-Barakzai (Abdur Rahman's tribe) vis-à-vis other tribes, combined with non-interference in tribes' internal affairs—provided they paid their dues—ensured a period of stability that lasted through Abdur Rahman's reign to the death of his conservative-minded son, Habibullah, in 1919.

*Independence and Ensuing Reform*

1919 saw full independence from the British and the ending of the subsidy. Amanullah, Habibullah's son, was enthroned in a significantly altered political landscape. The ending of the subsidy left Amanullah with little revenue, causing him to halt the stipends that had been paid to the Barakzai clans for generations.[83] He also had to drastically reduce the size of the professional army and rely on conscription, or hasht-e nafari, which reduced his ability to enforce tax collection. Hasht-e nafari literally means 'eighth man'—one in eight men from a clan or family was liable for call up at any one time to fight in mixed units. It was significantly different to the elegant solution introduced by Nadir Shah and Ahmad Shah Durrani, where service was well paid, with opportunities for plunder, and men fought in kinship-based units.

Amanullah was a much more reform-minded monarch, but he never had enough money to compensate for the speed and the depth of the modernising reforms he initiated. For example, he wanted to target regressive social practices, such as the sale of women for marriage to settle debt, as well as more technical issues, such as the introduction of identity documents. Significant reforms, such as these, would have had to have been done very slowly to be fully successful. However, as it was it merely introduced the reformist-conservationist dichotomy in the population that was to decimate Afghanistan over the twentieth century.

Amanullah's reforms were excessive and Zamindawar rose in rebellion in 1923, with more localised disturbances in the remainder of Pusht-e rud.[84] These took six months to quell, as none of the conscripted battalions in the south would fight the Alizai. The rebellion was eventually settled by troops from Herat, who executed the rebel leaders and deported groups of Zamindawaris to Turkestan,[85] which was by now becoming a dumping ground for Helmand's rebels. As a short-term measure, Afghan monarchs had found that once taken from their land, and thus their source of power, opposition groups were less troublesome. In the long term however, it did not help bind disparate groups into a state.

Amanullah was the last of his dynasty's line and, aside from a brief Tajik usurper, the throne passed to a separate Barakzai dynasty—the Musahibans—although they were still from the Mohammadzai sub-tribe.[86] The two monarchs from the dynasty, Nadir Shah and Zahir Shah,[87] did not immediately learn from the lessons of Amanullah and faced a number of serious rebellions in their early years, such as in the winter of 1938/9. The government was carrying out a campaign for compulsory (male) education, which was used as a rallying cry by Alizai mullahs who said that female education would be next—a red line for the tribes of the south. What started as an Alizai disturbance quickly spread to other tribes and there was a confrontation between the government and the tribesmen at Yakhchal, near Gereshk, which was eventually resolved when the government employed aircraft (bought from the British) against the tribesmen.[88]

Starting from approximately that point forward, social reforms were to be slow and pursued with a concurrent development bribe. The Musahiban dynasty started to be looked upon by many Helmandis as a golden age of stability. There were two main reasons for this. First, the (mainly agricultural- and land-based) tax burden on the population was slowly replaced by trade taxes, government monopolies and for-eign aid (the British subsidy in another form). By 1970, agricultural taxes represented one per cent of revenue.[89] Secondly the canal projects increased the quantity and value of land in Helmand dramatically.

## The Canals

The development of Helmand had begun with the reconstruction of the Saraj Canal (the Nahr-e Saraj) in 1910. The canal gave the district its present day name when it was created in the 1960s (Nahr means waterway). What was previously desert was then populated with non-Helmandi ethnic and tribal groups, including refugees who had recently fled the Soviet revolutions in Central Asia.[90] For this reason, many of the villages along the canal are named after kinship groups—

Uzbek, Turkmen, and Popalzai, for example. The government planned to continue developing the area during the 1920s, but was distracted by the internal unrest caused by Ámanullah's social reforms.[91] Once the Musahiban dynasty had ascended to the throne, the government was able to start building another Helmandi canal in 1936—the Nahr-e Bughra.

In the absence of the British subsidy, the Afghans planned to use American financial and technical assistance to build the canals and, more broadly, to balance Russia's influence in the north. The US would be taking over Britain's historical position. However, the Americans rebuffed the Afghan government. This forced them to ask the German and Japanese governments for help, which was given.[92] The Bughra project regularly had up to 7000 workers and ran concurrently with other small-scale developments in the area. Roads, bridges and telephone wires connecting the major settlements sprang up, marking the first externally advised development of Helmand.[93] However, with the onset of World War Two, the British insisted that the German and Japanese engineers be expelled.[94] The Afghans continued the project alone.[95]

The culmination of World War Two was marked by further applications for US assistance, but US government dithering resulted in the Afghan government privately contracting the US firm Morrison–Knudsen (MK) in 1945 to survey a Helmand-wide dam and canal system.[96] In a rather rushed fashion, and without the appropriate soil surveys, construction began in 1946. Within a short period, problems became evident. For example, the dam at the start of the Bughra had caused the water table to rise, creating a surface salt crust.[97] What were at first solvable technical issues were compounded by cross-cultural human factors. To save money, the Afghan government had agreed to do administrative and drainage work that they were not technically competent to do, but they 'neglected' to admit this to the Americans to avoid losing face. For their part, the Americans had difficulty in recruiting employees who understood the language and culture of Helmand, particularly how to 'deal' with Helmandis. The costs rose and the project looked set to discontinue, if for no other reason than that the Afghan government could no longer afford it.[98]

Events were overtaken when US President Truman announced his Point IV program in 1949, namely 'a bold new program ... for the improvement ... of [worldwide] undeveloped areas'.[99] US aims were not only to counter Soviet influence, but also to reshape the world to be more developed, something Zahir Shah immediately took advantage of. The US hoped that development would make the world less susceptible to hunger, poverty and war. To the US, these were technical and engineering problems rather than human ones,[100] resulting in 'development myopia'[101] that excluded other problems. The lessons of the first Bughra project were ignored and in 1952, the Afghan government created the Helmand Valley Authority (HVA),[102] modelled on the US Tennessee Valley Authority, to manage a project that was becoming enormous. The US paid for MK to do the work.

In northern Helmand, the 320-foot Kajaki Dam was built to provide electricity and irrigation water,[103] and several concrete-lined canals were built or extended for the regions nominated for development. These included the Bughra for Nad-e Ali and Marjeh, the Shamalan for Bolan, Aynak and Nawa, and the Darweshan for Garmsir. For hydrological reasons, the dam was built in Alizai territory, even though, as a group, they benefitted the least from the canal project. The most striking part of the project was that the two new areas, Nad-e Ali and Marjeh, were to be reclaimed from the desert and settled with a non-Helmandi population. This was the largest increase in agricultural land that Afghanistan, let alone Helmand, had ever seen; but the settlement of non-Helmandi groups threatened to upset the province's extant inter-tribal dynamics. It was also the most expensive project that the Afghan government had ever attempted. A fifth of government expenditure went to the HVA in the 1950s and 60s[104] and the president of the organisation received cabinet status.[105] But again, corners continued to be cut and the appropriate surveys were not commissioned.

The government of Afghanistan aimed to settle nomads, whom it saw as backward and extra-legal, in Nad-e Ali and Marjeh. Through settlement they could be subject to development, control and taxation, eventually making them government clients. The unstated aim was that it would disempower tribal groupings that had caused problems for previous governments.[106] Thus, the majority of settlers were Ghilzai, for example the Kharoti in Nad-e Ali and the Daftani in Marjeh (whereas the government of the time was almost exclusively Durrani-Barakzai). The indigenous Helmandis on the outskirts of the project (mainly Barakzai) would receive water from the new irrigation system that would enable them to double crop. For those groups that immigrated, each family was given thirty jereebs (six hectares), house

29

material, an ox, implements, seed, food and loaned money. Even so, some of the nomadic families had to be forced into settling against their will.[107]

Nad-e Ali was the first area to be settled in 1954. Most of the new-comers were settled in villages in cohesive, tribally homogenous groups of fifty to one hundred families (for example, Shin Kalay).[108] Other settlements were tribally or ethnically heterogeneous (for example, Zhargoun Kalay). Ironically, the kinship groups that were settled homogenously found their political voice—the exact opposite of government intentions. Those settled heterogeneously often experienced problems between kinship groups. In this first wave of settlements, about 2500 families were settled, 1200 of them nomadic.[109]

Many families stayed less than a few months. The land was as profoundly unsuitable for arable farming as the now-settled nomads. The lack of survey meant that the HVA had failed to discover an impermeable substratum or to anticipate that raising the water table would cause excessive water logging. The inadequate drainage meant that the land rapidly acquired salt crusts.[110] Again, technical problems were compounded by human factors: detailed cropping advice was not followed—more likely, not understood.[111] When the first off-season water arrived in the areas surrounding the projects, the farmers thought it was a 'gift from Allah'.[112] The government, in its hubris, had failed to understand the farmers' primitiveness—to the Helmandis, a dam was a metre tall and made of mud. The scale of the Kajaki Dam was inconceivable and many of the traditional, self-built irrigation systems were damaged, causing yields to plummet. These problems combined to provoke an exodus of settlers, and by 1960 only 30 per cent of the original settlers were still in Nad-e Ali.[113] In some areas, agricultural production had still not returned to 50 per cent of pre-1950s levels by 1969.[114]

The settlement of Marjeh in 1957–9 avoided many of the previously made mistakes.[115] The farmers were settled in contiguous homogenous blocks, thus striking a balance between complete heterogeneity, which caused ethnic and tribal strife, and the homogenous village structure, which enshrined power blocks as potential negotiators with the state.[116] In a further attempt to break up tribal structures and identity, the families were also informed that they could choose their own leaders, called wakils (literally, advocates). None chose to do so, however, preferring to remain under their existing tribal leaders.[117] Services, such as schools, were built[118] and a higher proportion of the settlers had farming experience.[119] US advisors, however, worked in separate American environments and very few spoke Pushtu, whilst many of the government officials were extra-provincial and only spoke Dari (Pushtu, rather than Dari, is the language of Helmand). The US advisors' education levels caused them to look down on the Helmandis as backward.[120] Overall, and as before, technical problems were compounded by cultural and linguistic issues.

Whilst the settlement of Marjeh was more successful than that of Nad-e Ali, the project was still a 'bleeding ulcer'.[121] The first settlements were followed by acrimonious blame games between the Americans and the Afghans. MK then employed an 'independent' firm—in reality, one of their affiliates—to conduct an audit that significantly highlighted Afghan shortcomings, whilst ignoring American ones. The Afghans terminated MK's services and rejected the report. In a high-risk strategy, and even though they wanted to disengage, the US government became directly involved, and in 1960 government engineers took over and accelerated the project.[122] Against the backdrop of the Cold War the US felt they could not admit that level of defeat.[123]

The canal projects had made Helmand even more important. Recognising this, the 'Gereshk' province was created by subdividing Farah province in 1960.[124] Gereshk was chosen as the capital to reflect the historical dominance and closeness to the monarchy of the Barakzai. It was a way of enshrining the power of the Helmandi Barakzai, which had been diluted as settlers arrived in the province. The US, however, looked at Helmand ahistorically, seeing only the canal projects. Thus in 1964, and under US pressure, the capital was moved to Lashkar Gah where the headquarters of the HVA were, and Gereshk province was renamed Helmand province.[125] The co-location of the HVA headquarters and the provincial government signalled that the canal project *had become* the province; indeed, in the 1970s, the president of the HVA was also governor of the province.[126] The HVA president had so much patronage power (due to control of the water supply) that had the offices been separate the provincial governor would not have been able to achieve anything that the HVA president did not agree to. This was an excellent demonstration of how patronage works in Helmand.

The movement of the capital to Lashkar Gah meant that, for the first time since the accession of the Barakzai monarchy in 1826, the Helmandi Barakzai lost power. As a way of compensating for this loss,

31

the government radically redrew the district boundaries in Helmand. The historical districts of Zamindawar, Gereshk, Now Zad and Garmsir were abolished and the number of districts increased. The new districts were given an 'order' or status, which dictated how many resources (staff, budget, services) they could draw from the central government and this, combined with where the boundaries were actually drawn, was used by the government to impose its influence and exert control. This was critical, as voting, which allows the creation of de jure power blocks from de facto ones, was introduced in the 1964 constitution.[127]

The old Barakzai district of Pusht-e rud or Gereshk was split into Nahr-e Saraj (the only 1st order—the best—district in the province), Lashkar Gah (the capital with its own rules for resourcing) and Nawa (4th order).[128] The district boundary for Lashkar Gah was gerrymandered such that the mixed tribes of the urban area were in the minority compared to the Barakzai: the Nad-e Ali boundary was drawn along the edge of Barakzai territory in Bolan and a slice of Barakzai Babaji (north of the Helmand River) was included. Thus, even while accommodating US influence, the Barakzai central government managed to maintain Barakzai control over the new capital of Helmand.

The other tribes were not so lucky. The ancient Alizai district of Zamindawar was split into Musa Qala, Baghran and Kajaki and granted only 2nd order, 4th order and sub-district status respectively. Now Zad (mixed Noorzai/Ishaqzai) became Now Zad and Washir districts with 2nd order and sub-district status. Garmsir, the only ancient district to remain in its previous form, was given 3rd order status. Sangin, a sub-district, was created in the seam between ancient Zamindawar and Pusht-e rud (it is not known from which exactly it stemmed), probably to protect the Alakozai (a tribe related to the Barakzai) from the Alizai. The thirty-seven different tribes and ethnicities of immigrants in Nad-e Ali and Marjeh were lumped into one 3rd order district.[129]

The district reorganisation was the central government trying to influence the distribution of resources in Helmand; that is, the district boundaries encompassed areas of land and gave control of them to particular groups, whilst at the same time giving the groups a set level of resources to administer them. The weakness of the division was that whilst it recognised the Barakzai interests and population size, as should be done in a democracy, this was not the case with the other kinship groups in Helmand. The historical Barakzai versus non-Barakzai and central Helmand versus non-central Helmand dichotomies were perpetuated.

The canal projects increased in scope during the 1960s. As well as redoing much of the work in Nad-e Ali and Marjeh, adding drains, sanitation and reforesting, large-scale USAID development projects were initiated. The Lashkar Gah hospital was built,[130] as well as a schooling system for central Helmand up to high-school level. By 1968, 30 per cent of boys province-wide were receiving education, and Helmandis were being trained to run the canal projects themselves.[131] Due to American cotton lobby restrictions on USAID, the British government was asked to build a cotton processing plant (a gin) in Lashkar Gah during the 1970s.[132] Finally, with the adoption of double cropping and the utilisation of tractors and fertiliser,[133] yields in central Helmand started to rise, and by 1966 they were increasing year on year.[134] Some of the original settlers who had left returned, applying for resettlement.[135] Whilst a marked improvement as all of these factors developed central Helmand, it was done at the expense of the outlying districts, thus altering the 'Helmandi balance' further. This continues in the present day, as we shall see in Chapters 5 and 6.

Outside the new districts of Nad-e Ali and Marjeh, the government wished to continue the project to the south with the Shamalan and Darweshan Canals. The canals had been unfinished at MK's termination and so the US government took over their construction.[136] The previous lessons had finally been learnt, but now a very different set of problems emerged, as, even though the soils were much more fertile than those in Nad-e Ali and Marjeh, and the incoming farmers more skilled,[137] much of the land selected for the project was already populated. Elders and technocratic government officials handled the required political process with mutual incomprehension.[138]

The government had to move families from their ancestral lands to build the canals and the associated infrastructure, only to move them back later, side-by-side with new settlers. The identity of their new neighbours was not advertised initially, and rumours were rife. Elders went to Lashkar Gah to complain, partly because they misunderstood what was about to happen and partly because they were about to lose government land that they had been illegally cultivating. They were brushed off.[139] Elders of communities who were connected to the government, usually by kinship, managed to get canal works diverted away from their land through their less well-connected neighbours' land. The government was striking at the heart of Helmandi power—land—by giving some of it away to outsiders. In many cases the government works vehicles were met with gunfire.[140]

Once resettled, indigenous kinship groups and groups of settlers clashed over land and water.[141] Desperately complicated patterns of land tenure resulted where the owner, sharecropper, mortgagee, miraw (water manager) and day labourer all came from different ethnic or tribal groups.[142] This lacked the attendant stability that traditionally ensued from intra- and inter-segmentary group dispute resolution. The government could not even provide its most basic function—arbitration—as it had caused the problems in the first place, not least by failing to issue the appropriate land documentation.[143] The settlers diluted the power of the traditional khans by, among other things, employing indigenous workers on their new land.[144] The connection of irrigation ditches to the government-built canals disempowered the miraws and landowners, whose power had been based on controlling water sources.[145] Thus, it was this unintended social revolution that laid the foundations for many of the land disputes that are still ongoing.

In 1973, Daud Khan, Zahir Shah's cousin, staged a coup and abolished the monarchy, making himself president. As a relative of the king, little changed in patronage terms in Helmand. He oversaw a further expansion of the canal project, even while the US–Soviet détente saw the US disengaging as rapidly as possible.[146] For Daud Khan, the canal project *was* modernisation, and between 1973 and 1978 the government settled a further 4000 families, creating new settlements from the Darweshan and Shamalan canals, and resettling families on two-to-ten jereeb plots from broken-up abandoned farms in Marjeh and Nad-e Ali. The smaller plots were not big enough for subsistence and the new immigrants were forced to work on others' land. Worse, the settlements' accelerated nature meant that families were ethnically and tribally mixed, with few of the services that previous settlers had enjoyed.[147] This brief, but intense, expansion of the project has left its legacy in the small-scale landowners who still exhibit disharmony with their neighbours.

The twenty years of the canal projects in Helmand left quite a legacy. In technical terms, the projects succeeded in creating a large agricultural base in southern Afghanistan—Nad-e Ali and Marjeh represent modern farming systems.[148] Land was given to 10,000 families,[149] and on an individual community scale, those settlers who chose to remain in Helmand have benefited: by 1975, 92 per cent of settlers were happy with their existence.[150] Aside from the settlers, many indigenous communities in central Helmand, who were mainly Barakzai, benefited from the increased access to irrigation water, markets and services that the canal project brought. The improvement to many people's lives cannot be understated.

However, the influence exerted by the canal projects also deeply altered Helmandi society, particularly the identity and cohesion of kinship groups. At district scale, Nad-e Ali and Marjeh were comprised completely of non-Helmandis and the central region was 30 per cent comprised of settlers. Further south, the Shamalan region was 26 per cent settlers and Darweshan 40 per cent settlers.[151] This caused the Barakzai to lose influence centrally through population dilution, although they managed to retain some of their previous influence due to the redrawing of the district boundaries. A similar situation befell the Noorzai further south, although they did not benefit from the boundary redraw.

Many of the nomadic groups that settled (for example, the Kharoti in Nad-e Ali) experienced a change in tribal leadership structure from quami to rutbavi, commensurate with their newfound landownership. Whereas previously they could have expected to change their leaders reasonably often, those leaders that led them into the settlements, or their descendants, are still leading them today.[152] This rutbavi (hierarchical) structure enabled them to negotiate more effectively, opposite to what the government had originally intended. Now they could envision political power that they had not previously held. However, the district boundaries were drawn in such a way that it was difficult for them to use it, creating disenfranchisement. In the later settlements, the government had preferred to break up the groups, creating smaller, poorer, heterogeneous communities. This, combined with the disempowerment of the landowners and miraws, was the most damaging aspect of the projects, as fractured communities were susceptible to internal conflict.

The real losers were those tribes that did not live in central Helmand. This very much followed a historical pattern and confirmed, for example, the Alizai narrative that the government was not interested in helping them. The district allocations further reinforced this. Central Helmand became a product of socio-economic modernisation leaving

35

the Alizai, Noorzai and Ishaqzai, in the north and south of the province, suffering a paucity of development. This division was to feature heavily in the violence that was to come. More subtly, the US and Afghan governments completely failed to understand that, by settling 10,000 families and creating an educated cadre to run the canal project from within Helmandi society, they were emphasising the conservative-reformist divide in Helmandi society that had first been crafted by Amanullah in the 1920s.

*Conclusions*

This chapter has given the historical context for the conflict that began in 1978. We began by describing an ideal: the Popalzai Durrani state, where the tribes, landownership and the state were in balance. In reality, it was almost certainly more internally violent than I suggest, however, it gives a stable ideal against which to compare succeeding historical developments. We then examined the Barakzai-Alizai dynamic in some detail, including how that dynamic interacted with repeated British interventions in Helmand and Afghanistan.

This was followed by a discussion of the reforms that Amanullah wished to implement and the associated rebellions in Helmand. This conservative-reformist dichotomy in Afghanistan still strongly echoes today. I remember visiting a Helmandi provincial chief of police in 2011, who had originally been trained by the Soviets but was at that time working for the Western-backed Karzai government. On his desk was a stylised photo of Amanullah, who was his hero; as we spoke, it was clear that he saw parallels between the three eras. I also had the pleasure of having recounted to me what happened when this particular man visited his subordinates out in the districts, many of whom were illiterate ex-jihadi commanders: he used to present them with a copy of this photo. Needless to say, Amanullah was not a hero to many of them!

The Alizai–Barakzai dynamics and the conservative-reformist dichotomy were greatly compounded by the canal projects, which complicated group identity and further upset the balances in Helmandi society. Whereas previously tribal identity had defined groups in Helmand, other factors such as education and settler-status also now became important. For example, the expansion of the education system had led to violence between Islamist and communist students in the Lashkar Gah Lycee, each of whom sought to overthrow the previous order and to replace it with their own political ideal. These three factors also interacted as, for reasons discussed later, the canal projects had a high degree of educated *and* communist inhabitants. These elements all added layers of complexity to the identity of individual Helmandis and groups, creating a tangled web of labels, relationships and motivations. This complexity laid the foundations for the conflict that is the focus of this book.

2

# FROM THE SAUR REVOLUTION TO THE
# SOVIET WITHDRAWAL, 1978–89

Jihad was not free.

Alakozai businessman[1]
Gereshk

Everyone had a [Khad] file ... [there was] so
much trickery between different mujahidin
[groups and leaders].

Hafizullah Khan
Hizb-e Islami Amir for Helmand

## Background

The 1978–89 conflict in Afghanistan has a very strong Western narrative, set within the context of the Cold War. The conflict, of which the Helmandi fighting was a subset, was understood in terms of an 'East–West confrontation'.[2] This was the age of the glorious mujahidin fighting their Soviet oppressors in a jihad. As the foreword to Sandy Gall's memoirs, written by Margaret Thatcher, begins, '... one of the most heroic resistance struggles known to history has been taking place ... in the mountains and plains of Afghanistan'.[3] This is not atypical of Western journalistic accounts of the era. Arthur Bonner, one of the very few journalists to travel to out-of-the-way Helmand, discussed the war in terms of the holy mujahidin fighting the atheist communists, even when investigating the incongruity of opium growing among the Alizai 'religious' figures of northern Helmand.[4]

The religious nature of the anti-Soviet resistance was repeatedly emphasised by Western journalists with, for example, Jon Anderson speaking of a 'peculiar fatalism of men for whom belief in God and paradise has replaced the fear of death'.[5] The Soviet side had a different angle and vocabulary, but the narrative was similarly strong. The 'limited contingent' was doing its 'international duty' in supporting 'worldwide socialism'.[6] The Afghans fighting them were labelled as 'counterrevolutionaries' or 'imperialist and Zionist agents'.[7] In soldier-slang, they were 'dukhi' (ghosts).[8]

The communist coup of 1978 ushered in an ideological government that was authoritarian and swift in its approach to implementing reform, specifically with regard to land redistribution and improving literacy.[9] We have seen what happened when previous Afghan rulers had taken such an approach to reform. The subsequent Soviet intervention was initially intended to last for six months, which was considered a sufficient period of time to stabilise the country and its armed forces before withdrawing.[10] Viewed through the Western prism of the Cold War, the Soviets were atheist communists who sought to subjugate Afghanistan as a client state. This 'intervention' caused the United States to begin funding resistance to an 'occupation', leading to an injection of resources that served to reinforce the narratives surrounding the war, according to which the Afghan resistance—the mujahidin—were holy fighters striving to liberate their homeland from the evil Soviets.[11]

In addition to this overall conflict between the Soviets and communist government forces on the one hand, and the mujahidin on the other, there were a series of further fragmentations to consider. The Afghan communists were divided into two factions, the Khalqis and the Parchamis—both based on Marxism-Leninism—with the Khalqis being the more fervent of the two.[12] The Afghan government's most efficient organ was the state security police, Khedmat Amniat Dulati (Khad), which was essentially an extension of the KGB and acted across all departments of the state in a 'counter-revolutionary' role. By counter-revolutionary, I mean not only combatting the mujahidin, but also those within the government it deemed to be insufficiently supportive of government or Soviet objectives. Of course, Khad was the first government organisation to be purged if a different faction or leader gained the upper hand in Kabul. Throughout most of this period it served as the main instrument of government policy.[13]

The 'freedom-loving' mujahidin, backed (mainly) by Pakistan, the United States and Saudi Arabia, were ranged on the other side of the conflict. The mujahidin were organised into seven parties with differing ideologies. Four of these were particularly important in the context of Helmand: Jamiat-e Islami (Jamiat), Hizb-e Islami (Hizb), Harakat-e Enqelab-e Islami (Harakat) and Mahaz-e Milli (Mahaz). Although Hizb and Jamiat members disagree as to which came first, the two parties are the closest in terms of ideology, which is Islamist in outlook and similar to that of the Muslim Brotherhood (Rabbani, Jamiat's leader, was the first to translate Sayed Qutb's work into Dari). They sought to establish a modern state, without a monarchy, based on Islamic principles.[14] Harakat and Mahaz were the so-called traditionalist parties. Harakat wanted a return to Islamic law, sharia, yet did not see any incompatibility between the monarchy and Islam. They were mainly comprised of clerics. Mahaz were known as the royalist party. They sought a return to the monarchy and were mainly comprised of people connected to the old order.[15]

Over time, the perception grew that Hizb were more reactionary and Jamiat more moderate, in an analogy to the Khalq and Parcham factions in the government. Both these dichotomies tended towards national ethnic polarisation as the war went on; Khalq and Hizb towards the Pushtun, and Parcham and Jamiat towards the Tajiks.[16] The Pakistani Inter-Services Intelligence (ISI) should be considered an exceptionally important organisation when it comes to the mujahidin parties.[17] It supported the parties to different degrees as suited Pakistani national policies towards Afghanistan. The ISI was able to do this as the US allowed them to distribute US aid without oversight. In effect, the United States paid while the Pakistanis played.

President Daud Khan was killed during a coup launched by the People's Democratic Party of Afghanistan (PDPA) in April 1978—a communist takeover. This was known as the Saur revolution. Because they dominated the army, the more ideologically extreme left-wing Khalq faction managed to seize power in 1978 and Noor Mohammad Taraki, a founding member of the PDPA, but not a member of the military, was proclaimed president. The twenty-one months of Khalqi rule were to have a drastic effect on Helmandi society. Following the Soviet intervention at the end of 1979, the Parcham faction gained power.[18]

It is difficult to say whether Khalqis deliberately planned to destabilise society by removing the power of the previous elite;[19] however, contemporaneous government newspapers give the impression that they had an almost fervent desire to reform society as fast as possible.[20] The Khalqis were also cognizant that they might face resistance, and so they moved as quickly as they could.[21] Following the communist narrative of class war, the Khalqis wanted to increase the power of the 'proletariat' (in this case, the farmers) against that of the capital class (the landowners). This also had the added benefit of disempowering the previous government's power base, the Durrani landowners, or khans. But the narrative of 'class struggle' made no sense to illiterate farmers.[22]

The Taraki government issued three decrees particularly relevant to our story. Decree number 6 referred to the regulation of rural mortgages and debt, and removed a key basis of the khans' power—by controlling credit, the khans were able to keep their tenant farmers in debt cycles. Decree number 7 imposed limitations on marriageable age and bride price, which changed marriage from a social institution to a transaction between two individuals, thereby criminalising a key Pushtun conflict resolution and power-regulation mechanism, namely that of kinship groups swapping women to settle disputes. Finally, decree number 8, which was probably the most damaging as it was the easiest to enforce, decreed land redistribution whereby estates over thirty jereebs (6 hectares) would be redistributed to peasants.[23]

This background, whilst true, is overly simplistic when applied to the conflict in Helmand. This chapter will explore this period through Helmandi eyes, exposing an almost completely different conflict: one where the Helmandis fought each other utilising and manipulating external ideologies in an attempt to leverage their local disputes. The chapter begins with a discussion of the collapse of the government in Helmand, caused mainly by the land reforms provoking individual resistance. We will then look at the Soviet intervention and the further increase in violence that this caused. Most of this was 'mujahidin'-'mujahidin' violence, and it will be explored though the lenses of the patronage of the different mujahidin groups and the control of the drugs trade. The chapter discusses government infighting, as well as the common tactic of splitting families across the 'government'-'mujahidin' divide. It was this practice that enabled the most efficient manipulation of external narratives. Finally, we will look at the Soviet drawdown and the militia programme that the Soviets enacted, as this was to have most serious consequences for the future stability of Helmand.

## Government Collapse and the Soviet Intervention

Decree number 8 was announced at the end of November 1978.[24] It outlined a programme of land redistribution, according to which all holdings over thirty jereebs were to be given out in packages of six jereebs. This was not enough to support a family of ten.[25] The land was to be distributed to the farmers who had previously been sharecroppers, thus inverting the rural hierarchy.[26] Thereafter, it was to be given to landless people in the village, the district, the region and finally nationally. The arbitrary redistribution cut-off was to have critical resonance in Helmand, as thirty jereebs had been the amount given to the 1950s settlers, so they were unaffected by decree no. 8.[27] It is not clear whether the Khalqi government was aware of the impact that this was to have in Helmand.

One consequence of the reform, for example, was that the communists found support in the canal-zones, generating the fifth largest provincial communist party in the country by 1980 (see Map 4). Helmand was the only major area of communist recruitment in southern Afghanistan,[28] probably because the landholders from the canal-zone escaped redistribution unless they had accrued more land than they had originally been given in the 1950s.[29] Those groups who had received land under Nadir Shah and Ahmad Shah (discussed further below), conversely, were major targets due to the size of their landholdings—some of the largest estates in the country were in the Helmand Valley.[30] This land had often been in families for 250 years,[31] and thousands of families and jereebs were affected.[32]

The land reforms were poorly thought out, and, to make matters worse, the accompanying communist narrative made no sense to the Helmandis.[33] As a Barakzai militia leader said to me, 'the mother of the problems that we have now is the land redistributions under Taraki'.[34] The reforms were based on an ideological model of a nuclear family that did not exist in Helmand, where extended families shared undivided inherited land. The reforms were also predicated on land area, but in Helmand this was not the most important factor in determining harvest; access to irrigation water was. If land was subdivided in a way which meant that water had to be obtained from a neighbour then it could become valueless and could even cause conflict, as cousins often owned contiguous land inherited from a common grandfather. Communal land, a vital part of the community, was not recognised. It seems clear from this that the ideologically driven government did not understand, or chose to ignore, land ownership dynamics in Helmand, thereby allowing some to take advantage of the ensuing chaos.

The redistributions themselves were carried out in different ways. In Malgir for example, force was not always necessary as there was a perception of government strength that had been carried over from the pre-revolutionary period.[35] In other areas the police or the depaye militia were used. The latter were a legacy from the Zahir Shah era:[36] militias of varying size (about 100 men in Nawa[37] and 300 men in Musa Qala)[38] that were led by the district head teacher and composed mainly of students. They worked under the instructions of the district chief of police. Purging the militias soon after coming to power, the Khalqi government then used them extensively to achieve its revolutionary aims.[39]

Yet, private actors often manipulated the land redistribution. The process as a whole was under the control of the Revolutionary Defence Committee in Lashkar Gah, with requisite sub-committees in each district to which people could appeal.[40] However, the membership of the committee was strongly biased towards certain local groups at the expense of others; Khalqis and their families always did well out of the land distributions.[41] In Nad-e Ali, for example, the leader of the land committee was Abdul Hakim (Kakar, from Chah-e Mirza) and the secretary was Amanullah Khan (Laghmani, from Loy Bagh), both of whom ensured that the land was distributed to their and their kin's advantage.[42] In other areas, groups of Khalqis spontaneously banded together and stole their neighbours' land, waiting for the theft to be ratified later by the Revolutionary Defence Committee.[43]

The land distributions took place against a background of arrests directed at anyone that the government deemed an opponent.[44] The communist government, viewing events through the prism of the earlier communist–Islamist violence in educational establishments, believed that anyone who resisted the government must be ikhwan (that is, a member of, or associated with, the Muslim Brotherhood).[45] This was a similar approach to that taken by the United States in the immediate post-2001 era, in terms of arresting people according to an ideological blueprint in which anyone who resisted the government was a 'Talib'.[46] In the event, the arrests simply served to push people into becoming what they had been accused of. It was not only those who had opposed the government that were arrested—even individuals suspected of having the potential for opposition were rounded up and sent to Lashkar Gah or Kandahar prison. This resulted in the arrest of tribal leaders, mullahs, sayeds, members of the old order, and Parchamis; in short, anyone with influence. In one incident, 100 Helmandi political prisoners were thrown out of a plane into the Arghandab reservoir.[47]

But there was a paradox. Even though the very poorest in Helmand stood to gain from the land redistribution, it was this section of society that ultimately formed the manpower for the uprising. This was because the rural mullahs and khans deliberately misrepresented the government's narratives. The public literacy programme, for example, was considered a key part of the reforms.[48] But the only people in the village who could read were the khan and the mullah, and they viewed the programme as an assault on their means of power. They saw their interests eroded, and traditional Helmandi narratives of government interference were easily exploitable to generate popular mobilisation. Helmandis began to respond to what they saw as a 'godless, imposing and cruel' government.[49] Many were persuaded by their landowning leaders that land redistribution was state theft, and that it was their Islamic duty to oppose it.[50] The narrative of the anti-Islamic flavour of the government is the same complaint as that levelled by jihadi publications associated with the post-2001 Taliban organisation.[51] For them, it is the same long struggle.

Government officials were being assassinated in Lashkar Gah within two months of the revolution.[52] In October 1978, the Baghran district governor, Ekhlas (Barakzai, Khalqi, from Malgir) was killed by Rais Baghrani (Alizai/Khalozai), the Baghran government agricultural cooperative leader[53] and a fellow 'Khalqi'. This was clearly a naked grab for power, rather than an ideological uprising. The government, not sure of the situation, sent a replacement, Jan Gul (Barakzai, Khalqi, from Malgir), who was killed shortly after. Baghran has been under Baghrani's control ever since.[54] In other northern districts, the government retreated into its administrative enclaves, allowing bands of criminals to take advantage of the vacuum. Local notables began to police their own communities. In Kajaki, Mahmad Khan (Taraki), a landowner, collected men to 'defend the population'. Nasim Akhundzada

(Alizai/Hassanzai), the son of a locally famous cleric, did the same in Musa Qala.[55] Shortly after, at the end of November 1978, land redistribution was announced.

In January 1979, Musa Qala fell. One night at 3 a.m., District Governor Zabit Aulleah (Noorzai, Khalqi, from Garmsir) went on patrol with 300 depaye, presumably to supervise land redistributions the following day (land redistribution had begun that month). He was ambushed by Nasim. The depaye's leader, Ghulam Dastgar Mahali, who was also the district head teacher, was killed along with 100 of his men. The remainder fled back to the district centre, or hukomat (literally: government). On the following day Nasim brokered a deal with the district governor, allowing him to escape. Nasim then attacked the hukomat, and after killing 160 people associated with the government, he duly proclaimed himself district governor.

Three days later, the army was sent in from outside Helmand and retook the hukomat, installing an administrator from Nangahar, Sher Gul, as the governor. After a month, the army was redeployed elsewhere, leaving behind police and the depaye. Within two months, Nasim had reoccupied the hukomat, executing thirty Hassanzai elders (those from his clan and the people who posed a challenge to his power) who had been working with the government. He buried them in the village square, over which he had a dining area set up for entertaining guests.[56] His quest for power conveniently coincided with the narrative of resistance to communism.

By June, Now Zad, Washir and Sangin were under attack. Now Zad and Washir fell to coalitions of local commanders. Similarly, Sangin fell to Abdul Khaleq (Ishaqzai/Mistereekhel, from Qala-e Gaz), Atta Mohammad (Ishaqzai/Chowkazai, from Myanrodai)[57] and Dad Mohammad (Alakozai, from Sarwan Qala). The non-canal-zone areas had fallen from government control by mid-1979. Garmsir, Nad-e Ali, Marjeh and Nawa were to remain under government control until after the Soviet intervention at the end of the year.[58] Lashkar Gah remained a 'bastion of the regime'.[59] The higher education levels and lack of large-scale land redistribution in the canal-zone made them less susceptible to rebellion.

Thus, the response to the government was one of local resistance.[60] Originally, resistance groups rose up without the help of the mujahidin parties along community or tribal lines.[61] The mechanism was that an individual actor—a military entrepreneur[62]—would leverage the perception of a power vacuum, created by weakened or non-existent government in a district, to improve his own position. For this he needed two things: men to fight and weapons/supplies to equip them with. With the rise of the mujahidin parties, the leader would later come to personify the interaction between local factors and external ones. This was because supplies were more likely to be given out to successful commanders with many men, and men would be more likely to follow a commander who was well stocked with munitions. This interaction fuses the local elements of men and on-the-ground information, on the one hand, with the external elements of funding and legitimacy bestowed by an organisation—a mujahidin party—on the other. But at first, it was a local, spontaneous usurpation of government power.

The 'organised' resistance of the mujahidin parties only came later, once the Soviets had invaded. At the time, most of the northern districts were falling from government control and the mujahidin parties in Peshawar were still forming and reforming, fighting for influence and trying to attract funding.[63] Local commanders used different communication networks in order to reach out to Peshawar for membership, recognition and funding. For example, Hizb was a party well known for recruiting among teachers and the educated youth.[64] Their members often sought links through school or university colleagues to Gulbuddin Hekmatyar (Kharoti), the leader of Hizb, and the supplies coming from Peshawar. Harakat was almost exclusively a clerical party,[65] with those that reached out to it often doing so through religious teachers or other mullahs that they had met at madrassas. Mahaz, led by Pir Gailani and widely seen as the royalist party,[66] organised itself along connections either generated around the royal government or through teacher–pupil relationships in Gailani's Sufi order.

These interactions between fighter and party were related to refugee dynamics. Helmandi families, forced to move by the war and declining outputs of the canal and karez systems,[67] adopted what is known as a split-migration strategy.[68] This involved moving the bulk of the family to a refugee camp—usually Girdi Jangal in Pakistani Baluchistan—while leaving workers, usually older men, to tend the land and keep it productive. The young men would, of course, be fighting, thus allowing the family to maintain its obligations to the jihad. This meant the family tended to their assets at the same time as keeping safe and reducing costs, because they were being fed through refugee handouts. All of the mujahidin parties maintained offices in Girdi Jangal, and the people who fled to the camps were quickly recruited, armed and sent back.[69] This interaction was later repeated with the post-2001 Taliban.

The following section comprises examples of mobilisation, looking at three key individuals. They are self-descriptions (or descriptions by close family members). Self-descriptions are often self-justifying, and there is almost certainly some ex post facto justification occurring here: these narratives match much of the anti-communist rhetoric common to the mujahidin parties. However, these personal stories should be considered alongside the government collapse discussed above and the descriptions throughout the book of the actions of these key men in the fighting that was to consume the province.

Upon Taraki's acquisition of power, Hafizullah Khan, from Bolan (see Map 5), immediately left for Peshawar, where he met with Hekmatyar and started his training in Attock, in the Pakistani Punjab. As he put it, '[then] there was only Jamiat and Hizb to choose from'. He described the following tale, occurring in about 1969, when he was sixteen, as formative. Ghulam Mahmad Niazee, a leader of the nascent Islamic movement in Afghanistan, had come to speak at the Lashkar Gah Lycee, and the 'non-Muslims' (that is, the communists) had tried to stop him speaking. The Islamist students fought the communist students and Niazee was allowed to speak. After leaving school, Hafizullah studied engineering at Kabul University, shortly after Hekmatyar had been expelled and imprisoned for murder. There was still a residual 'Hekmatyar network', ensuring that when Hafizullah went to Peshawar he was only looking for one man. Once he had been appointed Hizb's Amir (leader) for Helmand by Hekmatyar in 1978, his job, as he put it, was to 'organise the war'. As the mujahidin organisation developed, this meant facilitating the relationship between fighting groups and organisation-supplied funding and weapons. He began to organise depots in Girdi Jangal and Baram Cha on the border between Helmand and Pakistan.[70]

Malem Mir Wali was two years younger than Hafizullah and shared very similar experiences. He also blamed many of the disturbances at the school on the communists and described the atmosphere as very factionalised: 'the communists did not pray and had no respect for the teachers', he said. What was happening at the school in Lashkar Gah during the 1970s was a microcosm of what was happening at the universities in Kabul: 'you knew who the communists were and who the Muslims [Islamists] were'. After graduating from school in 1975, Mir

Wali went to teacher training college in Kandahar, completing his studies eight months after the Taraki coup. Many of his classmates in Kandahar had links to Hizb, and the training college was a hotbed of political activism. He spent 1979 completing his national service. Just before the Soviets invaded, he returned home to Spin Masjid to teach in the primary school. After six months of teaching, and once the Soviets began to base themselves permanently in Helmand, he began fighting with Hizb as Shaed Mansour's (Barakzai) deputy. When Mansour was eventually killed by the Soviets in 1984, Mir Wali took over.[71]

Nasim Akhundzada, mentioned above, affiliated with Harakat. He had known Nabi Mohammedi, the leader of Harakat, since well before the war, when Nabi had owned land and taught in Helmand.[72] As Sher Mohammad, Nasim's nephew, said, 'once [Nabi] had started Harakat [in September 1978] it was obvious who Nasim would go with, all the mullahs were with Nabi'. Once Nasim had begun to 'protect the population' he reached out to Nabi in Peshawar. When the weapons began to flow is not known, but what is clear is that, much like the Hizb mobilisation described above, there was a relationship between what was occurring in Musa Qala and a mujahidin party with a particular ideology. Moreover, it was the commanders who reached out to the mujahidin parties and not vice versa, adding weight to a main conclusion of this book: that local dynamics drive the violence, with support from outside ideological elements, in this case the mujahidin parties.

In contrast to the popular Western narratives surrounding the Soviet intervention and the glorious mujahidin, actual events in Helmand paint a very different picture. In Kabul, Hafizullah Amin (Kharoti) seized power in September 1979. The takeover was an echo of the Taraki coup and little change to official government policy was seen in Helmand.[73] However, as an ex-Khalqi said to me, 'Amin just altered the patronage network.'[74] Those who had been jailed under Taraki were released, while those who had previously supported Taraki were jailed or fled.[75] Land, the key mechanism of patronage in Helmand, was redistributed again. 'Trib[al] [membership] was very important', said a senior Kharoti tribal figure; their confiscated land was returned to them by order of (the Kharoti) Amin.[76] Others began to take their land back. In most cases the new owners of their land were the previous tenants; only those who had done something wrong—such as the Khalqis who had stolen it—were removed and killed, while the remainder were allowed to stay, readopting tenant status. In one case described to me, the local Hizb commander arrived at a deal with the tribal leadership: the mujahidin would get their land back for them, but they had to pay. 'Jihad was not free.'[77]

Concurrently, groups of resistance fighters began to interact with the mujahidin parties, and gradually ostensibly began to adopt their ideas. As a result, the population became able to indicate which party a commander was affiliated with,[78] even though most commanders 'wouldn't have been able to say who Hekmatyar, Zahir Shah or the Muslim brotherhood were or what they stood for'.[79] This worked both ways: 'the [parties] who gave [them] weapons had no idea how they were being used'.[80] This is a clear example of local actors exploiting the mujahidin parties for instrumental purposes; something they were able to do due to the latters' ignorance of the complexity of local politics. Soon, the Soviet intervention would massively increase the amount of funding that mujahidin parties received—before the intervention they were 'more or less dormant' due to a lack of funding[81]—which would subsequently increase the opportunities for exploitation.

In December, with the situation spiralling out of control, the Soviets intervened and enthroned the Parcham faction under Babrak Karmal. They planned for a temporary deployment to stabilise the situation, thus allowing them to leave.[82] From the Soviet perspective, troops were not necessary in Helmand as 'the government was really strong [there]'.[83] They also considered Helmand, and particularly northern Helmand, to be a strategic backwater.[84] As one senior ex-communist police officer commented, 'before I came to Helmand, I thought it was just Gereshk'.[85] The central Soviet aim, and the only one that was continued until the end, was to keep the route from Herat to Kandahar open.[86] But the Soviet installation of Karmal had made him a puppet in the eyes of the Helmandis (even more so than Taraki and Amin, although there was no change in official policy between any of the three leaders as discerned from Helmand).[87] The population consequently responded by evicting the government from the remainder of the countryside, including Nad-e Ali, even getting to the point where they were able to fire upon Safean, a southern part of the urban area of Lashkar Gah.[88]

The situation became critical. In mid-1980, the Soviets deployed up to 500 troops to Lashkar Gah. Bost airfield, hereafter referred to as the 'maidan', the word used by Helmandis, was developed as the Soviet headquarters in Helmand.[89] Up to that point, only the pre-intervention mentoring structure of two advisors per police or army kandak (battalion) was in place.[90] The immediate Soviet concern was to establish a defensive perimeter (a 'cummerbund'; see Map 5) around Lashkar Gah, Gereshk and the connecting road through Chah-e Anjir. Secondary to that was the re-establishment of some of the hukomats from which the government had been evicted.[91] This took until late 1983 and involved some of the fiercest fighting of the Soviet Helmand deployment. The Nad-e Ali hukomat, for example, was established and overrun several times.[92]

The mujahidin, as they had become labelled by that point, were eventually pushed back, and a series of posts was established through Nawa, Aynak, Bolan, Loy Bagh, Chah-e Anjir, Basharan and in the desert to the east of Lashkar Gah.[93] A similar series of posts was established around Gereshk, running along the Abhashak Wadi and through Abhazan and Deh Adam Khan (see Map 5).[94] The Soviets then established a second headquarters with an artillery detachment on a small hill just to the south of Gereshk—the Helmandis now call the hill '*taapuh*' (artillery).[95] Soviet troop numbers based in Helmand eventually rose to about 1,000[96] or 1,500[97] by 1987.

## Inter-'Mujahidin' Conflict in Northern Helmand

Shortly after the Soviet invasion, the various actors in northern Helmand began to fight among themselves. Whereas coalitions of local groups had ejected the government in 1978 and 1979, they began to fall out during 1981. This was not helped by the fact that commanders who were geographically proximate often subscribed to different mujahidin parties because they were trying to gain leverage in local disputes; the interaction with different mujahidin parties worsened these local conflicts.[98] Northern Helmand's mini-civil war is one of the dynamics from this era that is completely divorced from the overarching narrative of the mujahidin resisting the Soviets. Local commanders used Soviet and mujahidin party money to fight each other, with private feuds driving the conflict.[99]

This dynamic was understood by Khad, the government security service, and exploited ruthlessly in Helmand as per its official national policy.[100] As Jabbar Qahraman, one of my on-the-record interviewees (see Appendix 1), said to me, 'the mujahidin in Helmand didn't fight the government at all; they fought each other'. 'Khad had links with all of [the mujahidin groups], we just sat back and watched them attack each other', he said with a laugh. In the wider context, not as much ISI-supplied mujahidin party money made it to Helmand as to other areas. They too considered it a backwater populated with the 'royal' Durrani tribes that they were trying to disempower.[101] Finally, one of the most notable features of the Helmandi conflict is the strategy employed by actors within a family, whereby individual members would side either with the government or with the mujahidin, in order to protect their lineage. This continues to the present day.

Now Zad provides a detailed example of the political situation. The situation was complicated. There were three main tribal groupings and a host of smaller communities, each of which had multiple commanders. The Ishaqzai, probably the largest community, were led by Mullah Abdul Ahad and were affiliated with Harakat. Ahad soon made himself submissive to Nasim from Musa Qala in order to guarantee supplies.[102]

The Noorzai were clustered around two leaders, Haji Abdullah Jan and Israel Khan, both of whom had sought supplies from Hizb. Israel Khan was in a stronger position, however; Mahmad Ashem, his patriarch, lived in Lashkar Gah, and was deliberately supportive of the 'government'. Tor Jan, his nephew, was also a tribal liaison officer in Khad. Israel was the family member in the 'mujahidin'. This affiliation with both the government and a mujahidin party was later to prove useful when the mujahidin took over Lashkar Gah, with Israel a member of the attacking force—the 'communist' members of his family were saved (see Appendix 4 for Mahmad Ashem's family tree).'[103]

The third largest community, the Barakzai, was led by Malem Yusof and Zabit Jalil, an ex-teacher and army officer respectively. Hizb supplied them both.[104] 'Hizb' and 'Harakat' in Now Zad soon began to fight, although the reason behind this is obscure. Some eyewitnesses say that the dispute concerned 'money and drugs',[105] while others point to the killing of a 'Harakat' commander by 'Hizb', sparking revenge.[106] Mir Wali believes they began to fight because of a failed internal 'Harakat' arrest that caused two 'Harakat' men to seek asylum with a 'Hizb' commander who then refused to give them up to 'Harakat' because of the importance of offering asylum to the Pushtun. Whatever the precise reason as to why 'Harakat' attacked 'Hizb',[107] it appears from the evidence above that local factors instigated the conflict. Khad also played an important role, if not in instigating the conflict, then in massively supporting the 'Harakat' factions through Nasim Akhundzada.[108] Khad's dealings with Nasim deviate so much from 'Harakat's' and the overarching mujahidin narrative that they are worth exploring in some detail.

Nasim, his brothers and nephew were later to dominate Helmand, and they continue to do so in the present day. A large part of the family narrative is that they fought the Soviets, forcing them to leave, and that they then evicted the remnants of the communist government from Lashkar Gah.[109] This echoes the glorious mujahidin narrative and is often presented thus in the literature.[110] When I interviewed Sher Mohammad Akhundzada, Nasim's nephew, and asked him whether his uncle had accepted supplies from Khad, as many others had, he started laughing and, stumbling over his words, asked me, 'Which Khad?' As we both knew, there was only one Khad.

He looked me straight in the eye, and, without a trace of irony, said 'we [were] the cleanest mujahidin in the country; it was *pure* jihad.' Whatever Sher Mohammad might protest, the fact that Nasim Akhundzada accepted money and supplies from Khad to attack other mujahidin groups, particularly Hizb ones, is well known in Helmand. He was not the only commander to have done so by any means, but he was the primary recipient of their aid.[111] Rasoul, Nasim's brother, even later preached in northern Helmand's mosques against Hizb: 'Parcham and Khalq have become Muslims, but not Hizb', he said.[112]

So why did the government support Nasim? In central Helmand, the main mujahidin party represented was 'Hizb', particularly in Nad-e Ali and around Gereshk, and they consequently represented the greatest threat to the government in Helmand. On an ideological and a national level, the government knew Hizb the best from pre-Saur revolution clashes in the universities. They were also scared of them as they were the most organised, literate and funded element of the resistance.[113] One knowledgeable and well-connected interviewee believes that the Khad interest in Now Zad was piqued by the growth of 'Hizb' there in early 1980.[114]

However, a policy of putting Hizb under pressure in northern Helmand in order to provide relief for the government in central Helmand betrays a misunderstanding by Khad of the degree to which there was a clear leadership structure among the mujahidin in Helmand. Khad were blinded by the political complexity. It shows that they were following the well-known narratives surrounding the mujahidin—particularly their ideological and unitary nature—rather than understanding that their formation, organisation and ideological affiliation were driven to a much greater extent by intimate local factors. This was confirmed by a professional police officer who stated that 'it was only during Najib's time [1986 onwards] that Khad started to understand the differences in-between the different mujahidin groups'.[115] Because Khad did not understand the local context surrounding different 'mujahidin' groups actors like Nasim manipulated them. This appears astonishing when you consider that some Khad operatives were related to mujahidin commanders. But it makes perfect sense if you consider that the centre of gravity for the conflict is the tribal group, clan or family, rather than the ideological divisions that we are so familiar with.

The inter-commander war widened. For example, Abdul Rahman Khan (Alizai/Khalozai) was a major commander from Kajaki. He had experienced 'problems' with Nasim since before the Saur revolution, but he was also responsible for 'Hizb' in the north of Helmand and in charge of those 'Hizb' sub-commanders who were fighting Nasim's Harakat-supplied commanders in Now Zad.[116] As a khan he would have been more likely to follow Mahaz (the royalist party), as opposed to Hizb, whose main constituency was teachers, engineers and other educated professionals,[117] yet he switched from Mahaz to Hizb when the former could not supply him adequately.[118] When asked about the reasons for the discord between Abdul Rahman Khan and Nasim, responses vary from money,[119] accusations about one or the other of them being supported by Khad[120] or giving information to Khad,[121] territory,[122] pre-Taraki issues,[123] or that Abdul Rahman Khan was dragged into the fighting because his sub-commanders were fighting for their lives in Now Zad.[124]

Rais Baghrani (mentioned earlier in this chapter, regarding the murder of two district governors of Kajaki), the third major commander in northern Helmand, came from the Khalozai, the same sub-tribe as Abdul Rahman Khan. Originally a Khalqi, he affiliated himself to Harakat.[125] In order to escape Nasim's growing dominance, he subsequently affiliated himself with Abdul Rahman Khan under Hizb patronage.[126] Baghrani was later to 'join' Jamiat, the Taliban and, finally, the Karzai government.[127] Each change in organisational 'membership' was due to evolutions in his local political context, which he needed to either exploit or not be destroyed by—ideologies were/are irrelevant to him. Soon, Baghrani and Nasim also began to fight, potentially in response to the Nasim–Abdul Rahman Khan fighting. Khad were ever-present on the sidelines.[128] These dynamics have implications reaching to the present day. Different ideologies, governments and conflict narratives have come and gone, but Baghrani's and Nasim's families are still fighting, all the while interacting with whichever outside organisations and ideologies will help them in that local fight (as we shall see in Chapters 3–6).

Events in Sangin followed a similar pattern.[129] Sangin had fallen to an alliance of Abdul Khaleq, Dad Mohammad and Atta Mohammad in mid-1979 (all from the areas surrounding Sangin's hukomat), who had ejected the governor, Engineer Qasim (Achakzai, Hyderabad, Khalqi).[130] Rauf Khan (Ishaqzai/Mistereekhel)[131] was a fourth commander from the north of Qala-e Gaz,[132] and appears not to have been involved in the original overthrow in Sangin, yet rose to become the Mahaz Amir for Helmand due to his standing as the second most important leader in the Helmandi Ishaqzai.[133] Dad Mohammad affiliated himself to Mahaz despite being Alakozai. He was driven by a competition with Atta Mohammad (Ishaqzai) over Sangin's bazaar.[134]

Thus Dad Mohammad was soon to 'join' Jamiat for the remainder of the jihad, as Mahaz could not supply him properly.[135] Atta Mohammad was 'with' Jamiat, although he had briefly 'been' Harakat at the very beginning, and was soon to re-affiliate himself with Harakat.[136] Abdul Khaleq, from the southern part of Qala-e Gaz, opted for Hizb,[137] probably because he was in competition with all of them and was the furthest removed from Sangin. His southern flank also abutted central Helmand, which was a Hizb stronghold. As was the case elsewhere, the side switching and deal making in Sangin clearly demonstrates that private disputes between local actors were the primary factor when deciding to affiliate with a specific mujahidin party (see Map 6). As the conflict wore on, these disputes began to be more and more about one thing: opium.

Opium poppy is a traditional crop in northern Helmand. During the course of the 1980s its cultivation spread province-wide.[138] It was politically and economically vital, as the drugs trade ensured survival due to the revenues it could generate, thus buying a military edge in local disputes. Drugs money increased an individual's power and allowed for greater territorial control, which in turn meant more control over the narcotics business. Although Nasim controlled the traditional opium-growing areas, other mujahidin groups soon adopted the same strategy.[139] Some scholars have argued that Nasim coerced individual farmers into poppy production.[140] But this seems unlikely given the attraction of poppy growing for farmers in terms of increased and more stable revenue.[141]

Nasim did, however, tax opium production at 10 per cent, with additional taxes also being placed on its transportation.[142] Rasoul, Nasim's older brother and a cleric, offered Islamic justification for the growing of opium. He manipulated Islamic and anti-communist narratives: 'we must grow and sell opium to fight our holy war against the Soviet nonbelievers' and 'Islamic law bans the taking of opium, but there is no prohibition against growing it', he said.[143] Moreover, Nasim offered credit to farmers under the traditional salaam system,[144] whereby he bought the crop at the time of sowing.[145] The opium moved out along the same route that weapons came in, to the Girdi Jangal camp in Baluchistan, then to nearby refineries owned by Hizb in Koh-e Sultan.[146] Nasim even had an office in Zahidan, Iran, to handle onward movement.[147]

The poppy funding gave Nasim another edge in his struggles with rival mujahidin groups, and soon the clashes became not only financed by drug profits, but about drug profits; control of agricultural land, transport routes and bridges became essential. The farmers grew the crop for economic reasons,[148] but the commanders had to control the territory to tax them. (Nasim's fighters demanded in-kind payments of bread from farmers for 'protection', and so farmers needed even more to maximise the revenue from their land.)[149] This dynamic continues today, with poppy funds often being used not so much to pay for anti-government fighting, but with anti-government fighting being used to defend or gain elements of the narcotics business. By the time the Soviets left in 1989, the 'mujahidin' in Helmand were considered to be largely self-financing.[150]

Nasim claimed to have set up hospitals and clinics in the areas that he controlled.[151] Similarly, Nasim and other clerical leaders, such as Baghrani, expanded their madrasa networks to train military recruits for their mujahidin forces (Nasim's were known as the 'Sacrificers')[152] and a clerical-run civil bureaucracy.[153] Measures such as these can clearly be interpreted as part of a traditional strategy by Helmandi leaders to gain legitimacy in the eyes of the local population. Regardless of how they have accumulated their money or power, most leaders in

Helmand begin to act like tribal leaders and distribute patronage to establish the beginnings of patron–client relationships. This provision of 'political' services to the population marks the transition to warlordism. Incidentally, Sher Mohammad, Nasim's nephew, went to one of these madrasas in Zamindawar with Abdul Qayoum Zakir, a future leader in the Taliban movement and head of the Taliban Military Commission in 2012.[154]

### Central and Southern Helmand

Central Helmand was more stable in terms of large-scale inter-commander warfare due to the presence of an enemy—the government and the Soviets. However, there were numerous, smaller groups as a result of the local social heterogeneity, particularly in the canal-zones. The government held Gereshk itself, and a defensive line was established by the hydroelectric dam to the east, the band-e barq, which was guarded by one of the few remaining depaye militias.[155] The area around the dam was (and remains) socially heterogeneous, with a Barakzai majority. This had been a vital part of the previous monarchy's power base in Helmand, and there are many Mohammadzai villages. There is a smattering of Kakar villages, some Ishaqzai on the eastern fringes and seventy-five mainly Ghilzai families from the canal projects.[156] This local heterogeneity significantly diversified mujahidin party membership, often village by village.[157] Hizb, Harakat, Mahaz, Etihad and Nejad were all mentioned as having villages in the area that sought supplies from them.[158] There was small-scale skirmishing throughout the jihad, but the presence of the government kept them focused (see Map 7).[159]

In Malgir, to the west of Gereshk, there was a slightly different situation. Malgir and the areas around Paind Kalay were overwhelmingly Barakzai. Those that were not, were implants from the Taraki land redistributions, but these were often ejected once the government lost control.[160] The Barakzai clans in that area have traditionally allied themselves into two power blocs of different clans. The more powerful clans, the Akhundzadakhel, the Utmanzai, the Bayezai and the Sardarzai, worked together in a coalition led by Haji Khalifa Shirin Khan. These generally affiliated with Hizb. The second, weaker power bloc was led by Haji Abdul Agha and consisted of the Shamezai, Nekazai, Yedarzai and Masezai. These generally affiliated with Harakat.[161] Both of the power-bloc leaders were major landowners, for example, Khalifa Shirin Khan owned 1,600 jereebs (320 hectares). Such large historical landowners were not 'normal' Hizb commanders. Thus in Malgir, the pre-Taraki division was reflected in the choice of mujahidin party selection.

According to Mir Wali, who was later to dominate the area as the major Hizb commander, 'Harakat' groups began to form in Malgir in 1980 under Mahmad Wali. The 'Hizb' groups formed in 1981 under Shaed Mansor (Barakzai) and eventually became more powerful. There was also a smattering of Mahaz and Etihad groups, but these soon allied themselves with one of the two dominant factions.[162] There were no major clashes between the different groups reported to me, at least during the first few years of the communist government. This was similar to Babaji, further to the west and positioned on the border between Lashkar Gah, Nad-e Ali and Nahr-e Saraj districts, where the villages (all Barakzai) tended to get along peacefully, despite differing party membership—Babaji was mostly Hizb affiliated, with some Etihad, Jamiat and Mahaz villages.[163] In Babaji, the types of commanders fitted the different mujahidin parties' ideologies. For example, the Mahaz leader was Khwashdel Khan, a tribal leader.[164] The Harakat groupings were under Mullah Hafizullah.[165] The fact that the different groups remained allied was likely due to their proximity to the government stronghold of Chah-e Anjir.

Nad-e Ali was different yet again. The canal settlements had created a unique social mix with different tribal and ethnic groups populating different villages, while some villages were completely socially mixed. As Nad-e Ali had the most developed government infrastructure of any rural area in Helmand, there was a significant degree of interaction between the government and the population, which in turn led to a degree of Khad penetration, although this appears to have been on a much smaller scale than in northern Helmand. Overall, Nad-e Ali did not suffer from the major infighting that was present elsewhere. There were several reasons for this. First, the presence of the government meant that the different groups had a clear target for their activities, and most of the different groups in Nad-e Ali shared common cause due to the fact that they had arrived at the same time, whereas elsewhere in Helmand the settlers were mixed in with the indigenous Helmandis. Secondly, in Nad-e Ali—as per the royal government's aims[166]—the social power blocs were relatively small, which meant that any infighting could be contained fairly quickly. The 'Hizb-Harakat' fighting was not to reach Nad-e Ali for some years, and by-and-large it remained peaceful until then (see Map 8).

The Kharoti were the largest community in Nad-e Ali at the time of the Soviet intervention.[167] Like many communities, or lineages, they used a strategy of bridging the mujahidin–government divide by deliberately placing people in influential positions on both sides.[168] In their thinking, the unit of currency that must survive was the community group. Thus the Kharoti leader, Wakil Safar, was appointed a senator by Babrak Karmal.[169] Yet the village that he was from, Shin Kalay, and another closely related Kharoti village, Naqilabad, were utterly dominated by 'Hizb' groupings (Hekmatyar, the leader of Hizb, was also Kharoti).[170] Ironically, it was the arrest of the respected Wakil Safar during the Taraki era that had pushed the village to reach out to Hizb for supplies.[171] Shin Kalay provided multiple fighting groups led by commanders such as Dr Jailani and Baryalai, with each commander leading men from their lineages.[172] (See Appendix 4 for a Kharoti tribal diagram.) Naqilabad was dominated by Pir Mohammad Sadat who was widely respected as an exceptionally brave commander and revered for fighting hand-to-hand against Soviet soldiers in irrigation ditches.[173]

The third major grouping of Kharoti in Nad-e Ali was made up of those who had been settled by Noor Mohammad Khan (also a parliamentarian)[174] around Khwashal Kalay and Noor Mohammad Khan Kalay. Previously kuchis (nomads), they were slightly looked down upon by the other Kharoti, who had already been landowners before they came to Nad-e Ali.[175] The Kharoti in Shin Kalay and Noor Mohammad Khan Kalay had been feuding at a low level for years.[176] Although Noor Mohammad's son Haji Jamalzai originally joined Hizb 'for lack of other parties',[177] the villages soon broke with the rest of the Kharoti and affiliated with Harakat[178] under Mullah Baz Mohammad (Taraki) from Marjeh.[179] The switch in mujahidin party affiliation was driven by the low-level feud with Shin Kalay. This dispute was to prove surprisingly stable during the jihad, however, with only minor skirmishing between the groups, usually over who could get supplies from different sections of the population.[180]

This stability was largely due to the presence of a Kharoti shura (standing leadership body) across the two mujahidin parties represented within the Kharoti and covering those members of the tribe in the government, including Wakil Safar—in other words, Kharoti tribal interests were allied across the memberships of several different opposed organisations.[181] Disputes between different Kharoti mujahi-din groupings would quickly be resolved before they escalated and the tribe was able to maintain a foot in all camps while sharing informa-tion between themselves.[182] When I questioned senior Kharoti leaders in early 2009 as a serving British army officer (in uniform) about those members of their tribe in the 'Taliban' that we knew to be fighting us, they would shrug and explain that they had lost control of the younger, more wayward members of the tribe. Their explanation was that the 'Kharoti' supported the government, but the tribe was fragmented because of the war. They argued that differing ideologies (for example, Islamism versus democracy) were driving the split in their tribe.

I further explored this issue as a researcher in 2011–12 with the same elders (after I had known them for three years)—I think they had for-gotten our original conversation. I suggested that the alliance of a pan-tribal shura straddling government and non-government lines and shar-ing information was still in existence during the contemporary conflict between the Taliban and the government. They laughed, looked sheep-ish and agreed.[183] It was fascinating to compare their open acknowl-edgement, even glee, at the deliberate splitting of families during the jihad with their denials of a similar contemporary dynamic when I, the questioner, represented one of the opposed sides (as a British officer I was working with the Afghan government). This is clearly consistent with the tendency of individuals in Helmand to exploit the ignorance of and manipulate outsiders for their own interests.

The second most populous community at that time was probably the Noorzai, centred in Loy Bagh, under the leadership of Shah Nazar Helmandwal. He was also asked by Karmal to be a parliamentarian despite his 'membership' of Mahaz.[184] Within Shah Nazar's sub-tribe, the Gurg, his brother Haji Pida Mohammad, was a 'clean skin' (that is, affiliated to no one), and his nephew, Abdul Ahad, was an 'Etihad' commander, although this was a deliberate decision for family safety, as opposed to the unplanned 'Hizb'–'Harakat' split in the Kharoti.[185] Another sub-tribe of the Noorzai in Loy Bagh, the Aghezai, was also deliberately split; its members were mostly in the 'government'—indeed, one of them, Khano, later became the most influential militia leader in Helmand. Yet Mullahs Habibullah and Karim, two influen-tial members of the sub-tribe and Khano's relatives, were the 'Hizb' commanders for the area (see Map 9).[186]

The high level of local feuds in Loy Bagh, existing alongside strong Hizb and government penetration, meant that Loy Bagh was frequently a battleground.[187] It was destroyed twice during government offensives, and even doubled up as the hukomat when the real one was overrun.[188] The deliberately split kinship groups were a gift for Khad. It enabled them to manipulate family disputes, sub-tribe against sub-tribe and cousin against cousin.[189] As Khad were Parchami dominated, Hizb and Khalq were both competitors to them, albeit on different sides of the 'government-mujahidin' divide.[190] Of course, this worked both ways—it was not just Khad exploiting familial feuds, but members of the population attempting to manipulate Khad against their own personal enemies.[191] This meant that Loy Bagh became an impossible place in which to live—several people left and went to Chah-e Mirza in order to prosecute their jihad there.[192] This in turn led to their neighbours trying to steal their land—something else that Khad spotted and took advantage of.[193] As one senior Noorzai tribal leader described it, 'it was a civil war between families'.[194] Loy Bagh was a 'front line', and whose territory you lived in dictated your ideological leanings.[195] Interestingly, in Loy Bagh, Khad understood well the local political dynamics,[196] which meant that neither side was able to dictate the dynamics of the conflict; neither the 'government' nor the 'mujahidin' wanted to destroy the village, yet that was precisely what happened.

The last major group of Noorzai in Nad-e Ali were not settlers from the canal projects. Haji Lal Jan (Noorzai/Darzai, Harakat) led a group of Noorzai tribesmen from the village of Gundacha in Washir to Noorzo Kalay (so named after them), north of the Nahr-e Bughra, just as government control began to slip in central Helmand. Water stress had forced them out of Washir.[197] He knew the area because his brother, Qabir Khan, had been fighting with Harakat in Nad-e Ali.[198] They were cousins of Abdul Rahman Jan (Noorzai/Darzai), who was later to become much more prominent as the Helmand chief of police under President Karzai.[199] Another group that came at that time was an Ishaqzai community led by Rahmattiar that settled to the south of Khwashal Kalay in Jangal. As a Hizb commander, Rahmattiar had negotiated a deal whereby the Hizb Amir Hafizullah would bless what was effectively land theft.[200] Rahmattiar was to grow into the most powerful Hizb commander in the south of Nad-e Ali.[201]

Despite the differences between Rahmattiar (Hizb, Ishaqzai, land thief) and Jamalzai (Harakat, Kharoti, settler) in terms of background and provenance, there was no infighting reported between the groups in the early stages of the jihad. Khwashal Kalay (meaning Happy

Village) was shared on an amicable basis between Harakat and Hizb. Haji Mullah Paslow, leading the Popalzai community around Khwashal Kalay, was the third major commander in the area. Both Harakat commanders, Jamalzai and Paslow, received their supplies from Baz Mohammad in Marjeh.[202] The Hazaras, right on the southern tip of Nad-e Ali, were unified and fought with Wahdat, a Shia, Iranian-sponsored party, under Assadullah Karimi, the village teacher.[203] Marjeh was similarly fractured with Hizb commanders, including Obaedi (Daftani) and Muslimyar (Achakzai); Mahaz commanders, including Tor Jan (Alakozai); Etihad commanders, including Matouf Khan and Yahya (Noorzai); and Jamiat commanders, including Hakim Khan (Daftani); as well as the aforementioned Baz Mohammad who organised Harakat supplies in the area.[204] The social heterogeneity that the canal projects had created bred a plethora of mujahidin groups.

Moving further south, Nawa enjoyed a unique situation that meant that fighting was kept at a low level during the jihad. Aside from the settlers, Nawa is dominated by the Popalzai and Barakzai tribes, who enjoy good relations with each other (in Helmand). At first, many fighting groups affiliated themselves with Mahaz, a natural party for these two 'royal' tribes; however, an absence of supplies meant that they both subsequently aligned with Jamiat.[205] Jamiat in Nawa was led by Akhwaendi (Barakzai/Akhundzai), the party Amir for the province.[206] But the most important factor in Nawa's stability was that Allah Noor (Barakzai/Nooradinzai/Gurgezai), a relative-by-marriage of Akhwaendi (Akhwaendi's sister married Allah Noor's brother), was the Khalqi militia leader in charge of the southern part of the cummerbund that stretched through Nawa, protecting the district centre and Lashkar Gah.[207]

Allah Noor's brothers were in Jamiat, and Akhwaendi's brothers were in the militia, and 'a lot of women had been swapped between [their] two clans [over the years]'.[208] Consequently, there was little discord between the 'government' and 'Jamiat' in Nawa, largely because they were composed of allied clans! This also allowed both the government and the mujahidin to claim that they 'controlled' Nawa, thus enabling the actors on the ground to continue asking for funding. Any fighting that did occur in the area was between Hafizullah Khan's 'Hizb' commanders and Akhwaendi's 'Jamiat' commanders, who were backed up by Allah Noor—the 'government'. Yet this was mainly over who could control and tax the people in that part of the Barakzai belt,[209] and bears no resemblance to the overarching narratives surrounding the conflict.

Finally, we turn to Garmsir. As the gateway to Pakistan, Garmsir occupies a strategic position as a major mujahidin supply route for weapons travelling into, and for drugs travelling out of, Helmand. However, as elsewhere, the resistance in Garmsir started independently of political parties. Haji Aurang Khan (Noorzai), a tribal leader, had been Garmsir's first political prisoner, and when he was released after twelve months in jail he began to fight the government. In 1980, he 'joined' Harakat, using the village mullah's links to a Harakat mawlana (senior religious figure) named Zakiri (Hotak, from Kandahar) in the party's Quetta office. Aurang cooperated with mujahidin from other parties including Hazandar and Neamatullah Khan (both Alizai, Hizb)[210] and Alam Gul (Kharoti, Nejad).[211]

Despite this cooperation, they were unable to push the government out of the hukomat. In mid-1980 Mudomer Khan (Noorzai), a Harakat commander, enlisted the support of Nasim Akhundzada from Musa Qala to come down and evict the government.[212] Nasim left behind a 'Harakat' administration, but problems soon began to emerge. Aurang still allowed 'Hizb' to operate in the district and pass supplies as they had done before—after all, they were all mujahidin fighting the infidel communists. But Zakiri in the Harakat office complained. Aurang promptly left Harakat and became independent again. Sometime later (probably in 1982), once the Soviets had re-established the district centre, Aurang and his men re-joined the jihad with the Khales faction of Hizb.[213]

This chapter has so far summarised what was occurring in the different districts in Helmand in response to the communist takeover and ensuing Soviet intervention. This general discussion of the different districts reveals an intensely complicated political situation. Each of the areas had a slightly different mix of local factors—the presence of government in their area, the degree and type of social fragmentation based on tribal structures, length of time settled in the area, migration patterns, land ownership and so on—which resulted in a multiplicity of conflict dynamics.

In most areas, however, the role of private disputes and local actors in manipulating the mujahidin parties and the government was paramount. That they usually managed to do this is testament to the ignorance of the local complexity displayed by the government and mujahidin parties. The coping strategy employed by Helmandis over the last thirty-four years—membership of different opposed organisations from within the same family or lineage—demonstrates clearly how in these circumstances local factors were more important in driving conflict dynamics than external, ideological ones. For every example, though, there is a counter-example. Some families did genuinely split along ideological lines at the beginning of the jihad, only to reconcile later, but such examples are comparatively rare.[214] The chapter now moves on to discuss how the government attempted to control the situation.

### Government Infighting and Response

In a reflection of the intra-'mujahidin' fighting, there were major problems between the Khalqi and Parchami factions within the government.[215] Helmand was an important area for Khalqi recruitment, yet Parchamis dominated the national government. Therefore Kabul had to tread a careful line politically in Helmand, and chose to appoint Khalqis there as a reflection of the local political landscape. Zeyarmal, a Parchami Barakzai from Kandahar, for example, was appointed provincial governor in 1984, but was swiftly removed when it came to be understood that only Khalqis could work in that position.[216] The police, who were drawn from the villages of central Helmand, tended to be Khalqi dominated. Khad, which was mostly Parchami, did not trust the Helmandi Khalqis, leading to problems with information sharing and cooperation.[217] Worse, their Soviet mentors often took on the views of their mentees, causing factionalism within the Soviet establishment as well.[218] Of course, within these distinctions the degree to which people actually subscribed to their espoused ideologies must also be taken into account, as party membership was often a necessary part of career advancement. Parcham and Khalq are perhaps best considered as solidarity groups, rather than strict ideological factions.[219]

The Khalqi–Parchami relationship was a complicating factor for the overall Soviet–Afghan government relationship within Helmand. The latter relationship was generally good, particularly between the Soviets and the Parchamis. Soviet troops were stationed in Helmand for a period of two years and so were able to gain some familiarity with Helmandi local politics. In addition, the Soviet intervention had been prefaced by a decades-long relationship between the Soviet Union and Afghanistan, meaning that many of the Helmandi communists had studied in the Soviet Union and spoke Russian. As such, there was a degree of familiarity with each other's culture, and they would often socialise together in Lashkar Gah. The Soviets also had a number of Pushtu-trained linguists, as well as native Tajiks (Farsi, Dari and Tajik are all derivations of the same language that allow mutual comprehension). Finally, many of the Afghan communists were already members of the PDPA before the Soviets intervened, so a person's 'ideology' was better known, which increased general trust between the two camps.[220] However, while many Khalqis were willing to accept the technical and material help that the Soviets gave them, as Habibullah, an ex-Khalqi district governor in the Karzai era said, 'it was ok to cooperate on military stuff, but the politics were all wrong between [us and them]'.

The mosaic of different militia groups must also be factored into this broader picture. Allah Noor, from Nawa, was in the Grow Mudafen: the Revolutionary Defence Group.[221] These militias had fairly low salaries and were not particularly strict with regard to their ideological recruitment criteria[222]—while they were comprised mainly of students in Helmand, there were even some ex-mujahidin present in their ranks. The main factor holding them together was their salaries.[223] The band-e barq was held by another type of militia, a derivation of the Zahir Shah-era militias, the Depaye Khudai, which were essentially village defence forces[224] and were 'mainly mujahidin anyway'.[225] There were other types of militia, including the more ideologically focused, with PDPA membership a prerequisite to admission, such as the Depayan-e Enqelab.[226] At their peak, there were probably around 4,500 police and associated police militias in Helmand.[227]

While the early rebel bands were seeking supplies from their respective mujahidin parties, the government and their Soviet backers were fighting to secure central Helmand. The cummerbund came under the responsibility of the police,[228] although Khalqi militias held the southern sections.[229] Outside the police cummerbund, the Afghan army was deployed. Their brigade headquarters were based in Bolan[230] with kandaks in Khan Eshin, Khwash Kawa, Garmsir and the desert to the south of the Arghandab River. Their main role was the interdiction of mujahidin supply routes. Artillery was kept in Bolan, the maidan and to the south of Gereshk, and was regularly used to shell villages as punishment for harbouring 'mujahidin'.[231] Aside from their advisors in the police, Soviet troops also worked with the Afghan army, although the numbers of Soviet troops in Helmand were much smaller and would rise and fall depending on what was happening across the south and west of Afghanistan.[232] At most, the Soviets had a kandak in Lashkar

Gah and a kandak of spetznaz (Special Forces) working across the province with the Afghan army. Any major operations were usually conducted by extra troops brought in from either Kandahar or Herat.[233]

Central Helmand became the focus of many government and Soviet operations to 'clear' the mujahidin and establish security posts and district centres. Without exception, my ex-mujahidin interviewees would focus on the cruelty of the Soviet and Afghan troops, and particularly on the ubiquitous use of airpower and artillery.[234] This was usually used in response to 'mujahidin' attacks, and included the use of anti-personnel bomblets and mines in villages.[235] In one instance, the village of Zhargoun Kalay in Nad-e Ali was completely destroyed from the air.[236] Events such as theft and rape were also reported as commonplace.[237] Worst of all, massacres of the civilian population occurred, the largest of which is documented below.

Without access to Soviet sources, and given the time that has since elapsed, it is extremely difficult to pick apart different government and Soviet operations. From the perspective of the population, they had a short-term military focus, with the aim being to kill as many mujahidin as possible and not to hold territory.[238] The re-establishment of the hukomats in central and southern Helmand required longer-term operations, but not longer than two or three months.[239] The Afghan army and Soviet troops would then withdraw to their bases, leaving the police to hold the hukomats, often resulting in a 50-by-50 metre defensive perimeter.[240]

Operations in central and southern Helmand would generally occur approximately once every month and would be of a small scale.[241] In comparison, the less-frequent operations in northern Helmand were not intended to establish security posts.[242] These operations were conducted by units from Kandahar and Herat and sometimes involved thousands of troops.[243] Ex-communist interviewees repeatedly emphasised the fact that, in all of these operations, the Soviets made serious attempts to help the population with medical, agricultural and other support,[244] which was consistent with their narrative of 'international duty'. However, these attempts were not understood or appreciated by the population, given that they took place against a backdrop of indiscriminate violence.[245] It was these operations above all else, and the resultant damage to the irrigation systems, that drove people to move their families to Pakistan as refugees. Whether that damage was deliberate or accidental is a question of perspective.[246]

By far the worst event perpetrated by government and Soviet troops in central Helmand was the massacre in Khwashal Kalay, Nad-e Ali, which probably occurred on the second day of Eid al-Adha (10 October 1981).[247] The reasons for the massacre vary—some say it was carried out as an act of revenge in response to the killing of a Soviet colonel near Shin Kalay the day before,[248] while others maintain that the village of Khwashal Kalay had not provided its conscription quota,[249] or merely that the village was a centre of resistance that needed to be punished.[250]

Government and Soviet troops went through Khwashal Kalay, searching for people, before lining up 200 villagers.[251] The troops then proceeded to move along the line shooting each person in turn, with women being taken away for rape elsewhere in the village.[252] The troops then moved through the villages, in the process killing those who had escaped or avoided the line-up; they even turned their weapons on the villager's dogs, camels and donkeys. Eyewitnesses describe the smell as their most vivid memory of this terrible event; bodies were still being found two weeks later. That evening, people from the surrounding countryside crept into the village to bury the dead in the village graveyard on the desert escarpment to the west. The villagers were buried four to a grave.[253]

Many interviewees, including an interviewee from the government, acknowledged the fact that a deliberate massacre of around 200 people had occurred.[254] The one eyewitness to the aftermath that I interviewed said that the massacre was committed by a Soviet unit called 'seyara sarakuwa' (my transcription from their enunciation), but I have been unable to translate the phrase or find any more information regarding the unit. According to the same interviewee, the unit was involved in operations in Chah-e Mirza shortly afterwards in which Amir Jalat Khan (Kakar), a Jamiat commander, was killed with eighty-five of his men. That was the end of Jamiat in Chah-e Mirza for the remainder of the jihad.[255] Many of my interviewees were tough men who had done and seen terrible things, yet they became misty eyed and faltering when discussing the Khwashal Kalay Eid massacre. This level of emotion was not displayed when discussing any other events during the interviews. For that reason it was very hard to pick apart the details surrounding the event. For example, I do not know the number or identity of any Helmandis involved in perpetrating the massacre or the exact motivations. In a macabrely interesting way, this event does fit the overall Western narratives surrounding the conflict: Russian and communist atrocities were often highlighted.

At the national level, Karmal's inability to manage the situation eventually prompted his removal by the Soviets, who installed Dr Najibullah (hereafter known as Najib) in his place. He was the previous head of Khad.[256] The lack of progress or momentum at the national level was reflected in Helmand. Although the cummerbund was complete, there was a limit on what military operations could achieve in terms of getting the central Helmandi population to support what they considered an occupation government (the government was perceived by the rural population as a 'godless puppet government').[257] In return, many PDPA officials were utterly disdainful of 'tribalism', which they considered 'feudal and backwards'.[258] These were issues that were unlikely to go away while Karmal was in power or while the country was under Soviet occupation. Still the civil war raged in northern Helmand.

Yet normal life went on regardless. Those government employees and businessmen that were not ideologically committed to communism, or responsible for cruelty or atrocities, and offered a service that was needed in the rural areas—such as doctors or engineers—were allowed to travel with a party of elders in order to offer medical support or service the canal networks.[259] Schooling and health services continued in the centres of Lashkar Gah, Gereshk and occasionally the southern and central district centres, but these were precarious and sometimes evicted by mujahidin.[260]

Najib became general secretary of the PDPA in May 1986. Shortly afterwards, he launched his National Reconciliation Programme. The population was fairly cynical to new pronouncements, and with the change in rhetoric, people were not sure if it 'was just noise or whether it was an actual change ... certainly in the beginning there was a lot of talk and not much action'.[261] However, as Najib's rule developed, many, even some mujahidin commanders, began to consider him a good leader who was much more conciliatory in approach when compared to the dogmatic policies of the Karmal administration.[262] The National Reconciliation Programme was designed to bridge ideological differences between the irreconcilable mujahidin and government viewpoints, by softening hard-line government positions. Aspects of the programme included power sharing with non-PDPA parties or individuals, an amnesty for political prisoners and a new constitution modelled on the pre-communist constitution of 1964. Later on, Marxism was removed and replaced with Islam and the market economy as 'guiding principles' of the government and nation.[263] This overarching ideological framework was designed to encapsulate a much more pragmatic policy on the ground in Helmand.

This policy consisted of a three-pronged strategy that was heavily dominated by Khad. First, it evaluated its policy of support for mujahidin groups and decided to focus on supporting Nasim in his war to wipe out all the other mujahidin groups, particularly 'Hizb' groups. This was the hammer. Secondly, the anvil: Khad began to offer amnesty and arms to whole mujahidin bands, and the communities they were drawn from, if they agreed to come over to the government and form militias. These twin policies formed the main base of the government's strategy to reduce government–mujahidin violence in the province, and were complemented by the third prong: that of inviting mujahidin figures to take their place in the government.[264]

These policies were used as means to break the stalemate of the Karmal years and as a way to ensure the government's survival once the Soviets left.[265] However, they should also be seen as a rebalancing of power from the centre to the periphery (that is, from state to tribe). In a patronage system such as that which exists in Helmand's society, ideological manoeuvring has little effect without the threat of force or the benefits of cash and supplies. Thus the provincial council, once reformed, was still seen as a fig leaf because it had no funding to distribute.[266] Yet Najib's policies could be considered a success, at least according to government figures: between 1985 and 1987 the percentage of Helmand under 'government control' rose from 13.1 per cent to 24 per cent.[267]

Shah Nazar Khan, the leader of the Nad-e Ali Noorzai, from Loy Bagh and a Mahaz 'member', was appointed provincial governor in 1987.[268] Khad carried out the negotiations leading to his appointment. But while Shah Nazar was a significant tribal leader, he was not a particularly important 'mujahidin' commander. Despite being the provincial governor, he was not necessarily in the 'government'—he merely adopted the government label to support his own private interests. The remainder of his family continued their affiliations with the same 'mujahidin' franchises detailed previously, with his non-affiliated brother acting as a go-between.

Thus in 1989, during mujahidin infighting in Nad-e Ali, the 'Etihad' part of the family came under pressure from Rahmattiar's 'Hizb' groups. Shah Nazar used his relatives in Khad to contact the 'Etihad' part of the family and offer weapons. This was still the case when it became clear that the weapons were being used to attack Habibullah (Noorzai, Garmsir), the Khalqi chief of police in Nad-e Ali who was under a constant state of siege from the mujahidin. At that point, it was only Habibullah and his men that were enabling the 'government' to remain in Nad-e Ali.[269] The family's interests were much more important than Shah Nazar's affiliation with the government.

In northern Helmand, Khad further inflamed the Nasim–Abdul Rahman Khan tensions by increasing its support to Nasim at the expense of other commanders.[270] Even though Nasim 'did one thing for Khad and ten for himself' (that it, Nasim manipulated Khad),[271] the supplies had the desired effect, and by 1987 Abdul Rahman Khan had been forced out of Kajaki, to Malgir, where he based himself with Mir Wali.[272] At around the same time, Baidullah (Alizai/Khalozai), originally a 'Khalqi' district governor of Kajaki, but now a sub-commander of Abdul Rahman, defected back to the 'government' with his men and formed a militia in Gereshk. The fact that he was the first significant commander to do so means that he is still remembered today. Later on he was to defect back to 'Hizb' in Nad-e Ali and was eventually killed by Nasim.[273]

At the same time, Rais Baghrani joined Jamiat because Nasim was successfully blocking Hizb supplies reaching Baghran from Pakistan. Hundreds of people died in clashes between the two of them in the summer of 1988. His defection was a boon to Jamiat as it was another way of guaranteeing supplies to Ismail Khan in Herat, at the end of a very long supply route.[274] Slightly later, Rauf Khan (Ishaqzai, Mahaz) also defected to the government and formed a militia in Gereshk from his mujahidin band.[275] These glorious 'mujahidin' groups, fighting for their liberty and for Islam, were simply bought off with government cash.

Nasim began to expand and attack other 'mujahidin' groups throughout the province. Mir Wali was a particular target for harbouring Abdul Rahman Khan, and so Nasim reinforced the local Harakat groups in Malgir. This was the first time that the 'Hizb'–'Harakat' war had come to Malgir, which was exactly what the government had wanted to happen (although Mir Wali had fought Nasim before in Now Zad as part of the previous 'Hizb'–'Harakat' fighting).[276] Those mujahidin groups unaffiliated with either Hizb or Harakat quickly chose to join one or the other.[277] Nasim then persuaded Dad Mohammad

(Alakozai) in Sangin to ally with him; Mohammad did not leave Jamiat, but merely formed an alliance with Nasim.[278] Little persuasion was needed if the extra supplies would help him fight Atta Mohammad (Ishaqzai), his closest rival.

The Dad Mohammad–Atta Mohammad dispute dictated the story of Sangin. However, the combination of two leaders with similar names, and jihadi affiliations to the same two parties or splinters thereof, means that it is extremely difficult to identify the dynamics in Sangin during the jihad, and the following should be treated with a degree of caution. Interviews, secondary sources and discussions with Sangin experts fail to yield clarity, and it can be argued that the complexity of local politics in the area continues to contribute to the violence in the present day (see Map 6). In this story, the complexity of shifting alliances and deals was epic. The actors and groups in Sangin were willing to subscribe to any ideology in order to obtain weapons to help them in their quest for local dominance.

Atta had previously betrayed Nasim by leaving 'Harakat' to join 'Jamiat'. Rasoul, Nasim's brother, had then reportedly said 'I don't want to kill anyone except Atta; he is the devil.'[279] Thus the subsequent alliance between Dad Mohammad and Nasim benefited them both, as Atta and Dad were rivals. Atta Mohammad later 'joined' what the locals called kuchnai (little) Harakat (whereas Nasim was in loy (big) Harakat)—probably one of the splinter factions of Harakat led by Mansur or Malawi Moazen[280]—presumably because he was able to secure better supplies to fight Dad Mohammad.[281] At that time, Dad Mohammad and Atta Mohammad each repeatedly took control of the bazaar and lost it again. During the course of this, Atta Mohammad affiliated with Harakat, Jamiat and then kuchnai Harakat, while Dad Mohammad affiliated with Mahaz, before joining Jamiat and then forming an affiliation with Harakat. Privately, they continued to fight each other for much of the time.[282]

Hafizullah Khan, the Hizb Amir for Helmand, later claimed to me that Atta affiliated himself with Hizb as well. This is unlikely as Atta Mohammad, as well as fighting Dad Mohammad to the north, was also fighting Abdul Khaleq (also Ishaqzai, Mistereekhel) to his south, who was with Hizb.[283] Abdul Khaleq was eventually to die during this period in Qala-e Gaz, although whether this was due to government or intra-mujahidin action is not known.[284] As this was occurring, the other half of the Mistereekhel under Rauf Khan was persuaded to join the government (he was under heavy pressure from Atta Mohammad at the time).[285] Rauf then became the leader of one of the first tribal kandaks in Gereshk.[286] This war over Sangin, and its profitable drugs bazaar, has yet to be concluded at the time of writing in 2013. The conflict is still being driven by these local dynamics, although the ideological narratives of the conflict have changed several times.

Outside of Sangin, the Khad-funded 'Hizb'–'Harakat' war continued apace and Nasim began to dominate northern Helmand. Baghrani was contained in Baghran. Now Zad and Washir came under Nasim's purview.[287] Although there were attempts at mediation by Israel Khan (Noorzai, Etihad, from Now Zad) throughout the decade,[288] this was all-out war funded by Khad. At the time, Israel's family was split across 'Khad', 'Etihad' and 'Hizb', but it is not known what effect this had on negotiations, if any. Apparently, the Soviets (and presumably Khad) only realised just before they left that Israel's family was split in this way—this according to my interviewee, a member of the clan, and a member of 'Khad'.[289] The war was increasingly becoming about the most important komandan (Helmandis borrowed the Russian word for commanders) and where they could accrue resources in an utterly tangled web of manipulations and counter-manipulations.

It is worth considering at this point what Nasim gained as a result of this territorial control. He was certainly not the governor of northern Helmand in the sense that a Western observer would understand—he did not have direct, de jure control over all of the territory that he 'owned', for example. That territory also contained the networks of his vanquished foes who had been forced to accept Nasim's rule. The nature of tribal or militia warfare is that Nasim would have established himself as the dominant security actor in that space—the primus inter pares—and this would have given him some ability to levy 'Islamic' taxes on agricultural production, particularly the ever-expanding poppy fields. Some areas, like Baghran, he was unable to influence at all, while others he could only influence by proxy.

Nasim developed his rule though a series of inter-clan marriages. In this, he was seeking to be able to rely more on those commanders who controlled his sub-areas. The nature of patronage-based tribal militias is that there is a shifting system of allegiances, dependent upon what each individual commander thinks he can gain by loyalty to his patron. The fact that Khad injected a great deal of patronage into this system through Nasim allowed him to 'buy' more commanders, and 'acquire' more territory, which in turn allowed him to make more money from the poppy crop in a virtuous circle; however, the nature of these interactions makes them inherently unstable, as they are based on personal relationships.[290]

There was concern that the government would not be able to survive the Soviet drawdown,[291] and so the second part of the government strategy, starting in 1987,[292] concerned the increased formation of militias, which both diminished the recruitment pool for the resistance and increased government forces. The militias were employed to defend major population centres and government sites in Lashkar Gah and Gereshk, which were all that the post-Soviet government could realistically expect to hold. The Parchami-dominated Khad grew its 'mujahidin' kandaks, some of whom ended up in the army chain of command. The police grew their own 'Khalqi' militia kandaks.[293] For the tribal leaders, having members of the tribe in different parts of the 'government' and the 'mujahidin' was a perfect way to enhance their position. With a militia, they now had their own 'force' that they could move individual fighters into and out of, while maintaining government legitimacy and access to healthcare (critical for wounded mujahidin). For example, Jabbar Qahraman, the leader of the largest militia in the south, used to offer healthcare to wounded mujahidin in Kandahar.[294]

Thus recruitment by different 'government' organisations led to a patchwork of militias under different chains of command that progressively emasculated the professional armed forces in Helmand.[295] The militias were initially under professional control. Later, after the Soviet forces had left, a shift occurred where militias began to outnumber and control the 'professionals'. Eventually, the key division in Gereshk was to come under Allah Noor's (militia) control.[296] At the time of the Soviet withdrawal in February 1989, the militia situation was becoming increasingly confused, with groups changing their chains of command, or ignoring it altogether and doing as they wished.[297] As a former professional army officer said disgustedly, 'the Najib militias were just private armies'.[298]

The 'Khalqi' police militias tended to be based around Lashkar Gah in order to reinforce the cummerbund. Allah Noor, in Nawa and later in Bolan, was the largest of these at that time, but other examples include Khano (from the Noorzai/Aghezai sub-tribe from Loy Bagh), Khudai Noor (Noorzai, from Garmsir) and Usem Khan (Barakzai) who guarded his hometown's part of the cummerbund in Basharan.[299]

Khano had taken advantage of the fact that his brother was closely linked to a senior Khalqi by launching a militia.[300] He originally started with a kandak-sized militia and ended up becoming a major-general militia commander by the early 1990s. He later spawned an impressive Helmandi dynasty, including a son who studied as a 'refugee' in Ireland and was an Afghan MP in the 2005 session.[301]

The militias under Khad's control guarded what the central government considered to be critical strategic points. Thus there was a Baluch militia under Mir Aza (who was actually Pakistani Baluch) to help guard the frontier with Pakistan,[302] and there were militias in Deh Adam Khan to defend the band-e barq (hydroelectric dam).[303] Engineer Matin (Noorzai) was given the most important job of all: defending the Khad headquarters and supplying depots in Lashkar Gah and at the maidan.[304]

The militias that fell under Afghan army command clustered around Gereshk under the remit of the 93rd Division. This was because the government, like countless before it, recognised the strategic importance of Gereshk. The division began with an establishment of 2,000 men, but as the 'jihadi' kandaks grew this was expanded to 7,000, dwarfing the professional forces in the province.[305] But the government policy was working (for them). 'Mahaz', for instance, had lost Shah Nazar Helmandwal, Dad Mohammad and Rauf Khan, their Amir. By 1987 they were no longer a force in the province. However, the groups and individuals that had comprised 'Mahaz' were still in existence, but were now affiliated with new mujahidin parties or the government. As the Soviets left, the division was under the command of General Baba Tapa, a professional officer.[306]

Finally, sitting outside all of these structures was the brigade of militias under the command of Jabbar, but answering directly to Najib, based in Maiwand and supposedly responsible for security across much of the south once the Soviets left.[307] These conflicting chains of command were to lay the basis for much friction later.

While the inter-'mujahidin' war was continuing, and Khad was gradually increasing the number and importance of militias in the province, conventional operations still continued. This included an extensive operation in Sangin launched by Soviet and Afghan troops, as well as militias, from March to May 1988. Large government operations were among the only times that the mujahidin worked together to a common goal, and this time the Soviets were forced to reinforce themselves from Shindand airbase in Herat province.[308] The operation spread from Sangin to Qala-e Gaz in April and then Sarwan Qala in May. On the first of June, the Soviets pulled out.[309] However, it is hard to say what the long-term effects of operations like these were.

In this case, for example, some argue that the operation was to set up power lines,[310] which the 'mujahidin' took down once the 'government' troops had gone. Others argue that it was designed to provide a distraction for withdrawal later that year, and to allow the new militias some breathing space.[311] Whatever the reason, starting in February, 6,000 regular troops and militias fought towards Kajaki; effectively, the central Helmandis were paid to fight the northern Helmandis, reinforcing the old north–south divide.[312]

The conventional military operations, in short, simply, did not change the facts on the ground. When a mujahed was killed, his relatives would feel honour-bound to replace him with another male member of the family,[313] and so massive military sweeps were pointless. What broke the Karmal-era stalemate was the programme led by Khad that supported Nasim to force other mujahidin groups to join the government. An important example of this is the defection of Mir Wali to the government in 1989, as he was pressed in Malgir by 'Harakat' (Nasim) and Khad. Mir Wali became a kandak commander, with responsibility for the Abhashak Wadi part of the cummerbund.[314]

The withdrawal of Soviet and regular Afghan government forces from Helmand in 1988 was part of the first phase of the Soviet withdrawal plan,[315] which was preceded by a retrenchment of Helmandi district-level government. First, in June 1988 the government withdrew from Khan Eshin.[316] Garmsir was then abandoned in August.[317] The central districts of Nad-e Ali and Nawa were part of the cummerbund for Lashkar Gah and so were held. The last regular government force to leave Helmand was a Soviet spetznaz battalion that withdrew from Kajaki at the end of October 1988.[318] Nasim's men immediately (re-) occupied the dam.[319] By the end of October 1988, the government was only present within its central defensive line.[320]

## Conclusions

The Soviet era has tended to be viewed through the prism of the Cold War. The narratives of the virtuous, pure mujahidin fighting the evil, godless and cruel Soviets are well known. Here, I have shown the

Helmandi interpretation of those events, with a level of complexity inherent in local politics that almost defies analysis. And when external actors, such as the mujahidin parties and the government, are unaware of that local context, the latter is more likely to shape the dynamics of the conflict. This concept is repeated up until the present day.

Several examples of this were discussed earlier in the chapter, the first of which was Khad's support for rival 'mujahidin' groups and these groups' manipulation of Khad resources to aid them in their local disputes. This was certainly true at the beginning of the decade in northern Helmand. In areas where the government had better knowledge of the local complexity, for example Loy Bagh, neither side was able to shape the conflict dynamics; Loy Bagh was destroyed. The machinations of Khad demonstrate that individuals like Nasim were able to manipulate government policy for their own ends.

There was clearly a tendency for private actors to flip backwards and forwards between different parties and between the 'mujahidin' and the 'government'. Ideology was rarely a reason for patron selection. Choice of mujahidin party was often driven by private, pre-revolution disagreements, and commanders regularly switched parties due to on-going feuds. Finally, the deliberate practice of splitting communities across different, often opposed, organisations, in order to ensure lineage survival, shows that the 'tribal' group was much more important than what, to them, were ideological abstractions. A lack of knowledge of local complexity by both the government and the mujahidin parties facilitated these dynamics. In conclusion, the Soviet-era was portrayed as an East–West clash, but was in fact a conflict driven by local dynamics.

3

# FROM THE SOVIET WITHDRAWAL
# TO THE US INTERVENTION, 1989–2001

> I was told it was all about Islam; I can see
> now that they were lying; it was all about
> power.
>
> Ishaqzai ex-Mahaz commander[1]

> Talib: We want you to go [forward] under
> the Qur'an; we want the Qur'an to be raised
> up high.
>
> Khalifa Shirin Khan: We have [fought] the
> Soviets for fifteen years; we have been doing
> jihad; we are not kaffirs.
>
> The Taliban's second meeting<br>Gereshk, 1994

*Background*

The Soviet withdrawal from Afghanistan led to a reduction in the amount of international attention focused on the country. This resulted in a less polarised narrative than that of the 'East-West' Soviet–mujahidin clash, according to which the collapse of the Afghan government preceded a civil war in Afghanistan. This battle for Kabul—usually explored through a focus on the internecine struggle for the capital—involved a confusing array of political and ethnic groups, deals, intrigues and betrayals.[2] Appalling depredations were exacted on the civilian population. Data describing the conflict dynamics occurring outside of Kabul, however, are almost entirely absent.[3] In this chapter, I show that the Helmandi individuals and dynamics simply continue on their previous trajectories, rather than this period representing a different phase of the conflict. The habitual analysis is that this phase of the conflict represents a separate era, so too the Taliban era: because the West or the Soviets were not involved, it was a less civilised, more barbaric, more animal conflict.[4] I assert that this is a very Western-centric, orientalist viewpoint.

Scholars have viewed the rise of the Taliban—a movement of religious clerics who promise to restore order—as a direct reaction to the chaos of the civil war, even though it was acknowledged that they were a movement heavily supported by Pakistan. (Pakistan had switched its favourite client status from Hekmatyar and Hizb to Mullah Omar and the Taliban.)[5] The Taliban's ideology and political programme were focused on the provision of social order. Their ideology was closest to Harakat's—they were traditionalist and sought to impose their interpretation of Islam as the source of all laws. The West was particularly opposed to the movement's treatment of women.[6] William Maley captured the narrative of the new era when he reported that 'religious fundamentalism of a particularly virulent kind seemed to be on the march'.[7] Writings about the Taliban often focused on their religious nature, extolling, for example, the strength of their 'religious dogma'.[8] Journalists were even more direct in their prose, focusing on 'the weird society ... television sets hung up like hanged men'.[9] The Taliban formed an alliance with Osama bin Laden and al-Qaeda in their war against Ahmad Shah Masoud and the Northern Alliance. This was to be their downfall. Following the al-Qaeda attacks against the US on 11 September 2001, the US drove the Taliban from government.

This chapter discusses the continuing civil war in Helmand; first the conflict which occurred under the auspices of the Najibullah government in Kabul, and secondly that which occurred once Najibullah had stepped down. Lastly, we look at the Taliban era in Helmand (1994–2001). The most important difference between the three eras is the change in patronage networks as primary funders of the conflict: from

Khad and the mujahidin parties, through narcotics production funding the fighting, through to Pakistani funding through their Taliban proxy. The Taliban era is of particular interest. It was much calmer and more secure than other periods in Helmand. I argue that this was due to their knowledge of the local political dynamics enabling them to effect social control, rather than subscription to their religious, conservative ideology, which was not that different from that which came before, in any case. In all three periods, the same families, clans and militias were fighting, although they may have changed who they 'worked' for.

## The End of the Najibullah Era

The departing Soviets left a vast amount of weaponry in the hands of the militias in Helmand, including tanks and artillery, and this was to have a drastic effect on the balance of power in the province, giving more power to the central Helmandi groups who controlled the weaponry.[10] In central Helmand, 'government' patronage was an essential part of the economy. In a parallel development, the taxation of the growth, sale and transportation of opium had become the bedrock of the northern Helmandi economy—one source states that opium was taxed at approximately 5 per cent and that the average yield per jereeb was 16 kilogrammes. The same source calculates that this netted over 13 metric tonnes in opium taxes from the 1990 harvest in Musa Qala alone (it was taken in kind; the total harvest was 260 tonnes). This was mostly spent on the main expense for the various mujahidin administrations: supporting fighters.[11]

Nasim, for example, was the most powerful commander in the province, in recognition of which he was appointed deputy defence minister in the Afghan Interim Government based in Peshawar in February 1989.[12] But this position, and the legitimacy it conferred, did not alter his behaviour—he still followed the twin aims of supporting the production of opium and attempting to destroy any opposing mujahidin groups. He was later to have his ministerial funding removed at US insistence because of his role in the drugs trade. In the winter of 1989/90, however, Nasim presented himself unannounced at the US embassy in Islamabad and tried to negotiate with the ambassador by linking reductions in poppy growth to development aid. Although agreed (for $2 million), the deal was later cancelled as the US felt it could not be seen to be engaging with 'drug dealers'.[13]

The drugs war continued and in September, Yahya (Noorzai) a Hizb commander from Marjeh, tried to hold the bridge over the Helmand in Garmsir[14] in order to tax the passing trade.[15] Nasim attacked and decimated his forces, causing Yahya to flee to Pakistan, having reportedly suffered 400 casualties.[16] It was later rumoured—but remains unconfirmed—that he reinvented himself as a government militia commander in Lashkar Gah.[17] The conflict in Helmand was being dominated by the private war between Nasim and anyone who opposed him. Commanders affiliated themselves with either the 'Hizb' or 'Harakat' alliances (that is, for or against Nasim) depending on which affiliation would best preserve their individual political control (and hence profit) in a particular area. This is best shown by the fact that Nasim used to sell his drugs to Hekmatyar's 'Hizb' labs, which were located in Iran for protection.[18] Similarly, drugs funding did not immediately replace Khad funding or mujahidin party funding when the Soviets left. Khad still paid Nasim money, for example. Slowly, however, over the course of three years, drugs funding became relatively more important and the latter two sources of funding became relatively less important until they disappeared altogether in 1992.

The territory planted with poppy gradually grew in size, with poppy being harvested on a large scale for the first time in 1991 in parts of 'lower [central] Helmand'.[19] However, taking into account the loose, patronage-based methods of political control employed by Nasim (and all commanders), and the benefits that poppy cultivation would bring to the individual farmer,[20] this does not appear to have been forced on farmers (see Chapter 2). As an ex-Hizb commander told me with a grin, 'Rasoul [Nasim's brother] was never really able to force people to grow poppy [around Lashkar Gah]—he didn't really have that much control.'[21] Another interviewee in Gereshk, who, as he was not a 'Hizb' commander, was less biased when talking about Rasoul, pointed to the fact that farmers grew poppy to try and strengthen their economic situation, not because Rasoul ordered them to.[22]

The ailing government had completely retreated to the defensive cummerbund that had been established in and around the central districts (see Map 5). The situation was desperate. Twenty days after the Soviets left, for example, a 38-year-old police captain from Garmsir, Habibullah (Noorzai, Khalqi), was sent to Nad-e Ali as the district chief of police. He described it as the most awful period in his life and visibly shuddered when talking about it. He expanded, saying that he lost men 'every day, sometimes two, sometimes five, sometimes more'. He controlled a 300-by-300 metre area of the hukomat, he said, showing me, as I interviewed him, the very area he had lost so much blood defending. Habibullah said he was under daily siege by local mujahidin commanders such as Dr Jailani (Kharoti, Hizb), Haji Barakzai (Kharoti, Harakat; Haji Jamalzai's nephew), Rahmattiar (Ishaqzai, Hizb) and Abdul Ahad (Noorzai, Etihad).

Habibullah was forced to abandon the district centre around a year after he had been posted there. He and the then district governor, Mahmad Razer (from Chah-e Anjir, Barakzai), were forced to leave in the middle of the night as they had run out of ammunition and food. The supply convoys, which normally came across the desert from Lashkar Gah, had been unable to get through. He was jailed for deserting his post, but in a move typical of the survivors in Helmand, of which Habibullah is a prime example, he was released a week later and made the company commander of the tolay (company) guarding the prison. When I asked him to confirm that I had heard him correctly, he smiled at me as if I knew nothing about Helmandi politics, and that this sequence of events was perfectly normal!

At an overt level, the fight in Nad-e Ali appeared to be between the mujahidin and the government. But a deeper irony is that these mujahidin commanders, or their representatives, were later to become important 'elders' sitting on the District Community Council established in 2009, when Habibullah returned to Nad-e Ali as district governor. The council was designed to provide a checking and advisory role on the district governor, but the history somewhat hampered politics in the district. Apart from during the Taliban era, there were no centrally appointed, non-indigenous, non-'mujahidin' officials in Nad-e Ali between Habibullah leaving in 1990 as chief of police and returning in 2008 with the support of the British as district governor.

However, one event was to change security provision in Helmand drastically and, indeed, in Afghanistan as a whole: General Tanai, a Khalqi, attempted to launch a coup with the help of Hizb in Kabul against President Najibullah (a Parchami; hereafter Najib) on 6 March. As a result, Najib could no longer trust the Khalqis as partners in government, but he was unable to alienate them completely. Thus he began to change the balance of power between the militias and the professional security forces by reducing the amount of patronage the Khalqi Ministry of Interior had available to distribute. But this proved problematic insofar as the security forces in Helmand were historically Khalqi-orientated.[23] Two Khalqi interviewees identify this as the point at which stability in Helmand changed irrevocably for the worse.[24] Many 'Khalqi' police commanders simply reinvented themselves as militia commanders.[25] Indeed, Habibullah, a well-known ideological Khalqi,[26] simply switched patronage networks by leaving the police and forming his own militia—the 904th kandak—which guarded the Bughra between Babaji and Gereshk.[27] One ex-army officer described the army and police as existing only 'on paper' at that time.[28]

Militia commanders—individuals such as Khano, Allah Noor and Jabbar—became more powerful at the expense of professional policemen who were paid by the Khalqi-dominated Ministry of Interior.[29] Khano offers a special case though. His brother was a senior Khalqi and he was a 'Khalqi' militia commander. Yet Khano himself probably gained more than anyone out of the militarisation in Helmand, which was designed to offset Khalqi domination of the security forces. Private actors manipulated the government programme of militarisation, due to the government's ignorance of the identities and motivations of those actors. When the example of Habibullah is also considered, it becomes clear that the government policy of increasing the militarisation of the security forces had little meaning when, in reality, police commanders were simply becoming militia commanders. The security infrastructure was transforming, accelerating government collapse, and, as a result, Khano and Allah Noor ultimately became the de facto decision-makers in the security infrastructure after the coup.[30]

General Tanai was forced to flee to Pakistan after his failed coup d'état. Shortly afterwards, he came to Lashkar Gah, which at the time was probably the most important Khalqi powerbase in the country,[31] and led secret negotiations between Khano and Hafizullah Khan, the figureheads of the two central Helmandi ideological power blocs.[32] As Hafizullah put it to me, 'Tanai surrendered to Hizb ... Khano gave us money and weapons'. The ex-Khalqis that I spoke to described it as a rapprochement.[33]

The outcome of the negotiations was that 'Hizb' commanders and the remnants of the 'Khalqi' Helmandi government would work together against the 'Parchami', Khad-backed 'Harakat' alliance that was threatening them.[34] This agreement was reached while the rest of the national government was being purged of Khalqis and was fighting against Hizb.[35] It would appear that the central government was either unaware of this accommodation, or was forced to accept it. A very strange situation was developing where the two halves of the 'government' were openly working with opposed 'mujahidin' groups, against each other. Malem Mir Wali even tried to claim to me that he joined the government at this point, probably in order to increase the legitimacy of his move, but Hafizullah (and other interviewees)[36] dispute this, saying, 'I [Hafizullah] hated him for his [earlier] defection' (see Chapter 2).

The impact of Tanai's failed coup on conflict dynamics in Helmand was overshadowed by an event of even greater consequence. Nasim was assassinated near Peshawar on 25 March 1990.[37] Many scholars attribute his murder to Hizb, who killed him due to the reduction in poppy production that he had ordered after his deal with the US embassy in Islamabad (his poppy went to Hizb refineries).[38] The Helmandi version, as ever, is much more complex than this.

First, there is conflicting evidence as to whether Nasim ever reduced poppy growth in the areas that he controlled.[39] Additionally, the United States never kept its side of the bargain, and by the time that Nasim visited the embassy, poppy had already been planted for the 1989/90 season and had not yet been harvested at the time he was killed (although the effectiveness of his 'ban' would have only just become verifiable as the plants reached harvesting stage). Finally, Nasim, inevitably and as was the custom, would have built up stocks of opium as a form of capital savings. The more likely reason for the assassination is honour: just before his death, he accused Hekmatyar, the leader of Hizb, of 'betraying the jihad' by affiliating himself with Tanai.[40] Harakat eventually traced the assassination to a nephew of Abdul Rahman Khan, Nasim's old Alizai enemy, who then confessed that Hekmatyar had planned the killing.[41]

The mujahidin press was effusive in its eulogies of Nasim. The Afghan Information Centre's (AIC) *Monthly Bulletin*, set up by the esteemed Professor Majrooh[42] in Peshawar, said that Nasim controlled 18,000 men in the south-west of Afghanistan and was the only commander in the area not to have had his base captured by the Soviets. It was, according to the AIC, the biggest funeral ever for a commander. People 'all over the South' were sad to see him go.[43] Even the Jamiat-sponsored *Afghan News* claimed that he had 10,000 men and was keen to stamp out poppy cultivation.[44] Nobody mentioned his collusion with Khad or the murder of groups of elders. Nasim was immediately replaced by Rasoul, his older brother, at the head of their 'Harakat' patronage organisation.

In response, Rasoul publicly launched a 'general war' against 'Hizb' in Helmand, but in reality this was a series of attacks on people that Rasoul had previously fought and feuded with, or those who refused to submit to him.[45] First and foremost, Rasoul attacked the man he believed was responsible for his brother's murder: Abdul Rahman Khan, who was still in Malgir.[46] Rasoul then attacked anyone who was not allied with him, galvanising his sub-commanders to do the same— the conflict was to continue until Rasoul established himself as the provincial governor in 1993.

But the 'government' and the 'mujahidin' were becoming less defined by the day. A massive battle in Deh Adam Khan then ensued between Allah Noor, Mir Wali and Rauf Khan (on the 'government' side), with Rasoul and Khan Mohammad (Barakzai, from Deh Adam Khan) on the 'Harakat'/'non-government' side in August 1990.[47] The Nejad groups in Deh Adam Khan also joined Rasoul's alliance.[48] During this battle, an eyewitness stated that Najib personally intervened and sent a message through Khad in Gereshk saying that Rasoul should be supported against the 'Hizb'/'Khalq' remnants. Rasoul refused the offer of help. The 'Parchami' Khad were trying to bring down their own 'government' because they hated the 'Khalqis' so much. The unity of government was ceasing to exist.[49]

Fighting raged throughout the province. Rasoul launched attacks on Atta Mohammad in Sangin. Sher Mohammad (Ishaqzai, Harakat) from Shurakay, who was also the brother-in-law of the Khan Mohammad involved in the attack on Gereshk, attacked Abdul Khaleq (Ishaqzai, Hizb) in Qala-e Gaz. Malem Yusof was attacked in Now Zad.[50] Abdul Rahman Jan (Noorzai, Jamiat, Marjeh) described a defensive alliance against Rasoul's attacks. This was comprised of himself, Mir Wali, Atta Mohammad, Mato Khan (another Etihad commander in Marjeh, related to Haji Lal Jan from Nad-e Ali) and Malem Yusof—they would all support each other when Rasoul came to their area.

Rasoul's attacks spread to Nad-e Ali where 'Etihad' groupings and the remnants of 'Mahaz' joined the alliance with Rasoul against the 'Hizb'/'Khalq' forces.[51] This was driven by a feud between Rahmattiar (Hizb) and Abdul Ahad (Etihad).[52] Generally in Nad-e Ali, however, fighting was kept to a low level. As Harakat asserted its dominance over Nad-e Ali, the Kharoti 'Hizb' fighters fled to Pakistan, and the Kharoti 'Harakat' fighters were unavailable for duty until they had left.[53] The Kharoti pan-tribal shura was still working.

Other members of Hizb were not so lucky: Rahmattiar (Ishaqzai), from Jangal in the south of the district, was kidnapped by Rasoul and taken to Musa Qala where he was imprisoned for two years. Their front collapsed when Rasoul confiscated all of their weapons.[54] The small groups that were caught between the two opposing forces did not fare well; for example, Nejad disintegrated, with some joining the 'Hizb'/'Khalq' patronage networks, some joining the 'Harakat' network and some going home: '[Nejad's] jihad was over.'[55] Over the whole of the province, the factionalisation appeared to subside as groups either opted for the 'Hizb'/'Khalq'- or the 'Harakat'/'Parcham'-led groupings. The complexity of side-switching, however, as people either opted for or against Rasoul, rested on individual political contexts as people sought to secure alliances that would protect themselves, their business interests and their villages. Larger, ideology-based organisations had completely ceased to exist as unitary wholes. The government, for instance, was split into, and working with, different sections of the mujahidin. Further, the increase in drug funding meant that the individuals and fighting groups did not need government or mujahidin party patronage to continue fighting. The national government did continue to fund different parts of the provincial government, but it is not known how much knowledge they had of the Helmandi reality at that point.

The people of Helmand viewed these shifting coalitions with a sense of unease. Different parts of the 'government' were supplying different sections of the 'mujahidin', although it is not clear how much knowledge each side had of the other at the time. Later on, when Khad were forced to flee the province, Hafizullah went to the Khad headquarters in Lashkar Gah and reviewed their documents. What he saw shocked him: 'the mujahidin were completely penetrated by Khad,' he said, and 'almost everyone had a file' detailing 'so much trickery between different mujahidin [groups and leaders]'. The fluidity with which two bitter enemies, Hizb and Khalq, could align with each other left many to conclude that the spirit of the jihad had been hopelessly corrupted. As one former commander, who was twenty-three at the time of the Saur revolution, told me bitterly, 'I was told it was about Islam; I can see now that they were lying; it was about power.'[56]

It was during this period that the Helmandi population sensed that the provision of external resources—from Najib's government and from the parties in Peshawar—was coming to an end. These were being replaced with more organic sources of money, derived from the drugs trade or general predation on the population. The external funding had forced, or at least appeared to force, the splitting of clans and families across ideological divides (that is, one family sending a brother each to the mujahidin and the government). However, once this funding was no longer available, or when it was perceived that it would not be available forever, the groups and their leaders did not need to demonstrate allegiance to any particular organisation or ideology and sought stability through other networks. Thus, individuals turned to tribal networks, which, although they had been damaged in the period since 1978, were extant (of course some, like the Nad-e Ali Kharoti, had maintained their strength and unity throughout the jihad). Tribal shuras were held which pledged that there would be 'unity after war' and 'cooperation and consolidation'.[57]

Thus the different tribes asserted their leadership—the Popalzai in the south, for example, formed a tribal council in Quetta in January 1991 with judicial and financial commissions, claiming that, no matter the background, 'any tribesman can join'.[58] In Helmand specifically, and in addition to the Kharoti, the Noorzai in the central part of the province began to broaden channels between members who had been on 'opposing' sides during the jihad,[59] as did the Barakzai,[60] and, in Garmsir, the Alizai.[61] This was the reassertion of Helmandi tribal groups and alliances in the face of dwindling external interest and patronage. The dynamic was to repeat itself in Helmand at two other similar junctures: first, when the Taliban were forced out in 2002,[62] and second, as ISAF was leaving Helmand in 2012.[63]

Funding from Russia to Najib's government was cut off after the attempted coup in Moscow in August 1991. The government could only support itself by printing money. The Afghan air force was grounded in January 1992 for lack of fuel. American funding to the mujahidin was similarly curtailed.[64] Elsewhere in the country, the territory controlled by the government shrank and mass desertions ensued.[65] The 'Khalq'/'Hizb' grouping in Helmand meant that the government could hold on to its traditional area of influence—Gereshk, Lashkar Gah, Chah-e Anjir and the routes in-between—while the 'Harakat' grouping controlled the rest of the province. As Rasoul slowly expanded his area, many petty commanders began to switch allegiances to him, safe in the knowledge that they would still be able to collect their own taxes and live in relative autonomy once they had done so. Those commanders that were vanquished did not have this privilege extended to them.[66]

This lack of funding forced individual commanders to look for other sources of funding besides that derived from the opium trade. The most obvious source was to loot from the population, which was something that all of the 'government' commanders including Khano,[67] Mir Wali,[68] Hafizullah[69] and Abdul Rahman Jan engaged in.[70] Chaos ruled: fifty or sixty 'posts' had to be crossed to get to Kandahar from Helmand, each controlled by a different commander, and each one charging the equivalent of half a day-labourer's wage for passage.[71] It was 'impossible to move' due to the combination of banditry and larger-scale battles between the commanders, such as those which ensued when Dad Mohammad attacked Hafizullah in April 1991[72] and when Rasoul attacked Atta Mohammad in Now Zad (where neither of them were based) in July of the same year.[73] The commanders were ranging across the province fighting other commanders where they found them—hundreds were killed and wounded.[74]

I have no evidence that Rasoul's commanders were systematically looting at this time (as the 'government' commanders were). However, as they only controlled the rural areas there was less to loot. Certainly, travellers to northern Helmand in 1991 emphasised the fact that there was 'no robbing or stealing' and that 'people were free to come and go'.[75] Rais Baghrani, the preeminent 'mujahed' in Baghran, for example, established anti-bandit checkpoints along roads.[76] The dichotomy between those commanders who were in the 'government' and those who were outside the 'government' has undoubtedly affected how the population in Helmand feel about the concept of government—something that has worsened over time, particularly during the Karzai era.

The period between the collapse of Najib's government and the coming of the Taliban was known as the 'mujahidin nights' or the 'topak-iyan [gun men] era' in the south. One gentleman, who had already fled from Now Zad to escape the fighting and had settled in Deh Adam Khan, described how farmers would go to work in their fields with a Kalashnikov lain by their side due to the unpredictability of the environment. 'One house would be one way [supporting one faction], and the next would be the other', he said.[77]

*Post-Najibullah: the 'Civil War'*

When Najib's government finally handed over to a 'mujahidin' coalition in Kabul in April 1992, the few remaining Helmandi police and army officers simply took their uniforms off and went home.[78] Civil officials like Abdul Sangar, the district governor of Nahr-e Saraj, did the same.[79] In Helmand, the secret agreement between Hafizullah and Khano laid the foundations for the political formulations that were to follow. A meeting was called in Lashkar Gah by Gul Mahmad Khwashal (Noorzai, from Farah), who had been appointed provincial governor by Najib, replacing Shah Nazar Khan from Loy Bagh. All the major powerbrokers in the Rasoul-opposed alliance were present at the meeting: Khwashal, Mir Wali, Hafizullah Khan, Atta Mohammad, Sarwar Khan (Abdul Rahman Khan's nephew), Khano, Allah Noor, Rauf Khan, Jenat Gul (the professional army commander of the 93rd Division) and Akhwaendi. Everyone promised to work together and fight Rasoul, Mir Wali said in his interview with me. However, according to Mir Wali, another plan was already in motion.

Khwashal began to drag his heels in the meeting, saying that it would be impossible to defeat Rasoul. This was a delaying tactic because Khad and Khwashal had already made a deal with Rasoul, according to which he would enter Lashkar Gah through one of their posts on the cummerbund. Once Rasoul entered Lashkar Gah, things did not go to plan and there was house-to-house fighting between Khad and Rasoul's troops on the one hand and the 'Hizb'/'Khalq'/'Jamiat'/'Mahaz' commanders mentioned above, on the other. The fighting lasted all through the next day, with the Khad/Rasoul grouping eventually being pushed back to the maidan, where the Khad brigade was based.

With Khad and Rasoul contained, Mir Wali describes having to rush back the following day to Gereshk, which was under attack, before finally returning to Lashkar Gah and teaming up with Khano and Hafizullah Khan in Muhktar. The next day (the fourth after the meeting), this Khano/Hafizullah grouping took the hospital and the old Khad headquarters before attacking the maidan. Matin, the Khad brigade commander, escaped to Musa Qala with Rasoul's help.[80] Lashkar Gah secured, Mir Wali again had to head to Gereshk (suitably refitted with Khad weaponry and ammunition) which was under attack from one of Rasoul's commanders, Engineer Ghani. Ghani surrendered, and while he was jailed, the Barakzai troops underneath him immediately switched sides and pledged allegiance to Mir Wali—possibly an outcome of the tribal rapprochement process outlined above.[81]

The ending of Khad patronage for Rasoul was a problem and put him under pressure all over the province.[82] Khano and Hafizullah led an operation, supported by Sar Katib (Hizb) from Kandahar, to clear the province of 'Harakat' forces. Starting in Gereshk, they moved through Malgir, Babaji, Nad-e Ali, Nawa, Marjeh and finally Garmsir, installing district governors as they went.[83] Nahr-e Saraj went to Khalifa Shirin Khan (Barakzai, Hizb), the Malgir landowner;[84] Nad-e Ali to Khalifa Khwashkea (Noorzai, Jamiat, from Loy Bagh);[85] Nawa went to Mahmad Wali (Popalzai, Jamiat, Nawa);[86] and Garmsir to Abdullah Jan (Hizb, Barakzai).[87] This took three days, during which time many of the 'Harakat' commanders fled to Pakistan. They then raided Now Zad and Musa Qala, where they stayed for three days of pillaging. There was no intention of holding northern Helmand: it was revenge. Upon returning to Lashkar Gah, they announced the remaining 'government' posts.[88]

Hafizullah Khan was made 'provincial governor'.[89] Khano was finally given the position of 'chief of police' to reflect the de facto position that he had held for the last two years.[90] Allah Noor was promoted to 'commander of the 93rd Division'[91] and Rauf Khan was appointed an independent 'brigade commander'.[92] Akhwaendi was also part of the alliance.[93] Due to the vast stocks of weaponry that they were able to arm themselves with from government armouries, this grouping proved stable enough to stop Rasoul taking Lashkar Gah and Gereshk. Both Abdul Rahman and Mir Wali speak of being armed with ex-government weapons. One interviewee claimed that Mir Wali had inherited 1,100 weapons from the government, cached them, and still had possession of them as of 2012.[94]

Astonishingly, despite being the location of so much fighting and having received only minimal government and Soviet interest, Helmand was to become the last holdout of the communist 'government', personified by people like Khano and Allah Noor.[95] However, as the 'government' was mainly made up of 'Khalqi' and 'Hizb' commanders it was completely cut off from *the* government, which at that time was led by President Mujaddidi, the leader of the Nejad party, and dominated by Parchamis and Jamiatis (and was fighting for its life against Hizb). The government in Kabul was far too worried about dealing with the local threat from Hizb to even think about Helmand, which existed in limbo from the national sphere.[96] Helmand was effectively independent.

Many in Helmand tried to take advantage of this complete lack of government in the province and moved to occupy better land than they were already on. Several Noorzai commanders from Now Zad and Washir followed Haji Lal Jan in escaping water stress in northern Helmand. Lal Jan had originally come to Nad-e Ali in the chaos surrounding the Taraki revolution. His brother, Haji Qabir Khan, settled on land around the Bolan junction alongside Mato Khan, another relative.[97] Malem Sher Agha also settled nearby, in Zaburabad, stealing government (non-owned) land.[98] Abdul Razaq (Noorzai, from Washir, a cousin of Qabir Khan) also came and took 'a hundred households' worth of land in what was previously the Bolan 'desert'.[99]

Other commanders were given land in recognition of loyal service during the jihad.[100] All of these land gains were recognised a few months later by the Rabbani government, and crucially, are seen as completely legitimate today by the landowners, but not by their longer-settled neighbours. The previous jihad-era land thefts were also rec-

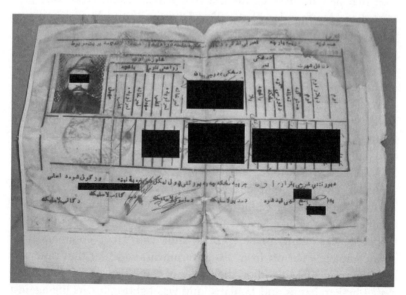

Figure 1: Rabbani-era land document

ognised officially, including those perpetrated by Haji Lal Jan[101] and Rahmattiar (see Chapter 2).[102] Official land documents were issued, meaning that these land thefts continue to create division and conflict today (see Figure 1).

The more progressive elements of Lashkar Gah society began to rue the day that Hafizullah took over. He began by looting the bank and stealing the streetlights for scrap.[103] Despite initially promising cooperation with the teachers, the girls' school was closed and was not to reopen until the Karzai government a decade later. Although there was some (secret) home schooling, most of the (former) communists (that is, the educated professional people like teachers) either fled or started making plans to leave.[104] Shah Nazar Khan, the Noorzai ex-provincial governor, was assassinated in his home by persons unknown.[105]

The killing bore all the hallmarks of the kind of political assassination favoured by Hizb commanders, but when I questioned Hafizullah about it, he looked at the floor saying that he knew nothing about it and mumbled something about it being a 'tribal thing'. I later spoke to a close relative of Shah Nazar's whom I knew well,[106] who told me that the actual killer had already been killed (in revenge), but that there were two other people involved who 'still need to be killed' and so he would not be able to talk to me about it until that work was done. He confirmed that they were members of Hizb, but it was the actual individuals who were important, not the organisations that they subscribed to. The very fact that I held the latter conversation twenty years after the event gives an indication of the innumerable intertwined and everlasting feuds that percolate through Helmandi society, and demonstrates the interminable and intimate nature of the conflict.

The government collapse also spawned a new interest in Helmand from the Iranian intelligence services. Shortly after the Najib government fell, a Sardar Baghwani reportedly held meetings with Allah Noor and Khano in Lashkar Gah.[107] This was the first report of Iran's interest in Helmand since the negotiations over the Helmand water treaty in 1973.[108] A decade later, Baghwani was reportedly in Helmand distributing arms,[109] and again in 2006 he supposedly came to meet with the 'Taliban' in Marjeh and Now Zad.[110] Iran has major strategic interests in Helmand, particularly with regard to the water that flows through the Kajaki dam.[111] This theme will be picked up again in later chapters.

In October, the fighting between Rasoul and the Lashkar Gah 'government' continued and there were violent clashes between Hafizullah's men and Rasoul's when Rasoul attempted to retake the maidan.[112] But even the threat of an external enemy failed to hold the 'government' together in the long term. Some say that the argument began over dividing the spoils,[113] while others maintain that it started when Gulbuddin, Assadullah Sherzad's[114] nephew, launched a rocket-propelled grenade at Sar Katib, the Hizb commander from Kandahar who was reinforcing Hafizullah. This was an act of revenge for an earlier killing when 'Hizb' and 'Khalq' were enemies. Gulbuddin was killed and Assadullah Sherzad wounded in the ensuing melee.[115] The battle lasted for eight hours in the centre of Lashkar Gah and 'lots of Sar Katib's men were killed … one roundabout had ten of their bodies on it'.[116] Contemporaneous secondary sources state that a difference in ideologies relating to girls' schooling caused the 'Hizb'/'Khalq' grouping to fracture,[117] but this was not confirmed in my interviews and was deemed unlikely by a neutral witness who was in Lashkar Gah at the time.[118] The feud described above is the more likely reason. Hafizullah had only been provincial governor for six months when he was ejected from Lashkar Gah. The 'Hizb' commanders then set up a base in Khushk-e Nakhud with their men[119]—the site of the battle of Maiwand against British–Indian forces 112 years before.

By this time, Rabbani, the leader of Jamiat, had been appointed president in Kabul, and it seemed prescient to have a 'Jamiat' face to the Helmandi 'government': they needed an alliance with a government that could support them. Thus the Helmandi 'government' morphed and Akhwaendi (Barakzai, Jamiat) was appointed provincial governor. The real power, however, was still held by Khano.[120] Akhwaendi was reportedly a man with very parochial interests whose only aspiration was to support his community in Nawa, rather than act like a provincial governor.[121] Another interviewee described him as 'a dangerous man [who] always had a group of eighteen-year-old [kids] with him'.[122] Shortly after the switch in provincial governor, Khano attacked 'Hizb' posts (until two days previously his allies) in Babaji, Nad-e Ali and Marjeh, and funding began to flow from the central government. This came from Kabul, encouraged by personal relations between Akhwaendi and Rabbani, and from Mazar-e Sharif, as a result of relations between Khano and Dostum.[123]

Akhwaendi's period in power appeared to represent a brief respite in the continual military action. This may have been because it was over the winter, and therefore not during the traditional fighting season. At the same time, it appears that Rasoul spent that winter building a broader alliance with 'Hizb' consisting of most of his former enemies from the previous decade: Atta Mohammad, Dad Mohammad, Mir Wali, Hafizullah Khan, Rais Baghrani, Obaedi and, crucially, Ismail Khan, known as the Amir of Herat.[124] The addition of Ismail Khan was a masterstroke, as the presence of a heavyweight player held the alliance together. It is worth noting, however, that Ismail Khan was also part of the national 'government' led by Rabbani. The national government was presumably unaware that different parts of itself in the periphery were attacking each other, thus allowing the old feud between Rasoul and the central Helmandi commanders to drive the conflict.

After the poppy harvest in 1993, the alliance led by Ismail positioned their forces in Delaram. Khano received word of this and immediately launched a pre-emptive attack on them, inflicting some damage.[125] Whether this was the original plan, or whether the pre-emptive attack had changed their plan, Ismail's alliance then attacked Gereshk, approaching from the east. Allah Noor conducted the defence of the cummerbund in Deh Adam Khan in June. The battle lasted twenty-two days and ultimately resulted in the fall of Gereshk to Ismail.[126] Both sides had tanks and other heavy weapons that had been left by the Soviets.[127] Each different private actor had their own alliances; as one of the militia commanders said, 'Iran was helping Ismail and Pakistan was helping Rasoul … what chance did [the militias] have?' He neglected to mention that the militias and Ismail were being supported by the Rabbani government. Allah Noor et al. fled to Lashkar Gah to try to work out what to do.[128]

During the week after the Deh Adam Khan battle, Rasoul went through Malgir, Babaji, Marjeh and Nad-e Ali, clearing them of the remnants of the 'government', leaving just Lashkar Gah and Chah-e Anjir in their hands.[129] The story then becomes more confused. At some point during that week Abdul Rahman Jan switched sides with his men, allying himself with Rasoul (he had previously been with the 'government').[130] He himself attributes this to his Jamiat links with Ismail Khan. The next decisive battle took place in Chah-e Anjir, where Khano and Allah Noor were cornered, with Abdul Rahman on Rasoul's side. Khano and Allah Noor both fled in the middle of the night, escaping to Mazar-e Sharif on a plane that Dostum supplied,[131] and one interviewee commented that 'Rasoul had tried many times to take Lashkar Gah, but was only successful when Abdul Rahman joined

him'.[132] As Khano left, he turned his heavy weapons over to Abdul
Rahman, even though he had just switched sides.[133] Many view this act
as decisive in Abdul Rahman's later rise to power (see Chapters 4–6).[134]
A senior Noorzai tribal leader interpreted this as a 'tribal act', as he
would.[135] However, there is perhaps another explanation identified by
another interviewee: the role of an Iranian intelligence operative in
brokering a deal between Khano, Ismail Khan and Abdul Rahman, all
of whom were Iranian clients.[136]

The groundwork that the previous tribal shuras had laid paid divi-
dends. As Rasoul entered Lashkar Gah, the members of the former
administration were absorbed by their tribal kin. Israel Khan, the
'Etihad' commander from Now Zad, for example, entered Lashkar
Gah with Rasoul and was able to guarantee the safety of those members of the clan who had worked with the government.[137] The previously held affiliations were ignored in the face of tribal solidarity. In
this, they were working with the grain of Helmandi society. No one
wanted to kill someone if they had a powerful family behind them: the
obligations for revenge would be too strong. The ideological labels that
people had adopted were not enough of a reason to kill them.

Abdul Rahman was appointed 'deputy provincial chief of police'
under Rasoul, with the latter becoming 'provincial governor'.[138] The
other jobs were divvied up at a meeting attended by Mir Wali in
Lashkar Gah. As recounted by Mir Wali, when Rasoul arrived at the
meeting he pretended that he did not know who Mir Wali was, a deliberate and serious slight designed to put the ex-'Hizb' commander at a
disadvantage. First, Baghrani was made 'commander of the 93rd
Division' and Abdul Ahad, the Ishaqzai Harakat commander from
Now Zad, was made the 'chief of police'. Atta Mohammad was made
the 'district governor' of Sangin.[139] 'Hizb' got the scraps. Khalifa Shirin
Khan and Abdullah Jan remained in Gereshk and Garmsir respectively,
and Malem Yusof was either appointed or remained in Now Zad. Mir
Wali was made the 'provincial head of culture and information', and
Hafizullah was not given a post. 'Khad' went to Dad Mohammad from
Sangin in recognition of his long-term alliance with Rasoul.[140]

The spin that the Rabbani (Jamiat) government in Kabul put on
these events is particularly interesting because they contrast with the
local reality. *Afghan News*, the Jamiat mouthpiece, proclaimed that the
'Herat to Kandahar road had been opened for use after government
forces had smashed several groups of armed bandits along the road'. It

went on to say that 'government administration had also been reactivated in Farah and Helmand', that 'all [of Ismail's alliance] decided to
join together and liberate the province from the militia forces of the
former regime', and listed the change in administration in Lashkar Gah
as a 'defeat for [Hizb] as [they were] close to the militias'.[141] Again, the
Helmandi reality is different: Ismail Khan, a 'Jamiat' commander affiliated to the government, had deposed another 'Jamiat' commander,
Akhwaendi, who was also recognised by, and affiliated to, the Rabbani
government. This gave Rasoul, a 'Harakat' commander, the provincial
governorship. The 'Hizb' forces in the area had actually been fighting
on Rasoul's side; the only defeat they suffered was in the division of
post-battle spoils. The national government had no hope of influenc-
ing events in Helmand that it could not understand; it could merely
follow them, accepting and recognising the 'facts on the ground' as
they occurred.

Rasoul's tenure was another period of greater stability for Helmand,
mainly due to the lack of large-scale, military manoeuvres across the
province. This stability allowed families to return, and by 1994, 50 per
cent of refugees had done so.[142] Rasoul was confident enough to offer
to send military support to the Rabbani government in its war against
Hizb for control of Kabul.[143] Some of the district governors were
changed to reflect the new order, for example, Mullah Said Gul (Alizai/
Khalozai), a Baghrani sub-commander, was appointed to Nad-e Ali.[144]
'Government' positions had ceased to have meaning, and several people commented on the fact that 'officials' stopped having defined positions and that the only qualification for a 'government' position was
being in a militia. This was the period of andiwali government (andi-
wal means friend in Dari): where nothing got done and friends of the
appointee filled all of the 'posts'.[145] In essence, this was a fully patronage-based organisation and the culmination of the process originally
set in motion by Najib's National Reconciliation (and militia) policy.

Officially, this was an administration of mujahidin unity including
'Hizb'. Those areas that were 'conquered' by Rasoul, such as Babaji,
joined the 'government'.[146] However, Rasoul coveted all the power for
himself, and a round of looting occurred with former 'Hizb' areas being
the targets. Thus the streetlights in Shin Kalay were stripped out and
taken to Musa Qala. Apparently, Haji Jamalzai, the Kharoti Harakat
commander, allowed this to happen despite having influence with
Rasoul. As far as he was concerned, '[my village] does not have street-

lights, so why should Shin Kalay?'[147] Even more bizarrely, there were 'Hizb' figures in the Helmandi 'government' (for example, Mir Wali), which was funded by the central government, at the same time that the government was under grave threat from Hizb in the environs of Kabul. Helmand was utterly disconnected from the national discourse.

Rasoul's tenure was short. He died of natural causes in Lashkar Gah on 6 September 1994 at the age of sixty and was immediately replaced by Ghaffour, his younger brother.[148] Ghaffour was not as dictatorial or hard line as Rasoul, who had lost a great deal of the support that Nasim had built up during the jihad.[149] As ever, control was exerted by proxy and Ghaffour, like Rasoul, never had direct control over Gereshk (where Khalifa Shirin Khan was still district governor and Baghrani the commander of the '93rd Division'). He did not have very much control in Nad-e Ali either.[150] Even so, Ghaffour, like Rasoul before him, condoned the settlement of a large number of Alizai tribesmen on government land in the southern Bolan desert.[151] Life went on much as before.

## The Rise of the Taliban

As Ghaffour was settling into his new job, a movement of religious students was emerging in Kandahar: the Taliban. The story—or myth—of their rise in Kandahar has been covered elsewhere and will not be discussed here,[152] but their takeover of Helmand is worth recounting in some detail as it demonstrates how they were able to take over so much of Afghanistan in the coming months. It also gives credence to the theory that in the initial stages of their growth as a movement the main motivating factor for the Taliban was securing the trade route to Central Asia, through Gereshk, for Pakistani trucking mafias:[153] most of their military activity focused on clearing the route between Kandahar and Herat.[154]

As the Taliban seized power in Kandahar, Ghaffour mediated between them and the soon-to-be ejected commanders who had been in charge there.[155] There was, however, no loyalty to Ghaffour and they approached Rais Baghrani, the commander of the '93rd Division' in Gereshk, and reached an agreement that he would affiliate himself with the Taliban, breaking his deal with Ghaffour. Six Talibs then organised an 'official' meeting with Khalifa Shirin Khan (the district governor), Khan Mohammad (an ex-Harakat commander) and Baghrani (the

'93rd' divisional commander). As described by an eyewitness, they used the soon-to-be well-known narratives of the Taliban, imploring them to work with the new movement and be good Muslims, saying, 'we want you to go [forward] under the Qur'an; we want the Qur'an to be raised up high'. Khalifa Shirin Khan was slightly incredulous: 'we have been fighting against the Soviets for fifteen years; we have been doing jihad; we are not kaffirs', he retorted. The meeting broke up.[156]

Nine days later, two cars came from Kandahar with ten Talibs. They proceeded to Baghrani's headquarters for lunch. After the meal, Baghrani and the Taliban set about removing the checkpoints on the main road between Gereshk and Kandahar that were manned by Mir Wali and other 'Hizb' commanders. This took two days, and on the third day they launched an attack on Mir Wali's positions in Deh Mazang and Abhashak. The fighting lasted for eighteen hours, and finished at 8 a.m. the next day when Mir Wali escaped westwards to Nimruz.[157] While this was occurring, Ghaffour was approached in Lashkar Gah by Taliban representatives.

The Talibs had been sent to negotiate the fall of Helmand and told Ghaffour that they wanted to cut a deal: the Taliban would remove Mir Wali and Atta Mohammad from Helmand and Ghaffour would be left to control the Alizai territory in the north of the province. In return, he had to give up Lashkar Gah.[158] Ghaffour considered what had happened in Gereshk and realised that he had no choice—with Baghrani on their side, the Taliban would be undefeatable, even though they had not yet sent any serious forces to Helmand.[159] Many interpreted this as a deal between Ghaffour and the Taliban,[160] and Abdul Rahman probably summed up the best how most people felt about it, 'Ghaffour and [Baghrani] went over to the Taliban; they did it because they were all mullahs.'

In fact, Baghrani had sold out Ghaffour to the Taliban, a new organisation supported by Pakistan, because he saw it as a way to get ahead in their feud. Ghaffour fled to Musa Qala and Taliban forces occupied Lashkar Gah peacefully.[161] The Taliban were clearly an organisation with a strong ideology, yet they also had very good knowledge of the local Helmandi context—as is evident from the secret negotiations with Baghrani and then the approach that they made to Ghaffour— which enabled them to shape the events in their favour. This was an entirely new dynamic and different to how we normally see the Taliban depicted. What made them successful was their local political knowledge rather than their ideology, which was not so different from Rais Baghrani's or Rasoul's.

By this time, the Taliban had moved forces in from outside Helmand and, with Baghrani, attacked Atta Mohammad and Dad Mohammad in Sangin who had allied in the face of the Taliban threat despite the bitter fighting that had taken place between the two over the last fifteen years. Both were defeated and fled west, Dad Mohammad with 500 of his fighters and Atta Mohammad alone; his fighters immediately went over to the Taliban.[162] These forces then pressed on to Musa Qala and evicted Ghaffour from there and Kajaki in mid-January.[163] It was here that one of Ghaffour's nephews, Sher Mohammad, fought his first battles as the commander of a few men. Upon Ghaffour's death, he was to rise and take control of the dynasty, eventually becoming provincial governor during the Karzai era.[164]

Ghaffour and his family were forced to flee through Baghran, where Baghrani made sure that they were attacked and plundered for their weapons, money, opium and women. This particular act, and the dishonour associated with it, still shapes events today.[165] At approximately the same time, the Taliban pushed to Marjeh, where Abdul Rahman had retreated from Lashkar Gah when Ghaffour left. They attempted to disarm him, provoking a furious response.[166] Abdul Rahman was pushed out to Washir, where he linked up with Malem Yusof in Now Zad. Both were soon defeated by the Taliban.[167] In the months of December 1994 and January 1995, Helmand fell to the Taliban, who then proceeded to disarm as many of the jihadi commanders as they could.[168]

Ghaffour fled to Herat via Ghor, where he allied with Ismail Khan.[169] Abdul Rahman and Mir Wali met them there.[170] They all wanted to retake Helmand in order to regain their interests in the drugs trade, upon which their power was based. Thus Ismail Khan and the Helmandis, as well as some Kandahari commanders, tried to reconquer Helmand in March and succeeded in occupying Gereshk, but they were quickly beaten back by the Taliban, losing over 2,000 men who were captured.[171] Despite serious trust issues between the Herat-based commanders,[172] a second assault was carried out in August, and by the 26th of that month Gereshk and Musa Qala were under their control.[173]

At this point the ISI intervened in the Taliban's favour, rushing men and materiel to them, including 1,500 new Toyota Hiluxes. The Pakistani army even gave artillery and helicopter support, probably for the first time.[174] Within a month, the Taliban had recaptured Gereshk and Ismail Khan's force disintegrated. Ghaffour, Mir Wali and Abdul Rahman all fled to Iran.[175] Ghaffour soon ended up in Quetta where he was eventually assassinated by the Taliban.[176] Abdul Rahman then fought briefly with the Northern Alliance against the Taliban, before going back to Iran. Mir Wali spent much of the next six years fighting with the Northern Alliance against the Taliban in the north of the country. Neither Abdul Rahman nor Mir Wali was welcome in Pakistan as they had fought the Taliban—when they visited they were forced to leave by the ISI.[177]

The Taliban brought an entire set of political appointees with them, mainly from Uruzgan.[178] Their first provincial governor was Mullah Mahmad Karim (Noorzai, from Kandahar). He was replaced shortly afterwards by Abdul Bari (Alakozai, from Deh Rawoud) who remained governor for the remainder of Taliban rule.[179] Generally, Abdul Bari was seen as a fair governor, albeit one who was disorganised and slightly corrupt.[180] In many respects the critical position was the governor for Gereshk, who also had responsibility for Sangin, Kajaki and Musa Qala: Mullah Mir Hamza (Noorzai, Deh Rawoud). Mir Hamza was highly respected by Mullah Omar, who referred to him as 'Haji Khan'.[181] Echoing history, such an important position—Gereshk was the back door to Kandahar—had to go to someone trustworthy. He was also respected by the local people as being serious and fair.[182] Mir Hamza's deputy was Haji Mahmad Azem[183] and the mayor was Abdul Haq (both Noorzai, Uruzgan). Abdul Haq's job reportedly centred on collecting the road tolls[184] upon which much of the Taliban treasury in Helmand rested.[185] The district governor was the commander of Taliban forces in the area.[186]

Beyond those key posts, however, government administration appeared to be little more than an afterthought. This is probably best summarised by an ex-Mahaz commander who said, 'the Taliban came into Helmand stating that they didn't want to do government, and they didn't'.[187] When the Taliban commanded by Mullah Ibrahim (Laghmani, from Garmsir) had reached Nad-e Ali and finished fighting with Abdul Rahman, Ibrahim simply became district governor. Characterised as intelligent and respected by the people, he was unfortunately replaced by Mullah Abdul Rahman (Noorzai, from Now Zad)[188] after about a year, who was in turn replaced by Mawlana Sahib (from Uruzgan) shortly afterwards. Mawlana Sahib remained in the post for the longest period, but was characterised by one of the senior tribal leaders in the district as desperately corrupt when dealing with land issues, and as being cruel, resorting to shooting people to maintain order.[189]

There followed four other district governors in Nad-e Ali, bringing the total to seven in seven years: Mullah Abdul Rahim (Ishaqzai, from Uruzgan), Mullah Sharwali (Daftani, from Nahr-e Saraj), Mullah Abdul Haq (Daftani, from Waziristan, Pakistan) and Mullah Saifullah (Alizai, from Uruzgan).[190] This was an astonishing turnover in personnel. Apparently, Nad-e Ali was considered a 'rest and recuperation' posting for Taliban commanders from the fighting in the north of the country. The district was also seen as a position in which they could make money due to the fact that there were, by now, interminable land disputes in Nad-e Ali, and the social heterogeneity meant that the need for an 'impartial' figure was greater than in areas where there was a unified tribal leadership. As one man who was fairly close to the Taliban administration told me, 'people had no choice but to allow the Taliban to solve [disputes] as they allowed no fighting ... [and] when they solved them they made money out of it!'[191]

The last central district of Nawa began the Taliban era with an unknown district governor who was soon replaced by the Mullah Ibrahim from Nad-e Ali. He was again highly respected by the population. One interviewee recalled that when Ibrahim's own brother killed someone, he ensured that justice was served and that the victim's family received the appropriate blood money. He did not abuse his power, and made sure that disputes over land and women were solved without the payment of bribes.[192] Yet beyond the central districts, the Taliban instituted a form of indirect rule by employing a district governor from a supportive, sometimes minority, community in the district, although they were also selected for religious achievement. Thus in Garmsir, Mullah Naim was appointed from the Alizai, a minority community.[193] In Now Zad, the Taliban district governor was Dost Mohammad Akhund (Ishaqzai, Harakat) who was the brother-in-law of Abdul Ahad, the main Harakat commander for Now Zad during the jihad.[194]

Every district had a shura (council), the composition of which varied depending upon local context—every district had a slightly different method of Taliban control. In many cases, Harakat networks quickly became Talibanised,[195] as Harakat and Taliban structures were both clerical, and Mullah Omar had been a member of Harakat. Broadly, both parties had the same type of people: mullahs and those who wanted a return to traditional village life. Yet while many of the Hizb or Jamiat networks were ignored or suppressed,[196] in other areas commanders of those parties would rise in the Taliban movement. This depended on the local political balance: in some cases the suppression was due to the fact that their previous enemies were now affiliated with the Taliban government.[197] This shows that the Taliban used detailed knowledge of the local political context in order to successfully rule.

In Gereshk for example, Mir Hamza reactivated Harakat networks to govern, thus relying on a minority of Barakzai from the smaller tribal coalition (see Chapter 2) and other tribes.[198] Ex-Harakat commanders like Mullah Atta Mohammad (Barakzai, from Malgir) and Saddiq (Ishaqzai) became minor Taliban officials.[199] Hizb-affiliated commanders were excluded, and thus Khalifa Shirin Khan, the mujahidin district governor, stayed at home.[200] The district shura consisted of 'influential' mullahs and elders from the district, but reflected the 'Harakat' bias expressed above[201] and had very little power anyway.[202]

Baghrani remained as commander of the division before moving to Herat to fight Ismail Khan, and then to Kabul to fight the Northern Alliance,[203] eventually becoming a 'Chief Mullah'.[204] Many of his sub-commanders went on to become Taliban sub-commanders, taking the prenominal mullah, thus, Mullah Janan (Alizai/Khalozai/Arabzai), Mullah Rauf (Alizai/Khalozai/Mirazai), Mullah Zakir (Alizai/Khalozai/Arabzai)[205] and Mullah Ahmad Shah (Alizai/Khalozai/Yahyazai), among others.[206] All were to feature prominently in the next fifteen years of the Helmandi conflict.

Finally, many young men came of age during the Taliban era and joined the movement. One such man was Lal Mohammad from Torghai, south of Malgir, who joined at a young age. Much later he was to become a militia commander for ISAF and the Karzai government and then change sides back to the 'Taliban' in 2012.[207] Much of this side switching was driven by issues with his neighbours. Ezmarai, the son of the head of intelligence for the Khalqi police, also became a petty commander in the Vice and Virtue organisation in Gereshk.[208] He was later to become the chief of police of Nahr-e Saraj in 2010 and was rumoured to run a brothel with the female prisoners. Mir Wali described Ezmarai as a 'money dog' and pointed out that he would go with whoever was in power—it appears it was no different with the Taliban administration.

The approach in Nad-e Ali was similar: empowering former Harakat commanders and working with minorities.[209] Thus Haji Mullah

Paslow, the Popalzai Harakat commander, was an official in the government, while his nephew, Akhtur Mohammad, was a judge.[210] From the Noorzai clan in Loy Bagh that had split so successfully during the jihad, the Aghezai, Mullah Karim (who was actually Khano's nephew, and had been with Hizb, although whether the Taliban knew this or not is unknown) acted as a mullah for the movement. Another ex-Harakat commander, Zakiri (Noorzai), acted as a petty commander.[211] Mullah Karim aside, the Hizb figures in the district were not represented in the Taliban administration. Some were persecuted. Rahmattiar (Ishaqzai, from Jangal), for example, was repeatedly arrested and tortured. In one incident in January 2001, he was blamed for a disturbance that was actually caused by Abdul Rahman, who had been running a low-level insurgency against Taliban rule in Marjeh, and thrown in prison in Kandahar. He was eventually freed by the Karzais at the end of the year (see Chapter 4).[212]

In Nad-e Ali too, as in Nahr-e Saraj, young men came of age during the Taliban era and joined the movement. One particular young man, Murtaza, was a Kharoti tribesman from Shin Kalay.[213] Shin Kalay was not well represented in the Taliban administration, mainly because they had been so closely aligned with the communists or Hizb, and the Taliban had considerable numbers of ex-Harakat people within their ranks. Murtaza, however, came from the smallest of six Kharoti clans in Shin Kalay, the Shabakhel (see Kharoti tribal diagram in Appendix 4). This was either a reflection of the Taliban policy of empowering minorities, or the fact that Murtaza saw it as a way of breaking out of his life as a member of one of the less powerful clans in the village.[214] Before long, Murtaza was in command of a group fighting in the north of the country and he was eventually arrested by the US and sent to Guantanamo.[215]

The central districts were split politically between ex-Hizb and ex-Harakat patronage networks, and the Taliban managed them by mostly supporting Harakat over Hizb networks. Most other districts in Helmand were similarly divided, but the Taliban managed them in different ways. In Sangin, Atta Mohammad's men had switched sides to the Taliban, so they formed the immediate political constituency. Akhtur Mohammad Osmani, who later became a famous Taliban commander, came from this Ishaqzai Chowkazai clan.[216] He eventually rose to become a treasurer to the Taliban and a close confidant of Mullah Omar (he was finally killed by ISAF in 2006).[217] Mullah Abdul Ghaffour, also from a minority tribe in Sangin, the Popalzai, rose to become the head of communications in the Taliban Ministry of Defence.[218] The same minority strategy was used in Garmsir, where Mullah Naim from the Alizai (approximately 10 per cent of the district's population were Alizai) was chosen, despite the fact that the Garmsir Alizai largely sided with Hizb during the jihad.[219] Thus when controlling the population, the Taliban were clearly able to act pragmatically on the basis of local realities and to dispense with the religious narrative that they ostensibly held and promoted.

Now Zad, however, offers a striking example where almost the entire district was supportive of the Taliban administration—indeed, some of the most powerful commanders involved in fighting for the Taliban nationwide were supplied by this district. In Now Zad, the Taliban employed Mullah Dost Mohammad Akhund (Harakat), who represented the faction of the Ishaqzai that had fought under Abdul Ahad (Dost was Abdul's brother), as the district governor.[220] Mahmoud Yunous (Ishaqzai) was from the same community and rose to become the commander of Kandahar Airfield and Hafiz Yunous (Ishaqzai) became the Taliban minister for mines.[221]

But the other communities in Now Zad also had power. One of the largest Taliban field commanders in the country came from the Noorzai community that had sided with Hizb: Mullah Salam from Tizne village. He eventually rose to become the Herat military commander[222] despite being despised by the residents of Herat and being seen as operating independently of control by the Taliban government in Kandahar.[223] The district had a lack of friction during the Taliban era due to this alliance between the Ishaqzai and Noorzai communities—quite an achievement after the infighting during the jihad. I asked a former Taliban Ishaqzai mullah how this came about. He attributed it to the large number of madrasas and religious students in Now Zad, although perhaps he is amplifying his own experience and applying ideological narratives to his own actions: 'when the Taliban came, all the students joined immediately'.[224]

Those who had not joined the Taliban from an established jihadi power bloc joined for a variety of other reasons, which created another layer in many communities' politics. Some, like Murtaza (Kharoti), joined as a way of increasing their standing in the community. Others joined because they wanted to take advantage of Taliban patronage in paying for fighters where there was little other employment—Atta

Mohammad's men in Sangin, for example. Some speak of ideological reasons for joining. The Taliban mullah from Now Zad discussed above is a good example of this, although he may have been self-justifying. He recounted to me that the Taliban had visited his madrassa and described the situation in Gereshk and Kandahar. 'Women are uncovered,' he said, 'they are all warlords and not true jihadists [in Gereshk].' But Kandahar was worse: the Taliban had gone to arrest a commander one evening and when they went into his room they found 'his chaiboy masturbating him'. As the-then soon-to-be Taliban mullah said to me, 'the Taliban showed me how people were not living properly'. He joined immediately and saw extensive service leading Taliban troops in prayer on the front line.[225] Most interviewees, however, agreed that the Taliban government was very similar to Rasoul or Ghaffour's style and ideology of governing: strict, Islamic and andi-wali.[226] Interestingly, unlike other periods covered in this book, they described it in terms of Taliban *co-option* of the population, rather than population *manipulation* of the Taliban.[227]

Helmand was stable under the Taliban. Local political control and disarmament of those not in the Taliban government allowed the Taliban to fulfil the narratives of social order that they espoused. My interviews show that the record of the Taliban with regard to fairness and justice was patchy at best, with some administrators being the epitome of fairness,[228] while others were as corrupt as those who came before or afterwards[229]—it all depends upon the official spoken about and the interlocutor. But stability seemed to be the same across the districts. The main thing that many Helmandis recounted was keeping a low profile, which meant that the Taliban left you alone.[230] 'Like before, it was done in the name of religion, but it was all about power', said one man who was a petty Talib.[231] Even the small number of communists who did not flee were safe, as long as they kept a low profile.[232] The emphasis was on stability, probably because for the entire time that the Taliban controlled Helmand they were fighting bitter wars elsewhere in the country, first against Hekmatyar and later against Masoud and Dostum.

There was, however, one aspect of Taliban rule that did not pass unnoticed by the population: the domination by Pakistani intelligence of the upper levels of the organisation's decision-making processes. The ISI was the source of much of the Taliban's funding, alongside road tolls and drugs.[233] One shopkeeper, who ran a shop in Lashkar Gah during the Taliban era, claimed he saw regular visits from the ISI. Allegedly, Hamid Gul, the former director of ISI, and at that point 'retired', was given a tour of Helmand by the Taliban.[234] Generally, however, the number of full-time Talibs in Helmand was low because manpower was needed elsewhere in the country.[235] This led to the greatest weakness of the Taliban method of government: conscription.

Conscription was how the Taliban maintained and delivered manpower in a flexible way. The draft was a common experience for Helmandis. Everyone knew someone who had been conscripted, and many of my interviewees had in fact been conscripted themselves.[236] The system of conscription was organised through the miraws (community water allocators) who were asked to draw up a list of males of the appropriate age. The miraws were the obvious choice for this job as they knew everyone in the community. The list was then passed to the local shura to issue the orders conscripting people. Individuals were ordered to report to Lashkar Gah, before being taken by bus to Kandahar and then onwards to wherever they fought (mostly Kunduz, or Mazar-e Sharif), allowing us to date their conscription from 1997 onwards.[237]

Many fled rather than face conscription, and there were even 'uprisings' in 1998 in response to the policy.[238] As conscription lasted for three months, most extended families had to give at least one person. In Shin Kalay around thirty-five were sent; one family sent two men, and although both returned, one had only three limbs.[239] From the small village of Kakaran in the north of Nad-e Ali, ten men were conscripted. Naqilabad, a previous Hizb stronghold, suffered particularly badly, having thirty men conscripted, of which only fifteen returned alive.[240] Conscripts were not paid for their service—only clothing, food and ammunition were given—although they were allowed to steal from the population in the areas where they fought in order to gather a salary.[241] The only way out was to pay: around 1,500 dollars was the going rate for not doing your 'Islamic duty'.[242]

The infamy that the Taliban were to acquire is, of course, largely attributable to their social policies. Yet while the measures they implemented appear extreme to outsiders, in the context of the seventeen preceding years of war in Helmand they were welcomed by the local population. Indeed, this was another aspect of Taliban rule that all of my interviewees commented upon, probably because they believed that it chimed with my understanding of the narratives surrounding the

Taliban movement (that is, they were telling me what they thought I wanted to hear). My interviewees also erred on the side of negative perceptions about the Taliban, because the West was fighting a 'Taliban' insurgency in Helmand at the time when the interviews took place—clearly they wanted me to know where they stood with respect to the Taliban. However, even though there was a divergence of opinion about whether the Taliban were too harsh in implementing their programme, everyone, without exception, welcomed the absence of crime and the increased stability.

Upon arriving in Gereshk, and before they had even begun to take over the rest of the province, the Taliban closed the barbers in the bazaar in order to prevent people from cutting their hair (long hair, according to them, was more Islamic). They also immediately issued a dictate banning reshwat, or the soliciting of bribes. They also understood the Helmandi mentality and took over the few remaining brick-built or concrete buildings—then, and now, a building not made of mud indicated the hukomat.[243] Many commented on the fact that they used to check people's beard lengths with their fists[244] and would not allow music.[245] But there was an under-society. As a Karzai-era district governor of Gereshk, who was rather fond of his viskey (which is what Helmandis call most alcohol), pointed out to me, Gereshk was then as it is now: 'you could still drink and get women, it was just hidden'.[246]

The rural areas were left to their own devices. In Babaji, for example, people only saw the Taliban once a month when two Talibs would circulate on a motorbike to 'check that no-one had any televisions'.[247] Even in somewhere like Shin Kalay in Nad-e Ali, which is close to the hukomat, the elders would often go a month without seeing a Talib; rural government was very 'loose-touch'[248] and based on spies—usually mullahs—and fear.[249] This was ably helped by the copious amounts of distrust that pervaded Helmandi society due to the corrupted jihad.[250] In areas like Gereshk, the strictures were more relaxed, but this probably reflected the indigenous males' attitudes rather than those of the Taliban.[251]

The Taliban stance on law and order was the most appreciated element of their rule. My interviews match the well-known narratives of the Taliban era: hands were cut off for theft[252] and beatings were issued for minor infringements such as failing to pray.[253] There was very little crime as a result.[254] But this was only slightly stricter than the clerical rule of Rasoul or Ghaffour, where cigarette smoking was allegedly punished with torture.[255] Many interviewees spoke very favourably of the Taliban in this regard—or rather the lawful effects on society of such measures—especially in comparison to the Karzai era that was to come.[256] As one of my closest contacts said to me, 'people were scared, but at least their home was not a war-zone'.[257] Another commented on the fact that 'you could go anywhere, *it was safe*'.[258] The Taliban increased the stability that Rasoul had established. People accepted that life was more peaceful under the Taliban,[259] and returned. Only 13 per cent of the refugees who had left the country had yet to return by 1999.[260]

Furthermore, there was not a huge difference between the infamous Taliban narratives on social order and morals and the Helmandi traditions. We should not see the Taliban as an external movement that was imposed on Helmand. It was much more organic than that: the Taliban were recruited from madrassas and refugee camps in Baluchistan, northwest Pakistan. These camps were mainly populated by people from the south of Afghanistan anyway.[261] The conservative values of the Taliban were similar to the conservative values of rural Helmand.[262]

The area where the Taliban utterly failed was in the provision of anything approaching sufficient public services. Although zakat (Islamic tax) was collected, it was not spent on the poor as it was supposed to, be and was instead used to help the Taliban with their wars in the north.[263] There were no schools or clinics built whatsoever,[264] but up to 500 madrasas were established province-wide, teaching over 100,000 students.[265] Yet despite the overtly religious focus of Taliban policy, there were still exceptions. The residents of Nad-e Ali, for example, used their connections to Mutmain (from Nad-e Ali), the Taliban minister of culture and education in Kandahar, to argue for the inclusion of secular subjects; something to which he agreed.[266] Overall, however, those services that did exist were provided by NGOs. These include the hospital in Lashkar Gah,[267] the first major repairs to the canal project since the 1970s, a gravelled Route 601 from Lashkar Gah[268] and several clinics throughout the province.[269] There was no building, however, in areas that had supported Ghaffour's rule, like Musa Qala.[270]

Perhaps the one issue that separated the Taliban from the population was the opium trade. When they took over in Helmand, the Taliban briefly declared poppy growing to be illegal, before recognising the revenue implications and re-implementing the 10 per cent Islamic tithe.[271] Taliban commanders themselves were soon involved in the trade.[272] Many became rich from the crop: one rumour circulating in 1999 told of 9,000 Helmandis who had gone to Mecca for Haj that year alone, presumably as a result of the drugs trade.[273] This continued until the Taliban opium ban in 2000,[274] the implementation of which was highly effective: the Taliban 'just beat people until they complied'.[275] Scholars disagree as to whether this was a ban to appease the United States and the international community, both of which were increasingly seeking to isolate the Taliban government,[276] or whether it was merely a Taliban ploy to increase the price of opium so that they could make a windfall profit on their stocks.[277] While opinion was equally divided in my interviews,[278] on balance it is likely that there is some truth to both arguments.

One elder, for example, recalls travelling to the West and being asked by Talibs as he left the country to make sure that people abroad saw his photos of the opium ban.[279] Yet other interviewees recall that before the ban the Taliban went to every household collecting two mahn (approximately 9 kilogrammes) of opium paste (worth approximately $252 before the ban and $4,500, or even $6,300, after the ban).[280] What ultimately convinced Helmandis that the Taliban were taking advantage of the ban was the fact that the latter did not seem to suffer and were still able to 'buy nice cars'[281] when Helmand was affected by a major drought in 2000.[282] This came at a time when a quarter of Helmandi livestock was dying due to a lack of water.[283]

Towards the end of the 1990s, people were starting to feel less positively about the Taliban government. The war in the north of the country between the Taliban and the Northern Alliance was interminable. In response to the drought of 2000, the Taliban reduced the flow through the Kajaki dam in an attempt to help, but this caused tensions with the Iranians.[284] The combined effects of the opium ban, the drought, and conscription created the impression that the Taliban government was about to crumble. It was against this backdrop that the attacks of 11 September 2001 occurred in the United States.

## Conclusions

This chapter has presented a detailed narrative of Helmandi history from 1989–2001. Normally, the beginning of this period, up until 1992, is discussed as the retreat of the communist government and the advance of the mujahidin. The Helmandi story is different: set against a background of side switching, manipulation and betrayal reaching eye-watering complexity, the 'government' split in two and allied itself with different mujahidin factions. The local political dynamics established during the jihad continued, and drove the struggle for power. Helmand essentially operated in a bubble, completely separate from the national government. Once the Rabbani government came to power, an attempt was made to re-establish central authority—namely the Rasoul/Ismail Khan assault on Lashkar Gah. This, however, appears to have been hobbled by a poor level of knowledge by Rabbani, leading to different sections of the government fighting each other.

The Hobbesian civil war period, from 1992–4, is considered a separate era in the habitual analyses of the Afghan conflict. In Helmand, it was business as usual: the same actors continued fighting each other and jockeying for power, although they sought funds and patronage from different sources. Interestingly, the stories told by the Helmandis of this era match the better-known narrative surrounding the 'Afghan civil war'. Within the context of Helmand, however, they simply match those told by Helmandis about other eras of their recent history.

Finally, the Taliban era offers us a very useful contrasting period of calm in Helmand. For most of their period in power (1994–2001), there was little large scale fighting in Helmand. This was down to their social control and their disarmament of the commanders who were not in their patronage network. However, most importantly, this social control was facilitated by their detailed local political knowledge. This is in direct contrast to the first part of the chapter when the communist government and the mujahidin parties had a poor knowledge of what was occurring in Helmand and were manipulated by the Helmandi actors. This greatly exacerbated the conflict.

4

# FROM THE US INTERVENTION TO THE RETURN OF THE ANGREZ, 2001–6

Either you are with us, or you are with the terrorists.

George W Bush
20 September 2001

With one bullet [Sher Mohammad] did many hunts.

Taliban sub-commander
Kajaki

*Background*

The events of 11 September 2001 prompted the United States to attack Afghanistan and drive the Taliban from power. The Taliban were replaced by the internationally-backed interim government of Hamid Karzai. The dominant Western perception of these years, particularly as promoted in the mainstream media, tends to focus on the apparent happiness of the Afghan population to be free of Taliban 'oppression'. Women, for instance, were shown discarding the veil in Kabul. This general optimism was tempered with some emerging concerns that the United States was relying too heavily on Afghan warlords, partly because its attention was diverted by the invasion of Iraq in 2003, and

111

that these warlords were preying on the population. The end of this period is usually defined by a re-emergent Taliban movement. Scholars saw this as a reaction to the warlords' predation.[1]

In the dominant media narratives surrounding this period, the Taliban were seen as opposed to Western ideology becoming established in Afghanistan. I treat it differently, although I do not deny that this was certainly a partial motivator for the central Taliban movement in Quetta. As I describe the conflict in this period, there were a series of very bad decisions made by Western actors in Helmand. They had almost zero knowledge of the environment they were operating in. Following on from my analysis in the previous chapters, this ignorance was extensively manipulated by the same Helmandi actors that had manipulated the Soviets and the mujahidin parties. As before, this manipulation allowed the conflict to get worse as time went on. By the time that the British intervened in 2006, near anarchy prevailed.

Firstly, I will look at the Taliban's exit and the re-establishment of the 'government' under the same commanders who formed the mujahidin unity government in the early 1990s. This time, of course, their patrons were Western, and this relationship and how it was manipulated will be explored. This dynamic reawakened the inter-commander war that had existed previously. I then go on to discuss how these factors—Western ignorance and behaviour, and the inter-commander conflict—lay the foundations for the rise of what I term the Taliban franchise. Of particular importance, and covered in detail here, are Western attempts to remove the mujahidin unity government (read: patronage network). The chapter will conclude with a discussion of the activities of Sher Mohammad, the provincial governor for most of this period. The parallels between Sher Mohammad's behaviour and that of his uncle, Nasim, in the sense of playing both sides against the middle, are striking.

*The Return of Mujahidin Unity*

During October 2001, the US began to bomb Helmand intermittently. Their primary target was the Daud-era military camp in Bolan, which was still used by Taliban military forces.[2] Beyond this, there was some bombardment of the outpost on artillery hill near Gereshk, where the Taliban kept some vehicles, and of their headquarters in Gereshk.[3] The cotton gin (factory) was also bombed, as it was one of the few buildings that remained standing.[4] The Taliban responded by conscripting men onto trucks in order to take them to Kandahar and the north to defend against an expected assault on Taliban front lines.[5] The population began to move away from the bombardment sites.[6]

Concurrently, Hamid Karzai, the head of the Popalzai tribe in Kandahar, held meetings with ex-mujahidin commanders in Quetta in order to build a coalition. Where support was pledged it was conditional on the United States backing Karzai—foreign money was the 'kingmaker'.[7] There was then a hiatus in Helmand until mid-November, when Mazar-e Sharif, Herat, Kabul and Jalalabad fell in a matter of days to former mujahidin commanders who had been in control before the rise of the Taliban. They were backed by US Special Forces. Karzai then moved into Afghanistan with a band of followers, including the son of the erstwhile provincial governor of Helmand, Rasoul: Sher Mohammad Akhundzada. According to (probably self-propagated) legend, they crossed the border on a motorbike and headed for Uruzgan province.[8] Sher Mohammad and a small group then continued to Kajaki and Musa Qala, where he began to organise fighters.[9]

Other Helmandi mujahidin commanders began to return independently. Hafizullah Khan left Pakistan and headed to Bolan.[10] Abdul Rahman Jan mobilised in Iran, presumably with Iranian support, before crossing Nimruz to capture Marjeh. As he recounts, Marjeh was taken from twenty Taliban fighters, one of whom was an Arab, and then lost to a Taliban counterattack from Lashkar Gah. Marjeh was captured and recaptured twice more, with a loss of eighty casualties on Abdul Rahman's side. If true, this story represents the only reported on-the-ground fighting with the Taliban in Helmand; the Helmandi interpretation of the intervention is that 'the US pointed a finger and the Taliban government fell'.[11] There was no coalition Special Forces activity in Helmand at this early stage, unlike elsewhere in the country.[12]

By the end of November it was becoming clear that the Taliban position in the south of Afghanistan was untenable. The non-Helmandi Taliban evacuated Lashkar Gah and Gereshk on 28 November 2001.[13] The Helmandi 'Taliban' mostly went home, while some went to Girdi Jangal refugee camp in Pakistan.[14] As they left, they handed control of Lashkar Gah to Israel Khan, from Ashem Jan's influential Now Zadi Noorzai family. He was immediately challenged by Hafizullah Khan from Bolan, leading to a standoff over the Bolan Bridge. A shura of elders decided that Israel should temporarily remain 'provincial governor' and Hafizullah should become his 'chief of police'.[15] Negotiations for the control of Helmand then began between Israel Khan, Hafizullah, Abdul Rahman and Sher Mohammad.[16] The new order had been defined by mid-December: Sher Mohammad, who had Karzai's endorsement, and hence also that of the US, was announced provincial governor. He entered Lashkar Gah with a militia comprised mainly of ex-Taliban fighters (he had mobilised old Alizai Harakat networks, which were generally Taliban-aligned).[17] Sher Mohammad, in his version of the story, claims that he personally pushed the Taliban out of Lashkar Gah, as does Abdul Rahman.

Kandahar fell on 7 December 2001[18] with the Taliban surrender negotiated by Rais Baghrani.[19] He had been fighting as a senior commander in Kabul and was asked by Mullah Omar, the Taliban leader, to negotiate with Karzai, who was in the mountains surrounding Kandahar. Once the negotiations were complete, Baghrani claims that Omar left Kandahar and that he went home to Baghran several days later, on the same day that Kandahar fell. Two of his commanders—Qayoum Zakir and Rauf Khadim—were not so lucky: they were given over to the Americans in the north by Dostum, and spent the next five years in Guantanamo Prison Camp in Cuba.[20] Murtaza, the Kharoti commander from Shin Kalay, was also caught in the north and sent to Guantanamo, to be released in March 2003.[21] However, Gul Agha Shirzai and the US Special Forces suspected that Omar had escaped with, and was being protected by, Baghrani. Shirzai threatened to send 4,000 men to Baghran to capture Omar, but Sher Mohammad offered to negotiate Omar's handover and the disarmament and public reconciliation of Baghrani. Baghrani has always maintained that Omar would never seek shelter with him as they were from different tribes Alizai and Hotak—and the chance of betrayal would be too great.

On 31 December 2001, US, and possibly British, Special Forces arrived in Lashkar Gah. They then moved to Baghran with Sher Mohammad to meet Baghrani and to attempt to search for Mullah Omar. Baghrani, confronted with his family enemy backed by the coalition, and with little choice but to comply, handed over 'seventy to eighty heavy weapons, including artillery, and eight to ten anti-aircraft guns; more than one hundred light weapons, including AK-47 rifles and rocket-propelled grenades; and two hundred tons of ammunition' as a token of public reconciliation. An advisor to Shirzai joked that the weapons offered were paltry when compared to the full stock of Baghrani's weapons, the collection of which would take weeks.

By 5 January, two reconciliations had occurred: Baghrani, 'the Talib', had publicly reconciled with the 'government'; and, privately, Sher Mohammad reconciled with him and allowed him to remain as de facto tribal leader in Baghran (the two families had been feuding for decades—see Chapters 2 and 3). These reconciliations were considered a trick by the US, which spent the next three years trying to capture or kill Baghrani—although they did get much of their intelligence from Mir Wali, who hated Baghrani for ousting him from Gereshk in 1994. Whether the US pursued Baghrani because he was 'Taliban', or whether Baghrani maintained links to the 'Taliban' as a way of hedging against the aggression of the US, Sher Mohammad and Mir Wali, remains unclear.[22]

Sher Mohammad, empowered with American funds and legitimacy, removed Hafizullah as chief of police and appointed Abdul Rahman in his place.[23] Abdul Rahman attributes his appointment to the presence of the ex-Jamiat Panjshiris controlling the Ministry of Interior. Dad Mohammad (Alakozai), from Sangin, was appointed head of Helmand's National Directorate of Security (the new Khad)[24]—a reflection of his client status to the Alakozai leader in Kandahar, Mullah Naqib, who was also part of the Karzai tribal coalition.[25]

Gereshk, for once, was not the primary focus of activity. An ex-Harakat commander from Deh Adam Khan, Khan Mohammad (see Chapter 2), immediately seized control there after having slipped over the border from Pakistan in the final days of Taliban rule.[26] Mir Wali arrived approximately two weeks later after taking part, or so he claims, in the Northern Alliance capture of Kabul. He had come via Peshawar, Quetta and Kandahar, and through the hands of Gul Agha Shirzai, the Kandahari Barakzai strongman who had the support of US Special Forces. At this point, the US armed Mir Wali and he established his patronage links to the fledgling US-backed Afghan government (although through a different route to Sher Mohammad). Mir Wali was appointed commander of the re-established 93rd Division.[27]

When Mir Wali arrived in Gereshk he called a meeting among (mainly) ex-Hizb commanders: Khalifa Shirin Khan, Abdul Raziq, Mirza Khan, Haji Kadus and Khan Mohammad were among those who attended.[28] This is the first time that Haji Kadus enters the story, and there is some confusion surrounding his origins. Many argue that he was a small-time Hizb commander, citing his closeness to Mir Wali.[29] However, Kadus (Barakzai/Shamezai) actually came from the other, 'Harakat' side of the tribal split in Malgir—that led by Haji Abdul Agha (Barakzai/Shamezai) (see Chapter 2). His father was a medium-level khan and his family were 'all Harakat'.[30] Mir Wali may have appointed him as his deputy in order to create a stable coalition; the two of them were to have a massive effect on Gereshk over the coming decade. It certainly had the desired effect of balancing Khan Mohammad's power—during the negotiations there was some posturing, and one of Khan Mohammad's commanders was shot in the leg, but Mir Wali was far more powerful and ultimately prevailed. Khan Mohammad was made chief of a police force that had been vastly reduced in size, as compared to Mir Wali's divisional command.[31] This reflected the power balance between the ex-Harakat and ex-Hizb networks in Nahr-e Saraj.

The events of 2001 had taken everyone by surprise in Helmand. This is one reason why the old commanders, who had wrought so much destruction during their previous tenures, managed to regain control. They retained the old networks that had been in place from the jihad and gained access to the considerable resources that stemmed from US patronage, including money and weapons, distributed by the CIA and Special Forces teams in the south. Combining the two reactivated the networks, demonstrating the importance of alliances with the United States. Ironically, the fact that the Taliban had removed the resurgent commanders in 1994 actually lent them some credibility with the US, but all relied on ex-'Taliban' for their support—it was impossible not to in a society such as Helmand's that had been so thoroughly co-opted by Taliban networks and patronage.

As elsewhere in the country, the fall of the Taliban was greeted with a sense of relief and of opportunity—the international community was finally going to help rebuild Afghanistan.[32] As such, tribal leaders began to reassert themselves and reintegrate former 'Taliban' forces. This was the second in a series of tribal rapprochements that has occurred during the conflict—the previous one being in 1991/2, and the most recent occurring in 2012 as ISAF began to pull out of Helmand. In some cases this was an automatic function of the acquisition of power; Sher Mohammad arriving in Lashkar Gah with the support of fighters who had formally fought for the 'Taliban' is a notable example of this. In others it was a deliberate policy of convening shuras to work through the issues involved. Thus Barakzai commanders and tribal elders convened under Khalifa Shirin Khan and Haji

Mudir Agha (from Nawa) in early 2002, and agreed to move forward and work together.[33]

In some cases these shuras were not able to broach the differences. In Now Zad, for example, the Ishaqzai shura (there were also other tribes' shuras in Now Zad) was unable to reintegrate those Ishaqzai tribesmen who had fought under Kakar commanders due to an unresolvable feud. Those members of the tribe were expelled from Now Zad and forced to seek government employment for protection. An important Ishaqzai Taliban commander, Rahim, gave his weapons back to the tribe. He was later to re join the Taliban, becoming their shadow provincial governor.[34] In other areas with different social terrain, different communities worked together through inter-tribal shuras. In Nad-e Ali, immediately after the departure of the Taliban, a multi-tribal militia was formed under the district shura to ensure security under Haji Jamalzai, the old Kharoti Harakat commander. Many of the men had connections to the previous administration, but in the atmosphere of 2002 anything was possible.[35] In a sense, when Helmandis talk of the broken expectations of the Karzai era,[36] they are talking as much about the broken expectations of those early tribal shuras and the spirit of cooperation that ensued as they are about the broken promises of the international community.[37]

Yet as had been the case with the previous mujahidin governments, those with positions of power and access to patronage needed to reward those who supported them. Thus district-level positions reflected the areas of influence of the top-level powerbrokers appointed by President Karzai: Sher Mohammad, Mir Wali, Abdul Rahman and Dad Mohammad. This was to protect their (geographical) powerbases. The commanders used patronage to mobilise men, upon which their ability to maintain power rested. This was very similar conceptually to how mujahidin commanders sought and maintained power during the jihad, and the way in which the mujahidin administrations were conducted between 1989 and 1994. Many Helmandis called it the 'second mujahidin unity government'.[38]

Khalifa Shirin Khan, who was close to Mir Wali, was appointed to Gereshk as district governor, and Meera Jan, an Abdul Rahman commander, to Nad-e Ali.[39] Gul Mohammad, Dad Mohammad's brother, was appointed district governor of Sangin.[40] Likewise, northern Helmand was considered important to the powerbase of Sher Mohammad; his brother, Amir Mohammad Akhundzada, was appointed governor of Musa Qala.[41] But with cousins-in-law in place in Kajaki (Haji Sherafuddin) and Baghran (Abdul Raziq),[42] Amir Mohammad effectively became the governor of the old pre-1964 district of Zamindawar (this is what the Alizai still call northern Helmand).

In those areas beyond the control of the 'big four', other, less well-connected people were appointed: Haji Abdullah Jan (Barakzai, Hizb) managed to regain his position in Garmsir[43] and Mohammad Nabi Khan, a Jamiat commander, was appointed governor of Nawa.[44] Hafizullah Khan, the old Hizb Amir for Helmand, who was detested by Sher Mohammad[45] and surpassed in importance by Mir Wali,[46] was not given any official positions.

Mir Wali was the most fortunate in terms of the position he attained; as divisional commander he had a large number of patronage positions to offer, and the 93rd Division largely became an ex-Hizb construct. Rahmatullah and Pir Mohammad Sadat from Nad-e Ali, for example, were appointed as his sub-commanders.[47] He also appointed Mir Ahmad and Mirza Khan, from Malgir and Gereshk respectively.[48] Sarwar Khan (Alizai), Abdul Rahman Khan's nephew, was a regiment commander responsible for the ring road from Delaram to Gereshk—a major moneymaking opportunity.[49] Each commander inflated the number of men 'under command', and so would receive, for example, fifty salaries for thirty men.[50] Further south in Babaji, Haji Gul Ehktiar and Sur Gul, his nephew, raised men and became sub-commanders, and they also had further sub-commanders, like Sayed Amir (Tsuryani) and Lal Mohammad (Barakzai), both from Torghai. Marriages were arranged to solidify links between different clans and different groups of armed men. Thus Kuchnai Agha (Sayed, from Saidabad), a 93rd commander, married his brother to one of Mir Wali's daughters. The relationship unfortunately came to an end when Hekmat, Mir Wali's son, killed Kuchnai Agha in a dispute over a chaiboy.[51]

Further up the valley, Abdul Khaleq's[52] sons, Qari Hazrat and Lala Jan, became the main Ishaqzai commanders.[53] These two men provide a good example of the link between security and drug production. Mamouk, another of Abdul Khaleq's sons, and Haji Aka (in the same clan) are both large-scale smugglers.[54] Similar to the role played by Mir Wali, but at a lower level, Qari Hazrat and Lala Jan personified the mechanism through which armed power, government legitimacy, mobilised men and drug profits were fused. In this, Mir Wali's links to Gul Agha Shirzai were to prove very useful: when the US wanted to establish themselves in Helmand, Shirzai made sure that Mir Wali was the natural choice.[55]

This played into a wider dynamic, however. The Barakzai were the main competitors to President Karzai's Popalzai in Kandahar. By supporting Mir Wali, a fellow Barakzai, Shirzai was creating a counterbalance to Karzai's main ally in Helmand, Sher Mohammad.[56] According to Sarah Chayes, the US was unaware of these power dynamics in the south; so intent were they on hunting down al-Qaeda and the remnants of the Taliban. They did not realise that by supporting Shirzai and Mir Wali they were creating problems for Karzai's tribal balancing act. This was because they saw Afghanistan in Taliban/non-Taliban terms.[57] Thus the first US Special Forces teams to reside in Helmand arrived at Mir Wali's office in the summer of 2002 and began to set up what later became known as Camp Price. As was to happen time and again throughout this phase of the conflict, individual Helmandi actors, in this case Mir Wali, were able to capitalise on US ignorance of local politics, thus allowing private motivations to determine the course of the conflict in Helmand.

According to Mir Wali, he tried to direct the Americans to the old army encampment on Artillery Hill, but the Americans wanted a base near the city. Mir Wali detached sixty men under Idris, Haji Kadus's brother, to guard the base for them in return for a fee.[58] But much more important than the money was the impression to the rest of the population that he, Mir Wali, was working with the foreigners and that he, alone, controlled access to their base. This mistake was made all over the country and gave the impression that the various warlords affiliated with the United States enjoyed impunity—which was often true. Initially the Americans operated on their own, but this changed when they lost two soldiers in Sangin during a reconnoitre operation in March 2003.[59] Mir Wali offered a solution: 'anywhere you go, take my men with you; they are familiar with the people, with the terrain; anyone you need will go with you'.[60] The US began to operate with militias made up of Helmandis.

In Lashkar Gah, Sher Mohammad did not receive the same patronage opportunities as Mir Wali. He did, however, control a large part of northern Helmand, without serious competition. As northern Helmand is a traditional poppy-growing area, this allowed him to dominate the opium trade and its profits. Mir Wali gained income from road tolls, US Special Forces, the Ministry of Defence and from the drug-growing areas under his control. Sher Mohammad gained from his position as provincial governor, which later allowed him to extract money from development projects. However, he mainly gained his income from growing and taxing opium in areas that he controlled—he maintained a series of drug militias, run by ex-'Harakat' commanders, many of whom had also been 'Taliban' commanders.[61]

Commanders such as Mullah Manan (Alizai/Hassanzai) were vital to Sher Mohammad's operation in Musa Qala.[62] Rahmatullah (Alizai/ Hassanzai) was responsible for moving the drugs to Baram Cha on the Pakistani border[63] and Pir Mohammad (Alizai/Hassanzai) was Sher Mohammad's bodyguard commander.[64] Other commanders included Mahmad Akhundzada (Alizai) and Abdul Bari (Alizai/Hassanzai).[65] Furthermore, Sher Mohammad maintained very close links with a major international drug smuggler, Haji Azizullah Alizai, later to be identified as a 'Significant Foreign Narcotics Trafficker' by the US president in June 2007.[66] They are allegedly cousins.[67] In a further twist to the tale, it was later rumoured that President Karzai's brother, Ahmad Wali Karzai, was living in Haji Azizullah's house in Kandahar.[68]

Initially, Mir Wali and Sher Mohammad were the two major players in the province, with Abdul Rahman and Dad Mohammad occupying the second tier of power. Abdul Rahman was dealt a more difficult hand, His 'police department' was effectively a series of local militias and was composed of groups like the Haji Jamalzai militia in Nad-e Ali, for example. The area that he controlled, mostly Nad-e Ali, Marjeh, Washir and Now Zad, was also significantly fractured in terms of tribal and jihadi party affiliation. Abdul Rahman was very much a junior partner to Sher Mohammad. Whereas Mir Wali was out in Gereshk, Sher Mohammad was in Lashkar Gah, as was Abdul Rahman, and both men kept some of their militias there. This initially created some tension between Abdul Rahman and Sher Mohammad.[69] Habibullah feels that an international dimension exacerbated this competition: Sher Mohammad looked to Pakistan and Abdul Rahman to Iran for support.

The 'police' were mostly drawn from certain family networks (see Appendix 4 for Noorzai tribal diagrams and family trees). Abdul Rahman's deputy was Ayub Khan, who was Israel Khan's brother.[70] Israel, in turn, is related to Arif Noorzai,[71] who is one of the most powerful figures in the south—one of his sisters is the widow of Ahmad Wali Karzai (Hamid's late half brother) and another is married to Sher

Figure 2: Sher Mohammad in 2012

Mohammad. Thus Ayub's appointment was entirely due to his tribal standing, which conferred a degree of tribal legitimacy and strength on Abdul Rahman's organisation. Being in the 'police' meant nothing if one was not backed up by a strong de facto powerbroker.[72] Like other major commanders, Abdul Rahman (Noorzai/Darzai/Parozai) placed loyalists in key positions. He appointed Sarwar Jan (Noorzai/Darzai/Parozai), for example, as chief of police in Now Zad, which was Abdul Rahman's tribal centre of gravity despite his (stolen) land being in Marjeh.[73] Hakim Khan (Daftani), an ex-Jamiat commander and a neighbour of Abdul Rahman, became the commander in Marjeh and then later in Nad-e Ali; it was an andiwali (friends') 'government'.

The ex-communists who had fled began to return as soon as the 'police' reformed. In the case of the Noorzai ex-communists, this had been part of Israel's original negotiations in Lashkar Gah: the Noorzai should become fully reintegrated into the new government.[74] A number of former policemen returned, such as Gulie Khan (Baluch), Ismail Khan (Hotak) and Habibullah (Noorzai).[75] While this was a positive step for the future development of the police—they were all well-trained, professional policemen—there were initially some private frictions between the jihadis and the communists.[76]

Abdul Rahman gradually started to shift his centre of gravity down to Nad-e Ali from Now Zad by allowing members of his clan to settle on stolen government land. He eventually became responsible for the theft of 20,000 jereebs[77] of land, much of which would have been redistributed to others as part of patron–client relationships.[78] This allowed Rahman to increase his control, as he effectively became the leader of a larger patronage organisation that controlled more land and drugs, allowing him to mobilise more men than ever before. For the 'police' especially, this dynamic enabled them to control more routes in Helmand, which in turn meant that they were able to dominate opium transport. The Helmandi 'police' came to be completely controlled by Abdul Rahman's network, and it was in this way that commanders who later became well known were recruited, such as Haji Baran, Dil Jan, Mirdel and Mahboob Khan. They were all Noorzai, all cousins and mostly from the same clan: the Parozai.[79]

As well as massively increasing his own landholdings in Marjeh (to be farmed by families from Now Zad), Abdul Rahman allowed relatives to divide up the area around the Bolan junction.[80] North of the Lashkar Gah road was given to Mato Khan (who was related to Lal Jan by marriage), a Noorzai commander who had fought in Jamiat with Abdul Rahman. His nephew, Abdul Raziq, was given the south side of the road—he came with 100 households.[81] Qabir Khan, already mentioned as Haji Lal Jan's brother, occupied the land a little further to the south, around Zaburabad.[82] Lal Jan himself, a cousin of Abdul Rahman, resumed control of northern Nad-e Ali, selling land in the desert[83] (see Appendix 4).

Even so, the 'police' were not a cohesive organisation. A 2002 UN report identified five separate 'police' factions that did not answer to the district chief in Nad-e Ali, Hakim Khan.[84] This was also one of the first observations that Habibullah conveyed to me when I met him for the first time in December 2008. The incoherence of the 'police' was due to the nature of their funding, which was fragmented, bottom-up and from many individual actors involved in the drugs trade. There were even reports of individual 'police' commanders running their own heroin-processing labs in Chah-e Mirza, Nad-e Ali.[85] The lack of any real police structure clearly contrasts with the older, more established network run by Sher Mohammad, in a region where much of the competition had been eliminated by his forefathers, as well as the mainly Barakzai-, Hizb-dominated 'organisation' led by Mir Wali, which was well supported by the government (unlike the 'police', the 93rd Division appeared to get paid regularly) and the Special Forces.[86]

However, every commander who had the power to do so (as a result of US patronage) stole land. Militia commanders divided up the area to the north of the Bughra canal. Haji Kadus, for example, parcelled up the land to the west of the Abhashak Wadi. Much of this land went to refugees from water stress (lack of irrigation water) from northern Helmand.[87] Sher Mohammad also allowed (mainly) Alizai families to settle in the Bolan desert from northern Helmand,[88] as well as stealing land in Musa Qala.[89] All the settlements created tension with the existing landowners, however: the Bolan settlers with the Barakzai near the river; those north of the Bughra with the canal-zone; settlers and those in Musa Qala with the Pirzai.

Dad Mohammad, the provincial head of the NDS (National Directorate of Security: the Afghan Internal Security Service), ran the smallest of the networks in the province. One brother was the district governor of Sangin.[90] Another, Daud, became the chief of police in Sangin. All ran private militias that guarded the family power base.[91] In the case of Dad Mohammad's militias, some began to be sponsored and armed by US Special Forces from mid-2003 onwards, as was the case of Karim Khan, one of his sub-commanders.[92] This was to prove beneficial to Dad Mohammad later on, when the Special Forces repeatedly intervened in his favour to help him retain his position as the provincial NDS head, even though the UN advised that he be removed for his abuses.[93] Astonishingly, and perhaps indicative of the lack of communication between different branches of the US effort and between different rotations of officials in the country, the US continued to support Dad Mohammad even though they believed he was implicated in the deaths of US Special Forces soldiers in Sangin in March 2003.[94] These issues will be explored in more detail later on.

The titles and positions that were bestowed upon the old mujaheds did not mean anything in a Western sense. Rather they were a mechanism of reflecting de facto power that facilitated access to government funding and legitimacy. From the perspective of Kabul, it was better to have the commanders inside the tent than out, but it was more than an organisational carve-up of Helmand—it represented a geographic one as well, with the client militias of the main players continuing to act out their alliances and feuds. This carve-up, and the resulting inter-commander competition it enshrined, reflected the profit from the opium trade. In a study of money movements in 2005, Edwina Thompson found that the centres of drug finance in Helmand were Sangin (Dad Mohammad), Lashkar Gah (Abdul Rahman), Gereshk (Mir Wali), Musa Qala (Sher Mohammad) and Baram Cha (on the border with Pakistan and critical for the logistics of the trade).[95]

This was the provincial backdrop for the emergency loya jirga (grand council) held in June 2002 in Kabul and the constitutional loya jirga in December 2003. There was some confusion surrounding the emergency loya jirga, with no list of candidates drawn up.[96] Further, the list for the constitutional loya jirga was reportedly manipulated by Sher Mohammad to ensure that it contained very few Barakzai and as many Alizai as possible.[97] Hamid Karzai was elected president of the interim administration once Zahir Shah had anointed him at the emergency jirga. He was popular, but it was felt that he could have done more to limit the role of the topak salaran (warlords). While this comment was directed at Northern Alliance figures like General Fahim, it should be taken in the context of a province where four warlords were in charge. The Helmandis also felt that they were under-represented in terms of delegates per district compared to areas in the north of the country, particularly Panjshir. The identification of Panjshir—later synonymous with the central government—as a source of contention and unfairness by Helmandis repeatedly surfaced in my interviews.[98]

At the start of the jirgas the Helmandi delegates felt free to talk, but as the process continued, they felt less able to talk openly in the presence of the northerners, particularly about national politics. At one point they stopped Wakil Safar, the Nad-e Ali Kharoti leader, from speaking, as they feared for his safety. This underscored the climate of fear that pervaded Afghan, and particularly Helmandi, society: the last twenty-three years of fighting, side switching, betrayal and discordance had eroded trust. Yet overall the process was seen as a significant first step: the delegates felt important and proud of their democratic role.

One delegate's comment, however, demonstrated a true understanding of how things were to develop over the next five years: 'the foreigners must like the topak salaran'.[99] Helmandi fears about the role of the US were exacerbated as the US Special Forces detachment established itself near Gereshk. Helmandi lexicon underscores the importance of this in much the same way as other eras added new words to the Pushtu vocabulary—'raaket' and 'komandan', for example, were Soviet-era additions. One of the notable additions in the 2000s has been 'specialporce', which is indicative of their ubiquity.[100] Their mission was to search for al-Qaeda and Taliban remnants. In Helmand, at least to start with, this meant a focus on Rais Baghrani, even though publicly he had reconciled. This was most likely because the US gained most of its human intelligence from his enemies: Mir Wali and to a lesser degree Sher Mohammad.[101]

## The Role of Westerners

The Special Forces lost no time. They offered a bounty to anyone who was able to bring in former members of the Taliban, or particularly, al-Qaeda. US troops did not understand how fractured the society in which they were operating was. They also failed to understand how offering a bounty would cause people to denounce anyone they were having a feud with, or even innocent people, in order to collect the money.[102] Once arrested, a prisoner would often end up in Guantanamo Bay prison. Early in January 2003, for example, Abdul Kadus, a seventeen-year-old orphan from Nad-e Ali, was arrested by Mir Wali's forces in what appears, from the Guantanamo documents, to be a 'sting' in order to gain the bounty offered. In an almost exact copy of this modus operandi, Mohammad Ismail, a sixteen-year-old, was arrested, also in Gereshk.[103] They share consecutive Guantanamo inmate numbers, although the records are unclear about their exact date of arrest.

At the end of January, Abdul Raziq was arrested in Lashkar Gah by the '3rd Commando, Afghan Military Forces'. Although the reason for his initial arrest is unknown, in Guantanamo he was accused of being a member of a forty-man terrorist 'unit' run by Baghrani, an allegation largely based on evidence from another detainee—Mohammad Hashim—that was probably extracted under torture.[104] Raziq was to die of cancer in Guantanamo nearly five years later.[105] This forty-man terrorist 'unit' became a spectre for US Special Forces. It had allegedly helped Osama bin Laden escape from Afghanistan and had assassinated the Afghan vice president, Abdul Qader, in July 2002. Its funding came from 'al-Qaeda'.[106] Many of the Helmandi detainees were accused of membership of this 'unit', yet, as far as I can tell, its origin lies in the Guantanamo interrogations of the Kandahari Mohammad Hashim.[107] Although the unit appears to have been driving US Special Forces operations in early 2003, the only place I have seen it mentioned is in the Guantanamo files, where it is repeatedly referred to. My interviewees never mentioned it (although I did not ask about it).

The arrests continued. In early February 2003, a Mohammad Nasim was arrested because he had a 'similar name' to Mullah Nasim, a Talib who had fled the north during the ousting of the Taliban.[108] Soon after, on 10 February 2003, US Special Forces launched a major operation in Lajay village in Baghran in an attempt to arrest Baghrani, but they were heavily ambushed. In response, the soldiers rounded up ten locals, some of whom were most likely involved in some way in the incident, along with several who were not. Most were released between 2005 and 2007.[109] They failed to catch Baghrani, but this incident was the beginning of a series of attempts, lasting until 2005, by US Special Forces to capture him.[110]

The inter-commander war began to be reflected in the Guantanamo arrests. For example, Haji Bismillah was Sher Mohammad's head of transportation in Gereshk. He was responsible for collecting tolls and issuing permits. Their families had intermarried and Bismillah's brother, Mohammad Wali, was Sher Mohammad's driver (he is currently one of the MPs for Helmand). It appears that he was arrested on a tip-off from Haji Kadus in Gereshk, who coveted the revenue-making position for himself. Bismillah was accused of being a member of 'Fedayeen Islam' (this is another 'group' that I have never heard of outside of the Guantanamo files). He was also accused of 'working' with Sher Mohammad (at that point the provincial governor) and Baghrani (it should be remembered that they despised each other) against the United States, as well as being a member of the forty-man 'unit'. He was eventually released in 2009 after taking Donald Rumsfeld, the US secretary of defense, to court.[111] Mir Wali and Haji Kadus were brilliantly playing the US off against their rivals.

The commanders, some of them illiterate, had realised that the US did not understand Helmandi politics at all. They all took advantage by offering false reports to the US forces[112]—a fatal combination of US ignorance and Helmandi greed. In a most amazing example, in March 2003, two US soldiers in Helmand were killed in Sangin.[113] The Special Forces were convinced that Sher Mohammad was responsible and asked permission from their senior command in Kabul to 'take him out', but this permission was denied. Their request had probably been the result of 'intelligence' from Shirzai and Mir Wali, who were their main sources of information.[114] Sher Mohammad's ally Dad Mohammad gave the Special Forces a Haji Jalil instead.[115] In this case, the US forces realised that they were being played, and began to suspect that Dad Mohammad himself may have had something to do with the attack that led to the loss of their soldiers. Haji Jalil, for his part, always insisted during US interrogation that he was a victim of a feud. Mir Wali further exploited the situation when he offered more men to the US forces to 'help' them.[116] (See Appendix 6 for selected Helmandi Guantanamo cases in context.)

The United States eventually stopped sending people to Guantanamo from Helmand. US policies and practice directly countered their narratives, according to which US forces were rebuilding Afghanistan. The arrests by the US Special Forces in some ways resembled the reign of terror instigated by the Khalqis in 1978, albeit smaller in scale.[117] The arrests had been a disaster in reputational terms; a disaster that was compounded by the use of Helmandis in US Special Forces militias to extend the Americans' reach beyond Camp Price to the rest of the province. In the worst case of abuse, an Abdul Wahid had been beaten to death in Camp Price, probably by the Helmandi militias working with the United States.[118] The militias were mainly led by commanders that Mir Wali had chosen from the 93rd Division,[119] although Dad Mohammad also supplied some commanders (which is astonishing given the US realisations above surrounding Haji Jalil, and serves to further demonstrate the incoherence surrounding the US deployment and mission). Commanders affiliated with the Special Forces included Jan Mohammad (Barakzai), Daud (Kadus's and Idris's brother), Ghulam Rasoul (a brother of Mir Wali), Abdul Sattar and Raziq, two ex-Hizb commanders, and Karim Khan, one of Dad Mohammad's cousins.[120]

In addition to Baghran, the focus of US Speical Forces for most of 2003 was Sangin, where they were based for six months.[121] Their enemies were almost all Ishaqzai which is not surprising considering that their 'local ally' there was Dad Mohammad (Alakozai)—they spent months trying to capture Haji Naser and Haji Bashar (reportedly two

Ishaqzai 'Taliban' commanders). They also spent time in Qala-e Gaz and Shurakay (both Ishaqzai areas), Mirmandaw (mixed Barakzai and Khugyani) and Hyderabad (Achakzai).[122] The Special Forces' first step was to set up a firebase in the compound of a Haji Fatah Mohammad, a Chowkazai Ishaqzai smuggler, and permanently install militia there.[123] The commandeering of Haji Fatah Mohammad's (Ishaqzai/Chowkazai) compound in Sangin marked a watershed in relations with the Ishaqzai, and patterns from the jihad era began to re-emerge. Although the Ishaqzai Mistereekhel clan (Abdul Khaleq's old clan) were firmly within Mir Wali's patronage network, the more northerly clan, the Chowkazai (Atta Mohammad's clan), were not. Both clans were involved in drugs: the Mistereekhel through Mamouk (a son of Abdul Khaleq)[124] and Haji Aka,[125] and the Chowkazai through Fatah Mohammad.[126] The fact that the Chowkazai did not have protection through any of the four main patronage networks, combined with their drugs wealth, made them an obvious choice for predation by the government commanders who had US patronage. Dad Mohammad told the US that the clan harboured members of the previous Taliban government (which is true: Osmani, from Jushalay, and previously the head of the Kandahar Corps during the Taliban government,[127] came from the Chowkazai).

It appears that US forces unknowingly went along with this manipulation and allowed Dad Mohammad to persecute them and steal their drugs. When the Chowkazai clan rekindled their links to the resurgent Taliban movement in 2005, it would become pertinent to ask whether the aggressive stance of the Special Forces and their Helmandi allies had pushed them to seek protection from the Taliban, or whether they had been 'Taliban' all along and the US had been correct in pursuing them. In other words, did the local fight or the ideological difference drive the conflict? On balance, the fact that they were trying to protect their drugs wealth indicates the former. After all, many former 'Taliban' were also working with the 'government', and particularly with Sher Mohammad.[128]

Once he had been evicted from his compound, Fatah Mohammad, the Sanginite drug dealer, retreated to Quetta and began to divert his considerable resources into the scattered Taliban movement. He was eventually to pay the running costs of the Gailani Hospital in Quetta, which is well known for treating 'Taliban' fighters injured in Helmand. This dynamic demonstrates the complicated nature of the relationship between drugs, the 'Taliban', the Taliban and the ISI. Officers from the latter organisation regularly come backwards and forwards to the hospital, making sure it is 'protected', as well as paying a fee for each patient that is treated.

His sponsorship of the hospital also allows Fatah Mohammad, a drug smuggler, to play a 'community' role, thus enhancing his image in the eyes of the populace, even though he is doing it to interact with the Taliban and support the 'Taliban' (who are his clan and aid his opium business) over the Afghan government/'government' and the West (who would predate on him).[129] The Alakozai–Ishaqzai dispute had its recent roots in the conflict over Sangin bazaar between Dad Mohammad and Atta Mohammad. The government–Taliban dynamic was merely a fresh ideological framework for an old fight.

US Special Forces eventually began to work in Musa Qala, with Sher Mohammad's people, on the basis of intelligence that he supplied.[130] This cooperation was driven by US money, but the situation was confused. Haji Bismillah[131] was still in Guantanamo, where he stood accused of working with Sher Mohammad against the United States, yet the Special Forces that had arrested him (or probably the next deployment) were working with Sher Mohammad. It appears that there was just as little communication between US deployments as there was between troops on the ground and the Guantanamo interrogators. Sher Mohammad would of course have been aware of this, but manipulated the Special Forces' ignorance to gain bounty money and pursue his own enemies in Musa Qala. This behaviour was to be a significant driver of recruitment to the Taliban movement in the district.[132] Tor Jan (Alizai/Pirzai), for example, a tailor, was beaten up by Sher Mohammad's men, pushing him to seek protection and support from the Taliban.[133]

Finally, US Special Forces took over responsibility for security in Gereshk town—this led to the death of Idris, the man Mir Wali had supplied to protect Camp Price, at the hands of the chief of police, Badr, in a gun fight. Idris's death occurred as he tried to take control of Gereshk's bazaar—in effect, a US-backed militia attacking and evicting the police.[134] Badr, linked to Ahmad Wali Karzai, was making so much money from smuggling drugs at this point that he was concerned about the effect on his transport network and had fought to keep Idris out of the bazaar.[135] Mullah Daud, Idris's brother, took over as the United States' 'man'.[136]

While these US Special Forces deployments continued, the members of the 93rd Division continued to collect bounties, up to $2,000 per ex-Taliban commander captured.[137] In Malgir, this led to arrests of people such as Khudaidad (Noorzai), Atta Mohammad (Barakzai), Shahzada (Baluch) and Mullah Janan (Barakzai)—all ex-Taliban low-level commanders who had returned home after 2001 and were living under President Karzai's 2003 amnesty for Taliban foot soldiers.[138] It even caused competition between different elements of the 'security forces'. In one instance, Mir Wali's men were trying to apprehend a Mullah Saddiq (Ishaqzai, from Marjeh). A car chase ensued across Nad-e Ali, which was considered Abdul Rahman's territory. Unfortunately, Mir Wali's men crashed their car into a canal near Zaburabad. Abdul Rahman's 'police' arrived and arrested Mir Wali's men. This was a major problem: arresting Talibs was 'police business', they said. Mir Wali had to apologise to Abdul Rahman to get his men back.[139]

The US-led militias acted almost entirely on intelligence that was generated from the people they worked with, namely Mir Wali and Dad Mohammad.[140] I repeatedly explored the issue of faulty intelligence driven by feuds and vendettas in 2011 and 2012. The attitude of those involved is perhaps best summed up by one of the more prominent militia commanders, who was still working with US Special Forces in 2012, when I asked him if there were still any feuds left over by the false targeting of the early days. 'All those sorts of problems are solved now', he said, laughing, 'they [the people we targeted] are all dead.' He then thought about this for a moment and clarified: 'maybe about 10 per cent of those problems remain', he shrugged.[141] In general, these Helmandi militia commanders, some of whom had been working with the US for ten years by the time I interviewed them,[142] appeared to be arrogant young Afghans who knew that they had US support in their activities. Even Mir Wali, the arch denouncer, said he could not work out why the United States was 'so stupid' (this is a very common narrative from senior Helmandis).

Yet not all of the work of the Special Forces was bad—it appears that they made efforts at traditional 'hearts and minds' activities that were commensurate with their espoused narratives. They set up regular temporary clinics and schools for locals;[143] but these were still fraught with issues of cross-cultural communication, and often 'the locals stole the money, the clinic wasn't built … they didn't want it anyway'.[144] The Special Forces also made an effort to compensate the

relatives of those they had accidentally killed during military operations.[145] But the key issues remained: bounties, false intelligence, militias and denunciations. As my oldest interviewee stated, 'people like
money ... money for information ... doesn't work in Afghanistan.
Afghans are happy to sell their own country. Everyone thinks: what
can I get out of this? These are the foundations of the last thirty
years.'[146] Exploring the comments of this sweet old man, I later had a
long conversation with a Helmandi militia commander[147] where we
discussed the US-led militias and whether they might have made the
situation worse in Nahr-e Saraj.

'The Taliban are the enemy,' he stated, 'but they are local people, it
is house on house fighting; the source of this war is the thirty years of
fighting that has created badai on badai [revenge on revenge].' He had
described the fighting as utterly local, yet as we had previously discussed the Taliban as being a Pakistani construct I asked him to explain
whether his enemy were locals or Pakistani-led Taliban, or both at the
same time. In other words, did they act according to local dynamics,
or more external ideological concerns? Although illiterate, his answer
described the conflict perfectly. 'Both,' he said, describing a view where
they were completely synonymous. He continued: 'if they are my
[local] enemies and I work for the government, then they are Taliban
[by definition—because the government's enemy is the Taliban]', and,
at the same time, 'if they are [ideological, external] Taliban, then they
become my [personal] enemies'. This was a perfect logic circle: according to him they were the same thing.

I then broadened this discussion to include the role of the United
States. He did not accept that the Helmandi commanders of the militias were using the US, except to defend their houses from the 'Taliban',
which he saw as perfectly legitimate. He said that the US had helped
them during the jihad and was helping them again, conflating *his* private war with *the* ideological war. I then discussed a specific case and
asked about Khudaidad, a Noorzai commander who had been arrested
and put in Bagram prison by the US-backed militias in 2004/5. He was
from a village called Noorzo Kalay just to the southwest of Gereshk.
After spending around three or four years in Bagram he was released
and returned to his community.[148] Moving forward to the present day,
and the 2012 US Special Forces deployment to the area, most of the
problems with the 'Taliban insurgency' seemed to stem from or pass
through that village.[149] When I mentioned Khudaidad's name to the
commander, he looked away and tried to change the subject.

He understood that I was asserting that they had manipulated the United States because of a private feud. It is only because of my detailed knowledge that outside actors do not normally have, that I was able to challenge him. When I later discussed Khudaidad and Noorzo Kalay with the US Special Forces detachment in 2012, they were not even aware of the history and background of the issue—as far as I could tell they had minimal institutional memory.

*Inter-Commander Conflict and Predation*

In the same way that the interventions of the British in the 1800s united the disparate tribes in Helmand, so too the post-2006 ISAF interventions have similarly pushed Abdul Rahman and Sher Mohammad together. But as can be seen below, they did not work together in the early 2000s. A Noorzai man I interviewed pointed out that once the British had arrived, Sher Mohammad began to use Abdul Rahman as a proxy to undermine the British and the provincial governors that they supported.[150] When I interviewed them in 2012, both went to some effort to impress upon me the strength of their alliance.

This alliance can partly be understood as a tribal issue: Sher Mohammad and Mir Wali are the most prominent figures in the two largest tribes in Helmand, the Alizai and the Barakzai (which is the largest depends upon who you ask), and they use tribal networks for recruitment and legitimacy. They also act like tribal leaders by, for example, solving disputes.[151] Abdul Rahman is the most prominent individual in the third largest tribe, the Noorzai. He thus holds the balance of power and his allegiance dictates the overall power dynamics. Links to the presidency are vital here too: Karzai receives Sher Mohammad, whereas Mir Wali is not welcome. Hafizullah Khan, the old Hizb Amir, attributes this to pederasty. He described Sher Mohammad as President Karzai's 'boypriend' (he even used the English word, giggling as he said it), suggesting that he knew someone who had seen Sher Mohammad 'in' Karzai's room when they were living in Quetta in the late 1990s.

The tension between the commanders began well before 2001 and returned to Helmand immediately after they returned. Abdul Rahman was slightly incredulous when he described Sher Mohammad turning up in Lashkar Gah in December 2001 with a number of former 'Taliban' in tow. During 2002, this developed into a full-blown power struggle for control of Lashkar Gah, Nad-e Ali and Afghan drug routes. Nad-e Ali was eventually ceded to Abdul Rahman's control,[152] but not before their competition almost developed into outright war. In October 2005, Rahmatullah, one of Sher Mohammad's militia commanders, was transporting a convoy of drugs across the desert to Baram Cha on the Pakistani border. Amanullah (Noorzai), one of Abdul Rahman's commanders and the 'policeman' in charge of the security of Lashkar Gah, intercepted the convoy and a gun battle ensued, during which he was killed.

When news of this event reached Lashkar Gah, the militias of Sher Mohammad and Abdul Rahman began to clash and there were sporadic outbreaks of gunfire in the city. This caused the deaths of twenty-two of Abdul Rahman's men and an unknown number of Sher Mohammad's. Noorzai elders went to Sher Mohammad and complained that his commander had murdered Amanullah, and the incident began to take on wider implications. Abdul Rahman's tribal elder, Abdullah Jan, had led the Now Zadi Noorzai under the Hizb banner during the jihad (see Chapter 2) and the shadow of the thirteen-year 'Hizb'–'Harakat' confrontation (1980–93) began to loom.

President Karzai summoned Sher Mohammad and Abdul Rahman to Kabul and warned them that the posturing had to cease. Relations between the two of them began to improve from then on. Karzai may have brokered an alliance between them to the exclusion of Mir Wali, who has been shut out of presidential-level politics ever since.[153] The newspapers reported that a 'police convoy' was ambushed by 'suspected Taliban', which fits the habitual framing of any fighting being as a result of the government-Taliban conflict. In reality, the governor's drugs convoy was intercepted by another drugs gang, who happened to be in the police.[154]

Beyond this dispute, Mir Wali and Sher Mohammad had had problems since 2001, reflecting age-old antipathies between the Barakzai and the Alizai and between 'Hizb' and 'Harakat'.[155] In addition to the manipulation of US Special Forces, both Mir Wali and Sher Mohammad raided each other's client militias and opium stocks,[156] while simultaneously trying to ensure that their actions were interpreted as consistent with the narrative promoted by the international community; thus attacks and violence would be perpetrated against the 'Taliban',[157] whereas stealing each other's opium stocks would be phrased as 'drugs raids against smugglers'.[158] When, finally, in June

2005, Sher Mohammad's office was raided by US-backed independent narcotics officers from the central government, 9 tonnes of opium were found.[159] Amusingly, this had previously been stolen from Mir Wali.[160]

Outright warfare, akin to the situation in the 1990s, was not possible due to the presence of US forces, and so a pseudo-war ensued that took advantage of the complexity of local politics to mask the true meaning of events from the US and international organisations. There was competition between Abdul Rahman and Mir Wali, for example, as to who provided lucrative 'security' on the national ring road. The original agreement was that Abdul Rahman's men would control the road from Gereshk going west and Mir Wali's would control the road from Gereshk going east. This fluctuated, with groups of 'Taliban' attacking the other person's checkpoints.[161] In this proxy war, Khan Mohammad, the chief of police in Gereshk (2002–3) and an ex-Harakat commander, often acted for Sher Mohammad in Gereshk. This caused almost continual problems, including open gun battles in the bazaar. Khan Mohammad was kept in this position by his patron, Sher Mohammad.[162]

The war between the commanders was largely about drugs. Due to their uncertainties regarding the future, Afghans had immediately planted poppies in the interim period between the Taliban and the Karzai government. As a result, in 2002 Nad-e Ali alone produced 8 per cent of the country's opium.[163] As the lead nation for counter-narcotics, the British sent a team in the spring of 2002 to coordinate and finance an eradication effort. At Sher Mohammad's request, they did not leave the Bost Hotel, thus exacerbating their ignorance of the local situation, and without verification, the process was horribly manipulated. Compensation was available, but this was directed to Sher Mohammad's allies. Other farmers, upon hearing of the compensation, assumed they were going to have their crops eradicated and stopped irrigating their fields, intending to rely on the compensation money which never came, and their crops died, leaving them destitute. In April, there were massive demonstrations in Lashkar Gah[164] as Sher Mohammad had used eradication to target his rivals' fields and compensate his friends.[165]

To a certain extent, the Karzai national government, and thus the international community, had little choice but to support the warlord polity, who were the de facto power holders. However, the interaction of unscrupulous Helmandi warlords and ignorant international support was very damaging to the concept of 'government' in Helmand. From the perspective of many of the disenfranchised in Helmand, it also reinforced a historical narrative according to which the Kabul government was distant, did not understand them and was not to be trusted.

The commanders did not just attack each other, they also attacked many communities and people who were not within the patronage networks of the four major commanders. This was in addition to the bounty-hunting dynamic set up by US Special Forces: the 'government' became predatory and used the excuse of the presence of Taliban in communities it wished to target. The four commanders targeted individuals who were deemed to be easy prey and entire communities began to be terrorised as 'government' militias grew in confidence. This was particularly true in Nad-e Ali, Sangin and Musa Qala.

In Nad-e Ali, these dynamics started with a feud between Kharoti 'Talib' Murtaza and Noorzai 'policeman' Haji Manan. This resulted in a rupture between parts of the Noorzai and Kharoti communities in Nad-e Ali. When British troops arrived in Nad-e Ali in 2008, it looked to us like a government–Taliban fight. To introduce the characters: Murtaza was a government-era Talib who had been arrested in Kunduz during the overthrow of the Taliban government and had spent some time in Guantanamo, before being transferred to Afghan authority in March 2003.[166] He was released shortly afterwards and returned home. Haji Manan was the nephew of Haji Lal Jan who had settled in Noorzo Kalay (see Map 8) during the jihad and was acting as a commander in the nascent police in Nad-e Ali (in reality a non-uniform wearing militia).

The narrative of the Kharoti is strong: 'Every Kharoti who is a Talib is a Talib because of police brutality.'[167] In my experience, this view is held throughout the community. Once Murtaza had been released from Guantanamo and returned to Shin Kalay, he began to be harassed by Haji Manan and his men. The fact that he had been in Guantanamo was used as justification for their harassment, although because he was a releasee he was apparently not subject to a bounty. This harassment became serious during Haji Twoyeb's (Noorzai) tenure as Nad-e Ali chief of police between mid-2004 and the end of 2005, when the police became progressively Noorzai-dominated.[168] Haji Manan used to raid Murtaza's opium stocks and bully his family, claiming all the while that he was a 'Talib' and against the 'police', despite the fact that Haji Manan, at that exact time, ran a heroin factory in Zorabad.[169] Manan finally arrested Murtaza and stole all of his opium, before having him imprisoned for a year in Pul-e Charki prison, Kabul. He was released at some point in early 2006 and went home. Shortly after, Manan raided his house and in the ensuing fight killed two of Murtaza's brothers, Abdullah and Nek Mohammad.[170] His nephew, Shaedzada, was arrested, but released after five months.[171]

Murtaza disappeared to Washir and began working to encourage other Kharoti to resist the government.[172] As an Afghan politician said to me, 'Murtaza was a good guy; he was forced to join the Taliban.'[173] One of those that Murtaza managed to recruit was Ibrahim, known by the nom de guerre Shakir. Shakir was twenty-two at the time. He was known in his village for playing a rabab (a type of guitar).[174] Afghan intelligence painted him as a minor thief who used to steal copper electrical wires.[175] Around 2005, Manan raided his family home and stole their stocks of opium. (Previously, Shakir had been arrested and beaten, before being locked in a tandoor [bread oven] for three days—all for being a 'Talib'.) This time he arrested his older brother, Ismail, who was twenty-seven, and accused him of stealing. Ismail was still in jail in 2012.[176] Once Ismail was arrested, Ibrahim had no choice: he was 'majboor', or forced, to fight the government as he had been dishonoured. He contacted Murtaza.[177] Ibrahim's father, Spin, was left in a state of despair at the situation and moved the remainder of the family to Quetta for safety.[178]

The Noorzai perspective is very different. In my frequent interactions with Haji Manan in 2008/9, he described Shakir and Murtaza as Talibs (of course, as a British officer, I was also eliciting that narrative from him). Upon reflection, his insistences were similar to the narrative of the Helmandi militia commander discussed above. Abdul Rahman, the provincial chief of police at the time, and Manan's boss and relative-by-marriage, explained it to me thus: 'their differences were about the fact that [Murtaza] was a friend of the Taliban and Manan was a friend of the government'. This is, of course, completely true, but rather paints the issue inside-out: it was their personal differences that caused Murtaza to adopt his anti-government positioning. Murtaza, Abdul Rahman said, had tried to kill Manan, and even managed to kill one of his brothers with a roadside bomb.

When trying to understand the dynamics at a later date, I came to understand that this series of events had become subsumed in a wider narrative of tribal discord, particularly for the Kharoti leadership. A senior Kharoti leader told me that the 'Noorzai'–'Kharoti' problems (as he defined them, at that point Nad-e Ali was a 'Taliban'–'government' battleground) had started because of Abdul Rahman and Tor Jan, his district chief of police in 2007–8 (also a relative-by-marriage).[179] Another Kharoti leader pointed out that it was during Tor Jan's time that the police picked up their reputation for brutality and that it was this that drove the rejection of the government.[180]

I came to know several Kharoti leaders well over the years. One in particular, with whom I had dealt extensively in 2009, I knew well enough to have a frank conversation. We sat discussing Shakir over chai and dried Kandahari mulberries. By this point, Shakir had been killed by British forces and had become something of an icon to the Kharoti community in Shin Kalay. The car in which he had died had been dragged to the desert outside Shin Kalay and was now a shrine. Before he died, he had operated against the British and Afghan government forces, at the same time as the Kharoti leadership was talking with British forces, claiming that he was a wayward child that they could not control. But he was very much supported by the tribal leadership in Shin Kalay. During one incident in which I was involved, we fed this particular Kharoti leader information in such a way in which it could be judged whether it reached Shakir. It took about ninety seconds. The Kharoti leadership was playing the same game that it had played during the jihad: interacting with opposed ideological organisations for the safety and security of their group.

Looking back with the elder to the time when the Kharoti and the Noorzai community narratives had begun to diverge, I described to him the efforts the British had made to try and kill or capture Shakir, and vice versa. By that point he had realised that the British knew he had been closely communicating with Shakir and he grimaced, wondering whether I was blaming him for any harm that might have been visited upon British troops. I was not; I said I was trying to understand why Shakir was fighting. Without mentioning Shakir's suffering at the hands of Manan, he began to discuss the district-level power balance: the Noorzai controlled the police; they used to be much less populous in the district, and now, after their illegal immigration and land theft, they claimed to be the largest community, and so forth. For him, it was a community-level war, but then, he was a tribal leader.[181]

Unfortunately, this was only one among a plethora of examples where government officials—charwakian—abused their public positions in the government, pushing the population away. The classic case of this in Helmand is that of the Ishaqzai in Sangin (discussed above), although the Kakars in Garmsir also provide a powerful example.[182] Sher Mohammad, moreover, is accused of massive land thefts in Musa Qala[183] just as Abdul Rahman was in Marjeh.[184] Attempts by tribal jirgas to mediate between the commanders and the population would often end in an agreement for compensation to be paid by, for example, Sher Mohammad. The judgement would then be ignored.[185]

*Manipulation and Demobilisation*

In addition to manipulating the US Special Forces to target their enemies, and manipulating eradication for the same reason, the Helmandi commanders also entirely hijacked development funding.[186] The common thread was a lack of on-the-ground understanding by the internationals. Apart from admirable efforts by the UNDP and Japan to sink wells and build schools irrespective of the political orientation of the communities in question,[187] aid would generally be diverted to allied communities and withheld from non-allied (or 'Taliban') communities.[188] The US Provincial Reconstruction Team (PRT)[189] was physically protected by Abdul Rahman's men, so it became impossible for non-allied communities to access US decision-makers or resources.[190] More generally, the fact that the internationals worked through the provincial authorities meant that they were blinded to the reality of politics in the province.

The foreigners initiating development projects completely underestimated the level of complexity inherent in Helmandi society, where disparities in wealth, or the misapplication of development projects to favour one group over another, could create massive jealousy.[191] As one gentleman said to me, 'jealousy is the biggest enemy of all [in Helmand]'.[192] For most Helmandis, the notion that the US was unable to understand the private political dynamics which were so obviously fundamental to Helmandi society was simply incomprehensible: 'the foreigners must have an ulterior motive for being here'.[193]

In one of the worst cases of this, a small USAID-sponsored contractor team began to offer province-wide cash for works in 2004–5 to provide a financial buffer for upcoming opium eradication. The metric of success was how many man-labour days they could pay through the scheme, which they ran through the provincial governorship. This resulted in, for example, Alakozai militias protecting (Alakozai) farmers in Sangin, while Ishaqzai communities had their crops eradicated. Examples of the naivety of the scheme abound: money was paid for ditch clearance schemes that they could not observe or verify, stumbling into the old Barakzai–Alizai dispute; and there was a massive over-focus on Nad-e Ali and Marjeh, because they received much of their local advice from an old USAID engineer from the 1970s, who clearly loved those areas of central Helmand.[194]

The politics of Gereshk between 2002 and 2005 are a perfect microcosm of the provincial-level dynamics of the same period. The most important and influential position in Gereshk is that of the chief of police. As has been the case for hundreds of years, whoever controls the bridge over the River Helmand also controls Gereshk. As an individual actor in Gereshk, 'police' membership was the most useful positioning possible. A diverse array of lower-level commanders all attempted to become chief of police in order to facilitate their core business interests, which were almost always drugs.[195]

For example, Khan Mohammad was the initial chief after the US intervention.[196] He was to last in post for around two years until late 2003 when Ahmad Wali Karzai pushed to have Badr Khan (Popalzai, Uruzgan), an acolyte, put in position. This followed the historical pattern set by the Mohammadzai dynasty: the monarch (or president, that is, Hamid) rules Kabul, a brother rules Kandahar (that is, the late Ahmad Wali) and a cousin (or acolyte, in this case, Badr) is sent to Gereshk. Previously the dynamics had been about defending Kandahar from Herat; now they were about ensuring the safe passage of drugs west to Iran.

Badr literally had to fight his way into position against Khan Mohammad, the old chief of police.[197] Badr and Gereshk had a tumultuous year, suffering a mini-insurgency caused by Khan Mohammad. It was during this period that Idris was killed by Badr as Idris tried to take over control of the bazaar with the help of US Special Forces—in other words, US Special Forces and Idris's militia tried to take over security in an area that was controlled by a presidentially appointed policeman. If the US Special Forces had understood what they were doing, then it is unlikely that this would have happened. The situation eventually became unsustainable and Abdul Rahman sent Amanullah, his Lashkar Gah head of security, as a stopgap to calm the opposing factions in Gereshk.

Amanullah's role was only temporary and, Haji Kadus, Idris's brother, was appointed the chief of police. The Special Forces, as Haji Kadus's main patron, were presumably involved in lobbying for the unusual situation where the deputy of the Army Division and the chief of police were the same person, and their paymasters were the US Special Forces! It was a stable arrangement in the sense that Haji Kadus controlled the main sources of violence, and it was to last until late 2004, when the 93rd Division was disbanded (see below). At about this time, Haji Kadus was sacked as police chief and went back to working for the US as a militia commander. He plundered the police armouries as he left.[198]

The US, however, retained influence in the police by using Sergeant Abdul Raziq as a commander of their 'District Response Team', which was a counterterrorism team, and part of the 'police'. Although he was only a sergeant (and an ex-Talib), he became the de facto chief of police because he had access to the resources of the Special Forces, even though a figurehead chief was already in place. Actions like these made Helmandis wonder what the US was up to, because its rhetoric of state-building did not match its actions.

It later became clear to the US that Abdul Raziq had been abusing his position in order to smuggle vast quantities of opium and he was dropped. However, it was only in 2009 that he was put in jail through the internationally-mentored 'non-corruptible' narcotics justice chain.[199] Khan Mohammad was also arrested a year before Abdul Raziq, but not before they had fought repeatedly as rival drugs networks, using 'police' membership as a means of protecting their business interests.[200] Although they remain in jail, their networks are extant and controlled by relatives: Abdul Khaleq (Abdul Raziq's brother) and Agha Mohammad (Khan Mohammad's eldest son) both continue the family businesses.[201]

These events provided the backdrop for a number of other stories, the majority of which centred on control of the drugs trade. The mayor's and district governor's positions suffered similar abuse from individuals or networks trying to exploit them for graft. Additionally, the people in those positions had to be careful not to 'rock the boat' as otherwise they risked becoming sidelined or worse. Said Dur Ali (Shia, from Abhazan), for instance, was the long-running mayor of Gereshk, not linked to any factions, and played a very careful balancing act. One day, his son was kidnapped by the 'Taliban'. Khan Mohammad stepped in and very kindly offered to 'pay' the ransom for him, thus neutering him. Khan Mohammad had engineered the original kidnap.[202]

As well as militia commanders affiliating with the 'government security forces' there were a number of private militias formed by ex-jihadi commanders. Mirza Khan Kakar was one such ex-Hizb commander.[203] He had been a sub-commander for Mir Wali during the jihad and, with Mir Wali's blessing, settled his mujahidin group and their families in north-west Gereshk, where they appropriated land and established a village: Mirza Khan Kalay. He used to clash regularly with Khan Mohammad's militia. In the early 2000s he had married into Mir Wali's family, greatly alleviating his feud with Khan Mohammad.[204] He then became the NDS case officer for Gereshk, which helped even more.[205] He was eventually arrested for drugs smuggling in 2011.

The final major dynamic in Gereshk was the role of the highway police, who were under a United States Protection and Investigations (USPI: a private security contractor) contract. This contract was paid for by USAID to guard the national ring road that had been built in 2003–4.[206] Prior to September 2004, Mir Wali had been in charge of security on part of the road, but the new contract was nationwide and Mir Wali had no choice but to vacate the checkpoints to this new force. A man called Masloom (Barakzai, ex-Khalqi, from Babaji) was the first commander, but once the posts were taken over they were immediately attacked by 'Taliban', causing the loss of several highway policemen. Masloom immediately accused Hekmatullah, Mir Wali's son, of being behind the attacks.[207]

Others also point to Mir Wali being responsible for this classic Helmandi act.[208] This was a demonstration of the local sentiment that 'if you are not going to include me in the security answer, I will become part of the security problem'. Mir Wali berated Sher Mohammad and President Karzai for failing to provide security with the USPI contract. When I later asked Mir Wali, whose Taliban had attacked the checkpoints, he said, in a sarcastic tone of voice, 'My Taliban; who do you think?' At some point a man called Ezmarai, who had been a delgai (platoon) commander under the Taliban, took over the contract, making him exceptionally rich, even though he had to pay Mir Wali a 'tax'[209]—money that Ezmarai later used to become Gereshk chief of police in 2010.[210] The USPI were utterly unaccountable and complaints against the organisation were legion,[211] including using their control of routes to affect drug smuggling.[212] It was eventually closed down in September 2007.[213]

The combination of the violent inter-commander competition, the skewed counter-narcotics operations, the abuse of the population and the aggravating role played by US Special Forces created a very unstable atmosphere. This was exacerbated by the removal of the four major commanders (and many other petty ones), under the UN administered Disarmament, Demobilisation and Reintegration Process (DDR), and by the resurgence of the Taliban movement, starting in late 2004. These consecutive processes combined to create a shift in patronage-seeking activity. Commanders changed from working under the 'government' patronage network (channelled through the four major commanders) to working under a 'Taliban' patronage network.

Sher Mohammad manipulated the DDR process:[214] Mir Wali and the 93rd Division were the first to be disarmed, losing thirty-five pieces of heavy artillery, among other heavy weaponry, at the end of 2004.[215] As was the case elsewhere in the country, however, Mir Wali handed in his oldest weapons and cached the rest, where they allegedly still remain.[216] Similarly, Dad Mohammad only surrendered a few machine guns.[217] Khano, by this time a shopkeeper, was disarmed personally by Abdul Rahman in Lashkar Gah in April, in a harsh repudiation of the relationship that had begun thirteen years earlier when Abdul Rahman grew to prominence on the weapons that Khano had given him (see Chapter 3).[218] This was about power and about the fact that Khano was an independent 'commander' in Lashkar Gah whom Abdul Rahman could not control.[219] Furthermore, Khano still controlled a faction of the police (his relatives) who had managed to use their militia-era linkages to join in the post-2001 era.

However, more important than the DDR process was the removal of the powerbrokers from their jobs. Mir Wali was removed from his position as he was disarmed—as divisional commander the two were, by definition, linked. Sher Mohammad, by contrast, remained in post until December 2005, when he was removed at the insistence of the British government, who were soon to deploy troops to Helmand as part of the NATO expansion into the south of Afghanistan.[220] Karzai then appointed him senator in Kabul. Abdul Rahman remained in post until 10 June 2006 and, critically, as they were part of the police, none of his men were disarmed.[221]

The de facto powerbrokers in the province were thus replaced in their de jure provincial positions. The more prominent and influential commanders entered the parliamentary elections. Dad Mohammad and Mir Wali were elected, as was Wali Jan, Abdul Rahman's son. Baghrani ran but was not elected, and Amir Mohammad Akhundzada, Sher Mohammad's brother, was disqualified because of his 'links' to unofficial armed militias. He then polled the greatest number of provincial votes through tribal support, leading to protests in Lashkar Gah.[222] Hafizullah ran and would have become an MP were it not for the rules reserving a certain number of seats for women—two female teachers, Nasima Niazee and Naz Parwar, beat him in the voting results. This was somewhat ironic as Hafizullah refuses to deal with Western women at the PRT in Lashkar Gah—only men. The voter turnout was 37 per cent, which was significantly lower than the presidential elections the year before.[223]

Once the DDR process began, a separate campaign of assassination was launched to remove any vestiges of 'government' from Helmand. This was universally accepted by my interviewees to be directed, if not in many cases actually conducted by, the ISI, Pakistan's intelligence service; however, in the media they were discussed as 'Taliban' operations emanating from across the border.[224] Whereas there had been assassination attempts on Sher Mohammad before in 2003[225] and 2004,[226] in the second half of 2005 a systematic campaign was waged against provincial notables including senior religious figures,[227] election candidates[228] and judges;[229] set against the on-going murder of policemen. Another attempt was also made on Sher Mohammad's life.[230]

Subsequent to this, the schools in Helmand were targeted, resulting in almost all of them being destroyed and the remainder closing down.[231] There were one or two exceptions in Nad-e Ali. School burning, the 'Taliban' and the influence that Pakistan exerts on the 'Taliban' are important issues for the Helmandi population. Helmandis accept that most of the 'Taliban' fighters and commanders are Helmandi, and most would not burn schools in their own communities. They point to a more extreme branch within the Taliban that is either entirely Punjabi (Helmandis call all Pakistanis Punjabis), or closely mentored by the 'Punjabis' (the ISI).[232] This issue will be explored more closely below. Finally, the Taliban distributed 'night letters' to place pressure on those who had not been assassinated. Letters would say such things as, 'Anyone who gets money from the government or the US, whether he is clergy, grower, officer etc., the mujahidin of the Islamic state will not spare him and will be punished according to the sharia.'[233]

By the end of 2005, the province was approaching near anarchy, and power began to flow back to the localities. Groups assumed responsibility for their own security, much as they had done when the state collapsed in 1978. This was encouraged by the same external influences leading the assassination campaigns, who suggested to groups that had lost out under the departing administration that they could regain their rights by opposing the government. Essentially, the Taliban narrative encapsulated well the multiplicity of reasons that people had to be annoyed with the 'government'. The ensuing provincial power vacuum meant that the government in most Helmandi districts had dissolved by the end of 2005.[234]

### The Rise of the Taliban Franchise and the Mahaz System

The Taliban resurgence in 2004–5 was primarily based on the reactivation of old Taliban networks from the previously ousted government. This was similar to the resurgence of the jihadi commanders in 2001, or even the dynamic of the 'civil war' period from 1989 to 1994. That too was driven by the activation and reactivation of different commanders' networks based upon new or different patronage flows. The mobilisation of 2004–5 also shared similarities with that of 1978 in that there were personal feuds (then created by the Khalqi predations, later driven by the warlords' predations) driving membership of opposed ideological organisations (in this case the Karzai government and the newly resurgent Taliban).

Links to the Taliban went both ways. As well as providing a forum for training and organisation in Pakistan, the exiled Taliban leadership sent emissaries forward to preach in mosques in Helmand,[235] where they would often cite the predations of the four leading commanders by name.[236] Once it became clear that Britain would be deploying troops as part of the extended ISAF mission, the Taliban activities reached fever pitch, and even Iran used its old links to invigorate resistance against the British; for example, Sardar Baghwani was seen again in northern Helmand exhorting young men to rise up.[237] Initially, the dispossessed ex-government Taliban formed links through their own personal networks to funding streams in Pakistan controlled by mahaz commanders (see below).[238] This was similar to how the rebels in 1978–9 used personal links to contact the mujahidin parties.[239] The main difference was that the Taliban was a single organisation (whereas there were many mujahidin parties), although the Taliban lacked a clear leadership structure. Taking the evidence below into account, the

Taliban could be mistaken for several different jihadi parties held together in a loose alliance—exactly what officially the mujahidin parties were. Only later did the Taliban attempt to reassert control and encourage cohesiveness.

The main difference, discussed below, between the 1978 government collapse and the 2005 government collapse is that many of the actors involved in the 'government' prior to the 2005 collapse switched sides, such that the post-collapse 'Taliban' contained people who had previously been antagonistic and even fighting each other. This did not occur in 1978. The 'government' commanders who had been divested in 2004–5 had taken the position that if they were not included in the security solution then they would become part of the security problem. Security was a zero-sum game and commanders could not opt out of a position in the new patronage landscape. They had to have at least one alliance with an organisational patron; they could not survive as a lone actor. Either they were being patronised, and hence protected, or they were not, and they would be fair game for those with resources and protection. Confusingly for the British when they arrived in 2006, Mir Wali and Sher Mohammad, the two greatest side-switchers to the 'Taliban', retained positions in the government as an MP and a senator respectively.

Individual commanders reformed affiliations through personal networks with mahaz commanders, who should be seen as analogous to the amirs that each jihadi party had in each province to represent them and organise supply.[240] Conceptually, it was the same setup. In 2005, the most important mahaz commander in the south of Afghanistan was Mullah Dadullah (Kakar, from Uruzgan),[241] closely followed by Osmani (Ishaqzai/Chowkazai),[242] from Sangin. There were others, like Mullah Baradar (Popalzai, Uruzgan),[243] Akhtur Mohammad Mansour (Ishaqzai, from Band-e Timor)[244] or Mullah Naim (Barich, Garmsir—not to be confused with the Alizai Mullah Naim, also from Garmsir who was the Taliban district governor there).[245] All were Taliban government-era officials or founding members of the movement, and all had fled to Pakistan in 2001.[246]

Dadullah was an exceptionally charismatic commander who was known as the 'lame Englishman'. This was because he had one leg and was incredibly devious.[247] Originally fighting in Kandahar, he moved to Helmand and fought under Nasim Akhundzada, returning after one year once Nasim was killed in March 1990 (see Chapter 3). During the

Taliban government, he had risen to command the so-called 'Helmandi Brigade'—shock troops—and had escaped capture in the north of the country in late 2001. By early 2006 he was the most important Taliban military leader in the south and was able to muster 300 'Taliban' to attack Sangin district centre and the (mainly US) troops that were defending it.[248] Dadullah was quoted as saying that his 'most lovely activity was the jihad and fighting the heretics face-to-face'.[249]

Enmities jarred the relationships between the four main mahaz commanders: Dadullah and Osmani did not get on[250] and Baradar and Dadullah were also enemies.[251] This led to a highly fractured situation in 2005. A district might have several 'Taliban' groups in it, which had mobilised for different reasons, and were working for different mahaz commanders (see Figure 3). Many of these groups were led by previously antagonistic commanders who had been on either side of the government–non-government divide, or were drug smugglers protecting their crop, or both. In addition, many families looked at the rapidly changing situation and opted to send at least some of their sons to the Taliban (often to different mahazes) to protect the family.[252] Before 2006 the population were aware of who was fighting, but not which mahaz they belonged to, very much like the situation in 1978–9 when the rebel groups had not yet formed their alliances with the mujahidin parties.[253] Ironically, the arrival of the British in 2006 helped the 'Taliban' consolidate and coalesce. From the perspective of the Helmandis, *the* historical enemy had just turned up for round three.

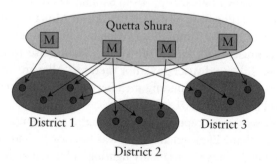

Figure 3: The Taliban mahaz system. Note that no one mahaz commander controls all the fighters in any one district

Nad-e Ali saw the earliest reactivations of the old Taliban networks, but one of the latest manifestations of major military activity. This can mostly be explained through the continued activities of Abdul Rahman. Despite his commanders being among the worst in terms of predation, they were still in government positions and so were able to supress potential 'Taliban' military activity. Even when removed in mid-2006, Abdul Rahman had built up such a successful network of relatives in the police (for example Tor Jan and Sarwar Jan, the chiefs of police in Nad-e Ali and Now Zad, respectively)[254] that he was still able to exert massive influence. As Abdul Rahman put it, 'Nad-e Ali was ok because my people were in charge of security … they are the only ones who know who the Taliban are.' In one sense he was not lying; he had simply omitted to mention the fact that it was his men who had pushed other communities in Nad-e Ali to seek affiliation with the Taliban in the first place.

The main problem in Nad-e Ali was the police preying on people, and this was mainly focused on members of the previous Taliban government.[255] In 2003, these ex-Taliban members started organising.[256] The first step in the reactivation of their networks was to travel to Quetta to ask for help from the newly reformed Taliban central shura. Once contact was initiated, a two-way flow would begin with Afghans living in Pakistan making the journey to Nad-e Ali and vice versa. Supplies of weapons were organised before being brought over from Girdi Jangal camp and cached. Small-scale military activities started in mid-2005, with some skirmishing attacks on government patrols as they moved around the periphery of Nad-e Ali (for example, Saidabad).[257] The levels of military activity were kept low due to Abdul Rahman's grip on security in the district. Later on, in 2006, 'Punjabis' (the ISI) would be seen in Nad-e Ali, although overall the organisation was very much in the hands of the local 'Taliban' commanders,[258] with the Punjabis working as advisors—every mahaz had their own set of advisors.[259]

In Nad-e Ali, an obvious example of a 'Taliban' commander is Murtaza, the Kharoti 'Guantanamo Talib', and previously discussed; however, Akhtur Mohammad (Popalzai), a previous Taliban judge, was also among those who made the journey to Pakistan.[260] Sardar Mohammad (Ishaqzai, and a relative of Rahmattiar, see Chapter 2) was involved in smuggling, and kept his options open by offering support.[261] Similarly, the Noorzai Aghezai clan in Loy Bagh (Khano's clan and known for splitting itself across ideological divides during the jihad; see Chapter 2), began to reach out using Mullah Karim. Karim's cousins were later to become the provincial chief of police and Nad-e Ali district chief of police—the faction that lost out when Khano was disarmed in 2005 had managed to regain power in the police in 2008.[262] The clan had successfully split itself again.

Other Noorzai groups suffered from unwanted splits. For example, Haji Lal Jan, a powerful ex-Taliban commander, suffered from a split in his own family, as a result of which he was forced to leave his village of Noorzo Kalay in 2005. Arab, his nephew by marriage, contested the leadership of Noorzo Kalay, despite being only thirty years old. But the divide is deeper than that. In the original migration from Washir in the early 1980s, Arab's family had come from Nakhooma Kalay, whereas Haji Lal Jan had come from Gundacha Kalay (both are in Washir), and the villages competed. Arab's interaction with the 'Taliban' was about sub-village power grabs, and nothing to do with ideology.[263] His uncles, Ghulam Saki and Mullah Habibullah, were both former members of the Taliban movement, linked to Dadullah's mahaz, and had arranged for Arab to go to Pakistan for training. He returned as 'commander' of Maat-e Que, his home area, and his base was in Washir under Abdul Salam (Noorzai commander of the Herat Corps during the Taliban government; see Chapter 3), where he raised a multi-tribal group of fighters. As someone from Noorzo Kalay put it to me, 'Arab was using the Taliban to improve his own position.'[264]

Towards the end of 2005, in an attempt to corral the movement, the central command in Quetta appointed Taliban district governors—for example, Mullah Mohammad Arif Akhund in Nad-e Ali[265]—to coordinate civil issues. However, the mahaz commanders continued to 'act … like kings',[266] and it was to be some time before the Taliban managed to coordinate the 'Taliban' better (see Chapters 5 and 6).[267]

Nahr-e Saraj suffered 'Taliban' instability at a much earlier stage than Nad-e Ali. In 2003–4, replicating the pattern elsewhere in the province, the ex-Taliban came under pressure from predation by Mir Wali and his bounty-hunting commanders. As was the case elsewhere, many of the commanders left Nahr-e Saraj and went to Pakistan seeking interactions with mahaz commanders that could provide them with training and weapons. A two-way flow of personnel and equipment then began between Pakistan and Nahr-e Saraj. Military activities started in mid to late 2005, although at first these were very low-key: two men on a motorbike carrying out an assassination, or a roadside bomb. However, in Nahr-e Saraj the new 'Taliban' were composed both of those who had supported the government previously and those who had not[268]—in other words, those who had been in the 93rd Division and those who had been persecuted by the 93rd Division.

Mir Wali and the 93rd Division were DDR'd (another 'word' that has entered the Pushtu lexicon along with 'raaket' and 'specialporce') in the autumn of 2004. This required a degree of coordination as parts of the Division were still being maintained by the US Special Forces as militias. It appears that the US detachment had begun to realise by this point that it had been manipulated over various issues including the Guantanamo arrests. This caused the US to replace its alliance with one Helmandi—Mir Wali—whom it blamed for its troubles, to one with a lesser man: Haji Kadus. This meant that they were affiliating themselves with the smaller faction of the tribal split in Malgir. The alliance with Haji Kadus was to last for the next eight years, with the Special Forces nicknaming him 'The Dous' (he was very popular with the US Special Forces operators that I met). The ignorance of the international community in prosecuting the DDR programme and of the United States in switching support to Haji Kadus has shaped the conflict in Nahr-e Saraj ever since.[269]

Once the Division's weapons were handed over, the Special Forces raided Mir Wali's house and confiscated his personal weapons. This was organised by Haji Kadus, who was usurping his ex-boss's position.[270] At the same time, the United States purged its client militias to remove anyone who was loyal to Mir Wali or had any previous association with 'Hizb'.[271] Mir Wali also reported to me that he found out at that time that Haji Kadus was planning to kill Hekmat, his eldest son. The US did not understand that Haji Kadus was launching a coup against Mir Wali. Kadus commanded their militias and his brother Daud guarded Camp Price, thus ensuring that only the people that the brothers wanted to meet the Americans got to meet the Americans.[272]

Many of those 'Hizb' elements, particularly the Ishaqzai, were put under pressure once the 93rd Division was DDR'd. This included Qari Hazrat and Lala Jan, his brother, who were 93rd commanders for the Mistereekhel clan of the Ishaqzai in Qala-e Gaz. Now that they no longer had the protection of the 93rd patronage network, their drugs interests run by Mamouk, another brother, came under pressure from Dad Mohammad and his militias—much like the Ishaqzai Chowkazai clan's interests had been since 2001.[273] Dad Mohammad was later removed from his post six months after Mir Wali and disarmed in June 2005, giving up his weapons just one week before the deadline required for participation in the national parliamentary elections.[274] His brother, Gul Mohammad, managed to remain in position as an official in Sangin until he was killed in mid-2006.[275]

Sher Mohammad was only removed in December 2005. Before he was removed he realised that the Mistereekhel drug interests were unprotected because of the DDR of the 93rd Division.[276] This uneven disarmament opened up some opportunities for a little extra predation and harassment.[277] Thus, whereas the two Ishaqzai clans—the Chowkazai and the Mistereekhel—had fought each other during the jihad (see Chapter 2), they were now pushed on to the same side. Qari Hazrat (Mistereekhel) affiliated himself with the Taliban and became a significant commander with both Ishaqzai clans behind him.[278] It is interesting to note how this looked from an Alakozai perspective: 'the Taliban, the smugglers and the Ishaqzai are all the same thing', a well-connected Alakozai scribe said to me.[279]

The disbanding of the 93rd Division had destroyed the tribal coalition created by Mir Wali—that between the two tribal groupings led by Khalifa Shirin Khan (the Akhundzadakhel, the Utmanzai, the Bayezai and the Sardarzai: the more powerful grouping previously affiliated with Hizb) and by Haji Abdul Agha (Shamezai, Nekazai, Yedarzai and Masezai: the less powerful grouping previously affiliated with Harakat). Mir Wali was Bayezai (stronger grouping/'Hizb') and Haji Kadus was Shamezai (weaker grouping/'Harakat'). Now that the 93rd Division had been disbanded, and as a result of Haji Kadus's coup against Mir Wali, those from the stronger grouping were affiliated with the Taliban; 'Taliban' commanders were 'Hizb' people such as Hazrat (Barakzai/Sardarzai) and Zapran (Barakzai/Bayezai).[280] The weaker grouping, however, contained the US militia commanders; the militia commanders were 'Harakat' people such as Jan Mohammad (Barakzai/Shamezai)—in fact, Kadus, Daud and Jan Mohammad all came from the same village: Khugyani in Charkandaz.[281] These age-old political competitors (since well before 1978) now became labelled 'government' and 'Taliban'.

It is unfortunate for the Americans that they supported such a narrow faction and pushed their enemies from the other part of the tribal coalition into forming an affiliation with the Taliban. Did Haji Kadus persecute those from the stronger grouping because they were affiliated with the Taliban, or did they affiliate with the Taliban because Haji Kadus was persecuting them? Ultimately, it was driven by the intra-Barakzai competition that was much older than, and nothing to do with, either the Taliban or Haji Kadus's persecution. Nonetheless, the situation accelerated, and before long village elders were organising their own defence and asking either Haji Kadus or the 'Taliban' for support.[282] Haji Gul Ehktiar and Sur Gul, his nephew, were such examples of ex-Hizb commanders who joined the 93rd patronage network, and after the disbandment of the division looked to ally with the 'Taliban' for protection.[283]

DDR, in short, was a disaster in Nahr-e Saraj and was entirely to the Taliban's benefit.[284] The 93rd Division split, with a small Barakzai rump remaining with the US Special Forces (affiliated with the government), but with the vast majority of the Barakzai and other tribes' commanders affiliating with the Taliban.[285] These two alliances then continued to fight each other for the next few years. The United States drove the militias under Haji Kadus to attack Qari Hazrat, then a member of the 'Taliban', often against Mir Wali's wishes (he was, by that time, the MP for Nahr-e Saraj).[286] Haji Kadus also exploited his family's Harakat links to open negotiations with Sher Mohammad. In case the US dropped him, he would need a powerful sponsor to best Mir Wali, who now hated him.[287] The Taliban organisation was a franchise, utilised to protect other private interests.

Interviewees agreed that 'everything that Qari Hazrat did was for Hizb, not Mullah Omar'.[288] Qari Hazrat worked under several 'organisations' at the same time: he 'had several bosses—Mullah Saddiq [the Taliban district governor—see below], Mir Wali, his own tribal drug interests and Gulbuddin [the leader of Hizb]; but Mullah Omar [the Taliban leader] got blamed for everything that went on in Nahr-e Saraj'.[289] Even members of 'Hizb' agree: 'most of the [Nahr-e Saraj] Taliban are actually Hizb fighting for themselves, in the name of the Taliban'.[290] Jabbar Qahraman, an MP for Helmand, also agrees that former Hizb members of the 93rd Division joined the 'Taliban' in 2005. He was later part of an abortive attempt in 2007 with Michael Semple, an EU diplomat, to reintegrate them into the police (see Chapter 5). However, when questioned about the 'Taliban' in Nahr-e Saraj in fact being affiliated with 'Hizb', Mir Wali proved evasive over the issue. He turned my question back on me and spoke about the growth of the Afghan local police in 2011–12 (see Chapter 6), and said

151

that you must have local forces that know who the Taliban are in order to fight them. It should also be noted that 'Hizb' in Nahr-e Saraj, while previously a mujahidin organisation, now represent a solidarity group of ex-mujahidin. They no longer espouse an ideology or exhibit institutional organisation; but the personal bonds between the fighters remain strong.

The Quetta Shura Taliban knew DDR was occurring and took advantage by appointing a Taliban district governor a month later. Initially, this was Mullah Saddiq (Ishaqzai, ex-Harakat), who was described above at a time when he was being chased by Mir Wali's men, and then Sur Gul (Barakzai, ex-Hizb), who had been part of Mir Wali's 93rd Division. This illustrates that in this case the Taliban in Quetta understood well the local political complexity. First, they relied on their previous constituency there (that is, ex-Harakat networks), but when the Hizb-aligned tribal confederation sought protection from the Taliban, because Haji Kadus had taken the Harakat-aligned confederation into the 'government', they quickly changed their representative in the district. The outcome was the complete inverse of the previous political situation in the district.[291]

What happened in Nahr-e Saraj was ultimately linked to what was happening in Sangin, through the Ishaqzai community who straddle the border between the two districts. The Ishaqzai dynamic was such that Qari Hazrat provided the on-the-ground leadership of the two previously antagonistic clans (see above), with Osmani and Akhtur Mohammad Mansour helping provide the link to the Taliban Quetta Shura. Additional funding was provided by drug smugglers such as Mamouk and Fatah Mohammad.[292] This Ishaqzai community was heavily predated upon by Dad Mohammad and Sher Mohammad, who were disarmed and removed much later than Mir Wali (who had been 'protecting' the Mistereekhel Ishaqzai). This story eventually came to a nadir when thirty-two members of Dad Mohammad's family were ambushed and killed when they went to collect the murdered body of Gul Mohammad, the ex-Sangin district governor in June 2006.[293] The massacre has been described in various ways: a drugs hit, a Taliban hit and an Ishaqzai–Alakozai dispute.[294] The evidence presented in this chapter suggests that it is a combination of all three.

Musa Qala followed a similar pattern to Nahr-e Saraj, where individual commanders affiliated themselves with the Taliban for protection. There were many people who had been persecuted by Sher

Mohammad and his brother, Amir Mohammad, who was the 'district' governor of the Alizai areas in the north of Helmand (Zamindawar). Mullah Salam (Alizai/Pirzai), later to become famous for switching sides yet again, was a former Taliban commander who had been the district governor of Kajaki during the Taliban government. His land was appropriated by Amir Mohammad, and Hassanzai (their sub-tribe) tenants were moved on to it. Mullah Matin was another Pirzai commander who began working with the Taliban to protect himself.[295] During 2005, the depredations became so extreme that a group of elders asked the Taliban for protection,[296] and there was a groundswell of people joining the 'Taliban' under people like Mullah Salam to protect themselves from Sher Mohammad's network.[297] Because Sher Mohammad had allied himself with the United States, there was the further motivating factor of a US firebase a short distance from Musa Qala, from which artillery was occasionally fired at the 'Taliban'.[298]

### Sher Mohammad Akhundzada

Sher Mohammad was removed from the provincial governorship in December 2005 at the insistence of the British.[299] Sher Mohammad then ordered his commanders to begin fighting the British under the Taliban franchise. Many had come from the Taliban in the first place. This is considered common knowledge in Helmand,[300] and was even confirmed by the first UK taskforce commander, Brigadier Ed Butler. When I questioned Sher Mohammad about it, and in particular pointed out a *Telegraph* article[301] that referred to his purported admission of this, he categorically denied that he had ordered his men to the Taliban and touted his anti-Taliban credentials. I again raised the issue of the *Telegraph* article and asked if he had met Damien McElroy, the author. He had, but, 'that journalist lied and twisted it; he was Angrez [*sic*] wasn't he … I hate that journalist.' Taliban commanders, however, point out that by being 'Taliban' as well as 'government', Sher Mohammad was protecting drug interests.[302] As one put it, 'with one bullet he did many hunts'.[303]

Sher Mohammad not only ordered his men to work with the 'Taliban', but he also provided massive financial support to their operations—many Taliban commanders even went so far as to say that Sher Mohammad became a mahaz commander himself (despite being a senator in Kabul).[304] Sher Mohammad's commanders who began to work for the 'Taliban', or under Taliban patronage, include Mullah Manan.[305] Rahmatullah, mentioned above in the incident where Abdul Rahman's commander Amanullah was killed, also moved to Baram Cha to work as a 'Talib-smuggler'.[306] Hafizullah provided me with the names of other commanders who entered the 'Taliban' franchise from Sher Mohammad's at that time: Abdul Bari (Alizai/Hassanzai) and Mahmad Akhundzada (Alizai). As this information comes from Hafizullah (Hizb), these names should be treated with a degree of caution. Overall, though, it is clear that Sher Mohammad was playing both sides at the same time, much as Nasim his uncle had done during the jihad (see Chapter 2), and that the ignorance of the British in insisting that Sher Mohammad was removed caused him to work more with the organisation that the British were opposed to—the Taliban.

The re-emergence of the Taliban in Helmand province is not difficult to explain. Warlord predations on former Taliban commanders that caused them to form affiliations with the ISI-sponsored Taliban provided the background dynamics. The power vacuum created by the warlords' removal coupled with a destabilisation campaign orchestrated by the ISI played a close supporting role.[307] But the actual shift between the two patronage organisations, from majority government-control to majority Taliban-control, was caused by the commanders switching sides and forming new alliances: Mir Wali in 2005, Sher Mohammad at the end of 2005 and Abdul Rahman in 2008.

In the case of Sher Mohammad this was deliberate and was probably motivated by his hatred of the British, both historically (see Chapter 1) and for insisting that he be removed from his job. In the case of Mir Wali, his sub-commanders switched sides for their own protection. The evidence shows that Mir Wali allowed this to happen and took advantage of it. Everything was driven by local context. For example, later, in Malgir, US Special Forces worked with a previously 'Harakat'-aligned coalition led by Haji Kadus against mainly 'Hizb' groups. But in Musa Qala the 'government', and the British when they arrived, fought the old 'Harakat' networks of Sher Mohammad. These personal dynamics drove the fighting against the British when they arrived. The Taliban in Pakistan simply provided funding.

Sher Mohammad was replaced by Mohammad Daud as provincial governor, an English-speaking technocrat from Helmand, but with no tribal base. He was deputised by Sher Mohammad's brother, Amir Mohammad, making it very hard to escape the influence of the previous governor.[308] Sher Mohammad detests the British for his removal and called them 'nah poh', which translates as 'stupid, unintelligible, slow-witted, unintelligent, uneducated and ill-informed'. 'They do not understand Helmandi politics at all,' he told me, 'we are both on the same side.' He was not lying; he was just affiliated to both sides at the same time.

Once appointed, Daud led the 2006 eradication programme supported by the newly deployed Afghan National Army (ANA) and Abdul Rahman's police. The crop in 2006 was twice as large as that of 2005, and his intent was to eradicate the poppy that was grown on government land by government officials. The fact that this coincided with the British deployment was regrettable timing.[309] The ISI-sponsored Taliban were offering to fund resistance to the eradication forces using protection of the poppy crop to gain farmers' support.[310] The eradication, led by Amir Mohammad, began in Dishu and then moved into Khan Eshin and Garmsir.[311] It later moved into areas like Sangin, which at that point was in the throes of outright warfare between the Afghan National Army and the 'Taliban'.[312]

Overall, less than 10 per cent of Helmand's 40,000 hectares of opium poppy was eradicated and the process became corrupted by business interests. Central Helmand, the domain of Abdul Rahman, was left untouched, largely because his police were providing the protection for the eradication force. The same occurred in Musa Qala, Sher Mohammad's domain. Province-wide, poor farmers were targeted rather than richer landlords or those with connections to government, while in Sangin the eradication proved incendiary and allowed the 'Taliban' to protect poor farmers from government eradication. This was in fact Ishaqzai tribesmen facing down an Alakozai-led eradication effort.[313]

*Conclusions*

Of all the periods in Helmand's history discussed in this book, the period following the events of 11 September 2001 clearly demonstrates that private interests, and local disputes, have played a highly prominent part in driving the Helmandi conflict. As this chapter has shown, local actors were able to exploit the ignorance of the international community—and to some extent, even the Taliban—regarding local issues and personal conflicts in order to achieve very specific, local aims. In this way, and despite the value-based, ideological rhetoric that the international community and the Taliban espoused, both became embroiled in what was, in effect, a localised civil war. Furthermore, that ignorance made the conflict worse as local actors were able to prosecute their feuds in indirect ways and with greater resources than they would be able to accrue otherwise.

# 5

# FROM THE RETURN OF THE ANGREZ
# TO US RE-ENGAGEMENT, 2006–9

> People rose up; some came with guns,
> some with knives, some with sticks; we
> went to defeat them.
>
> Redacted
> (speaking of the battle of Maiwand)

> Why Helmand? The Angrez could have
> gone to any province.
>
> Helmandi Senator[1]

## Background

The British deployed forces to Helmand in 2006 in order to support the government and deliver reconstruction and development to the population as part of a programme of NATO expansion throughout Afghanistan. During this period, the overwhelming media narrative of the conflict focused on the fierce fighting between ISAF and Afghan government troops, and the resurgent Taliban. As per the 'insurgency narrative' (see Introduction) the government forces, and the British, were seen to be protecting and advancing democracy, and women's rights, and countering the growth of narcotics. The Taliban, still considered a unitary actor, were opposed to the government and the British, and fought in the name of Islam.

In this chapter, I will tell the story of the first three years of the British deployment as seen through Helmandi eyes. In addition, I will juxtapose the Helmandi view with my experiences serving as a British officer from 2008 in central Helmand, working with many of the Helmandis discussed in the text. Certainly, it will become clear to the reader that the British were able to discern few of the political dynamics at first—that took many years. To use myself as an example, and I was more informed than many foreigners by dint of the political nature of my job and Pushtu language skills; my understanding of the conflict completely changed between 2008 and 2012. To put this in context, in 2012 a Helmandi that I knew well laughed (kindly) at me when I intimated that I was reasonably well informed. According to him, I knew 'about 1 per cent [of what went on]'. This ignorance in many cases led us to be exploited by Helmandi leaders; Helmandis continually manipulated me.

I begin the chapter by discussing why the British chose Helmand (and what the Helmandis thought of this). The choice of Helmand, not surprisingly, frames the whole campaign for the Helmandis. The rest of the chapter covers consecutive eras of the campaign, with slightly increasing levels of British knowledge, but never really enough to stop them being manipulated. First, the deployment to northern Helmand and the 'Taliban' response it generated. This is contrasted with the calm that existed in central Helmand, at that time under 'local' control. I then discuss two attempts by the British to do some 'political' work with their increased understanding, reminiscent of the operations that Khad used to mount (see Chapter 2). While this was occurring, the Taliban in Quetta were attempting to reorganise the Taliban into a more unitary organisation (also discussed in detail).

The chapter finishes with a discussion of the British focus on central Helmand, the ensuing fighting, and the gradually continuing increase in British knowledge of the local political context. I conclude, based on my analysis here, that the British never reached the levels of local political knowledge required to prosecute the type of war that they wished to (that is, a counterinsurgency). Arguably, increased knowledge might have led them to the conclusion that the conflict was a long-standing civil war between Helmandi factions that they had unwittingly become involved in, rather than a conflict that fitted the 'insurgency narrative'.[2]

*Why Helmand and Why Northern Helmand?*

The British mission, as part of the expanded NATO/ISAF mission, was to bring increased security and stability to the province and to check the narcotics trade.[3] As the lead nation in the coalition for counter-narcotics, it was felt appropriate by Tony Blair, then prime minister, that Britain deployed troops to Helmand (as it was such an important centre in the narcotics trade).[4] However, the most important factor in the selection of Helmand was NATO politics between the Canadians, the British and the Dutch: the Canadians wanted Kandahar, and the Dutch Uruzgan.[5] The mission was intended to last for three years at a cost of £808 million,[6] with significant numbers of British forces being deployed from May 2006 onwards. The initial plan was to secure a 'lozenge' around Gereshk and Lashkar Gah and demonstrate their reconstruction efforts to the population.[7] US Special Forces were still to remain in the province under their counterterrorist Operation Enduring Freedom mission.

Unaware of these decisions and machinations, the Helmandis heard on the radio that the British were returning after 126 years. What they heard seemed incongruous to what they knew of the British.[8] There was even confusion in the Afghan 'government'. A Helmandi senator asked me, 'Why Helmand? The Angrez could have gone to any province.'[9] On a more personal level, a senior and well-educated provincial official remembers sitting on his grandfather's knee as he was told stories about the battle of Maiwand, where his grandfather had fought. 'People rose up; some came with guns, some with knives, some with sticks; we went to defeat them', he said.[10] He then recalled a meeting with British officers in early 2006. A young intelligence officer asked him what the Helmandis thought of the British in light of their shared history. The provincial official replied that the Helmandis hated them, causing the officer's face to turn red with embarrassment. Not wishing to offend his guest, the official continued, 'but that was then, and this is now ... now you have come to help'. He later explained to me that because he was a government man, and that was the government policy, he followed it. Yet he was thinking 'why are they *here?*'

The British troops focused on three issues as they toured the province to explain their deployment. First, security: the incoming 3,000 British troops and a further ANA brigade would ensure security, including patrolling the border with Pakistan to stop the Taliban and their supplies coming into the province. Second, development: in contrast to the United States, who had directly implemented projects themselves, the British would be channelling development money through the provincial government in order to strengthen its mechanisms and its relationship with the population. Third, counter-narcotics: this was an acute concern for Helmandis. As the British were touring the province, the 2006 eradication campaign was in full swing. The British line was a classic fudge: 'no UK military personnel will be eradicating poppy; however, part of the UK mission is to support the [Afghan] government in its counter-narcotics efforts'.[11]

It is hard to judge now what the majority of Helmandis thought about the return of the British at the time. My interviewees (later) discussed it in a universally bad light, focusing on revenge for Maiwand, and traditional British perfidy. But much has happened since 2006, and oral history is the 'facts' of the past retold through the lens of the present. Contemporaneous US diplomatic cables referred to the positive reception that the British received as they arrived, and to an atmosphere of hope that the British were going to help solve some of the very serious problems in the province.[12] 'It is true', one US diplomat wrote, 'that Afghans have a long memory for history, and a few Afghans even comment on the (unfortunate) British colonial history. In general, however, the great majority of Afghans understand and support the modern-day British role here.'[13] It is of course impossible to know how astute the writer of those cables was or whether the Afghan words of welcome were hiding other thoughts.

The British entered a situation that was spiralling out of control. Indeed, in April, a British reconnaissance patrol was attacked in Now Zad, a month before they had even taken over responsibility for the province from the Americans. Their attackers turned out to be 'policemen', and there was a question as to whether the attack occurred because the 'police' thought that the British soldiers had arrived to confiscate their opium stocks.[14] Patrolling began in Gereshk at the end of April and was met neutrally.[15] Elsewhere in the province the situation continued to deteriorate: Baghran 'fell' to the 'Taliban' on 29 April (it was the first district to 'fall' in 1978 as well).[16] Concurrently, there was a large amount of other military activity. US Special Forces were still based in the province and highly active, although uncoordinated with the British.[17] In mid-May, a large US-led operation was launched to put pressure on the Taliban to ease the entry of the British and other coalition troops into the south. It had the reverse effect. Similar to a Soviet sweep operation, and with large amounts of airpower, it had the effect of massively 'stirring things up' in Helmand.[18] To the Helmandis, the economic development that the British had promised seemed oddly juxtaposed to the massive military operations that they could see around them.[19]

It appeared that northern Helmand was about to revert to 'Taliban' control. Governor Daud told the British that the towns in northern Helmand were under attack by the Taliban. The British had to deploy there to stop them from capturing a district centre and 'raising the Taliban's black flag'.[20] Yet the shadow of the previous Helmandi government loomed. In Musa Qala, for example, the police were under the command of Abdul Wali Koka (Alizai/Hassanzai)[21] and the district governor was Mohammad Wali, whose brother was Bismillah and was still in Guantanamo (see Chapter 4)—both were heavily linked to Sher Mohammad, and their bad behaviour was the spark of the uprising for most of the 'Taliban'.[22] They came under attack on 18 May. British troops responded by deploying to Musa Qala, with Amir Mohammad, the deputy governor, and his militia. After securing the town they headed north to Baghran. Amir Mohammad had told the British that the 'Taliban' had come from there.[23] This may have been true, but in reality he was most likely targeting his old family enemy, Rais Baghrani. The conflict was being driven by their feud, but the dynamics were overlaid for British consumption with the abstract government–Taliban fight. It appeared that the British were unaware they were being manipulated.

A few days later Now Zad was to come under attack. Sarwar Jan (Noorzai), a relative of Abdul Rahman Jan, was the district chief of police and represented the old warlords' rapaciousness.[24] He was described as a 'very, very cruel man'.[25] Now Zad was an important area for the Taliban due to the fact that major commanders like Abdul Salam (Noorzai) and Rahim (Ishaqzai), the Taliban provincial governor at the time, came from the district.[26] By 22 May, a small number of British troops had deployed to the hukomat to reinforce the 'police'.[27] At the beginning of July, locals began to leave Now Zad and the British began to be attacked there as well.[28]

In Sangin, a similar pattern had prevailed. Sangin's district chief of police was an ally of Sher Mohammad, Khan Mohammad (Barakzai, ex-Harakat, ex chief of police in Gereshk).[29] Gul Mohammad, Dad

Mohammad's brother, was the former district governor,[30] but still an 'official' in Sangin.[31] In mid-June he was murdered by the Ishaqzai 'Taliban' (see Chapter 4).[32] The family response exploited the common Western understanding of the conflict: Dad Mohammad, at that point an MP, insisted that the remaining members of his family were rescued from the 'Taliban'. Moreover, warning that it was about to be overrun by Taliban, President Karzai and Governor Daud insisted that the British deploy to the district centre.[33]

In an attempt to take advantage of this situation, Khan Mohammad also insisted that he be extracted—the Sanginites had accused him of raping a little girl and were trying to kill him.[34] The British moved in reluctantly on 21 June. They were not keen to be involved in what they understood to be a private feud.[35] When they arrived they held a shura with the locals who told them that they were not wanted and asked them to leave. The British spent the next few days building their defences until they began to come under attack at the end of the month, allegedly from Ishaqzai tribesmen, in response to a Special Forces operation to the south of the district centre.[36] At around the same time an American convoy was ambushed to the south of Musa Qala district centre, resulting in another large battle where the British again began to come under attack.[37]

While the provincial government and the British were distracted in the north of the province, another group of militants from Pakistan crossed the border and captured the Garmsir hukomat on 16 July. According to the Afghan government and two interviewees, they raised the flag of the Jamiat-e Ulema, a Pakistani political party with close links to the Taliban, and a deal was struck to allow the police to leave.[38] Pakistan denied the event had ever happened whilst the Taliban claimed it as *their* victory. It is not known what role Naim, the ex-Taliban governor for Garmsir, played in this odd adjunct to what was occurring in the province. On 18 July, government officials and police fled Nawa, which the Taliban also claimed as a victory.[39] Both hukomats were swiftly taken back by the ANA with ISAF air support.[40] The district centres experienced government collapse in the same order as they had in 1978 (see Chapter 2). And as with the collapse of the communist administration, there was no major fighting in Gereshk, Nad-e Ali and Lashkar Gah that year.[41]

The deployment of British troops to Helmand had not gone as intended. Despite the removal of the four rapacious commanders in

2004–6 (Abdul Rahman was finally removed on 5 June 2006),[42] they still managed to maintain significant patronage networks of sub-commanders within the organisations and areas that they used to control. However, these networks had been weakened significantly by their patrons' removal. This meant that the groups and individuals that the commanders used to predate upon sought Taliban patronage to attack them in revenge.[43] The British factor served to complicate matters even further. The British knew that they had come to Helmand to support the government and fight the Taliban, but they did not have enough knowledge about Helmand's politics to understand exactly who the 'government' were and who the 'Taliban' were. When they arrived in Sangin, for example, they were immediately told where the 'Taliban' were by the 'government', but luckily the local ANA commander warned the British platoon commander that they were being used to settle a private feud.[44] In the eyes of the Ishaqzai in Sangin, the Pirzai and the Khalozai in Musa Qala and almost everyone in Now Zad, the British had arrived and immediately started supporting the topak salaran (warlords).[45]

When they deployed to the north, the communities did not understand why British soldiers were suddenly arriving in their villages[46] and the British had no idea as to who their friends or enemies were.[47] This situation was compounded by the absence of reconstruction projects[48] combined with the civilian casualties that resulted from the use of airpower to defend isolated British positions—18,000 pounds of explosive (around twenty-five airstrikes) were dropped by the British on Now Zad during that summer alone, flattening the bazaar.[49] Thus from the perspective of the population, the British narrative did not match their actions. They also could not understand why they 'supported' the warlords' sub-commanders, with whom the population had major grievances. By this point, the Helmandis were twenty-eight years into their conflict and there was no patience for a historical enemy.

People began to leave northern Helmand for safer areas[50] and the 'police' (militiamen of the warlords) began to leave or switch sides— even though they were loathed by the population, the police hated the British even more, and the warlords could no longer pay them.[51] Governor Daud was to complain repeatedly that year about the 'tribal wars' in the north of the province,[52] but to the British the problem was interpreted through the Taliban–government prism. There were ominous signs, however, that ISAF was inciting the same general resistance that the Soviets had incited. When a joint French–ANA patrol was attacked north of Sangin in May, for example, they reported being ambushed along a 7 kilometre-long stretch of road as 'every man and woman [came] out of their compounds to fire at them'.[53] In many cases, the local population assumed that ISAF was deploying in order to stop them growing poppy[54] (see Figure 4).

## The 'Taliban' Response and a British Retreat

The Taliban leadership in Pakistan (hereafter the 'Quetta Shura') took advantage of the situation in Helmand with a considerable degree of skill. A Taliban spokesman stated that 'we are here to destroy the British. We will hunt and kill them. We will not let them go back to England and say that they have defeated the Afghans.'[55] It was an evocative narrative that resonated strongly with the Helmandis. It brilliantly contrasted with the reconstruction and counter-narcotics narrative. Jihadi publications published in Pakistan extolled the same narrative and stated that 'the

Figure 4: Children's graffiti in Lashkar Gah, 2008, depicting UK involvement in Helmand (note 'Chinook' helicopters)

British had not generated a hand span's worth of security for the people at the same time that they brought the dirty slogans of democracy'.[56] The past had a strong resonance, particularly among the Alizai:[57] 'we gained our freedom one hundred and sixty years ago [sic] and we shall remain free ... we do not accept the claim that they are here to rebuild our country ... they have done nothing for us',[58] said one Taliban commander in Musa Qala. Much later, when I attended a shura of 300 Alizai elders in Lashkar Gah, the anti-British exploits of Akhtur Khan and Abu Bakr Khan during the 1800s were remembered with a proud twinkle in the eyes of those attending.[59]

The fighting was becoming unsustainable for the British—they were not equipped to maintain isolated outposts under constant attack.[60] The population also wanted an end to the violence. The original uprising was attracting fighters from other areas, which was leading to more and more violence. Dadullah, the most important mahaz commander in the south, had gone to Waziristan in May 2006 and negotiated for militants to come to Helmand in order to fight NATO and British forces.[61] Correspondingly, British sources describe the arrival of Pakistani fighters in northern Helmand towards the end of June and the beginning of July, where they acted as mentoring teams to the locals.[62] This was the much-vaunted Taliban offensive in the summer of 2006.[63] This stream of foreigners in 2006 was to become a flood in Garmsir in 2008.[64]

Musa Qala elders, led by Haji Shah Agha, approached the British to negotiate a ceasefire. In public they stated that they had done so because they were weary of seeing their district destroyed by fighting between the British and the Taliban.[65] Yet in practice they aimed to eject the Sher Mohammad-linked police chief and district governor.[66] British forces and the Taliban would withdraw from the district and allow the elders to maintain security with a militia comprised of their 'sons'.[67] In return, the Afghan government would offer development projects in the area. The elders particularly wanted a canal, like the US-sponsored canal projects that had been given to central Helmand (northern Helmand is experiencing desertification and this is a recurrent demand of the northern Helmandis).[68] The agreement was signed in September and the British pulled out in October, handing the hukomat over to the elders. The Afghan national flag would continue to fly,[69] but the deal was not supported by the US who saw it as a retreat for ISAF and the international community. Governor Daud retorted that the British were a provocation that had now been removed.[70]

Taliban media in Pakistan painted British actions as a retreat, and noted the differences in the US and British positions. They also seized on British statements to the effect that 'if us leaving generates stability in an area, then we will do it elsewhere', and pointed out that this made it very clear who was generating instability in Helmand. According to the Taliban leadership, the withdrawal of the British from Musa Qala was a step towards 'freeing' their country.[71] The argument that the British rather than the Taliban are responsible for the instability in Helmand is a constant refrain among most Helmandis that I have spoken to, and the deal proved popular among elders in other northern districts. Ceasefires, with British troops remaining in place but not patrolling, were struck in Now Zad and Sangin.[72]

Sher Mohammad immediately began to lobby against the deal, as he had lost influence through the removal of his officials. When I later interviewed him, he was vehement, accusing the British of handing the town over to the Taliban. Shortly after the deal, he had sent delegations to meet with the newly enlarged Provincial Reconstruction Team (PRT) in Lashkar Gah. One delegation included Koka, the erstwhile Musa Qala chief of police, who brazenly complained that the elders' shura was comprised of drug dealers and Taliban. He said that he hoped ISAF could return, but of course with US troops, not British ones (Helmandis usually tailor their message depending on their audience: he was speaking to a US officer and would have been aware that the United States was not supportive of the British deal). On the same delegation was a female Helmandi MP, who pointed out that now that the deal was in force girls could no longer go to school.[73] She was manipulating ISAF's stated aims in the conflict, even though girls have rarely gone to school in Musa Qala.

There was too much pressure on the deals and they ultimately collapsed, leading to more fighting. Now Zad's took about three weeks, Musa Qala's collapsed in February and Sangin remained peaceful until March 2007.[74] The collapse of the Musa Qala deal has been blamed on the Americans killing a 'Taliban' commander in or near the exclusion zone surrounding the hukomat. The 'Taliban' claimed he was within the negotiated exclusion zone while the Americans maintained that he was outside of it. It is difficult to identify who the 'Taliban' were at that stage, but two interviewees point to the fact that Sher Mohammad's men were continually probing across the exclusion zone's boundary in attempts to scupper the deal.[75] Once it collapsed, however, Haji Shah Agha was murdered and Musa Qala went back to 'Taliban' control.[76]

Fighting resumed in Now Zad throughout 2006 and 2007. Once the deal in Sangin broke down in March, there was a large British operation in an attempt to 'clear it once and for all', seemingly reminiscent of the 1988 Soviet operation discussed in Chapter 2. The town was reported as 'utterly devastated' after British troops attacked and then blew up compounds (that is, people's houses) from where they had been fired at—behaviour that was somewhat different from the publicly promised reconstruction mission.[77]

While the fighting continued in the north and the south of the province throughout the winter of 2006–7, central Helmand remained peaceful.[78] As with the Soviets before them, the British did not have nearly enough troops to garrison the province and instead conducted massive clearing operations that were not linked to any political objectives apart from killing 'Taliban',[79] much as had been the case with the Soviet operations against the mujahidin. The main difference was that the Soviets did very strong political work through Khad (see Chapter 2), which was entirely absent during the early British period.[80]

One such British operation occurred over the summer of 2007. Direct parallels were drawn between this operation and the experience of being in the area when a Soviet operation moved through.[81] The aim was to clear the ground between Gereshk and Sangin and to 'push the Taliban north',[82] which demonstrated a lack of understanding about the nature of the 'Taliban'.[83] Crucially, however, by imposing an abstract sense of cohesion on an enemy force that was anything but, the British were hardly in a position to understand the effects that their operations would have. By now, the fighting was largely fuelled by resistance to the British more than anything else.[84] For this, Helmandis use the terms 'mukowmat', which means 'resistance', but also 'be-tasleemeduna', which translates more poetically as 'without submission'.

## Calm in Central Helmand

Lashkar Gah and Gereshk were still under central government control; 2007 was the period during which US Special Forces were supporting Police Sergeant Raziq, enabling him to be the de facto chief of police (the US was supporting him with so many resources that he was able to dictate to the Nahr-e Saraj chief of police; see Chapter 4).[85] The highway police under Ezmarai were guarding the national ring road.[86] To the southwest towards Nad-e Ali, Haji Kadus (Mir Wali's old deputy) had reinvented himself as a 'police' commander of 300 men after being asked by some Barakzai elders in Malgir to defend them.[87] He established a series of checkpoints running through the centre of Malgir all the way to Loy Mandah.[88] Haji Kadus had appealed to Assadullah Wafa, the provincial governor, for funding to fight against the 'Taliban', but in reality he was protecting the Barakzai against mixed communities to the north, and fighting those elements in the Barakzai community opposed to him (see Chapter 4). The governor gave him a stipend under a (now unknown) militia programme. This funding was supplemented by the Special Forces.[89]

Nad-e Ali also remained secure. Although Abdul Rahman had been removed from the provincial chief of police position in June 2006, his cousins Tor Jan and Haji Lal Jan remained in the police in Nad-e Ali as chief and deputy, respectively. They were funded largely through drug interests and kidnapping,[90] meaning that they were able to supress whatever movements the 'Taliban' made, while at the same time sowing the seeds for future Taliban dominance. 'Police' control of the road network, through checkpoints, allowed control of drugs transportation through the area. Most people in Nad-e Ali, apart from those directly linked to him, agree that Tor Jan's tenure was marked by exceptional brutality and by a widening of the targeting of predation to everyone in the community (see Chapter 3).[91]

The practice of kidnapping individuals for ransom was of particular note. Abdul Khaleq's (Mulakhel) father, for example, was taken to a prison in the desert and later freed for 600,000 kaldars (Pakistani rupees: about $6,300). Mohammad Fahim and his father Juma Gul (Daftani) were later kidnapped. Because they resisted 'arrest' their ransom was two and a half times as much (1.5 million kaldars). After the Murtaza incidents (see Chapter 4), the Kharoti had started patrolling their village at night for protection, so the police did not target them. The kidnaps were conducted at night by 'policemen' out of uniform, and the practice reached such proportions that a shura was called by a Kharoti elder, Atta Mohammad, where he demanded that the kidnappings cease and threatened to take the complaints to the 'provincial government, to Kabul, to ISAF'.[92]

In August 2008, Tor Jan was killed by a suicide bomber sent from Pakistan, the first that Nad-e Ali had ever seen.[93] It was described by the locals as 'a gift from the Taliban'.[94] When I arrived in Nad-e Ali that December as a British army officer, we had no information about these local machinations. We operated as per the Western narrative: that the 'Taliban' had taken over the district.[95]

### British Attempts to do 'Political' Work

By December 2007, the Afghan government and the British had decided that Musa Qala had been under 'Taliban' control for too long and a joint operation was planned to retake the town. The Afghan public blamed the Angrez for its fall to the 'Taliban' in the first place.[96] For the first time some political work, similar to Khad operations, was carried out by the British. They identified a Taliban commander, called Mullah Salam, who was ready to switch sides. There was also a concerted effort to kill or capture specific 'Taliban' commanders using Special Forces raids in order to impair the coordination of the defence of Musa Qala,[97] after which Mullah Salam would be made district governor. President Karzai saw the deal as a 'grand alliance' that would unite two of the three warring sub-tribes of the Alizai in northern Helmand (the Hassanzai and the Pirzai) as well as bridge the government–Taliban divide.[98]

The operation was completed successfully with British and Afghan government forces occupying the town and installing Mullah Salam, but it then emerged that not everything was quite as it appeared. There was some confusion over which of the three Mullah Salams from northern Helmand was involved. One was a petty Alizai/Pirzai commander with thirty men, installed by the British, from Shah Karez village. Another Salam was an Alizai/Khalozai ex-Rais Baghrani commander, and the brother of Zakir, who had gone to madrassa with Sher Mohammad and was in Guantanamo. The third Salam, a Noorzai, from Tizne village in Now Zad, had been the Taliban corps commander for Herat during the Taliban government.[99]

There is strong evidence that President Karzai thought that the Mullah Salam in question was the Alizai/Khalozai commander.[100] By an astonishing coincidence that is too strong to ignore, Zakir, his brother, had just been processed for release from Guantanamo. He and Rauf Khadim had maintained their cover stories and it appears that the American interrogators had no idea how senior they were, and so they were released on the same day.[101] Their transfer date was 12 December

2007—the same day that Afghan and ISAF forces occupied Musa Qala.[102] It is not known if Karzai both knew of Zakir's imminent release and tied it up with the fact that, as far as he knew, his brother was attempting to switch sides. Reportedly, Karzai was talking to a 'Salam' before the deal went through,[103] but it is not clear whether he was talking to the petty Pirzai commander Mullah Salam, who was pretending to be Zakir's brother, or whether he spoke to Zakir's brother, who played along because he thought that it might help his brother's release. Karzai may not have linked these two events at all, or may not have known what he was doing, but the coincidence is still stark.

What of Sher Mohammad's role (as an advisor to Karzai)? When I asked him if Karzai had got the wrong Salam, he smiled, surprised, and nodded, muttering 'maybe, maybe' under his breath. From his reaction, I was under no doubt that this was what had occurred, but that Sher Mohammad's links to Zakir (a major Taliban commander at the time of interview) meant that he was not going to discuss it with me. Sher Mohammad had pushed Karzai to accept the deal; this was a perfect opportunity for him to remove the 'Taliban' administration in Musa Qala and have Commander Koka, his man, reinstated.[104] In a final twist to the tale, Zakir and Rauf were later released from Afghan detention—allegedly because Sher Mohammad and Baghrani, respectively, had paid their release 'fees'.[105] Guantanamo had a powerful influence on Zakir: 'I have strong feelings of revenge in my heart … until this fire of revenge is quenched, the jihad will continue.'[106]

Mullah Salam, the petty Pirzai commander, was appointed district governor. He quickly proved ineffective and spent much of his time feuding with the Hassanzai Koka.[107] Their militias clashed regularly, and even though it was inappropriate for Salam to have a militia as district governor, it became very difficult to remove him as he was such a high-profile reconciled 'Talib'.[108] The fact that he was actually the 'wrong' Mullah Salam was quickly forgotten among the Western community, but not among the Helmandis.[109]

Judging by Sher Mohammad's reaction to the Musa Qala accords, he lost power to the anti-Sher Mohammad Pirzai group. The retaking of Musa Qala in December 2007 led to the reinstatement of Koka (Hassanzai) and the reconciliation of Salam (Pirzai), both with their militias. Thus the Pirzai–Hassanzai dispute still reigned in Musa Qala, it was just that both clans had representatives on the 'Taliban' side and the 'government' side, with the British stuck in the middle. We know that there were clashes between Salam's militia and Koka's 'police',[110] but 'Taliban' commanders also point to clashes between groups controlled by different mahazes in Musa Qala[111]—this may be due to Hassanzai and Pirzai groups joining different mahaz commanders due to their own feuding. These government–government clashes, combined with the Taliban–Taliban clashes, paint a different story to the normal government–Taliban dichotomy that is used to describe the conflict.

To complicate matters further, Sher Mohammad is also considered a mahaz commander by many Taliban commanders, at the same time as being a senator in the Kabul government.[112] One Alizai elder told me very seriously that, 'he was not scared of [Mullah] Omar's Taliban, but he was very scared of Sher Mohammad's Taliban'.[113] There are strong echoes here of the situation during the jihad with the Noorzai and Kharoti leaders in Nad-e Ali, who held senior positions in the 'government' at the same time as waging war on the 'government' through their family networks. In this case, Sher Mohammad affiliated with both the Taliban and the government in order to protect his business interests—his drug network.[114]

The dealings over Musa Qala had shown to many perceptive Helmandis that the British, the Americans and the Afghan government were not acting in concert, and there were divisions that could be exploited.[115] The British, as the historical enemy, lost out to this dynamic and ended up becoming the 'whipping boy' for wider dynamics that were not their fault. This was to become patently obvious with the impending declaration by Karzai that Michael Semple was persona non grata. The fact that he was Irish was irrelevant; as far as the Helmandis were concerned he was British. Even Jabbar Qahraman, an MP for Helmand and heavily involved with Semple in the events that led to his expulsion said, 'of course he was British'. Hafizullah Khan agrees.

Semple was the deputy to the European Union's special representative to Afghanistan. He and Jabbar Qahraman, in concert with the British in Helmand, partly understood local dynamics in Nahr-e Saraj (that is, that many of the 'Taliban' were ex-93rd Division 'Hizb' fighters and commanders). As Qahraman said, 'it was all about ex-mujahidin in Qala-e Gaz, Shurakay and Zumbelay … so I helped them out'. Starting with just two groups of fighters led by ex-93rd commanders, a scheme was designed whereby the fighters would train briefly at a desert camp. They would then begin joint patrolling with the police (who in many cases were also ex-93rd/ex-'Hizb' fighters). If these two groups were successful then others would follow. The central government in Kabul was kept fully informed though liaison meetings with the NDS.

Unfortunately, Assadullah Wafa, Daud's replacement as provincial governor, found out about the deal at the last minute and told President Karzai that the British were negotiating a deal with the Taliban—he was annoyed that he was not going to be able to take a cut from the large amounts of money involved.[116] Semple was expelled and the deal was off. Karzai raged against the British, further encouraging their position as a recipient of 'rightful' blame.[117] One of the longer-term and more depressing aspects of the deal for the British was that the understanding of the overlap between 'Hizb' and the 'Taliban' in Nahr-e Saraj was forgotten and had to be rediscovered in 2010 (see Chapter 6).[118]

## Taliban Structures

The British intervention had been a godsend for the Taliban movement.[119] The presence of foreigners, particularly the British, whose injudicious use of firepower was reminiscent of Soviet military operations, made funding and recruitment non-issues for them.[120] The British deployment helped the Taliban with their public relations. In the early days of 2006, like in 1978, the funding was local, provided for by zakat (religious donations from the population).[121] Almost all of the individual fighters came from the local villages and fought to defend their own homes.[122] The community replaced fighters if they were wounded or killed.[123] An individual's position within the 'Taliban' was dependent on his position in Helmandi society; so the best person to replace a commander or fighter would often be his brother, for example, rather than his second-in-command.

The Taliban's rootedness in Helmandi society, and its organic nature with respect to that society, is something that ISAF have consistently failed to understand, or which they have simply deceived themselves about. ISAF understood the Taliban in institutional terms without understanding the intimate links that define the organisation. Mahaz commanders operate through a series of personal relationships with local elders and a certain commander's group would only be able to operate in the area with the permission of the local community.[124] In

2006, Delgai (group/squad) commanders were also often local, although as time progressed commanders began to rotate into different areas as the Quetta Shura attempted to gain control over the unwieldy resistance organisation(s).[125] The most important position at this stage was the mahaz commander, as he was the channel through which outside funding flowed. In Nad-e Ali, for example, a joint decision was made in the early years between the district elders and the mahaz commanders not to attack the British, but this was apparently reversed when the 'bad behaviour' of the British was observed once they deployed in numbers.[126]

The individual motivations to fight the British were legion and well known: fighting foreigners,[127] defending the opium crop,[128] history,[129] cultural insensitivity,[130] righting perceived slights,[131] enjoyment and, particularly, revenge.[132] Every man had personal reasons for fighting, but in a society where the threshold to violence was low, many men were fighting. In a large number of cases people were fighting because of private feuds or inter-community violence, often generated or exacerbated by the warlords. Taliban commanders specifically mention the fact that the British were affiliated with the communities or commanders who had previously been oppressing them.[133] From the British point of view, they were not affiliated with anyone apart from the government, but it took time for them to realise just how partisan and non-cohesive the 'government' was in Helmand.

This was further complicated by the Afghan 'officials' that the British were working with. As was noted earlier, local 'officials' were manipulating the British, telling them that that village, those people, those fighters were '*all Taliban*'. British intelligence gathering was manipulated by false reporting, just as the Soviet's had been decades before; the social dynamics were simply too opaque to be understood by outsiders.[134]

The Quetta Shura and the ISI encapsulated the multiplicity of personal motivations for fighting in a strong narrative that resonated with the population.[135] Dadullah, their strongest commander, personified this narrative. When he came into an area, his presence alone would increase the attacks against the government and the British.[136] He also galvanised funding through his exploits and through links with al-Qaeda.[137] As an icon of the resistance he became a target for ISAF and was eventually killed in May 2007.[138] His killing exposed dangerous fractures within the Quetta Shura Taliban—Dadullah, who was Kakar, had been in competition for fighters, commanders and funding with Osmani, who was Ishaqzai.

Rumours soon began to circulate that the intelligence that led to Dadullah's death had been provided by an Ishaqzai tribesman. This followed on from Osmani's death, at the end of 2006, which was blamed on intelligence provided by the Kakars.[139] At the time, there was a great deal of discussion within the ISAF community about whether to kill or capture Dadullah, or whether he could be useful as a negotiating intermediary. Ultimately, however, the fact that he was so iconic and had played a unique role in the cohering of multiple different uprisings, combined with his links to al-Qaeda and to the contemporaneous Iraqi resistance (mainly for roadside bomb technology), meant that he was killed.[140] While Dadullah was effective, the fractures that he provoked were problematic for the ISI—this was exemplified in the rumours surrounding Osmani's and Dadullah's deaths. Starting at around the time of Dadullah's death, the Quetta Shura attempted to centralise their funding structure to one patronage chain, and away from the previous fractured mahaz system.[141] Although there existed a range of reasons for doing so, their primary objective was to stop destructive infighting between the mahazes; further centralisation, through the control of funding, would also allow the Quetta Shura and the ISI to be able to make a greater claim to be responsible for the resistance.[142]

As the fighting grew in scale when more British, and later American, troops were deployed to Helmand, more resources were needed—more than zakat was able to provide—and this gave the Quetta Shura a chance to dictate its terms through patronage. As part of this centralisation drive,[143] the Taliban reissued its code of conduct, or Layeha, in 2009 (the original was released in 2006, and consisted mainly of behavioural rules rather than structural ones).[144] The 2009 Layeha set out the existence of a central treasury and banned the creation of new mahazes or groups, instead placing the emphasis on a series of provincial and district-level nezami (military) commissions (discussed in detail in Chapter 6). Other non-military councils (religious, financial, political, cultural, educational and so on) were also outlined.[145] The Quetta Shura was trying to adopt a more institutional form of organisation as opposed to a patronage form,[146] similar to that which the international community were trying to institute in the Afghan 'government'. The Taliban were actually trying to remould the 'Taliban' into what the Western narratives described them as: a centralised, directed insurgency.

## The British Reassessment: A Focus on Central Helmand

At the end of 2007 and the beginning of 2008, it became clear to the British that their tactics would have to change. They began attempting to operate in a different way, with less violence and with a greater focus on the reconstruction that was one of the stated reasons for their campaign.[147] But the British realised that they could not generate enough troops to operate in this way—less reliance on force (particularly airpower), meant that greater numbers of troops were required (there were around 8,500 British troops in Helmand in mid-2008).[148] In order to help facilitate the change in tactics, the United States deployed over 2,000 marines to Helmand. Many went to Garmsir to secure the district centre. They also started mentoring the police in five districts across the province and patrolling the border with Pakistan.[149] Previously, in 2007, the Danish had also taken over responsibility for Gereshk and Nahr-e Saraj with a further 750 soldiers.[150] Increases were eventually to see ISAF troop numbers rise tenfold from the original deployment of 3,000.

In March 2008, Governor Wafa was removed and replaced with Gulabuddin Mangal. An ex-communist technocrat, Mangal was considered a great improvement over Wafa by ISAF,[151] yet many Helmandis focused negatively on his communist past.[152] In one of his last acts as governor, Assadullah Wafa appointed Habibullah district governor of Nad-e Ali, recalling him from retirement in Garmsir. The last time a former communist had held any kind of government post in Nad-e Ali was, in fact, when Habibullah had been evicted by the mujahidin in the early 1990s, when he was district chief of police.[153] The situation in Nad-e Ali in early 2008 was fractious, but it was nowhere near as bad as Habibullah's previous posting there (see Chapter 3).

In the spring of 2008, central Helmand was still stable, leading ISAF to concentrate on other areas of Helmand. Garmsir was flooded with 'Punjabis' and 'ISI', probably as the result of US operations there.[154] One interviewee even recounts meeting an ISI colonel in Quetta, whom he knew from the jihad days: the colonel was ebullient as he had 'just been across the border … doing a little jihad'.[155] British journalists in Garmsir also commented on the high proportion of foreigners fighting that summer.[156] The British, however, were focused on Kajaki, where they were trying to transport a third turbine to the dam in order to increase its output. This was considered important for the reconstruction of southern Afghanistan by ISAF. The Alizai of northern Helmand, however, wanted an irrigation canal (see Chapter 6).

Back in central Helmand, poppy eradication was still continuing, as it had done almost every year since 2002. During the 2008 eradication season, Abdul Rahman's poppy was targeted because he was no longer in the 'government'. It was estimated that he lost 20 per cent of his 'extensive' crop.[157] As his poppy was eradicated Abdul Rahman contacted Rahim Ishaqzai, the Taliban governor for Helmand and a fellow Now Zadi, and negotiated a deal whereby the 'policemen' guarding the checkpoints in Marjeh would become 'Taliban' and other Taliban would be allowed into Marjeh.[158] His relatives still controlled the 'police' because he had skilfully shaped the organisation to be supportive of his interests during his tenure.

It was a similar side-switching manoeuvre to those by Mir Wali and Sher Mohammad before him (see Chapter 4). However, the British understood it in terms of the 'insurgency narrative': the police had abandoned their checkpoints to the Taliban.[159] Abdul Rahman supported this narrative vociferously when I spoke to him later, and stated, 'there was no deal; we were so few; they surrounded us ... they were not local Taliban ... they were ... Punjabi, Arab, Chechen ... they were not Helmandis'. Abdul Rahman consistently refutes the idea that most 'Taliban' are local and instead maintains that they are 'all foreigners and Al-Qaeda'. This adherence is partly because he was used to dealing with Westerners before 2006, when Westerners only understood very simplistically what was going on in Helmand. Helmandis who currently deal with Westerners have dropped these simplistic explanations and now sometimes talk of local 'Taliban'. Thus, as the Westerners have improved their understanding of local Helmandi politics, the Helmandis have mirrored them, matching their understanding.

Over the summer of 2008, Marjeh gradually became a no-go area for the government and for ISAF. By August, it was fully in the hands of the 'Taliban'.[160] Abdul Rahman maintained a dialogue with Mangal, the new governor, throughout the events. He told him that he was worried because the 'Taliban' were growing in influence in Marjeh and there was nothing that he could do: Mangal should deploy more troops.[161] The ANA were eventually sent to Nad-e Ali in mid-August to shore up its defences, as Marjeh had 'fallen' on the seventh of the month. This was based on a poor understanding of who the 'Taliban' were. Tor Jan, however, who was the chief of police in Nad-e Ali, was a relative-by-marriage of Abdul Rahman—if they had wanted Nad-e Ali to 'fall' then it would have done so.

The ANA, supported by British mentoring teams, deployed to the district school building that was to become their base for the next year. They were able to move up to 7 kilometres from the district centre. The ANA soon suspected that the local police were 'Taliban' supporters; in a sense, those that were closely linked to Abdul Rahman were. Shortly after, the hukomat was then attacked from the west, from Shin Kalay, by 'Taliban', although this was probably the Kharoti militia that had been established to protect the village from the predations of the police.[162] Dr Jailani, the old Hizb commander, gave up his clinic between the hukomat and Shin Kalay for the 'Taliban' to use as a meeting room and checkpoint.[163]

The local situation was hyper-complex, involving several factions within the 'police', and multiple feuds and alliances.[164] The first faction was that linked to Tor Jan, the chief, and Abdul Rahman; they were linked to the 'police'-cum-'Taliban' in Marjeh. Another faction, linked to Haji Lal Jan, the deputy chief, were virulently anti-'Taliban' as they had been forced out of their village by Arab, a nephew of Lal Jan, who had joined the 'Taliban' to gain ascendency in a sub-village dispute.[165] This second faction had partly been the cause of the Kharoti tribal militia's founding, which was affiliated with the 'Taliban'.[166] Presumably, the 'Taliban' attacked the district centre due to the presence of the ANA and the British—Murtaza, the Kharoti commander, was quoted by Abdul Rahman as using the Taliban's narrative and saying, 'you have brought foreigners, kaffirs; we are obliged to do jihad', although it could have been because of the Manan–Murtaza feud (Chapter 4). To complete the circle, Abdul Rahman Jan and Haji Lal Jan were cousins-by-marriage.[167]

The normal description of a government–Taliban dichotomy did not match this extraordinary milieu. Once the British had deployed, the situation was soon dominated by the fighting between the mainly Kharoti 'Taliban', based in Shin Kalay, and the mainly Noorzai 'police', based in the district centre. This continued until December, by which time the British had reinforced their troops in Nad-e Ali, but were unable to leave the hukomat due to the resistance that their presence generated. The British were like a magnet to those locals who were linked to the Taliban, causing a similar reaction to that which had occurred in 1980 with the Soviets and in 2006 with the British in northern Helmand.

For Habibullah, being trapped in the district centre and surrounded on all sides by Taliban (or mujahidin, as they still called themselves) was nothing new.[168] However, it was not the deteriorating situation that acted as the principal motivator for the British moving into Nad Ali, but an audacious attack on Lashkar Gah occurring on 11 October 2008. The attack, which targeted the provincial governor's compound, began when the British received intelligence that 1,000 'Taliban' were planning to attack Lashkar Gah. This translated to 300 'Taliban' seen moving north through Nawa, along the right bank of the Helmand towards Bolan, opposite Lashkar Gah. They were intercepted with helicopters and around 150 were killed. The 'Taliban' escaped back to Nad-e Ali. Having been repulsed, Lashkar Gah came under rocket attack four days later, but from a police checkpoint in Bolan that was then destroyed with a British airstrike. The 'Taliban' activity stopped.[169]

The Western narrative of a 'Taliban' attack on Lashkar Gah[170] and the tracing of the militants back to Nad-e Ali were the casus belli for an expansion of the British intervention in the district. The British press were clear: this was a Taliban attack on Lashkar Gah.[171] However, things were not as they appeared. The attacks had been organised and financed by Sher Mohammad and Abdul Rahman.[172] Even Habibullah, a long-time Abdul Rahman ally, admitted to me, 'that attack … was [Sher Mohammad] and [Abdul Rahman] … the aim was to create chaos and prove they were the only people who could lead the province'. It is also worth pointing out that Habibullah knew all of this when we, the British, arrived in Nad-e Ali in 2008, yet neglected to tell us.

I later asked Abdul Rahman about who had organised the attack on Lashkar Gah and he began to guffaw, before becoming serious. 'I was in Kabul', he said 'I don't know anything about it.' This is an interesting admission from someone who claims to be among the only people who can solve the security issues in Helmand as 'only we know who the Taliban are'. I asked if it could possibly be something to do with Sher Mohammad. 'Sher Mohammad has no links with the Taliban', he said, despite having earlier pointed out that he had numerous links with the Taliban. 'It is Mangal propaganda', he added.

When I challenged Sher Mohammad he immediately said that 'it wasn't me … it was the Taliban … my police helped defeat it'. Yet the British, and Mangal, the provincial governor, did not understand that Abdul Rahman Jan and Sher Mohammad were manipulating events for their own gain. These two events caused the British deployment to

Nad-e Ali in December 2008, which hugely affected the shape of the conflict as it led the British to focus on central Helmand at the expense of northern Helmand.

In an unrelated but concurrent incident, the school in Shin Kalay was razed to the ground with a mechanical digger. Unlike the other schools in Nad-e Ali, the school had been built privately by a Western charity run by a former villager who now lives in the United States.[173] When I arrived in Nad-e Ali shortly after, the official story was that the Taliban were responsible. We were even shown around the ruined school by the elders who were lamenting Taliban cruelty. Habibullah said, '[the residents of Shin Kalay] are not up for education ... they are all Talibs', implying that they had pulled their own school down. In many respects he was right.

Other schools in the district had also been pulled down or heavily damaged by the Taliban in the preceding twelve months. There were two exceptions to this. First, the school in Saidabad which served the Shia Hazara community, because Iran's support for insurgent groups in Helmand was predicated on the protection of Shia communities, and those Taliban groups that were involved in burning schools were more likely to be those which received foreign sponsorship (see below for a discussion of types of Taliban).[174] Secondly, Loy Bagh's school escaped destruction due to the fact that Mullah Karim, a prominent Noorzai in Loy Bagh, was a key Taliban interlocutor in the district.[175] However, the school in Shin Kalay represented a special case, and while probably not a metaphor for school burning, this story demonstrates the difficulties with development in Helmand.

The school was built in 2004 by Green Village Schools (Shin Kalay means Green Village), a US charity run by Dr Mohammad Khan Kharoti.[176] It had 1,200 pupils, one-third of whom were girls. The school had been built on the land of Habib, Dr Kharoti's brother, in the northern half of Shin Kalay. The plot of land next door was owned by Daria Khan, a distant relative of Dr Kharoti, from another clan. Daria was jealous of the prestige that the school brought to Dr Kharoti and Habib in the village and sought to have it destroyed, framing his actions within Islamist ideology. He was eventually killed in a battle with British forces near Khwashal Kalay, in the spring of 2009.

When another person from the village was in Quetta in 2007, he heard that Daria had been there and had reported to the ISI that 'girls with big breasts are going to school in Shin Kalay and this is shameful'. Daria was using Islamist narratives to manipulate the ISI. He had previously threatened the teachers with death if they continued teaching at the school, but this was brushed off—Daria's nieces and nephews went to the school and his mother tried to restrain him. According to an interviewee, Daria publicly stated that the school brought Western influence and that this was something that should be stopped.

Later, in the summer of 2008, strangers came to the school and filmed it. The villagers said that they had been sent by the ISI. By this point the 'Taliban' were in control of the village, but it was self-defence, anti-police, village 'Talibs' who were working against the government in a franchise relationship.[177] Two days before the school was destroyed, two Punjabi-speaking men came and toured the school. They returned the next day with a much larger group of men, condemned the school as a 'Bush nest' (referring to the US president) and began to destroy what they could with their hands. The teachers fled for their own safety.

The group of 'Punjabis' returned on the following day with a bulldozer and began to destroy the school, before looting what they could over the course of the next two days. Unfortunately, at the time, and probably due to the on-going events in Lashkar Gah, ISAF helicopters were overhead while this was taking place but failed to intervene, creating the impression that ISAF did not care. That evening, once the Punjabis had gone, the villagers themselves further looted the school.

After these events, an elder from the village who was amenable to the school rang a contact in the Taliban's Quetta leadership and asked why the Taliban had committed this crime. They denied knowing anything about it and pointed to their policy forbidding the destruction of schools.[178] The leadership rang Malem, the Taliban governor for Nad-e Ali. He confirmed that it had happened, but claimed not to know who had done it. Thus even the local representative of the Taliban was ignorant of the events—this is what allowed the internal feud to drive the school destruction by the ISI. Malem was sacked by the leadership for allowing the school to be destroyed.

No one knows definitively who the Punjabis were, or even whether Daria was involved. These are the suspicions and rumours that the villagers express when they are not too scared to talk about it due to the factions and trust-deficit extant in the village. People did not fight back because they were scared of being publicly labelled pro-government: 'no-one is united in the village at all; everyone has connections going in every direction'. However, all interviewees confirmed that this was an act that was driven by jealousy and feuds within the village, rather than an external, 'Taliban'-sponsored operation. As one interviewee said, '[Dr Kharoti] is a good man, but the [Kharoti of Shin Kalay] are such sons of bitches … he got no support from the community.' (See Figure 5.)

The conclusion that many villagers have come to is that there is a faction within the village that went directly to the hardliners in the ISI. The ISI then sent a team over and commandeered Afghan government equipment in Marjeh to pull it down, even while the village was in the hands of the Kharoti 'Taliban'—in other words, the ISI was manipulated by an internal village feud due to a lack of on-the-ground knowledge. Even the tribal leadership was not particularly concerned by the events: they were able to access education elsewhere for their children and, as is fairly common in Helmand, they 'were not interested in the poor people's children learning to read as that would undermine [the tribal leaders'] position'. In a final twist, twenty or

Figure 5: Shin Kalay school in December 2008

thirty village teenagers began to work with the 'Taliban' groups in the village because they had nothing to do during the day with no school to go to. Some of these were killed when British and Afghan government forces took the village in December.

The British-led operation in Nad-e Ali in December 2008 marked the end of the British focus on northern Helmand and the start of a focus on central Helmand. According to the British, Nad-e Ali had fallen into the hands of the Taliban and the government, supported by ISAF, was going to get it back.[179] The force was made up of 1,500 soldiers, and led to the establishment of three British bases surrounding the district: in Trekh Nawar, to the west of Khwashal Kalay and in Maat-e Que. During the operation the British attempted to attack and defeat the 'Taliban' sequentially in the villages of the district. Initially focusing on Shin Kalay, and encouraged by Habibullah, the district governor (see Introduction), the British troops faced stiff resistance from the mainly Kharoti defenders under commanders like Ibrahim and Murtaza.[180]

It quickly became clear to the defenders that the British intended to assault the village rather than engaging in the kind of probing operations that had been pursued previously. The tribal elders told their men to stand down to avoid further destruction, but not before they had suffered seventeen dead.[181] Recruitment for the defence of the village was spread across the different clans (see Appendix 4), as were the casualties: one from the Saleekhel, five from Shabakhel (Murtaza's clan) and one from the Toreekhel (Wakil Safar's clan), for example. These casualties caused many of the clan heads to send sons to the 'Taliban' because of the nature of how fighting men are replaced by Helmandis (that is, families replace their own dead with relatives). One elder who was closely involved with the resistance used a Pushtun proverb to describe the recruitment: 'from drops of rain comes a flood', that is, everyone contributed what they could and the resistance was strong.[182] Interestingly, the casualties from the 'Taliban' were largely members of the poorer and less influential clans in Shin Kalay and it is therefore possible that it was these clans that provided one of the main sources of 'Taliban' recruitment in the village.[183]

When the British troops entered Shin Kalay they spoke with the villagers. The British adhered to their understanding of the conflict and looked to see where they could help; after all, they were there to support the Afghan government. This meant that they had entered the village with Noorzai police in tow. The residents of Shin Kalay were disgusted; they had been fighting to keep the police out. The British narrative—that they stood for good governance, fairness and reconstruction—did not sit well with the Kharoti view of the police who had just arrived with the British. Yet despite this, and in a typical display of Pushtun hospitality, the villagers thanked the British for 'liberating' them from Taliban dominion, which had destroyed their school, even taking them to the site and giving them a tour (see Figure 5). The British were later to find out, from Habibullah, that their colonel had been poured tea throughout the meeting by one of the Kharoti 'Taliban' commanders.[184]

Several days later, the British assaulted Zhargoun Kalay. The intervening period allowed the 'mujahidin-Taliban' (an interviewee Freudianly said 'mujahidin' instead of 'Taliban', when discussing these events) to prepare the defences of the town along the same lines as during the Soviet era. A shout went out to other communities across central Helmand that the Angrez were coming and the village needed help defending itself.[185] Groups came from as far afield as Nawa and the fighting was chaotic with many commanders operating against the British. These included Mullah Haji Ibrahim Akhund, Malem, Mullah Abdullah Akhund, Haji Lala, Mullah Mohammad Khan, Mullah Ghulam Mohammad Akhund, Mullah Mohammad Haq Akhund, Qari Awal Khan, Mullah Toofan Akhund, Mullah Abdullah Akhund and Malawi Farouq.[186] The 'Taliban' suffered heavy casualties. Four fighters were killed and another two wounded from one group alone. The British used artillery and dropped a bomb on the village during the course of the battle, which resulted in civilian casualties including the death of several members of the same family.[187] The British also took casualties that day.[188]

After two days of fighting, the British entered the village with the Afghan police. The police quickly demonstrated why the population hated them. I personally witnessed the district chief of police Abdul Sattar and his 'chaiboy' loading a fine-looking dog onto the back of his truck with a group of sullen villagers looking on. Walking over, we gently asked the chief about the dog and he answered that he had just found it and was going to keep it and take it back to his headquarters. We nodded towards the villagers and suggested that perhaps this would not be appropriate. His response suggested that he simply could not understand what we were trying to explain to him—as far as he was concerned, he had just taken this village and he was entitled to whatever he wanted. The dog was given back to the villagers.

At the same time as the battle for Zhargoun Kalay, the British moved an Estonian company up to Chah-e Anjir. To NATO, the Estonians were a valuable part of the coalition in Afghanistan.[189] To the Helmandis, the Estonians were Soviets (see Figure 6). In fact, some of the Estonian soldiers had actually served in Helmand during the 1980s with the limited contingent.[190] When the Estonians arrived in Chah-e Anjir they found a small band of policemen under Rahmatullah, keeping the 'Taliban' (mainly Kharoti from Naqilabad) out of the town. ISAF was puzzled as to how the town could be kept in government hands with such a small group of policemen.

They were not aware, however, of the familial links that cut across the 'government'–'Taliban' divide. Rahmatullah was from the Noorzai/Aghezai clan from Loy Bagh—Khano's clan. His paternal uncle was Abdul Sattar, the district chief of police, and Assadullah Sherzad, the new provincial chief of police, was his cousin: a solidly 'government'

Figure 6: Soviet and Estonian Vehicles side-by-side in Chah-e Anjir

family. However, Abdul Karim, the Aghezai 'member' of Hizb during the 1980s, was now on the Taliban shura for the district. This meant that he was able to manipulate the patterns of conflict in the district. The family wanted to maintain control of Chah-e Anjir because of the lucrative drugs market there.[191] It was the same old game.

After Zhargoun Kalay and Chah-e Anjir, the British moved quickly to Chah-e Mirza. There was no resistance and the British set up camp in a field opposite the mosque in Zorabad. Haji Manan, Haji Lal Jan's nephew, soon presented himself to the British as the police commander for the area (the British had not shared the operational details with the police beforehand as they did not trust them). Manan had not been back to the area since the 'Taliban', led by Arab, his relative, had evicted him and Haji Lal Jan (see Chapter 4). The British had absolutely no idea who he was nor any knowledge of the stories surrounding Manan and the persecution of the population in Nad-e Ali. Prima facie, however, he was dressed smartly in his uniform—something of a rarity within the police.[192]

The British held a shura in the village. The villagers were openly and vociferously disgusted with Manan, something that is unusual in a society which places a high emphasis on not insulting people in public, and particularly people who are known to be cruel and vindictive. The elders stated that they were keen to have ISAF ensuring security together with the ANA, but not the police. By now the British were beginning to understand how the local population felt about the 'police', but they were trapped between their understanding and the official narratives of the conflict. Officially, they had to work with the police in order to improve them, yet this provoked massive resistance from the locals, whose lives they were also there to improve. It was not just that there were some problems with the 'police' that were causing frictions with the local population; the 'police', or rather the individuals that comprised the 'police', were the raison d'être for the population's resistance. It was proving very hard for the British to balance these aspects of their mission; the population was largely incredulous when the 'police' turned up on the heels of the British assaults and enjoyed their support. It confirmed their worst fears, and confirmed what they knew from history about the Angrez. The population, in many cases, was affiliated with the Taliban in order to protect themselves from the 'government'.

The British were further confused the next day, when the elders reversed position and retracted their comments on Manan. They added that 'for cultural reasons' they would not be able to accept the British in the area, but they would be happy to have Manan ensuring the security of the village. They were attempting to manipulate the British by using the media narrative, that was emerging at the time, that ISAF troops were 'culturally insensitive' (many Helmandis listen to the BBC).[193] The British ignored them and later found out that Haji Manan had privately spoken to the elders and told them that the British had arrived to eradicate next year's poppy crop, but that he could protect them.[194] Finally, the elders approached the British discretely and tried to bribe them to leave. They ignored the elders again and continued with their original plan of establishing a base on the canal crossing point at Maat-e Que.[195]

For many in the population, the 'Taliban' were resisting British aggression. Many of my interviewees estimate that around 95 per cent of the fighters in the 'Taliban' in Nad-e Ali were local fighters,[196] and one man, well acquainted with the fighting in Nad-e Ali, listed a 'hatred of outsiders interfering' coupled with 'boredom ... through unemployment' as the primary motivation for joining.[197] The paradoxes were the same as that in Musa Qala in 2006: the 'police' are linked to the 'Taliban', but the population are also working with the 'Taliban' to keep the 'police' out. 'Taliban' and 'police' are just labels for local factions and do not adequately describe the conflict. Outsiders do not generally have a detailed level of knowledge of local dynamics, and the British certainly did not in Nad-e Ali in 2008, resulting in their continued manipulation.

The beginning of 2009 ushered in a new approach from the British, pioneered in Nad-e Ali. A community council was formed that was comprised of notables from the district that would carry out some government functions such as basic justice, allocation of development money, and security advice for the district governor. The council was to be elected from a shortlist vetted by the NDS. The NDS, in consort with Habibullah, wanted to strike people off the list due to their affiliation with the 'Taliban', including Pir Mohammad Sadat (Kharoti, ex-Hizb, from Naqilabad). The British insisted that he should be included for exactly that reason: they wanted both the 'government' and the 'Taliban' to be represented. In the final deliberation, the council was considered by the population 'a commanders' council', comprised of the mujahidin commanders who had survived the jihad and leveraged their position to become community leaders.[198] It broadly reflected the society in Nad-e Ali, even though Abdul Ahad from Loy Bagh engaged in extensive manipulation in order to install more of his supporters on the council.

Almost all of the commanders had been involved in ejecting Habibullah from Nad-e Ali in the early 1990s. These included Dr Jailani, who was appointed to the security sub-committee despite having a son fighting with the Taliban against the British.[199] Others, such as Abdul Malik (Popalzai), were sent to the council as representation for powerful ex-Taliban figures, in this case, Haji Mullah Paslow, his uncle.[200] There was, however, some representation from the old tribal leadership: Mirwais Khan (Kharoti) was Wakil Safar's son and Abdul Ahad was the nephew of Shah Nazar Khan, the murdered Najibullah-era provincial governor. Habibullah was allowed to nominate someone from the community as the twenty-fifth member and, in an unexplained move, appointed Abdul Karim from Loy Bagh, despite knowing that he was a local representative of the Taliban movement.[201]

The British gradually arrived at a better understanding of Nad-e Ali's micro politics. They persevered in the expectation that the situation would improve if community representatives and the 'Taliban' engaged in dialogue with the government. The British very strongly believed that there would have to be a political outcome to the conflict.[202] The council also managed the interface between institutional and patronage government: the district administration would be organised along institutional lines and the shura would be a patronage mechanism, distributing development funding through the elders. Overall, many of the community leaders were confused about the purpose of the shura—the leaders would meet anyway, if they needed to. Yet they went along with it because it enabled them to ensure that they received their cut of development funding.[203]

The Nad-e Ali district shura represents an interesting turning point in the British approach to Helmand. They were extolling a more inclusive counterinsurgency-style approach, where political work would provide the framework within which development and military force would be used. This was what their stated narrative had been since 2006, but it was really only during 2009 that the British began to match their actions to their words. Thus, once an area had been cleared of insurgents, development work would begin and attempts would be made to improve the Afghan government, to make it more responsive to the needs of the population.[204]

Conceptually, the new British approach was based on the ISAF counterinsurgency strategy. In this, the population was a mass that was stuck between the two competing 'offers' of the Afghan government and the Taliban. ISAF defined the 'government' and the 'Taliban' as separate, albeit factionalised, organisations. This was implicit in ISAF's role: their mandate was to support the Afghan government, leading them to define the situation through the prism of their own existence, much like the Soviets had before them. This is why the 'insurgency narrative' exists and is so resilient: it is linked intimately to ISAF's self-image and role in Afghanistan. In this narrative, ISAF hoped to win the population over by improving the Afghan government and building infrastructure, such as schools and clinics.[205] This was a significant improvement on previous British understanding and behaviour, but it failed to recognise the pshe-pshe (group-on-group) nature of the conflict.

Once the operation was over, most of the British troops who had promised that they would not leave Nad-e Ali, left Nad-e Ali. A very small number of troops remained in the district. (Even though the Americans had started to increase their troop numbers in Helmand, the British were still stretched.) Within weeks, the British were hemmed in their bases. Shin Kalay became a no-go zone for the government and the British. With fighting around the village once again, some of the tribal leadership negotiated with, or told, Ibrahim, the main Kharoti 'Taliban' commander at the time, to position his group to the south of the Kharoti tribal lands and fire on the British when they went south from the village towards the 'tribal boundary'. This meant that when the British used artillery or other heavy weapons it would not affect the Kharoti. The demarcation was marked by a canal lined by a road.[206]

While the leadership was dealing with Ibrahim, they were also negotiating secretly with the British, who were trying to secure Kharoti tribal guarantees of security for a potential rebuilding of the destroyed school. The elders negotiated in good faith, asserting that they would not be able to protect the school as they were scared of the 'Taliban'. What they did not tell the British was the hidden reason: that due to jealousy between families in the village, there was no way that they could guarantee the school's safety. At the same time, the same elders were also negotiating with the NDS, passing information on booby traps set by other non-Kharoti Taliban groupings.[207] It was extraordinarily complex.

Ibrahim's activities convinced the British that they needed to expand to the south of Shin Kalay and retake Khwashal Kalay. It had previously been 'taken' in the operation in December. By now the British were beginning to understand that the population and the 'Taliban' were not as far apart as they had previously believed; the politics were not as opaque. Not wishing to fight the population, British officers deliberately leaked the plan to select elders, safe in the knowledge that the 'Taliban', many of whom came from the communities that the elders represented, would hear about it. In the event, there was barely a shot fired, and the fighters withdrew to the south and set up another defensive line.

Meeting with the villagers afterwards, it was clear that there were two issues. The villagers were terrified that their poppy was about to be eradicated and they were also incensed that a US Special Forces raid had killed several members of a family the night before—an operation that the British troops had only been informed about minutes before it was due to occur and could not control.[208] To reassure the villagers that they were not interested in their poppy, after the shura, some British officers partook in an informal lesson in how to harvest the crop. As far as they were concerned, this was an important force protection measure: they were likely to get attacked less if the villagers believed that they did not want to eradicate their livelihoods. Later, when the story was recounted informally to the counternarcotics team at the Foreign Office in London, they were appalled. How could British troops, representing the lead on counter-narcotics in the international coalition, do such a thing? It was gently explained to them how conflicted the twin policies of counterinsurgency (aim: win the population) and counternarcotics (result: drive the population away) were.

The British were also told at the shura that Assadullah Karimi, the Hazara leader from Saidabad, had been kidnapped by the 'Taliban'. This looked like another government–Taliban fight, but it was later discovered to have been facilitated by Ishaqzai tribesmen from Jangal—they had manipulated the Taliban to settle some scores.[209] The Hazara and the Ishaqzai/Popalzai had been in a long-running feud in the south of Nad-e Ali over land and water rights. Since the arrival of the Ishaqzai community and more Popalzai families during the jihad, the Hazara had been forced to live in their 'dirty' (that is, saltier) water, affecting their yields. This was because they were downstream on the canal network (water runs north to south in Nad-e Ali). Although the issue had been solved by a shura during the Rabbani government, it continued to be a constant source of tension and would occasionally flare up, with raids and kidnapping. The Popalzai and the Ishaqzai in the south were closer to the Taliban than the Shia Hazara (Paslow, the Popalzai leader, was an official during the Taliban government). Assadullah Karimi was eventually released two months later on payment of a ransom to Abdul Bari, the Taliban district governor, mediated by Qasim, an Alizai elder from Zhargoun Kalay.[210]

Meanwhile elsewhere, in Spin Masjid, Malgir and Babaji, the Haji Kadus militia had collapsed in mid-2008 because the provincial government had stopped paying their stipend. Kadus claimed that he had supported it himself for as long as possible until running out of money.[211] The militia then splintered, and some of the groups continued defending their own villages in Babaji. The 'Taliban' in this case came from the north of the tribal divide between Babaji and eastern Nad-e Ali district (see Map 10). Previously, however, the Barakzai militia had over-taxed the (non-Barakzai) locals north of the divide. But they were less able to defend themselves without the governor's stipend, and so the Barakzai villages collected money to keep them supplied with ammunition. The line eventually collapsed when two of the militia commanders, Malem Anwar and Hamid Gul, fell victim to a blood feud. Some of Anwar's men accidentally shot and wounded Hamid Gul's son. They were not able to maintain unity even in the face of the 'Taliban' threat and had to flee to Lashkar Gah.[212]

Once it became clear that the militia was beginning to crumble, Qari Hazrat, the Ishaqzai Taliban commander and originally in the 93rd Division, contacted Haji Kadus and they discussed how to divide up Malgir between them, with Qari Hazrat protecting the 'Hizb' communities. Officially, however, Haji Kadus, was still working with the Special Forces who were actively trying to kill or capture Qari Hazrat. Mir Wali was stuck in the middle. He wanted the control, and negotiating potential, that Qari Hazrat could give him in the area, yet did not want Haji Kadus to gain anything.[213] When I asked Mir Wali about this, he denied everything, including ever having met Qari Hazrat, which is almost certainly untrue. To the British, the events in Spin Masjid, Malgir and Babaji looked like a Taliban takeover, similar to that which had occurred in Nad-e Ali.

This understanding necessitated action from the British. Also, privately, they were worried that the influx of US troops to Helmand was diminishing their 'influence' in the province, 'particularly with the Governor'.[214] They were also worried about the reputation of the

British military in light of the public perception that the United States had to help them out again, as was perceived to have been the case recently in Basra, Iraq.[215] Thus they planned an operation to retake Malgir and publicly linked it to the forthcoming Afghan presidential elections. If they could secure more territory for the Afghan government, then more people would be able to vote, thus legitimising the election. In the event, just 150 people voted from Spin Masjid, Malgir and Babaji.[216]

Before the operation commenced, the British concluded a private deal with Haji Kadus, exploiting their greater understanding of the conflict. However, they were unaware of his links to Qari Hazrat and arranged for Kadus to join the police, taking the rank of major. Once the operation was completed Kadus would also be responsible for the Parchow area close to Gereshk. He would, once again, be mentored by US Special Forces.[217] During the operation, for an unknown reason but potentially linked to the British deal, the 'Taliban' groups controlled by the Sattar and Naim Barich mahazes did not fight. To some Taliban commanders this looked like a deal had been struck between the British and the Taliban: their mahaz commanders had ordered them not to fight. Yet Sher Mohammad's mahaz—whether through ignorance of the deal or hatred of the British—continued to fight, which in turn caused a rift between Sher Mohammad and the other mahaz commanders, that had to be mediated by Zakir.[218]

During the operation, the furthest the British got west from Gereshk was Haji Gul Ehktiar Kalay. They established their base in Gul Ehktiar's house because it was the most defensible building around, not aware that his nephew, Sur Gul, was a senior 'Taliban' commander.[219] Sur Gul had even been arrested by the British in 2006, but as he had pretended that his name was Asir he was released to the NDS. Mir Wali then paid a bribe to secure his freedom. The British wished to be seen as fair and so began to pay Gul Ehktiar rent. The rent money had two consequences. First, it inflated Gul Ehktiar's importance in the area. Secondly, some of the money soon found its way, through Sur Gul, back to the bombs that were blowing up British soldiers.[220] This issue was never resolved, despite British suspicions, and the British pulled out three years later. This dynamic confused the locals, to whom it was obvious, and they assumed that the British must have been working with the 'Taliban'.[221]

While the Malgir operation continued, the Americans moved into Nawa in massive force. By the autumn of 2009, both the British and the Americans had 10,000 soldiers each in the province, with the British holding the centre and the north, with the exception of Now Zad, and the Americans in control of Garmsir, Nawa, Marjeh and Now Zad.[222] This increase in US troops created friction between the Americans and the British over their respective modus operandi, and particularly over the geographical areas in which development money was spent.[223] This tension was picked up much earlier by the Helmandis over issues such as the Musa Qala accords, but now that there were more US troops in the province the divisions became very easy to read.

The Helmandis did not believe the ISAF narrative of coalition unity and they tried to take advantage of the divisions (in a similar way to how the Khalqis and the Parchamis used to manipulate their Soviet mentors; see Chapter 2). Helmandi leaders would often insult the British to the Americans while emphasising how grateful they were that the Americans had taken their place, yet the same leaders would then tell the British that it was terrible that the Americans had come and that they would much prefer to carry on working with the British.[224] Unfortunately, many British and American officers fell for these ploys.

*Conclusions*

This chapter has traced the early British involvement in Helmand from 2006 to 2009. Despite increasing knowledge of the highly local dynamics, the British still continued to be exploited by different Helmandi factions and leaders. This allowed these local dynamics to drive the conflict, rather than the government–Taliban divide that the British (and other outsiders) understood. The stories told here, particularly those surrounding Sher Mohammad's dealings with the Taliban and the government; Abdul Rahman's side-switching and the multiple hues of 'Taliban' in Nad-e Ali; and the events surrounding the destruction of Shin Kalay's school, all provide examples of the levels of complexity involved and the difficulties that this presented for outsiders. However, it was not just the British: Abdul Rahman Jan manipulated the provincial governor, Mangal, and individuals in Shin Kalay manipulated the ISI and the Taliban.

However, the British understanding of these dynamics gradually grew, and they tried to better align their actions (less firepower) with their narratives (reconstruction). Moreover, British commanders tried to use their newfound knowledge of the local politics to achieve what they wanted without fighting. But this was only partly successful: more often than not, they were still duped by local 'officials' and Helmandi notables. Their continued failure can be attributed to the fact that although they had an increased understanding of the conflict, they were wedded to the 'insurgency narrative' as a framework through which to interpret the evidence they gathered (and the Helmandis understood that this was how they perceived the conflict and told them what they wanted to hear). This 'insurgency narrative' spawned ISAF's counterinsurgency strategy—a critique of which, drawing on Helmandi sources, forms the next chapter.

6

# FROM THE US RE-ENGAGEMENT

## 'COUNTERINSURGENCY', 2009–12

> Most people who think about Helmand
> develop mental problems, because the
> politics are so strange and complicated.
>
> Ex-jihadi commander, Nad-e Ali[1]

> Surely you could have solved this by now?
>
> Attributed to President Karzai[2]

*Background*

Unlike previous chapters, this one is organised thematically. Here, I discuss the 2009 ISAF counterinsurgency strategy that was premised on the 'insurgency narrative'. As previously discussed, the 'insurgency narrative' states that there is a legitimate Government of the Islamic Republic of Afghanistan (GIRoA), which is recognised and supported by the international community, but which is violently opposed by a movement of insurgents, called the Taliban, who have sanctuary in Quetta, Pakistan. From this perspective, the Taliban are religiously inspired insurgents who are opposed to the democratic and women's rights that the GIRoA embodies and promotes. For example, Tony Blair's memoir paints a binary view of Afghanistan, pitting 'fanaticism' against 'modernisation'.[3] This can be dismissed as rhetoric or conscious simplification, but it appears that Western militaries, above all the US military, believe(d) in a simplistic good-versus-evil narrative.[4] General Jones, President Obama's national security advisor, described the conflict as, 'a clash of civilisations ... a clash of religions ... a clash of concepts of how to live'.[5] Even Major-General Flynn, the erstwhile commander of NATO intelligence in Afghanistan, while lamenting the US intelligence focus on the Taliban at the expense of the wider country, still wrote of 'distinctions between the Taliban and the rest of the Afghan population'.[6]

To implement their new approach, ISAF troop numbers in Helmand rose to around 30,000 in mid-2010. In this chapter I will analyse the three themes along which this counterinsurgency strategy was prosecuted—security, development and politics[7]—through the eyes of the Helmandis. Broadly speaking, in counterinsurgency one is meant to provide security to the population while providing them with improved governance and development, thus drawing them away from the insurgent. My argument is that although the Americans and the British understood Helmand better than ever before, because they were wedded to their counterinsurgency strategy they failed to correctly interpret the conflict once again. To them it was still an insurgency. Helmandis, the greatest natural politicians that I have ever met, understood how ISAF conceptualised the conflict and presented information to them within an insurgency/counterinsurgency conceptual framework. This enabled them to continue manipulating the outsiders, as before.

First, I discuss security, looking at operations by ISAF (including the controversial 'capture or kill' raids) as well as operations by the Afghan government. By way of contrast, I include an analysis of what the central Taliban leadership were trying to achieve at the same time. None of these three organisations understood Helmandi politics to the degree that they were able to successfully influence events on the ground. Next, I consider development efforts in the province. Through Helmandi eyes, this would not be complete without a discussion of the ensuing corruption. A case study of money movement in Gereshk, whilst not specifically focussing on development, is used to illustrate how divergent the ISAF and Helmandi views were on the issue of corruption, and how poorly ISAF understood the underlying dynamics. Of course, the divergence of these views, and the role that ISAF played in the graft that it was ostensibly trying to stop, meant that corruption was exacerbated. I then consider some of the politics of the ISAF intervention and withdrawal alongside those of the province; by this point they had become somewhat intertwined. Even so, the Westerners did not fully understand what was going on, and the perspectives of the Helmandis and the internationals were dramatically different.

Lastly, I explore and analyse the common Helmandi narrative: that the British are working with and supporting the Taliban in order to destroy Helmand. Whilst I accept that it does not fit strictly within the framework of the rest of the book—namely that outsiders do not understand Helmand and are therefore manipulated by local actors— I consider this key narrative the result of the poor British understanding of simple (to the Helmandis) local realities and the divergence between British statements (reconstruction) and actions (use of firepower). In short, the Helmandis could not believe that the British were *that* stupid. To them, and in line with their historical understanding of the British, the Angrez *must* be up to something. From the Helmandi perspective, it was more likely that the British were working with the Taliban to destroy Helmand, than that they had arrived to reconstruct their province. This is the Helmandi conclusion to the most recent phase of the conflict.

## Security

By the beginning of 2010, the British were consolidating their position in central Helmand. Since the Nad-e Ali operation in 2008 (see Chapter 5), the area under British and Afghan government control had slowly expanded. The counterinsurgency strategy dictated that they 'needed' to be living among the population in order to protect them. They also began to reduce their use of violence.[8] Finally, they were marrying their actions with their rhetoric of initiating development projects, opening schools and refurbishing clinics. The population welcomed this.[9]

In February 2010, British, American and Afghan troops launched a large-scale operation to establish an Afghan government presence in Babaji, Naqilabad and Showal for the British, and in Marjeh for the Americans. This was predicated on the tenets of counterinsurgency, with the US general-in-command asserting that he would have a 'government in a box' ready to deliver services (for example, health, and education) in Marjeh.[10] In addition to a high rate of Special Forces

raids targeting individual 'Taliban' commanders, the British deliberately leaked operational information to specific elders. At that time, in
line with the 'insurgency narrative', the British understood the government and the Taliban as having separate 'offers' to which individuals
and groups could subscribe. They used their improved understanding
of the local politics and appropriately contextualised the leaks for each
community.[11]

Thus, when dealing with communities that interacted with the
Taliban, such information was delivered in the form of a threat
whereby resistance would be met with violence—such as the Kharoti
of Naqilabad and Showal. Those that were seen as closer to the government, such as the Barakzai of Babaji, received the information in
the form of planning meetings for the post-operational development of
the area. Either way, the result was the same: the 'Taliban' would know
roughly when the British were coming and might choose not to fight.
In the event this is precisely what happened. The British were trying to
manipulate the Helmandis as they understood them. This later back-
fired when the leaks were interpreted as the British working with the
Taliban, as is discussed further below.[12]

In Babaji, the British aim was to re-establish bases along the same
line as the Haji Kadus militia checkpoints (see Map 10). They understood that the old militia checkpoints had managed to keep the
'Taliban' from attacking from the north, and thought that replacing
and reinforcing them would be beneficial (see Chapter 5). However,
Babaji was full of inter-community mistrust and violence between the
Barakzai and non-Barakzai communities.[13] The British had unwittingly
affiliated themselves with the Barakzai communities in this inter-community conflict; they even used Barakzai men previously associated
with the militia as guides for their troops. This was an old mistake.
The elders from the mixed tribal communities to the north of the militia were appalled that the British were affiliating themselves with the
Barakzai community that they were fighting.[14] One of the guides, in
particular, was notoriously cruel.[15] Yet the British were not only
attacked by the mixed communities to the north, shortly after, and in
resistance to the 'foreign occupation', the British were also being
attacked by elements from the Barakzai communities (that were also
feuding with the guides that the British had chosen).[16]

During the course of 2010, the British and the Americans redoubled
their attention on the army and police in Helmand. Success in counter-

insurgency depends upon properly trained indigenous forces.[17] Early in the year, the British had established a provincial training centre for police recruits in an attempt to standardise the force and break the links to the patrimonial powerbrokers. More British and American forces were also diverted to mentoring and training, rather than conducting their own operations. By the end of 2010 the only large-scale operations were those where the majority of the planning and effort was divested by the Afghan forces themselves.[18]

These operations would typically be into areas like Yakhchal, south of Gereshk, or in the desert to the west of Nad-e Ali. Both areas had high rates of poppy growth. The areas were targeted deliberately: these were communities that nobody in the government cared about and they also lacked connections in the provincial capital or in Kabul.[19] The provincial government stated that the desert was full of 'Taliban'. But the operations were often followed by eradication and under an official Afghan government scheme, Governor Mangal received a cash bonus for his administration that was tied to how much opium was eradicated in each growing season.[20]

The increased government control within the canal-zone had enabled eradication, leading many rich landowners in Nad-e Ali to set up farms in the desert that were farmed by refugees from the north of Helmand.[21] Some of this 'desert' community was also formed of those people who had bought the land that was partitioned up by 'government' commanders, such as Haji Lal Jan, in the early 2000s. He allegedly still 'taxes' that community.[22] All of the communities sank tube wells, but as no ecological survey has been conducted of the area it is unknown what the long-term effects will be on the water table (that is, whether too much water is being drawn off to be sustainable). When travelling over the area by helicopter in the summer of 2012, it was clear to me that large areas had recently been marked out for cultivation. I saw a very large-scale operation, with perfectly straight lines running for hundreds of metres, spread over several square kilometers.

Helmandi poppy farmers blamed much of the eradication and the resulting operations on Mangal and the foreigners—the Americans and the British—for paying him to destroy their livelihoods.[23] There was also tentative evidence of a tribal divide between those within the canal-zone and those without. Within the canal-zone, the settlers were majority non-Helmandi Ghilzai, whereas the desert dwellers were Helmandi Durrani, mostly from the north.[24] Although the reasons for this divide are currently unclear, it may be due to acute water stress in northern Helmand, forcing migration south.[25] One man likened it to tribal war, where Mangal was allegedly eradicating the Durrani's poppy, while favouring the Ghilzai people who were the majority inside the canal-zone of Nad-e Ali. It is the sharecropping Durrani in the desert who currently suffer the worst effects of eradication and conflict.[26]

In reality the 'Taliban' in the desert were farmers defending their poppy crop, something that senior district police officers admitted to me one evening over Indian whiskey and red bull (a Helmandi special-ity). During the day, two 'Talibs' had been brought in dead, killed in battle when they had attacked the poppy eradication operation. When I inspected the bodies it appeared, at least from the state of their hands, that they had been involved in agriculture for all of their lives. They were dressed in opium-stained clothes and were brought in with ancient single-shot rifles. One had been run over rather than shot. As we discussed the event that evening, the senior officers were clearly unhappy. 'What can we do?' they shrugged. 'The government tells us these people are Taliban, but we can see that they are farmers' they lamented. It would have been rude, as a guest (in Helmand), to point out that treating them as Taliban was a self-fulfilling prophecy. But they knew anyway and were paid large amounts of money from Mangal's eradication bonuses to subscribe to the government narra-tive; this was up to US$1,000 per day according to receipts and cash that I witnessed. It was a depressing conversation to be involved in.

More broadly, a central part of the ISAF strategy involved killing or capturing individual Taliban commanders.[27] Prior to 2009, ISAF had attempted to use Special Forces in southern Afghanistan to capture or kill individual members of the Taliban. This strategy was premised on the belief that killing or capturing specific people, coupled with a deep knowledge of their social networks and Taliban structure, would allow ISAF to manipulate the Taliban movement. The strategy was occasion-ally effective. Rahim (Ishaqzai, Now Zad), the Taliban provincial gover-nor for Helmand, for example, was persuaded to give himself up after several of his colleagues were deliberately killed in quick succession in 2008.[28] Yet because of the Iraq war, and the diversion of resources that this involved, the programme was very poorly resourced.

Two aspects of this strategy changed in 2009. First, more Special Forces units and assets, such as satellite cover, were deployed to Afghanistan after being withdrawn from Iraq. Second, there was a redoubled focus on capturing or killing roadside bomb layers and 'facilitators' as these were causing most ISAF casualties.[29] These changes took place at the same time that General McChrystal (the former head of US Special Operations Forces) assumed command of ISAF troops in Afghanistan, which in turn led ISAF to refocus on counterinsurgency. Officially, targeting was a key mechanism allowing the government and ISAF to better protect the people.[30]

Increased resources meant that Taliban leaders began to be targeted more heavily. The new system was designed on 'tempo' and 'accessibility' rather than the more bespoke arrangement that had existed previously. This meant striking ever-lower individuals in the 'Taliban' hierarchy, but this had very little strategic effect on the Taliban movement as a whole. The increase in tempo meant that ISAF was unable to devote the resources to understanding how the movement worked at a holistic level. The heavy focus on the roadside bomb threat was based on limiting ISAF casualty figures as far as possible, but the opportunity cost was that they were unable to manipulate the Taliban movement.[31]

The targeting strategy was officially based on a Taliban that was inflicting cruelty on the Helmandi population. However, these raids often killed 'Taliban' fighters who were no more than resistance figures for their communities.[32] This included Murtaza, the Kharoti commander from Shin Kalay, who was arrested at the end of 2009. Shakir, his subordinate commander from Shin Kalay, was killed in a separate incident. Both were resistance figures. Kharoti villagers turned Shakir's car into a shrine situated close to a bridge recently built by the British and draped with the green flags bestowed on a martyr's grave.[33]

In another example, Akhtur Mohammad, the nephew of Haji Mullah Paslow and the leader of the Popalzai in Nad-e Ali, was killed. The clan had previously sent Abdul Malik, another nephew, to the community council in order to maintain a channel to the government. ISAF was correct in believing that he was a 'Talib'; however, the killing of Akhtur Mohammad closed the door to working with that community.[34] Operations to kill or capture 'Taliban' were often entirely divorced from the social terrain that shapes the conflict in Helmand. Capturing or killing 'Taliban', while ignoring or being unaware of their position within Helmandi society, meant that ISAF was not as able to shape the conflict as it thought it was.

In Kabul, President Karzai continuously upbraided the US, insisting that the raids caused civilian casualties.[35] A senior US general had to assure Karzai privately that 'categorically [they] had confidence in [their] intelligence and believed [they] knew who the enemy was'.[36] Yet I witnessed the 'wrong' people being killed by raids in Helmand on several occasions, and this was almost always the result of poor intelligence and of people using ISAF to settle their feuds. Helmandis often attempted to manipulate me in order to have their enemies killed. On one occasion, two American soldiers had been killed by a bomb. Shortly after, a Helmandi gentleman that I was in contact with began to explain to me that the components for that bomb had been stored in a particular individual's house. It eventually transpired that the other man was a neighbour with whom he had a land dispute.[37]

*The Response: Taliban Consolidation*

The narratives surrounding the Taliban are relatively straightforward. The Taliban are a movement of Islamic fundamentalists who seek to oppress women and fight democracy. According to this interpretation, there are divisions between those Taliban who are ideologically committed and those who are merely fighting for money or revenge. The Taliban are described as coherent and centralised.[38] But, as discussed below (and in Chapters 4 and 5), the reality of the Taliban structure in Helmand is different. It is important to understand these differences, as it explains why ISAF have failed to defeat the Taliban: they simply did not exist in the way in which ISAF understood them to. First, we begin with the ISAF narratives surrounding the Taliban, before describing the reality and how the central Taliban leadership tried, and failed, to make the 'Taliban' conform to something more like the ISAF conceptualisation. (It is ironic that the Taliban leadership tried to turn their organisation into something that ISAF already thought it was, doubly so when we consider that ISAF was basing its countering strategy on this mischaracterisation.)

The first narrative is that concerning the aslee (real) Taliban. These are the group commanders and those above them—in other words, the members of the Taliban who have links to the Quetta Shura. They are sometimes also called akidawee (ideological) Taliban, although these would be more properly considered a subset of the aslee Taliban, as not all of them fight simply in response to jihad obligations.[39] The aslee Taliban are closely linked to the ISI and they provide 'professional' skills such as bomb construction and facilitating the movements of suicide bombers. They also commit acts that local Taliban would not usually countenance, like burning schools.[40]

Daakhelee (internal Helmandi) Taliban comprise the vast majority of the 'movement'. Most estimates claim that they make up 95 per cent of the manpower of the 'Taliban'. They are involved in the fighting for various reasons, including revenge, evicting foreigners, boredom, unemployment, feuds and other grievance factors.[41] Many other individuals attach themselves to this construct and operate as 'Taliban', or are described as 'Taliban' by the Afghan government and international forces. These can be farmers defending their poppy crop; criminals; smugglers; militias; patronage-seeking fighters who used to work for the government and so on. They often get conflated under the Mullah Omar Taliban banner; as one interviewee put it, 'they do the [crime] and Omar gets the blame'.[42]

The more nuanced view shows a struggle for control of the 'movement'.[43] The Taliban in 2006 was based on a mahaz system (see Chapter 4), which is a patronage system that maintains figureheads in Quetta to source and distribute military supplies. These mahaz commanders will have a number of fighting groups, but they will not always be in the same area, and could be spread across the whole of southern Afghanistan (see Chapter 4).[44] The most important element of the mahaz system is its personal links to particular commanders and areas. This is analogous to the situation in 1978–9, when commanders would develop and use links with those who were in a position to fund them. The standing of a commander depends on his standing in the society; Qari Hazrat, the son of Abdul Khaleq, a famous Hizb commander, is a good example of this. The role of social prestige explains why replacements for fighters and commanders who have been killed would be drawn from the same family, starting with the closest male relative. This can be interpreted as revenge, but another reason why the Taliban movement seek out and offer jobs to close relatives of killed fighters is this exceptionally close link between the Taliban at ground-level and the society. The Taliban are simply harnessing revenge as a motivator.[45]

In a similar way, some mahazes and commanders will have different relationships with the ISI. This too can be a source of friction, particularly with regard to the provision of foreign Pakistani fighters.[46] Pakistani fighters, previously identified in northern Helmand in 2006–7 and Garmsir during the summer of 2008, used to be either given to, or arranged by, individual mahaz commanders to use as they saw fit. Since 2008, however, the number of Pakistani fighters has dropped dramatically.[47] Each mahaz also has its own ISI mentor and military trainers.[48] However, this should not be seen as representing Pakistani endorsement of the mahaz system, but instead reflects the fact that they are simply accepting its existence and attempting to exert what leverage they can—some mahazes and groups have refused ISI mentoring.[49]

This 'system' created a very confused landscape with several fighting groups operating in the same area but answering to different leaderships and funding. This can be considered analogous to the different jihadi parties operating in contiguous space during the 1980s. And just like the inter-mujahidin group fighting that occurred in the 1980s, this too now occurs with different Taliban commanders who belong to different mahazes.[50] This infighting caused the Taliban central leadership to decide to enact a centralised nezami—meaning military or organised—system in 2008.[51] This was eventually led by Zakir. Funding was diverted down this single chain in order to decrease factionalisation— the Taliban is a patronage organisation and was attempting to enforce one patron. The nezami system (and Zakir) would choose which fighting groups received weapons and funding.[52]

The mahaz system should be seen as the Helmandis reaching out for patronage in order to help them fight their local enemies, including the British. By contrast, the nezami system should be seen as outsiders reaching in and trying to influence the conflict using patronage. The two systems have been competing with each other since 2008/9 (at the time of writing in early 2013).[53]

The Quetta Shura's plan for a centralised structure was laid out in their 2009 and 2010 Layehas. New mahazes were banned and a clear command hierarchy was articulated, with more detail provided on the rules and responsibilities of the military commissions—the embodiment of the nezami system at district and provincial levels.[54] The nezami system is mainly funded by charitable donations from individuals in the Middle East,[55] which are routed through ISI mentors who sit on the Quetta Shura.[56] Supply for this system is handled by the Pakistani military until it reaches the Pakistani border 'overtly',[57] from where it is moved by smugglers to the groups operating in Helmand. This is the same as the mahaz system except that the mahaz commanders also have other sources of supply.[58] Outside of Helmand and some other southern provinces, the implementation of the nezami system has been successful. Helmand, however, has managed to resist the system's implementation.[59]

This is due to two factors specific to Helmand. First, Helmand generates vast sources of income: through drugs, ISAF supply contracts and development funding. The mahaz system, which is better integrated with society, is more able to use this income to maintain a degree of independence (see Chapter 3's discussion with regard to the Ishaqzai or Kharoti interests and their reasons for working with the Taliban). A key part of this dynamic is represented by those 'government' commanders who altered allegiances and became 'Taliban' commanders.[60] The best example of this is Sher Mohammad, who plays a role in funding the 'Taliban'.[61] Several interviewees even went as far as to identify him as a mahaz commander.[62] Secondly, Helmand's social structure—the rutbavi (hierarchical) Pushtun tribal system (see Chapter 1)—is highly commensurate with the mahaz system. The rutbavi system is based upon land ownership and the cycling of resources up and down a hierarchy to maintain social cohesion.[63] This is mediated by key individuals, who usually pass on their position through family links: so too, the mahaz system.

The resilience of the Helmandi mahaz system has led to a strange hybrid that is neither mahaz nor nezami (see Figure 7).[64] This hybrid situation has created a confused Taliban command system in Helmand. As the Quetta Taliban have attempted to centralise their supply, and hence the fighting, the mahaz commanders have attempted to co-opt that system. This is similar to how individuals co-opt the Afghan government system in Helmand. Further, if an order comes down through either the mahaz or nezami systems, it must be checked with the other system before it is carried out.[65] This is exactly analogous to the nations in the ISAF coalition having to check their ISAF orders with their national chain of command. This situation is nowhere better illustrated than in the case of Zakir.

Once Zakir was released from Guantanamo and the Afghan prison system in 2007–8,[67] he stepped into a Taliban that was beginning to implement the nezami system. In 2012, he appeared to occupy a position both as a mahaz commander and as the leader of the Taliban military commission (that is, as the head of the nezami system).[68] This is particularly the case where the Zakir mahaz is most prevalent: in Sangin,[69] Musa Qala[70] and Kajaki[71] districts. In those districts, Mullah Salam,[72] Zakir's brother, was both his mahaz commander and his

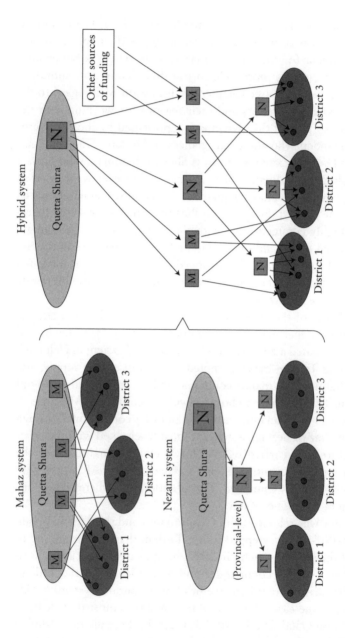

Figure 7: The hybrid mahaz–nezami system.[66] Note that in the hybrid system some commanders receive funding only from the nezami system; however, most are 'dual-hatted'. Mahaz commanders receive money from the Quetta Shura nezami head (that is, Zakir) as well as having independent sources of money. This means that commanders on the ground have to liaise up two chains of command before following orders. Note M = Mahaz, N = Nezami

nezami commander.[73] Interviewees were often keen to point out that they came under the Zakir mahaz system rather than the (Zakir) nezami system: the 'Taliban' is an organisation based on personal relationships.[74]

In central Helmand the situation was different and highly complex. In Nad-e Ali and Marjeh, Naim was considered the most powerful mahaz commander.[75] He was the Taliban provincial governor as well—a vestige of the pre-nezami governance system. Sher Mohammad was also seen as a mahaz commander,[76] alongside Motassimbillah Agha, Noor Ali, Mansour, Baradar, Zakir and Sattar.[77] This plethora of mahaz commanders should be seen as analogous to the multiplicity of jihadi parties during the 1980s in Nad-e Ali, which was in turn reflective of the social structure. To further complicate matters, the nezami commander in Nad-e Ali was Juma Khan, but he was also a member of Tayib Agha's mahaz.[78] In Nahr-e Saraj, Sattar and Janan were seen as the most active mahaz commanders.[79] Sher Mohammad was also seen as a mahaz commander there,[80] as well as Dadullah, Mansour, Baradar and Zakir.[81] There were only one or two groups that came under the nezami system in Nahr-e Saraj,[82] which is commensurate with the findings of the Gereshk model (see below). There, the 'Taliban' groups chose to act as independent groups—they could make more money by filtering funds out of Gereshk than from the nezami system.

A conclusion from this complex discussion is that the social terrain dictates where particular mahazes have fighting groups. Zakir's mahazes and overall control, for example, predominate in areas where American troops were based until the summer of 2012. It was he who said that he had 'a strong feeling of revenge in his heart' after his experiences in Guantanamo.[83] Likewise, at the time of writing, Sher Mohammad's mahaz, despite his substantial links to northern Helmand, has groups in Nad-e Ali and Nahr-e Saraj, where the British are deployed. It was Sher Mohammad who told me that 'the British are so stupid … when they go, we will still be here … I hate the British' after being removed as provincial governor at British insistence. Between the two of them they cover most of the province (see Conclusion). Because Zakir's men consistently point out that they follow him in his 'mahaz' capacity rather than his 'nezami' capacity (contrary to what the Taliban/ISI desire), it can be argued either that the Taliban Quetta Shura (and the ISI) do not have good enough knowledge of Helmandi politics to enact the nezami system of control, or that the mahaz system is too strong and ingrained in 'Taliban' organisation in Helmand, or both.

During 2011, it appeared that elements of the Quetta Shura were attempting to pursue negotiations with the Americans. A result was the opening of a Taliban 'office' in the gulf state of Qatar.[84] Tentative investigations show that the ISI was unaware of this. As a result, they diverted funding and support away from the Quetta Shura towards another Taliban shura in Peshawar. The Taliban Peshawar shura has been long-standing, but due to the Qatar negotiations it has now established a leadership position over the Quetta Shura. The only major commander in the south still receiving money from Peshawar and Quetta is Zakir.[85] This is because Zakir is the head of the Taliban military commission; however, the interviews cited above show that Zakir's commanders see themselves as part of his mahaz rather than his nezami system. There is a possibility that Zakir is using the Taliban funding to support his own personal power interests in northern Helmand, and generate his own patronage organisation.

The Taliban is evolving as a movement (see Figure 7). The Peshawar shura, staffed by young 'professional' (military) individuals who are not known to the international community, provides the interaction with the ISI and the foreign backers of the Taliban.[86] The top of the nezami system is represented in Peshawar, and this links to Zakir in the Quetta Shura, who controls the nezami system for southern Afghanistan. The old mahaz commanders now have to come to Zakir for money, as head of the nezami system.[87] However, on the ground, the mahazes are still independently active, as well as fighting for Zakir. And because funding only travels down the nezami channel everyone else at the top of the structure is side-lined, including old Taliban government figures.[88] 'Quetta is just not providing as much money anymore.'[89] This lack of funding has contributed to a decline in the violence in some areas of Helmand.[90]

The ISI's redoubled focus on the Peshawar shura and the nezami structure has allowed Iran to strengthen its interactions with other mahaz commanders as they become disenfranchised by the ISI.[91] As one alliance weakens, another patron steps in to fill the void. Much like Pakistan, Iran also has strategic interests in Afghanistan, which it seeks to achieve by supporting elements of the 'Taliban'.[92] In addition to the Kajaki dam dynamic outlined below, Iran also aims to protect and aid Shia communities in Helmand. A good example of this is the protection of the (Shia) Hazara school in Saidabad.[93]

Finally, some Taliban commanders point to a deal between Sher Mohammad and Iran to supply resistance groups in Kajaki that are attacking the Americans.[94] There are also rumours that Sher Mohammad and his childhood friend Zakir[95] have been discussing how to 'split Helmand' between them once the foreigners leave.[96] If true, it is this that will dictate the future of Helmand, particularly in the north, rather than the Afghan government or ISAF.[97] This merits further investigation.

*Development and Corruption*

The most significant outcome from the increase in American attention to Helmand was an astronomical rise in development spending in the province.[98] This automatically led to an increase in corruption, even though 'corruption', or baksheesh ('gift'), has been a large part of patronage societies like Helmand for a long time.[99] According to the narratives of international organisations (for example, ISAF), corruption is seen as an Afghan problem, mostly caused by the drugs trade.[100] Yet Helmandis blame ISAF and the international community: 'the foreigners don't know how to get things done; [and] the people who sort things out for them take all the money and put it in their pockets'.[101]

There was definitely a shift in 'corruption' over the 2008–12 period. When I first arrived in Helmand in 2008, many elders had learnt very quickly that the claims process, where they could claim for damage to property from ISAF due to military operations, represented an easy way of making small amounts of money, such as $500. During the conversations that I held with them in 2012, those very same elders tried to press upon me how good their new construction company was, and implored me to use my contacts in the PRT to help them gain reconstruction contracts. Another young man related how his family used to ring their relatives in Europe for money to help with weddings and other living costs; now their relatives in Europe were ringing them to gain contracts.[102]

Corruption is seen by Helmandis as originating in Kabul. It is driven by a vacuum effect, whereby more senior people in a patronage chain would demand payment from their subordinates in order to guarantee the tenure of said subordinates.[103] The foreigners provided poorly targeted money at the bottom, it moved upwards until it reached someone whom the international community protected, or supported in their post in Kabul (therefore had relative impunity), thence it left the country to Dubai (examples will be given below when discussing this dynamic in Gereshk).[104] As a very old man (by Helmandi standards) pointed out to me with a sigh, 'before 2001, Afghans didn't understand how the outside world worked; now they have all got bank accounts in Dubai'.[105] Helmandis estimated that the bribes they had to pay in 2010–11 were three times what they were under the Sher Mohammad government of 2002 to 2005.[106]

This growth in corruption was exacerbated by the tendency for ISAF to overpay for contracts due to the fact that they were unaware of local costs. In 2009, for example, the British were paying 650 dollars per dumper truck load of gravel in Nad-e Ali. The contractor had scooped this out of the River Helmand and transported it some 10 kilometres:[107] I estimate that this cost 30 dollars. The top policeman in the province explained to me that many Helmandis viewed this lack of prudence as stupidity, and as an invitation to pilfer more.[108] In any case, the PRT had such limited knowledge of the local politics that projects were often awarded to contractors who were unable to work in the relevant area because of community disputes.[109]

Lastly, the district councils that ISAF established became significant foci of corruption. The ISAF aim of empowering Helmandis to decide their own development projects[110] did not match how the Helmandis saw the councils. To them, the 'representative' elders stole from their own 'communities', or attacked other elders' projects with the 'Taliban' in order to dissuade them from taking on more projects.[111] These dynamics fed jealousy in a society as fractured as that of Helmand.[112] The speed at which development money was spent meant that it often failed to be targeted at specific communities or linked to particular political objectives, as it should be in a counterinsurgency.[113] Development projects were meant to buy the loyalty of Helmandis. In practice, and as Stuart Gordon has documented, development spending simply increased the instability that it was meant to reduce.[114]

One example of this is Mirwais Khan, the son of Wakil Safar, who stole the wheat seed meant for his community and sold it. Mirwais was arrested for this and spent a year in jail.[115] This gap in leadership allowed Haji Barakzai to move into a greater leadership position among the Kharoti.[116] In another example, Karim, one of the Nad-e Ali council members most closely linked with the Taliban, was also head of the development sub-committee. He used his positions to make money by manipulating security, and refused to allow the road to be resurfaced between Loy Bagh and Lashkar Gah unless he received a cut. If not, he would get the 'Taliban' to destroy it.[117]

In 2010, the Americans took over Sangin, Musa Qala and Kajaki in order to allow the British to consolidate in central Helmand. Towards the end of 2011, the US began to conduct operations to clear the road between Sangin and Kajaki. For them, the US$266 million contract to refurbish the dam was a lynchpin of their strategy in southern Afghanistan.[118] In one sense the operation to restore the dam was emblematic of everything that ISAF did in Helmand. It was visible development for the people delivered by the Afghan government in partnership with international forces. Internally to the coalition, however, there was a turf war between USAID and the US military about who could deliver more aid: the US were driven by internal feuds just as much as the Helmandis.[119]

The Helmandis saw it differently. The Alizai who lived around the dam would not benefit from the development, whereas the residents of Kandahar would. Instead, many Alizai wanted an irrigation canal.[120] They also had no interest in foreign forces working in their area, as it was felt that the presence of foreigners would lead to the eradication of poppy.[121] A well-connected former Khad operative pointed out that almost everyone fighting in Kajaki against the Americans was a daakhelee Talib—a resistance fighter. When fighters were killed, local people would collect money for the family.[122] The day after the Americans arrived in force, Mullah Salam, Zakir's brother (mentioned above when he was released from Guantanamo), was walking around the Kajaki bazaar talking to shopkeepers and collecting food offerings for his fighters.[123] This narrative of resistance allied neatly with Iran's strategic interests in northern Helmand.

Iran considers Kajaki a strategic interest and it seeks to influence the flow of the Helmand River through the dam. This is because water from the Helmand is ecologically essential for the Iranian Sistani region.[124] However, according to the ISAF plan, the development of the south of Afghanistan relies heavily on the Kajaki dam generating power for this area of the country, and especially Kandahar. They seek to 'boost the supply of water and electric power to both provinces'.[125] This, importantly, means that there will be less water available for Iran, potentially in contravention of the 1973 agreement between the two countries.[126]

Iran has consequently sought to prevent the reconstruction of the Kajaki dam by sponsoring fighting groups to target any international or Afghan government presence.[127] This also allows Iran to give the 'Great and Little Satans' (the United States and Britain, respectively) a bloody nose.[128] Thus while it may seem paradoxical that the Americans were having to fight their way through the locals in order to spend $266 million on generating electricity for millions of Afghans, a legacy of 'not wanting government', along with Iranian support, meant that resistance to the project was particularly strong.

The Americans began to pull out of Helmand almost as soon as the operation in Kajaki was over. The troops deployed as part of the US 'surge' were being withdrawn after just two years, with the deployment departing at an extremely rapid pace—by the end of the summer of 2012, there were only small numbers of US troops still based in northern Helmand. At the time this research was conducted, it was unclear whether the US would achieve its aims in Kajaki because of 'security concerns'.[129] The US relied heavily on its narrative of reconstructing the Kajaki dam without understanding the local concerns around poppy eradication, resistance and the desire for a canal in Zamindawar. This also partly explains why Iran was able to sponsor local fighting groups to achieve its aims in Kajaki.

Development was intimately linked to self-aggrandisement in Helmandi minds. One of the greatest divorces between Helmandi and Western understandings of development occurs with Governor Mangal. According to ISAF, Mangal was a great technocrat, who was reforming institutional government in Helmand and bringing much-needed development to the province.[130] But according to local opinion, during his time in office, land deemed undeveloped would either be appropriated or residents would be evicted from 'government' land.[131] Helmandis saw this as a direct result of Mangal's closeness to the British, and later, to the Americans, rather than being in spite of this. Interviewees stated that 'development projects' often resulted in people being relocated from their land.[132]

British, and later, American, officials focused on Mangal's technical abilities and his ability to operate in an 'institutional' way in comparison to some of his predecessors.[133] For ISAF, 'service delivery' was seen as a key part of what the government of Afghanistan could offer the populace.[134] However, diplomatic cables released by WikiLeaks show that ISAF became aware of allegations surrounding Mangal at some point around October 2009, but chose to do nothing about them. One cable stated that: 'it would be surprising if this type of corruption occurred without Mangal's knowledge or perhaps even his complicity'.[135] Sir Sherard Cowper-Coles, at that time the UK special representative to Afghanistan and Pakistan, concurs: 'we did nothing when we began to receive indications that Mangal wasn't as clean as we liked to believe'. 'We realised late', said Sir Sherard to me, 'and by then it was too late … we were invested.'

Mangal was finally removed in September 2012.[136] His sacking may have been linked to another series of protests over his governorship in Kabul in May and June. At that time, there were was also a spate of television talk show discussions,[137] press conferences[138] and newspaper articles about him.[139] Although reflecting general Helmandi feeling, these events were organised and financed by Sher Mohammad and Jabbar Qahraman. By this point, Mangal had allied himself with the 'Hizb' figures in the province as a bulwark against Sher Mohammad, and counted figures like Mir Wali and Hafizullah Khan as allies. This was clever political manoeuvring. Mangal's legacy was perhaps best summed up by a Helmandi senator: 'he seems to be better than the others have been … but Mangal is British'.[140]

Mangal's behaviour demonstrated how closely linked ISAF could be to one person's style of governance (through ignorance and by doggedly sticking to their counterinsurgency strategy). Gereshk provides a clear systemic example. Gereshk is a perennial concern for President Karzai because it sits on the strategic Herat–Kandahar highway.[141] The city's strategic location means that it generates vast amounts of income, and so many seek to control the city. In the ISAF era, this dynamic has taken on further importance because it is the only route through which supplies can pass from Karachi, the main ISAF seaport, to Camp Bastion, the main ISAF logistics base in Helmand. Thus, since 2001, Gereshk has had a vast array of different officials, particularly chiefs of police, partly because the position allows factional interests to legitimise their militias in official 'government' structures. This is sometimes exacerbated by ISAF's unwilling or unknowing involvement.

The model shown in Figure 8a shows the movement of money in Gereshk.[142] This demonstrates the interaction between development funding, control of the security landscape and the purchase of 'government' positions. Stability, defined as an absence of factional violence, is generated by the uninterrupted flow of money through the model. The international community calls this money flow corruption. The model has three main moneymaking activities (or inputs). These are drugs money, development money and the money from ISAF supply contracts. There are a number of other subsidiary inputs, such as corruption of the wheat seed distribution. In the pre-ISAF era, drugs money formed the bulk of inputs into the system.[143] However, in the post-surge era, with 30,000 troops being supplied through Camp Bastion, it can be argued that ISAF supply contracts form the majority of the monetary inputs to the system.[144] It is exceptionally difficult to quantify these figures, however.[145]

Conceptually arrayed above the income-generating layer is a level of security actors. These are men like Haji Kadus, Khan Mohammad or Ezmarai who either control or have controlled major factions in the 'police'. Many of these men rose to power by leading militias sponsored by US Special Forces in the period between 2002 and 2012, with Haji Kadus being a notable example of this (see Chapter 4). The relationship between de facto factional interests and de jure security forces can be considered like the petal-shaped structure within Figure 8. Individual actors and groups will try and gain a position within the 'police' in order to further their own interests. This allows them to interact with the state and gain 'legitimacy' and funding. Often they will maintain a half-in/half-out policy, giving them maximum scope for action. Membership of the 'police' simply denotes a label to enable other activities, rather than any form of ideological attachment to the government.

The private security actors gain income from the moneymaking activities. The mechanism is usually a mafia-style operation ('mafia' is another word that has been adopted into Pushtu during the ISAF intervention). A security actor, for example, might approach a contractor who is responsible for building a village school. They might inform him that it costs 20,000 dollars for the school to be protected from the 'Taliban'. In the case of Haji Kadus, he might tell the contractor that he must use a particular type of aggregate. This is because Kadus has 'retired' from the security business and now owns an aggregate mine 200 metres north of Camp Price. The mine is protected by the same militia force that protects Camp Price: he is still skilled at signalling to the locals that he is linked to the foreigners.

The same dynamic occurs when ISAF supply convoys are delivered to Bastion by Afghan contractors.[146] In this case, control of the 'police' checkpoint through which the convoys must pass is vital. Abdul Sattar

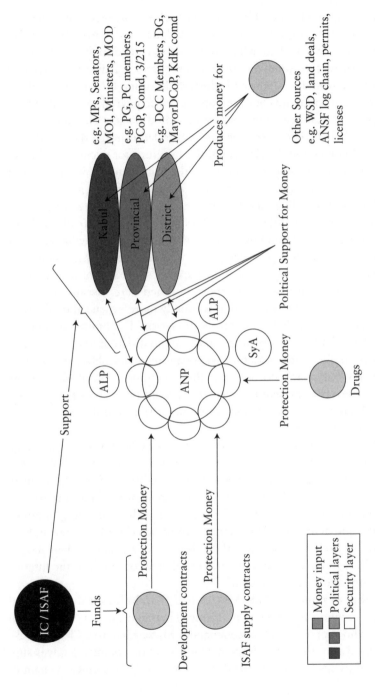

Figure 8: The Gereshk model. The petal-shaped structure is the half-in/half-out model of de jure/de facto militia positioning

215

(Barakzai, ex-Hizb, ex-Kadus militia) who controlled the Abhashak checkpoint, for example, made 10,000 dollars a day from ISAF trucking (gross). When Shadi Khan took over as chief of police in 2011, his first visit was to Abdul Sattar in his checkpoint. This is the reverse of what one would expect from Helmandi decorum. ISAF later found out that Abdul Sattar was not even on the police payroll. A deal had been in place for over two years where he would remain 'checkpoint commander', as he had been when he controlled it in the days of the US Special Forces and the Kadus militia. In return for a 'cut', the chief of police would maintain the illusion to the British and Danish that Sattar was part of the 'police'. Sattar was eventually removed in 2012.[147]

The most revealing aspect of the Gereshk model is the absence of the 'Taliban'. In many other areas actors and groups opt to ally with the Taliban and their funding because that is what best enhances their interests. In Gereshk, however, there is so much money available that the most lucrative option is almost always some sort of private moneymaking activity similar to those outlined here. Because most are related to control of the road, it is usually more beneficial to ally with the 'government' (which controls the road). The limited number of 'Taliban' that there were in the city were no different to other security actors, and in many cases they were paid by major players in Gereshk to carry out attacks to persuade the government and ISAF to allow those players to present themselves as a solution to security problems. Mir Wali is the most obvious example of this. The Taliban 'groups' were just tools for hire.

Above the security layer is arrayed a 'political' layer. In the model, this is split between the district, provincial or capital (Kabul) levels. The role of the political layer is to receive money from the security layer that extracted it from the income generators, and in return, to provide political protection for them through politicking, appointments and acquittals. The relationship between Abdul Sattar and the Gereshk chief of police described above is one example. This money would then pass through the provincial chief of police to the interior minister and thence to Dubai.

Other examples include Mir Ahmad (Barakzai), on the provincial council, who supported many former Hizb figures, and Mir Wali, an MP, who supported militia commander Mirza Khan (see Chapter 4).[148] Abdul Raziq, the jailed drug-dealing US militia commander, was supported by his brother on the district council.[149] This upward chain of payments was combined with the repeated outsourcing of development contracts through chains of sub-contractors. This resulted in situations where as little as $100,000 of the $1 million paid by ISAF to build a police station in Rahim Kalay (east of Deh Adam Khan) was actually spent on the bricks, mortar and labour—the rest went on kickbacks and dilutions.[150]

From the perspective of the Helmandis, ISAF plays a critical role in this process. Much of the money entering this model comes from ISAF projects and contracts in Nahr-e Saraj district. The money will travel upwards through the model until it reaches someone considered to be 'immune'. This immunity will often rest on interactions with the international community. The best example of this is President Karzai, who remained in his position with international support despite being widely seen as having committed electoral fraud in the 2009 presidential elections.[151] As far as Helmandis are concerned, the dynamic of ISAF putting money in at the bottom and protecting the people who extract it at the top is equivalent to money laundering: they see ISAF as laundering its own money (see Figure 8).

Moreover, in many cases ISAF officials know that an Afghan official is corrupt, and other Afghan officials know that ISAF is aware of this. The reasoning of the 'internationals' is that it is better to keep an official whose foibles they are aware of. Yet for the Helmandis this is simply evidence of the international community's double standards. They know that ISAF is aware of specific instances of corruption but chooses to do nothing about it.[152] The 'open secret' in Helmand of ISAF complicity in corruption is highly damaging to Helmandi perceptions of the government and ISAF.[153] Furthermore, there is often denial among some ISAF officials about ISAF's own role in corruption. Their narrative is that 'Afghan' corruption is caused mainly by the drugs trade.[154]

*Politics*

ISAF inactivity over Mangal was partly due to his skill in manipulating ISAF and the media. From the beginning of his tenure, Mangal maintained the position that if he were removed then Sher Mohammad would replace him.[155] As the British had insisted on Sher Mohammad's removal in the first place, this would be an unacceptable loss of face. It would also damage the ISAF position of working with the Afghan government against the Taliban while combatting narcotics (Sher

Mohammad was deeply involved with both the Taliban and narcotics). The appointment of Sher Mohammad would force to the surface the issue of whether the government–Taliban dichotomy was the correct way to understand the Helmandi conflict. Mangal realised this very early on, and played on it brilliantly, manipulating the British and Americans.[156] ISAF was blinded by Mangal playing up his institutional side.

President Karzai played an important role between Sher Mohammad, Mangal and ISAF. He regretted removing Sher Mohammad in 2005[157] and was incandescent with rage when Gordon Brown, the British prime minister, visited him and forcefully lobbied for Mangal forcefully, saying that he would pull British troops out of Afghanistan if Mangal were removed. 'Mangal is not your governor, he is ours', Brown reportedly said.[158] Sir Sherard Cowper-Coles also confirmed that Brown lobbied President Karzai several times, but suggested that it was Karzai who repeatedly pointed out that Mangal was Britain's governor, rather than Brown.

This continued for several years with Mangal reporting regularly to the British and Americans that he was desperately worried that Sher Mohammad would take over his position if he were sacked. The British were 'deeply concerned' that Sher Mohammad would come back to the province.[159] Karzai did keep Mangal in place, but detested the British, and the Americans, for the interference; he would have preferred Sher Mohammad to have been kept in post, not least because he was able to provide electoral support as part of Karzai's southern tribal coalition.[160] Karzai also detested Mangal for his closeness to the Americans and the British.[161] For his part, Sher Mohammad repeatedly organised schemes and protests in an attempt to unseat Mangal. While these overt politics continued, the foreigners missed the point that the Helmandis were making, namely that Mangal enjoyed a very poor reputation among local people.[162]

District-level politics were similarly complex. In Nad-e Ali, for example, fresh elections for the district council were held in 2010 to take advantage of the new areas that were now under government control (see Chapter 5). The disenfranchised communities living in the previous deserts surrounding Nad-e Ali in Bolan and the Bowri to the west were included in the electoral areas. This was a sensible move in terms of enfranchising the population, one of the aims of counterinsurgency. However, it incensed the population of 'central' Nad-e Ali who were 'legal' landholders with documents issued by Zahir Shah. They considered the desert dwellers as be-rasmiat (unofficial).

In the elections there were few changes in terms of who was elected. The two most notable changes were that Helmandwal, the nephew of Shah Nazar Khan, the erstwhile provincial governor, was removed from the Chair. He was replaced by Haji Barakzai (Kharoti), the nephew of Haji Jamalzai, the ex-Harakat commander from Noor Mohammad Khan Kalay. The space opened up by the death of Wakil Safar, and the arrest of his son Mirwais Khan, meant that different power centres in the Kharoti were able to rise to the fore.

The second change was that Pir Mohammad Sadat was voted out by his community in Naqilabad. Ostensibly, this was because, as the community said to the British, he was too close to the 'Taliban'. This manipulation was later shown to be untrue—he had tried to dominate the agricultural cooperative in the village over another candidate.[163] Overall the elections were seen by Nad-e Ali's population as having a positive outcome. This was especially true in respect of a Kharoti man who was elected to a government position of power within the district.

Finally, in July 2010, and twenty-six years after a similar Soviet announcement, ISAF declared that it would be withdrawing its forces by 2014.[164] As with the Soviets, they based their withdrawal plan on political reconciliation with the enemy (in this case, the Taliban), the growth of militias and increasing the competence of the army and the police. The militia programme was predicated on groups of roughly thirty men protecting their own villages from outside insurgents. This reflected the ISAF narrative that the Taliban were outsiders oppressing defenceless villagers. Yet the ISAF plan was inconsistent. They sought to strengthen the Afghan 'government', yet giving guns and training to people outside the 'government' would have the opposite effect. However, because of the high percentage of local 'Talibs', the programme has succeeded in reintegrating lots of previous daakhelee 'Taliban' fighters.

The Afghan Local Police (ALP) programme was first established in Helmand by British forces in January 2011.[165] The programme came after a long line of other militia programmes in Helmand.[166] Under law, the ALPs were to report to the district chief of police. They were recruited from the local communities and 'vetted' by the elders and the NDS. They would only operate in their local area. After a year, ALP soldiers would be encouraged to join the police, thus linking the communities to the police.[167] Many considered them analogous to the Najibullah militias (see Chapter 2).[168] However, ALPs are much smaller and more poorly armed. A more considered view is that they were very similar to the depaye militias under Zahir Shah (see Chapter 2)—in fact, in one case, the same group of people who had joined the Soviet-era depaye in Deh Adam Khan later became members of the ALP there.[169]

In the two main districts under British control (there were no ALPs in Lashkar Gah), ALP development was pursued differently, leading to different results and different problems. There were, however, two shared characteristics. First, there was a lack of British 'due diligence' in investigating exactly who it was who was forming these militias that they were arming. Secondly, the British sought militias on individual sites within each district in the hope that they would contribute to (separate) micro-gains in local security. The British did not consider how to divide the limited ALP establishment across the district in order to pursue a holistic security effect, in concert with the established Afghan army and police presence.[170] This meant that different groups of local elders (and different British officers) were competing for an ever-decreasing establishment.

In Nad-e Ali, the community council was strongly opposed to ALPs.[171] All of the members of the council voiced the same reason for this opposition, namely, that in such a heterogeneous district, once one community received permission to raise an ALP, everyone would want one, and then people would not be able to travel outside of their own villages and communities.[172] Habibullah, the district governor, could see that the British officers were keen on the scheme and so overruled the objections of the locals. He forced the programme through the district council by appealing to minority interests. For example, in Loy Bagh, an ALP commander from the minority Achakzai was empowered over the heads of the majority Noorzai: Habibullah had long had problems with Loy Bagh Noorzai figures such as Abdul Ahad Helmandwal and Mullahs Karim and Zakiri.[173] He reportedly said, 'if you don't get the men to do it, I will get them from somewhere else'. Habibullah eventually had to bring men from Musa Qala, where his brother was district governor.[174]

As a senior Noorzai tribal leader said to me, '[the ALP are] not with the support of the community'.[175] Officially, this is a prerequisite for the establishment of an ALP site. In the south of the district, both the Hazaras and the Ishaqzai were allowed to establish their own ALP militias, thus arming both sides in the long-running water dispute. The dispute's main protagonist on the Hazara side—Assadullah Karimi—was made the commander of the Hazara militia.[176] In Loy Mandah, the family of the district education director dominated the ALP; he was able to establish the ALP because his family had previously been targeted by another local family and the ALP offered his best form of defence.[177] In short, British ignorance of the dynamics allowed local politics to dominate the formation of the ALPs, rather than the ALPs serving to reinforce and strengthen the organisation of the Afghan government.

But it was not all bad: the ALP programme conceptually took the place of the reintegration programme. A large number of interviewees from across the social spectrum agreed that one of the main reasons that Nad-e Ali became more peaceful during 2011 was the rollout of the ALP programme. Many local 'Taliban' enrolled as militia fighters.[178] In addition, in those areas where the 'Taliban' were still active, deals were struck between the former insurgents and their now reintegrated brethren.[179] Yet there was a fundamental paradox in the British implementation of the policy. Communities that were 'known' to be linked to the Taliban were denied militias. Thus, on the advice of Habibullah, the Kharoti were not allowed to participate in the programme—the greatest historical 'supporters' of the Taliban in the district were not allowed an ALP. As Habibullah put it: 'they are all Taliban'. The manipulations continued.

Two prominent ex-Hizb Kharoti commanders explained wearily to me that they had seen this all before. The government did not trust them, otherwise they would have an ALP; the police still thought of them as Talibs.[180] Other communities joked that there was no point in having a Kharoti ALP and that the government might as well arm the Taliban.[181] But these were the same people who pointed out to me privately that the other ALPs were all former 'Taliban'. One Helmandi MP looked ruefully at the situation and wondered if it would spark the Kharoti to form their own militias for defence, much as they had done in 2007–8.[182]

The final result of the ALP programme in Nad-e Ali was that it allowed Abdul Rahman Jan to increase his control. Haji Lal Jan, his cousin, managed to present himself as the police officer in charge of the Nad-e Ali ALPs,[183] and the district chief of police, Haji Omar Jan, was a key acolyte of his. Haji Omar Jan's brother controlled all the militias in Marjeh. As Abdul Rahman said, 'all the [militias] are my people;

that is why there is security'. The ISAF narrative of bringing good governance in the wake of the rapacious warlords was somewhat contradicted by the fact that those same warlords regained security control through the ALP programme.

The development of the ALP militias was different in Nahr-e Saraj district. Immediately after the scheme was announced, US Special Forces converted their militias into ALPs, accepting the new labels (and funding). This meant that the previous militia commanders—Sarai Mama and Jan Mohammad—became the ALP commanders. Jan Mohammad also ran the militia that was guarding Camp Price and was the commander of the District Response Team, which was similar in concept to the original militias raised by the Special Forces.[184] Officially, they were part of the ALP programme. However, while the US continued to supplement their wages and supplies, in practice they were still considered Special Forces militias.[185] Jan Mohammad, for instance, used to visit the chief of police, as a subordinate commander should, but always turned up in US uniform to make an unsubtle point about who was in charge. 'Joining' the ALP was a rebranding exercise, like the many times before that the US Special Forces militias had been rebadged.[186]

Elsewhere, in Spin Masjid and Malgir, the militia commanders were largely ex-93rd Division. Many of them were also recent ex-Talibs, such as Lal Mohammad, who was a relative-by-marriage of Sur Gul, the Taliban district governor for Washir. Interestingly, the elders from the community only identified them as being appropriate for militia leadership late in the process, whereas they had originally said that there was no one who would be appropriate. Ostensibly, it took time for their confidence to be raised sufficiently for them to risk supporting the ALP programme. Secretly, the elders were managing their own reintegration process using the ALP programme. Lal Mohammad, for instance, had worked under Taliban, 93rd Division and ALP patronage networks by this point, with some of his side switching dictated by a land dispute with a Noorzai neighbour, Dad Gul.[187]

The ALP programme was entirely to Mir Wali's benefit, as he bragged to me when I met with him. He equated the security that existed during the tenure of the 93rd Division with the security that had been generated by the ALP militias. The programme recycled some of the security actors' armed interests away from the 'Taliban' and temporarily towards the 'government'. While beneficial for overall security, the provincial police hierarchy was solidly ex-communist by this time and they had problems exerting their control over the new militias that they were meant to command. From the point of view of the individual communities, the same actors were still wielding guns in their villages (Lal Mohammad being a case in point). It did not matter whether they were 'Taliban' or 'government'.[188]

The overall reaction to the ALP programme in Helmand was mixed. Many were concerned about the ability of the government to control the militias: 'the radio says that in Ghazni the [ALP] are going wild. So far in Nad-e Ali they are behaving, but that is because ISAF are here ... we will see.'[189] The injection of yet more weaponry into society was also not always viewed favourably.[190] Others stressed to me the importance of more training for the militias. This would make them more professional and accountable to the Afghan state.[191] Officially, the ALP programme had contributed to an increase in overall security where they were deployed, because they kept the 'Taliban' out of local communities. In reality, this was at the cost of paying many 'Talibs' not to fight (because they were members of the ALP).[192] The old warlords won the most out of the programme as they managed to get their men into the programme.[193] Many viewed the ALPs as a gamble on the part of ISAF, the consequences of which may well have to be dealt with by the Helmandis themselves at some stage in the future.[194]

Over the summer of 2012, the British started to look more closely at the ALP militias. They began a more intensive training and mentoring programme for them in an attempt to bind them to the Afghan 'government' and minimise the potential of them 'going wild'. There had been chronic problems with Afghan government pay for the individual militias and, upon the realisation that they were paying their enemies not to attack them, the British invested a great deal of effort to encourage the Afghan system to pay up.[195] Whether or not pay was the cause, some of the militias started to switch patron to the Taliban again, starting with Lal Mohammad in Torghai, who simply went back to working with Sur Gul, taking two men, a PKM machine gun, five Kalashnikovs and two motorbikes with him.[196] Another ALP militia later 'defected' in Musa Qala.[197] For this and other reasons the training and recruitment of new ALPs was halted nationwide in September 2012.[198]

The growth of ALP militias and the increased attention given to army and police training was part of a framework of transition to Afghan control. Lashkar Gah, which had in practice been controlled by the Afghan security forces for a number of years, was the first to 'transfer' officially in July 2011.[199] Most of Nad-e Ali had transferred by December of the same year. Nahr-e Saraj transferred lead security control in late 2012 and 2013.[200] Transition was a sign that the British forces that had generated such resistance over the previous five years were finally leaving, but many Helmandis were not sure if they could believe it.[201]

Many were convinced that the 'real' reason for the British presence was different to the stated one and assumed that this would be another trick. If the British did leave, it was assumed that the security forces (with the exception of the army) would splinter and dissolve back to their communities, pointing to the fact that ISAF patronage was the binding factor.[202] Others were convinced that there would be further inter-group warfare as they competed for water and poppy.[203] The most pessimistic suggested that the 'government would last an hour once the foreigners leave'.[204]

Alongside this primarily ISAF-driven withdrawal process, the Afghan government was also carrying out its own parallel political process by appointing local powerbrokers or their proxies into government positions (this is analogous to what happened in the Soviet era; see Chapter 2). For example, in the period between 2010 and 2012 they appointed relatives of Sher Mohammad as district chiefs of police in Kajaki, Washir and Baghran (Faisullah, Mirdel and Hayat Khan respectively).[205] Koka still remained in Musa Qala.[206] Sher Mohammad's brother, the erstwhile deputy provincial governor, Amir Mohammad, was made provincial governor of Uruzgan, a neighbouring province.[207] Interestingly, and mirroring this process, Abdul Rauf, a major Alizai Taliban commander, and originally Zakir's boss when both were in Rais Baghrani's 93rd Division in 1994, was appointed the Taliban governor for the same province.[208] Further west, Mir Wali's son, Hekmatullah, was appointed chief of police in Sangin. This was probably a stopgap on his way to becoming the Gereshk chief, a role that his father had lobbied hard for him to be appointed to.[209] Mir Wali denied this when I met him, indicating the peeling paint in his house as a sign of his poverty: 'there was no way I could afford the bribes', he said.

The Helmandi population have considered the changes wrought by ISAF and government plans. They are wary of the future, as the past has taught them to be. During 2012, the tribal leaderships in Helmand began to invite their members to a series of tribal shuras. These were a repeat of those shuras held in 1992 and 2002, when the communist and Taliban governments were overthrown. The format was similar. Members from both 'sides' (in this case the 'Taliban' and the 'government') sat down together and reaffirmed that they were all Noorzai, or Barakzai, or Kharoti, or Alakozai, and that they should work together. In many cases this reached an impressive level of complexity, with the shuras opening offices in Lashkar Gah and Kabul, and producing manifestos with positions on such things as women's rights, relations with other tribes and, most importantly, positions on reconciling 'Talibs'. The shuras were a formalisation of a time-honoured process: individuals subsuming themselves within the mass of the tribe in an uncertain future.[210]

## The Helmandi Conclusion: The British are Working With the Taliban

I consider the narrative outlined below a key result of the process that I have outlined in this book: namely that outsiders do not sufficiently understand the conflict in Helmand to stop themselves being manipulated. It demonstrates that the British view of the conflict (and therefore their actions) was so far removed from the Hemandi understanding that Helmandis considered them to be trying to destroy the province through an alliance with the Taliban, rather than their purported aim of reconstruction. This section explains the Helmandi conclusion to the post-2006 conflict.

Elsewhere in Afghanistan there are well-established narratives about ISAF, and particularly the Americans, supplying the Taliban. According to these narratives, two main mechanisms are involved in this process, the first of which is American sponsorship of ISI, which in turn supports the Taliban. The second concerns the profligacy associated with the indigenous supply contracts that are used to supply ISAF bases.[211] In Helmand, the rumours take on a different angle: that the British are supporting the Taliban and the US is fighting the Taliban. At its most extreme, this leads some to claim that a proxy conflict between America and Britain is taking place in Helmand. I have found these views to be widely held across a large section of Helmandi society, from Helmandi senators[212] to educated tribal leaders who have often dealt with the British,[213] to senior members of the Afghan police and army who are working with the British.[214] The overwhelming majority of Helmandis that I asked strongly believe this to be true.[215]

One of the most profound moments I experienced during the research for this book occurred in London, when interviewing a member of the Helmandi diaspora. He explained to me that when he first heard the 'rumours' he considered them true. Furthermore, the rumour threatened to unseat his identity as a Helmandi refugee, who had been living happily, prosperously and legally in the UK for some years. He could not countenance one of his countries purposefully destroying the other, and set out to investigate the matter himself. He found no 'evidence' in Helmand that would lead him to believe that the British were *not* working with the Taliban. Only the internal UK debate conducted in the media, involving images such as the corteges moving through Royal Wootton Bassett, allayed his fears. Of course, the majority of Helmandis have no access to that debate.[216]

The belief gained currency in Helmand in mid-2009, at the same time as the US began to increase their presence in the province. It partly replaced the earlier belief that the British had only come to Helmand for revenge, although the ideas co-exist to some degree.[217] The core of the narrative is that the US fight the Taliban more aggressively than the British, and by extension they must be more 'serious' about the Taliban than the British.[218] This is reflected by Taliban commanders who comment on the fondness of British troops for talking rather than fighting.[219] The British would be able to rebut these accusations. To them, the conflict was an insurgency, and so politics rather than force should be at the forefront; when the US arrived they had vast resources concentrated in a small area and so were able to do much more; and, privately, the British would point to the 'gung-ho' attitude of American troops.[220] In line with the ISAF narrative, the British were using 'courageous restraint' to protect the population.[221]

However, the basis of the rumour created by the arrival of the US troops was much further back in history. Here, I discuss historical factors that have led to the Helmandis interpreting the mismatched ISAF and Helmandi understandings as evidence for the British working with the Taliban. In the discussion below, when I use the word Taliban, I am referring to what the Helmandis would call aslee, or real, Taliban—that is, those members of the Taliban with close links to the Quetta Shura leadership involving funding and direction. For the Helmandis, it is considered obvious that the Quetta Shura Taliban are controlled and directed by the ISI.[222]

Primarily, this belief has as its basis a profound hatred of the Angrez. This is one of the most common Helmandi narratives. Jean Mackenzie, an intrepid American journalist who worked for the respected Institute for War and Peace Reporting training Helmandi journalists in Lashkar Gah from 2006 to 2008, put it thus:

In Afghanistan, word of mouth is everything, and Helmandis appear to have a deep, visceral aversion toward the British that defies rational explanation. The constant and abiding rumors [sic] that the British are supporting the Taliban with funds and weapons stem, most likely, from this deep well of historical hatred.[223]

I, too, can attest to this from personal experience when I spent time in Kabul socialising with Helmandis that I know well. I felt deeply humbled when I experienced the strength of the antipathy reserved for the Angrez. Mackenzie is right, but it is only the foundation.

Many Helmandis currently hold the belief that the British never gave up colonial control of Pakistan after the partition of British India in 1947. To them, it was a charade, designed to mask British power in the region. 'Why would they voluntarily give up power?' they ask rhetorically. This is irrefutable proof that the British control the ISI and the ISI control the Taliban. I was not able to discern whether this belief was strongly held at the time of partition, or whether it has been unconsciously created or reinforced by recent events.

Moreover, the Pakistani army is modelled on the British army; in fact, the Pakistani state has changed little since the British left. To Helmandis, it is also well known that Britain gives aid to Pakistan, which frees up Pakistani state spending to be cycled to the Taliban, which comes back across the border in the form of lethal aid.[224] In this, the Helmandis are factually correct. The Americans have largely escaped similar accusations in Helmand, presumably because of the 'deep well of historical hatred' that springs directly from the Afghan experience of British imperialism.

More recently, the Helmandis have been brutalised by thirty-five years of war, during which their own government paid them to kill each other on a large scale (see Chapter 2). This has led to a gradual breakdown of even the most basic trust, with one man stating pathetically to me that, 'I don't know who my friends are, and haven't for years.'[225] From the Helmandi perspective, this was followed by a period where the US spoke with the highest of ideals about rebuilding Afghanistan, only to beat people to death in custody, send children to Guantanamo and allow some of the most despicable people in Helmandi society to rise to the top through their sponsorship and ignorance. Then came the British intervention, where the rhetoric of development did not match the reality of violence.

In alleging British collusion in supporting the Taliban, Helmandis specifically point to the deal in Musa Qala between the British, the elders and the 'Taliban'. This was followed shortly after by the arrest of Michael Semple for talking to the Taliban and organising training camps for them.[226] As Hafizullah Khan put it, 'How could Semple work safely all over Helmand? And now he lives in Pakistan.' Soon the rumours were well established and had reached President Karzai. He claimed that unidentified foreign helicopters (reportedly British) had been transporting Taliban fighters from Helmand to the north of Afghanistan.

The 'helicopter' rumours were the first of the rumours to reach the international press.[227] The reports were reflective of underlying feelings, as well as serving as the basis for further rumours. They were also exploited by the Iranians and the Pakistanis. The Iranians quoted 'unnamed' diplomats saying that British helicopters were involved. They also alleged that the British had executed one of their Afghan interpreters who was knowledgeable about the operation.[228] The ISI played a much subtler game, telling the Taliban commanders they supplied that the money and weapons originally came from the British.[229]

Others realised that this was a profitable narrative that could deflect attention away from their own inadequacies. Mullah Salam, the reconciled district governor of Musa Qala, stated that the British had been moving Taliban around Musa Qala in helicopters because they were seeking revenge for Maiwand and were interested in the mineral riches of the province.[230] As Jabbar Qahraman (who does not believe the rumours) said, 'of course it is a lie … but it is a useful lie … even Karzai believes it!' The rumours were helped by the Helmandi perception that British rhetoric did not match the reality of their intervention in the province.

Events and dynamics that could be put down to British ignorance were attributed to Angrez perfidy. The Haji Gul Ehktiar story discussed in Chapter 5 is illustrative of this. Only long after the British began paying rent to Gul Ehktiar did they realise that the money was finding its way into armaments that were killing its soldiers. During this period, Sur Gul, Ehktiar's Talib nephew, had been bragging in his village that he had received the money from the British![231]

Everyone I spoke to had a story—usually an eyewitness story. A twenty-something Noorzai tribesman in Nad-e Ali, who has some friends fighting the British, told me that he himself had seen British troops dropping an ISO container full of supplies in Marjeh. Later, a

Talib friend of his had shown him a mobile phone video depicting a weapons cache full of 'British' weapons that had been given to the Taliban.[232] In another example, there was a set of ISI 'Punjabi' operatives in Nad-e Ali conducting a resupply of some Taliban fighting groups in broad daylight. While this was going on, there were British helicopters overhead, but nothing was done.[233]

Hafizullah Khan told me that 'a friend' had seen the British occupy a compound. Shortly after, they vacated it, leaving it full of ammunition for the Taliban. A Helmandi senator insisted that he had seen the Taliban passing by British vehicles and did not understand why they did not fire.[234] An elder claimed that a Talib had shown him a video of British officers talking with Taliban commanders, offering them $200,000 if they would not attack. The Talib then asked for $3,000 for the video; the elder tried to broker a deal with 'Channel 4' for them to buy the video but they refused saying it was 'too dangerous'.[235] There are many more examples.

Of course, not everyone believes these stories.[236] Jabbar Qahraman snorted when I asked him about it. Sher Mohammad, Mir Wali and Abdul Rahman all affirmed that it was ridiculous, which is interesting when contextualised in light of their 'Taliban' links: their double-dealing has probably contributed to the Helmandi understanding of how people with lots of power act. Habibullah Khan, who has worked with British troops for the last four years, also thinks it is untrue. But they can all understand why the majority of Helmandis believe this narrative. 'It is like a white and a black man walking together' said Abdul Rahman, talking of the fact that both ISAF and Taliban supplies come through Pakistan.

These powerful Helmandis can understand how international and British actions could be misconstrued by the populace. But they are also more aware of the potential for incompetence of international forces. They do not suffer so much from the 'man on the moon' effect, whereby incredulity follows from the world's most powerful nations being unable to defeat a 'couple of Talibs'.[237] Even President Karzai used to say to Sir Sherard Cowper-Coles, the British ambassador, 'surely you could have solved this by now?'[238]

What those individuals who do follow the narrative are doing is reinterpreting 'evidence' in light of their understanding of the strategic environment. This eventually snowballs as evidence is found, based on the original assumptions, which then becomes proof for the original assumption, and so on. For the many that do subscribe to the narrative, it is strong: a man in Nawa recounted to me how the police in Babaji had driven some distance to hand their Taliban prisoners over to the Americans rather than to the British, who they felt would immediately free them.[239]

Helmandis have a developed reasoning as to why the British would support the Taliban at the same time that they are deploying troops to 'fight' said Taliban. An educated mullah who worked for the Taliban government was convinced that the British and the ISI wanted an 'Islamic civil war' in Afghanistan, so that Islam in Afghanistan was 'weak'. 'They think that if there is an alliance between groups in Afghanistan then there will be bombs in London'.[240] A degree-educated Helmandi gentleman tried to explain to me very patiently that this stemmed from history and the desire of the British to avenge their previous defeats in Afghanistan, against the will of the US. This was leading to a civil war 'within NATO', with the British wanting NATO to break up. With Afghanistan weak, the British could re-establish their empire. I submitted that the British public were unlikely to stand for such deceit with the casualties and costs that it would entail. He responded that the British public were in on it and that they saw it as a reasonable cost of the war against NATO, if they could regain the empire.[241]

There are still parts of this narrative that need explanation. For example, why do the Afghan security forces continue to work with their British mentors? Two interviewees pointed to the fact that the war in Helmand was between roshan-fikran (progressives) and Taliban—if the roshan-fikran did not accept the help of the British then the Taliban would win. The police and army hated it, but had little choice.[242] But the strongest paradox is this: if, as I have argued extensively, the 'Taliban' are part of Helmandi society, rather than an external organisation trying to impose itself, then surely the population would know that the British were not supplying the Taliban (because the Taliban and the 'Taliban' are closely linked)?

It is hard to answer. Some 'Taliban' commanders even believe that there is a deal with British forces and are rather piqued when the British break 'the deal' and attack them.[243] In an extreme case, a 'Talib' had been given a claims card (to allow him to claim money from the British for damage to his house). He believed, and boasted to his 'Talib' friends, that as the card allowed him to enter the British base and have conversations about money, he was being recruited by the British.

(How poor must the interpreters have been in those interactions?) Later on, his house was searched by very polite British troops (new counterinsurgency doctrine: the population are the prize), who failed to find his Kalashnikov. This reinforced his belief. He now believed that he was an agent: the British would soon be along to de-brief him. Shortly after, British Special Forces killed him, whilst he still believed that he was working for them. His group of fighters then interpreted their friend's death as a US strike, against a British asset.[244]

I am unable to fully explain the paradox that I identified above. I think that the difference comes down to perspective. To Helmandis, when they use the word Taliban, they mean aslee (real) Taliban—those with substantive links to the Quetta Shura and/or the ISI. For aslee Taliban, spreading the narrative that the British are supplying them is part of their job, because it marginalises their enemy and erodes the links between British and Afghan government forces. So, an aslee Talib who is in charge of a delgai will tell his local fighters that the British are working with them in the knowledge that this will get out into the society. This was made worse by the British telling elders about their military operations in order to reduce fighting, in the knowledge that it would get back to the Taliban.[245]

For their sake, individual 'Talibs' feel rather pleased with themselves that they are using 'British' weaponry and ammunition against British soldiers.[246] It is a variation on the apocryphal Afghan saying: that they are going to use the Pakistanis [the Taliban] to get rid of the Americans, and then they are going to deal with the Pakistanis. Are they 'using' the British and the Pakistanis to fight the roshan-fikran, the Americans and the British themselves, before moving onto the Pakistanis? This issue, more than any other in this book, makes me think of what one of the interviewees most aptly stated: 'most people who think about Helmand develop mental problems, because the politics are so strange and complicated'.[247]

# CONCLUSION

Our main difficulty is with ourselves ... no Afghan regime or
political party will ever be very much different from the Afghan
society to which they belong.

Zahir Shah[1]

If men define situations as real, they are real in their consequences.

William Thomas[2]

This book set out to tell the Helmandi story of the last thirty-five years
of their conflict. Through this, it sought to demonstrate that outsiders
have never really understood the conflict in the way that Helmandis
have. Finally, in intervening without the required knowledge of local
politics, outsiders have made the conflict worse. This is as true for the
Soviets and the Americans as it is for the British, the Pakistanis and the
mujahidin parties; to a lesser degree it is also true for the Taliban leadership, particularly once they were geographically removed to Quetta
in Pakistan after 2001.

In the Introduction I outlined three broad eras in the conflict that I
define as a continuing civil war: that of maximum Soviet influence
(1978–89), that of dominant Pakistani influence (1989–2001) and that
of Western influence (2001–12). Each of these eras has had its own
'official narratives'. For the most recent Western phase, I termed this
the 'insurgency narrative'.

In all three eras, Helmandi actors and factions have exploited the
lack of detailed knowledge of Helmandi politics (and doggedness in

233

sticking to their own official narratives) displayed by outsiders, to manipulate them into funding their continuing conflict. The degree to which the US, the British, the Soviets and to a lesser degree the Pakistanis have had their aims in Helmand province thwarted is testament to the strength and opacity of these local dynamics. In what future historians may consider a grand irony, the 2009 ISAF counterinsurgency surge—an attempt to redefine the momentum of the war—did just the opposite and strengthened the primacy of Helmandi politics in driving the conflict.

This book presents an idiosyncratic viewpoint that is not often articulated.[3] But it is not in any way exceptional. It is simply based upon sitting down with people over the course of a few years, and attempting to understand them over a cup of tea, in their own language. Nor is this book conclusive, and it should be considered as no more than a first step: to repeat what a Helmandi I knew well said to me, 'Mike-sahib, you know a lot [about Helmand], but it is about one per cent [of what is going on]'.

### Why was there a Failure to Understand the Conflict?

The merits of the Western intervention in Afghanistan will be debated for some time. An important question that may occur to readers is why America and Britain were unable to understand what was occurring in front of them in such a 'medieval society'.[4] How did they fail to understand the Helmandis' conflict? Why did they stick to the 'insurgency narrative' so single-mindedly? How were they manipulated so easily by so many people, most of whom were illiterate? At risk of being a victim of my own experience, this can only be attributed to one thing: language. Edward Said articulated it well when he described in 1978:

...the most current transformation overtaking Orientalism: its conversion from a fundamentally philological discipline and a vaguely general apprehension of the Orient into a social science speciality. No longer does the Orientalist try first to master the esoteric languages of the Orient; he begins instead as a trained social scientist and "applies" his science to the Orient, or anywhere else.[5]

To 'social scientist', I might add intelligence analyst, Human Terrain Team member,[6] spy, diplomat, agent handler, development expert, academic, military officer and journalist—almost all of whom do not speak Pushtu or Dari. The vast majority of the interface between foreigners and Helmandis is managed by interpreters: either diasporic Afghans or young Kabuli men who speak English (often Tajiks or Hazaras). Neither of these would necessarily have the appropriate skills or knowledge to understand Helmandi society. More importantly, even if they did understand it, they are being paid by the foreigners who utilise their skillset, thus they have no incentive to challenge the understanding that their 'master' has of his environment. In the case of the young Kabuli, he does not want, for example, to take the risk of not being able to support a large family network with his salary.

Both British and American militaries have trained some linguists to appropriate standards. I was one of them. But these tended to go into specialist 'understanding' roles, rather than as decision makers, and there were simply not enough of them to sway the 'insurgency narrative' of the conflict. This is where it could be argued that the Soviets understood slightly better what was occurring in Helmand, allowing them to, for example, manipulate the groups in northern Helmand. They had previously trained Afghan officers in Russian, and had the benefit of two-year tours (rather than six months in the case of the British Army). There were also some Soviet Tajiks in their army (Tajik and Dari are dialects of the same language). Further, Soviet officers and advisors would live out in Lashkar Gah and dine regularly with their Afghan counterparts.[7] This would be impossible under the security arrangements in place currently in Afghanistan for Western officials.[8] That said however, even Soviet advisors were considered 'simple-hearted and naive. Not knowing the situation in the country, they listen[ed] first and foremost to their own advisees'.[9] This echoes the feelings that I saw some Afghan mentees privately reserve for the Western 'mentors' they were assigned in Helmand.

But worse, the 'insurgency narrative' was not even internally consistent: when reading Rajiv Chandrasekaran's *Little America* or Bob Woodward's *Obama's Wars*, which describe the US strategic decision-making processes in some detail, one is struck by how basic incoherencies in the official narrative arise, are not resolved, and are instead obscured by machinations internal to the US government. The obvious example is why, under a counterinsurgency strategy to protect the population, they sent a third of their force to an area (Helmand) with 4 per cent of the population.[10] These understandings lead me to conclude that the intervention in Afghanistan was not as important as Western leaders stated in their public pronouncements. If it were really important, perhaps threatening national survival, then arguably Western countries would have made an even bigger effort to understand the local politics of the conflict in Helmand (and Afghanistan).

This further extends to operations in Helmand. For example, one might ask whether Western militaries 'bent themselves out of shape' to achieve success there. There is evidence that they did to a degree; for example, increasing the number of troops trained in reconstruction and development, or increasing the number of Pushtu linguists.[11] However, changes in structure to the militaries, and here I talk of the British military, were not made. The British army deploys to Helmand on six-monthly rotations, which vastly reduce the level of understanding that it is possible to acquire. Furthermore, personnel enjoy a two-week leave period during those rotations. In Northern Ireland, a country where the British Army understood the language, there were two-year rotations. In British India, to take the most extreme example, political officers used to do ten-year tours!

This issue is linked to the fact that neither US nor British troops went to (specifically) Helmand for their stated reasons. As outlined by Professor Michael Clarke, the selection of Helmand for the British was an internal NATO process with other members of the alliance.[12] This is perhaps why the British (mistakenly?) deployed to an area of such historical significance. Unfortunately, the Helmandis were not privy to these discussions, and so attributed the most obvious reason they could see to the British actions: revenge.

Similarly, the US Marine Corps chose Helmand not because that was where troops needed to be deployed to best prosecute the war, but where there was an acceptance for their deployment from their British allies (as opposed to their Canadian allies who did not want them in Kandahar) and a degree of wanting to demonstrate what the Marines could do vis-à-vis other parts of the US military.[13] Both of these moves were dictated by the internal machinations of Britain, the US and NATO, and did not match the official narratives of the conflict. In both these cases, the Helmandis could sense the discord between what the British said and what they did: this contributed to the 'conspiracy' rumours discussed above.

It is worth asking why the 'insurgency narrative' understanding of the conflict did not become supplanted with a more nuanced narrative developed from an understanding of the Helmandi politics. There appears to have been a degree of self-perpetuation of the official narratives, even in the face of widespread doubt over the course of the war expressed in the (British) media. This can partly be explained by the same reasons that media narratives become self-perpetuating the world over; for example, the use of specific terms to communicate assumed concepts ('Taliban' for example) or very poor media access to the conflict zone.

However, I believe there is another reason associated with interventions like the British and American interventions in Helmand. ISAF intelligence reporting, particularly that from human intelligence, relies on a Western person to interpret the evidence (and ask the questions). An interview (...*inter view*) is constructed between two people and so, to some degree, one gets answers to the questions that one asks. It is reasonable to assume that if intelligence personnel have the 'insurgency narrative' of the conflict in their head when they are asking the questions, they are more likely than not to receive answers that reflect those questions, hence reinforcing their original premise. This hypothesis would be further compounded by denunciations: the 'source' will frame his denunciation of a local enemy in the appropriate official narrative. Of course, I also accept that the same trap may have befallen me, only with a different understanding of the conflict in my head.

This mode of intelligence gathering, and the associated analysis that goes with it, represents a good example of cognitive closure, where one seeks to remove ambiguities in the environment by applying templates to simplify understanding and 'close' the issue.[14] Cognitive closure of this sort would be made doubly worse by the reliance on interpreters to interact with Helmandis. That this may have continued even during the surge, with, one assumes, an associated increase in intelligence assets, brings into question the degree to which the intelligence effort in Helmand was dominated by the official understandings of the conflict.

Even outside of specific intelligence interactions, I witnessed a theme of Afghan interlocutors telling their Western 'counterparts' what they wanted to hear. This is what another advisor that I worked with termed 'ISAF theatre' (theatre for ISAF). This could be for purposes of manipulation in the case of Afghan government officials, or in the case of the villager, simply that they do not know what to say to the foreigner because what he is saying so strikingly clashes with their worldview. Many times I have asked questions of Helmandis (both in and out of uniform) and received the reply, 'what do you want me to say?' usually accompanied by a confused look. It then takes some time to explain to them that I am after *their* narratives and stories, rather than repetition of *others'* narratives. For a time, Western forces ran to the mantra of 'Ask an Afghan!' when they were confused about which particular course of action to take. This was a laudable improvement on the largely military approach taken previously. However, it unfortunately resulted in the reflection of their own narratives back at them, but strengthened because the Afghans 'told them so'.

I believe that the psychology of Western actors on the ground in Afghanistan and Helmand merits its own special study, and I can only hope to relate a few observations here. The particular issue that I would like to explore is what appeared to be a huge example of self-deception by many foreigners working in Helmand. In most cases they could see that there was a discordance between the official narratives of the war and what they saw in front of them. They, unfortunately, did not have the luxury of speaking Pushtu, or the indulgence of unlimited time to explore this discordance (as I did), yet they appeared to collectively self-deceive over what they were seeing before them.

Sir Sherard Cowper-Coles, the UK ambassador to Afghanistan and then the UK Senior Representative to Afghanistan and Pakistan (both during the ISAF period), very honestly put it thus: 'I was guilty of [self-deception] too … I lived the lie … it [the job] was fun … I allowed myself to be self-deceived'. He continued, 'it was fun for many others who came out as well … officers [gained] lots of experience … obviously this wouldn't work if we were conscripting middle-class kids [as soldiers, because they have more of a voice in society]'. I fully subscribe to Sir Sherard's description as representing my self-deception when I was serving in Helmand as a British Army officer.

This was exacerbated yet further by the fact that many of the British or American officers had to look their men in the eyes before going out on patrol with them, and holding the ambiguity and juxtaposed understandings in their heads was not conducive to motivating their men (of course, officers have faced this challenge since the beginning of time). This, for me, was made clear after discussing the conflict several times with one commanding officer of a British battle group in Helmand. He was so articulate about the 'insurgency narrative' of the war and argued it so convincingly, that I was convinced that he believed it. I think, at the time, he did. (I was working as an advisor, out of uniform, at the time; part of my job was to conceptualise the war with senior British officers, so I do not think he was deliberately lying to me.) However, when I met him some time later, he looked rather sheepish when discussing his previous views; I believe he had convinced himself.

This issue and the bending-out-of-shape issue above should be considered together. I think there is a case to be made that the Helmandis were able to sense our lack of resolve (in some cases before we ourselves sensed it) and that it contributed to them thinking that ISAF was there for nefarious reasons, or that they were supporting the Taliban. Many times when discussing those rumours with Helmandis, they would point out that we could solve the conflict if we, for example, sealed the border. That we weren't carrying out measures like these was evidence of our perfidy. Apart from their thoughts relating to our nefariousness they were being perfectly sensible: we were, however, more ignorant (and more stretched) than they could have imagined.

More broadly, there were issues with Western positioning that led to them adopting the narratives that they did. ISAF was set up to support the Afghan government. That was its mandate. Psychologically, the easiest way for ISAF, or individuals therein, to process the idea that the 'organisation' (that is, the Afghan government) that they were supporting was not an organisation, but a fluid franchise construct, was to categorise, for example, a 'policeman' who did not fit their idea of how policemen should act (that is, they were drug dealers) as an aberration, rather than a common example of what 'policemen' were actually like in Helmand. We often used to joke that the trick in Helmand was to find the 'policeman' who wasn't corrupt.

So too with our understanding of the 'Taliban'. (For example, the 'Taliban' commander who, under the leadership of his elders, ISAF knew to be protecting his community.) ISAF could only support the 'government' and fight the 'Taliban' when they treated these two examples as aberrations, and focused on the organisations themselves as worthy of supporting or defeating (respectively). But this book has shown that these aberrations *are* the dynamics: they are central, not peripheral. ISAF was not set up in a way that could understand that, as it was sent there with a mandate to support the government. As a senior UK official said to me, 'we had to support [the governor] … because he was the governor'.

It was easier psychologically to go along with the official narratives, because truly understanding the Helmandi viewpoint, as discussed in this book, would remove their own raison d'être for being in Afghanistan—I term this the self-psychological security argument. This would be like the British Army accepting that it was fighting a resistance movement that was facilitated by outside funding—they are not in the business of colonialism or occupation anymore and so, logically, upon accepting the resistance narrative they should leave Helmand. Our own identity has stopped us properly understanding what is going on in Helmand.

This was recognised by some Soviets as well. Artyom Borovik, an exceptionally perceptive observer of the Soviet intervention in Afghanistan, wrote that, 'we bombed not only the detachments of rebels and their caravans, but our own ideals as well'.[15] The Helmandi police officers who (metaphorically) closed their eyes when it became clear that they had killed some farmers defending their livelihood from eradication makes another powerful example (see Chapter 6).

Finally, there is an element of those not wishing to cross the Rubicon in their descriptions of Afghanistan. I personally know several well-known (Western) scholars and 'independent' organisations who limit what they say about the Pakistani, Iranian and Afghan governments' perfidy in the conflict, for fear of (violent) retribution (they have offices in Kabul, or wish to continue working there in the future). The media too, have great difficulty travelling in, and investigating, Helmand and Afghanistan. They often rely on 'embeds' with western militaries, which significantly limits their ability to hold truth to power. Even though the media does criticise the war, the criticism often falls within the terms of the debate set out in the UK; it rarely fundamentally reassesses the lenses through which we view the conflict.

## The Consequences of Failing to Understand the Conflict

Such is the discordance between the two understandings; it is as if ISAF and the Helmandi population have been fighting different conflicts. If one considers violence in war to be a means of communication, then there has been very little deliberate communication of intent that hit home between ISAF, the Afghan government, the Taliban and the Helmandis. 'Conspiracy' theories grow from these non-meeting narratives. The rumours that ISAF was working with the Taliban should have been a warning sign that there was something wrong with how the conflict was being interpreted and understood. At the time, it was dismissed as a conspiracy theory that did not fit the official narratives, rather than being understood as something of essence, simply because that was how the Helmandis defined their situation.

These non-meeting narratives are no better exemplified than by a shura that I attended in Lashkar Gah in 2011, between a senior ISAF general, Provincial Governor Mangal and 300 Alizai elders from northern Helmand. The advertised aim was that the elders would get a chance to air their concerns with the government and with ISAF as a prelude to closer cooperation. The experience of the shura, where I was sitting with the elders, was very different.

After the introductory prayers, a series of senior Alizai leaders were invited to represent the 'Alizai' concerns. As is the case in a segmentary tribal society, many of the concerns were parochial, concerning particular roads or projects. But, there was a thread running through all of their comments: water. The karezes (underground water channels) in northern Helmand have been desiccating for twenty years (whether due to global warming, population stress or not enough maintenance due to conflict is unknown). This has caused the large-scale migration to central and southern Helmand documented throughout this book.

According to the elders, there was a plan for a Zamindawar canal (as the Alizai call northern Helmand), drawn up at the same time as the other canal projects during the 1950s–70s. One of the elders went so far as to say that building a canal, with the associated employment, would permanently occupy half the young men (fighters) in northern Helmand. The overall story was one of Alizai disenfranchisement over the development works of the middle of the last century.[16]

After several elders had expressed the same sentiments, Governor Mangal began to speak. To most in the room, it was clear that his speech was not directed towards the elders, but to the senior ISAF general. He did briefly mention the Zamindawar canal, but only to say that it was a big project and that it would have to be looked at. 'It was', he said, 'linked to cooperation with the population and security being sufficient that work might start', thus putting the onus on the elders. To be completely fair to him, this is acceptable behaviour for a politician, even if it did make the elders feel that their concerns had not been heard.

'However', he continued, 'the road to Kajaki from Sangin is being built as we speak, and this is being done so that the turbine for the Kajaki dam can be fitted, thus bringing electricity to Kandahar'. He then began to berate them, pointing out that they should be helping the foreigners fit the turbine, not shooting them. Of course, the Kajaki dam refurbishment was a major ISAF objective, and so Mangal knew that he should at least nod to it in the presence of the ISAF general. The turbine issue, however, occupied three-quarters of his speech. As we spoke, there was some murmuring amongst the elders that he was not listening to them.

Next, the senior ISAF general spoke through an interpreter. 'I am often asked why we are here', he began. 'I will tell you. There is a city called New York ...' and he then went on to describe the attacks of the 11 September 2001. 'Terrorists', he continued, 'over the last thirty years, Afghanistan has been plagued by terrorists [that is, the mujahidin, who had been supported by the US] ... and I am here to clean the terrorists from Afghanistan'. By this point the elders who I was sitting with were in open disbelief. The elders were mostly ex-mujahidin, and so were the terrorists that the general spoke of. *Surely he didn't just say that?*

I turned to the man next to me, an old greybeard from Now Zad, and asked him what he thought of what the general had just said. The man was laughing so much, so ridiculous was the opening gambit of the general's speech, that he had difficulty in stuttering a reply: 'this man does not understand our problems at all'. We turned back to the speech. The general was saying that he took advice closely from Alizai elders, and they had told him that he needed to build the road to Kajaki and upgrade the turbines at the dam. He then discussed the government-Taliban conflict. 'The Taliban are losing', he concluded.

There are so many extra layers of meaning behind the events of that day, well beyond the obvious discordance of narratives between ISAF, the Afghan government and the Alizai elders. These layers demonstrate well the consequences of having an incorrect conceptual understanding of the conflict in which you are engaged. This story is almost infinitely complex and I myself do not understand all of the extra layers of meaning in this case. I describe some of them in the following paragraph to illustrate the complexity.

Thus, I had recently met the Alizai elders from whom the general took advice: a laudable action in counterinsurgency where you must work *with* and *for* the people. Those elders—unbeknownst to the general—were all relatives or close associates of Sher Mohammad Akhundzada, and were deliberately placed as the general's advisors. Sher Mohammad was therefore advising ISAF to head to Kajaki in force (through his relatives), but the elders may have been simply reflecting ISAF preferences back to them. However, he was also working with the Iranians to destabilise the area. Finally, the Alizai (whom Sher Mohammad claims to represent) also want a canal, and are locked in a zero-sum battle with the Iranians—any water that goes down the Zamindawar canal is water that is not flowing into the Sistani region of Iran.

This milieu of actors playing each other demonstrates that if you attempt to place a simplistic framework over events, as the general did, you risk appearing irrelevant or stupid. As we were leaving the shura, I was talking with some ISAF colonels, who were deeply fed up with 'another f— canal', because that is 'all they keep asking for'. When there is no communication that actually hits home, frustrations abound on all sides. This seems like an extreme depiction, but it is an echo of many such events that I have had the privilege to observe over those four years.

The major aspects of the ISAF strategy were predicated on their understanding of the conflict: that the Taliban movement was relatively cohesive, so too the Afghan government. Most importantly, these assumptions defined the type of interventions that Western countries had in Afghanistan. Thus, the West fought a counterinsurgency in support of the Afghan government (whether or not they did in the early stages is another matter). Moreover, because the Afghan government was legitimate, the Taliban were the enemy, who by definition were illegitimate.

If that assumption is shown to be just that, an assumption, ISAF should not be supporting the 'government', as they are not a cohesive organisation to support. Equally they cannot fight the 'Taliban', because they are also only a shifting, patronage-based franchise 'organisation'. This is what Emile Simpson terms 'political musical chairs' in his apposite book *War From the Ground Up*.[17] Taking this idea further, it can be argued that ISAF could have intervened in a peacekeeping-type role between the 'government(s)' and the 'opposition(s)'. Unfortunately, in conforming to their official narratives, they ended up supporting individuals and groups who made up the 'government', who were no better than the groups who made up the 'Taliban'. In many instances the 'government' acted worse towards civilians because they had the West behind them.

As a concept or strategy, counterinsurgency as practiced by NATO in Afghanistan has three broad thrusts: protect the population, improve governance, and develop the country. All of these are also predicated on the assumptions outlined above. Looking at it from the Helmandi perspective, the population might well ask, 'how can you protect us from ourselves when we are resisting you?' This idea was recognised during the Soviet era as well.[18] Neither the Soviets nor ISAF had conceptual space in their doctrines for large sections of the population resisting them, so instead they were painted as Maoist-style insurgents from outside who were terrorising the community.

Moreover, improving governance becomes a nonsensical task when the individuals or groups in the government are using ISAF to prosecute their own micro-conflicts. Lastly, development: authors such as Stuart Gordon have published extensive scholarship showing that development funds in Helmand actually increase factionalisation and conflict and lower the legitimacy of ISAF and the Afghan government, because they are so misappropriated and are viewed by the population as another part of Helmandi patronage politics.[19] This is all because Westerners do not understand the conflict and are continually manipulated by the Helmandis.

This was true in almost every aspect of the ISAF concept of counterinsurgency. Take, for example, the Special Forces targeting strategy. It sought to degrade the Taliban's leadership; but a super-decentralised, patronage-based organisation is not vulnerable to any sort of decapitation strategy.[20] The importance of the social context of the 'Taliban' was also largely overlooked by ISAF. Most commanders killed were replaced by their closest male relative because which family was operating in which area (lineage-wise) was critical.

The Taliban were mostly from the population, and in many cases ISAF killed people who were defending the population from ISAF or the police, making them instant heroes. Furthermore, the killing of 'Taliban' commanders who joined because of, for example, issues with the police was inelegant: their brothers who replaced them were sworn to avenge them, rather than fighting for political reasons. This targeting strategy may have removed hope for the reintegration of those families or clans into the government, especially whilst ISAF remains in the country. These are the reasons why the targeting strategy has had little effect on the 'Taliban'.[21]

Furthermore, British and American forces found a natural propensity for doing big 'sweep' operations, much like the Soviets. Often, these were done with the reported aim of 'demonstrat[ing] ISAF … ability to operate freely across [the area]. This provide[d] reassurance to the local national population and also contribute[d] to growing uncertainty and fear amongst the remaining insurgents operating in the area'.[22] This Orwell-speak is non-commensurate with the structures, composition and aims of the 'Taliban' as described within this book, and is more akin to conventional warfare, which is, of course, the raison d'être of Western and Soviet forces. In many cases these operations only managed to aggravate the Helmandis and widen the gulf between their understanding of the conflict and the 'public' pronouncements of ISAF.

Looking more broadly, the evidence suggests that the Quetta/Peshawar shuras should be seen as a funding bridge between a vast number of very low-level disputes in Helmand and money from the Gulf (that seeks to damage the West, among other things) and money from Pakistan (that seeks to keep Afghanistan unstable due to fears of India/Pushtunistan). In a sense, those actors in the Gulf and Pakistan have hijacked the Taliban ideology. Thus, if you remove the Taliban patronage chain, it will be replaced, because the disputes will still be continuing on the ground, and the donors in the Gulf and Pakistan still wish to fulfil their aims. Unfortunately, ISAF have done very little to solve low-level land or water disputes in Helmand, instead seeing 'improved governance' and 'socio-economic development' as panaceas.

These ideas bring into question whether the much-vaunted Taliban reconciliation process, including the opening of the office in Qatar, will deliver any benefits. The evidence presented here suggests that it will not. Even if the top tier of the Taliban decide to make peace with the Afghan government (assuming that the Pakistani government allows them), they have very little control over individual actors fighting in Helmand, the overwhelming majority of whom are fighting for personal reasons. 'Talibs' who are fighting to protect their drugs crop are unlikely to stop because someone in Quetta tells them to. Reconciliation of that top tier of Taliban will simply turn off a funding tap that will be turned on again by someone else. This was demonstrated in this book by Iran's courting of the mahaz commanders in Helmand when the ISI stopped independently funding them in favour of the centralised nezami system.

The British and the Americans each had their own national weaknesses that stemmed from their adherence to the 'insurgency narrative'. For the British, it was Sher Mohammad. They ignored him once he was removed at their insistence, because he was seen as a negative influence on 'governance'. This was because he was considered an example of the predatory government that existed before ISAF arrived in the south of Afghanistan. But as a principled standpoint it rested on the British concept of the now-legitimate governance of Governor Mangal, supported by ISAF. The British meeting Sher Mohammad would have weakened Mangal's position. But it was because Mangal had so much uncritical British support that he allegedly acted in the way that he did.

But Sher Mohammad was a power centre, probably the most powerful man in Helmand, whom the British simply should not have ignored. Interestingly, the very fact of meeting with Sher Mohammad, and understanding his motivations as an individual, may have forced the British to re-examine whether the official government-Taliban dichotomy was appropriate in Helmand. Incidentally, and underlining the degree to which NATO was uncoordinated in Afghanistan, it made the British look utterly impotent when it emerged in 2012 that the Americans had been speaking to him for some time.[23]

One of the Americans' key strategies was targeting what they termed the narco-insurgent nexus, that is, the idea that the drugs trade is one of the main financial contributors to the Taliban. The US military were convinced of the importance of this relationship, even though the CIA did not give it much credence.[24] I do not wish this to be seen as an apologia for the drugs trade, it is not. I do wish, however, to highlight that the moral ambiguities surrounding the production of drugs, where growers face destitution or worse if their crop is eradicated, are very far from the narco-insurgent nexus theory outlined above.[25]

There are several flaws in the narco-insurgent nexus concept, all centred around the cohesiveness of the Taliban and the ignorance of the fact that the reason why many officials joined the government, particularly the police, was so that they could protect their roles in the opium trade. These facts, however, were viewed by the US as subsidiary rather than central to understanding Helmand. However, the problem with targeting opium production is that *everyone* is involved in it. Opium *is* the Helmandi economy.

Of my interviewees, bar one or two in the diaspora, all were involved at some stage in the opium trade in Helmand. Targeting opium because it supplies the Taliban is analogous to closing a supermarket because it stocks fatty foods and fatty foods kill people: no one will have a job and the neighbourhood will starve. Going after the drugs trade was always going to generate more antipathy than it was going to resolve; ISAF was addressing the wrong part of the problem.[26] It generated more resistance. From the population's point of view it was repugnant that ISAF was protecting the government that made money from the drugs trade whilst eradicating farmers' poppy fields, because 'the money went to the Taliban' (who many in the population saw as defending them). The fact that one could pay the government not to have their fields eradicated completed the feelings of gross injustice felt by the population.[27]

The most important decision taken by America with respect to Helmand was that to surge up to 20,000 troops there in 2009–12. Reading accounts of the decision-making at US cabinet-level, it is clear that they were operating with an idea of the Taliban as a cohesive organisation: they followed the 'insurgency narrative' (indeed, they propagated it).[28] Nationwide, the surge was considered part of a strategy to force the Taliban to the negotiating table, through putting them under more pressure.[29] The evidence presented here however, suggests that the Taliban are a resistance movement that draws on extra-territorial sources of funding, and thus Taliban strength is a reflection of Western strength. The surge allowed ISAF to move into more areas of Helmand, allowing more Helmandis to fight them. It also necessitated more supply and brought more development, both of which injected money into Helmand's war economy making the problem worse rather than better. Corruption went up several-fold with the surge.

The overarching focus on counterinsurgency meant that the real issues in Helmand—the tribal balance with the Kandahar and Helmandi Barakzai, the Alizai and President Karzai's Popalzai; the drought in northern Helmand; the theft and occupation of land in central Helmand; the Iranian interests in the Kajaki dam; the increase in power of the Noorzai; the perceived disenfranchisement of the Alizai, and so on—have not been resolved. Dealing with those issues would have been the real counterinsurgency: no amount of 'institution building' or 'clearing, holding and building' would have solved them. These issues are going to shape the future for Helmandis.

## Implications for Western Counterinsurgency Doctrine

The degree to which the Helmandi war privileges the local nature of conflict-drivers may well offer an especially extreme case. It has been particularly violent for a particularly long time. However, I think this can be explained by the hyper-factionalisation present in Helmandi society (partly caused by the high levels of illiteracy). This is compounded by the sheer quantity of resources (that is, opium revenue) available at ground level and the degree of outside interest due to geo-strategic location. However, these factors are present elsewhere in Afghanistan and I posit that the arguments of this book can be transferred Afghanistan-wide.

If my arguments are correct, this book has major implications for 'Western' counterinsurgency theory and doctrine.[30] These doctrines are largely based upon Maoist descriptions of insurgency and highlight the importance of ideologies and organisation to motivate insurgents.[31] The British Army definition of an insurgency, for example, is 'an organised, violent subversion used to effect or prevent political control, as a challenge to established authority';[32] it was from this that the 'insurgency narrative' was drawn. But this is not what is occurring in Helmand. In treating the conflict in the way that they did, the US and Britain were imposing a view of the war that bore little resemblance to the local understanding. The clearest example of this was of the British ignoring the Helmandi historical hatred for them because it did not fit their understanding of the official narratives of the war. To paraphrase Clausewitz (still taught at British staff college), they were trying to turn the war into something that it was not.

US and British counterinsurgency doctrines treat concepts of factionalisation as peripheral rather than central. Yet in Helmand, the opposite appears to be true. Factionalism is a defining feature of the conflict, on both the 'government' and the 'non-government' side. Ignorance of these issues, the importance of which was highlighted two-and-half thousand years ago, is shown by Sun Tzu who wrote, 'if you know the enemy and know yourself, you need not fear the result of a hundred battles'.[33] Ignorance of this knowledge reduces the ability of outside interveners to influence and shape the conflict. One might lazily describe this as 'making it worse'.

This book underscores the importance, when intervening in an internal war, of understanding the local politics—its actors, groups, narratives, feuds and alliances. This must be understood over and above the official, ideological sphere. The next theoretical step is seeking to understand how to integrate the local and the ideological, in order to escape from the phenomenon that I described in the Introduction, where interveners would use the term 'Taliban, but...' or 'government, but...' and then continue to treat the 'Taliban' or the 'government' as cohesive organisations.

Counterinsurgency theory must seek to learn how to integrate the 'but' and make it central to everything that counterinsurgents do.

However, it is likely that, for understandable reasons, the British and American top-down bureaucracies will find it hard to be so responsive to local factors. Even the Taliban and Pakistan, who are outside actors with significant knowledge of the local environment, fail to dictate events in Helmand, as can be demonstrated by the failure to fully implement the nezami system for Taliban organisation there.

The rumours surrounding the British role and whether they are working with the Taliban offer a crucial example. They provide key insight into Helmand's war, and offer an example of what happens if outside actors do not understand the political context of where they are operating. To a Western readership, this 'rumour' is so ridiculous as to be worthy of nothing more than dismissal, yet I argue that the integration of such rumours and opposite perspectives is vital. The objective 'truth' surrounding the rumours is not important: it is whether the Helmandis believe them, why they believe them and whether their perspective can be better understood by exploring them that is important. I assert that the recent stage of the Helmandi conflict can only be fully understood, with all the detail described in this book, through what for Helmandis can only be described as a central paradigm: the Angrez are supporting the Taliban to destroy our province.

Fusing the local and the more common ideological narratives regarding the Taliban and the ISAF intervention in Helmand into an analytical construct will be an essential, if most difficult, task for future scholars and counterinsurgents. Extant counterinsurgency theory implores us to understand the human terrain[34] in order to defeat an insurgency.[35] But it is more than that—the human terrain *is* the insurgency.

*The Future*

Violence in some districts in Helmand, such as Nad-e Ali, saw a massive drop over 2011 and 2012,[36] even if overall levels of violence in the country are much higher than they were prior to the US surge.[37] In many cases, and pointed out to me by my interviewees, this was a numbers game. In some areas of Nad-e Ali there was an ISAF base on every road junction—in other words, the vast increase in ISAF forces treated the symptoms of the conflict very well, but it is yet to be seen whether this will translate into a similar treatment of the causes. Another key factor was recruitment of former 'Taliban' into the ALP, but this will work only so long as the ALPs are paid. There were less

# AN INTIMATE WAR

supplies too coming from Quetta, because of the switch to routing funding through the Peshawar shura. But perhaps the most important reason for the current drop in violence is that ISAF is leaving: the Helmandis have achieved their aim. They are now preparing for the next round, in what has so far proved to be a cyclical conflict of remarkable robustness.

As when the Najibullah government was collapsing and the Taliban government was ousted, the Helmandis are looking to their tribal leadership to provide stability into the next era. External actors tend to separate groups of Helmandis and leaders by using patronage power, although they often think that this implies ideological loyalty. Now that those outsiders are moving on, it is time for the Helmand polity to morph back into its natural units, just as before, and reinforce kinship groups. This will continue until the next external actor is able to coalesce groups of Helmandis around an ideological, and more importantly a patronage, banner. Then, as before, Helmandis will split and send their sons to the different sides, often to fight each other. This is the only way to ensure that the lineage, and the land associated with it, remains intact.

Many—especially the Indian government—are worried that the Taliban will take over (or be given by ISAF and the Afghan government) areas like Helmand.[38] They are only right to be worried if they mean by Taliban that Helmandis will begin once again to exert more control over their local areas. As shown here, the 'Taliban' are largely local, mainly motivated by fighting other Helmandis or resisting foreigners. Once the foreigners have left Helmand, many of those fighting them will go home, their work done. The underlying dynamics, however, will continue.

The majority of the issues that drive the conflict have been de-prioritised by ISAF and will continue to drive low-level conflict for years to come—what is required is long-sighted, low-level, comprehensive and fair dispute resolution. Beyond that, some issues whose roots lie in hundreds of years of complicated history—the Barakzai-Alizai power balance, for example—require yet further attention. Iran will continue to interfere in northern Helmand, as long as its concerns over the Helmand River's water are ignored.

The theft of desert land and the creation of a two-tier community inside and outside the canal-zone is a new dichotomy that has been created by this revolution of the Helmandi conflict. The thousands of

250

tube wells that have been sunk in the desert are most probably lowering the water table. Judging by the continued complaints of Alizai leaders, there are already tens of thousands of people in northern Helmand who do not have enough water to comfortably survive. These hundreds of thousands of people without adequate water in Helmand will feed the continuation of the conflict.

Overall, ISAF sought to strengthen the government in Helmand. They believed they were strengthening it against the Taliban, with the population stuck in-between, but unfortunately they were buffering the government *against* the population. The big players or families who have run the province over the last thirty years, largely those who rose to prominence during the jihad, are still running the province. The choice that the Afghan government now has, as every Afghan government has had over the last 250 years, is whether to co-opt them or take them on.

The ISAF intervention has shown that in the presence of another patronage network—the Taliban—they will just rearrange themselves on the 'other' side according to their local disputes. Now that ISAF is going, and the Afghan government is about to lose much of its combat power, co-option has already begun with, for example, the appointment of people such as Amir Mohammad Akhundzada as governor of Uruzgan, or Hekmat, the son of Mir Wali, to be chief of police in Sangin. A further, key question remains over what will happen with the Zakir/Sher Mohammad contacts, and whether this is a drive to assert their dominance over the south of Afghanistan. I see their negotiations as analogous to the 'Parcham-Harakat' and the 'Hizb-Khalq' alignments in the early 1990s. An indicator of their intent would be whether they have arranged marriages between their families. Many of my interviewees felt that Helmand was heading for the third round of the mujahidin 'unity' government.

However, with the 2012 signing of strategic agreements with the Western powers, India and China, it appears that the Afghan government will survive nationally once NATO withdraws most of its combat forces. Using the 1989–92 Najibullah government as a guide, as long as the funding remains the government will survive. But what will this look like in Helmand? A lot depends on the presidential election, scheduled at the time of writing, for 2014. If the winner is another southern Pushtun, but from another tribe, then the tribal alliances in play in the south will shift, creating new dynamics. That aside, the

Afghan government will have mostly the same interests in Helmand as before: Gereshk and Lashkar Gah must stay under government control, for trade and legitimacy, respectively. Outside those areas there will be different bespoke levels of control.

In areas like Nad-e Ali, Marjeh and Nawa that, because of the canal system, prefer some input from the government, there will be government control in the district centres and along the main roads; however, the villages will govern themselves, as they always have done. If they require anything from the government, they will go to it in the district centre (not for nothing is the district centre literally known as the hukomat or 'government' in Helmand). They do not want the government to come to them. As before, the main service that they require from government is fair, impartial dispute resolution. Northern Helmand, by contrast, will be de facto independent with local district governors and police chiefs. They will fly the flag of the Afghan government and will swear nominal loyalty to the Afghan government, but it will be meaningless.

These arrangements will last until the next injection of funds and ideology to Helmand causes the actors and groups to divide, once again, according to their local feuds and alliances: foreigners will come, and foreigners will go, but life will continue much as before.

# APPENDICES

# APPENDIX 1

# INTERVIEWEE DESCRIPTIONS

1.1 On-the-record interviews

These interviews were conducted with six prominent figures in the Helmandi story and one key British individual. They were conducted in Helmand, London and Kabul. Their purpose was to gain an understanding of how these key protagonists felt and thought at particular junctures in Helmandi history. Here follows a brief self-reported biography of the individuals in question. I have added comments where appropriate.

*Malem Mir Wali (Barakzai/Bayezai)—'MMW'*

Mir Wali is fifty-eight and from Malgir, Nahr-e Saraj. He went to primary school in Spin Masjid and then the 'Lycee' secondary school in Lashkar Gah. He then went to teacher training college in Kandahar during which time the Taraki Revolution occurred. He completed a year of conscripted army service and then returned to Spin Masjid to teach at his old primary school. He taught for six months, during which time the Soviets invaded. He began to fight under Shaed Mansour (Hizb). Shaed was martyred and he became commander, before rising to be in charge of Hizb in Malgir and the surrounding area. In 1987 he accepted an offer from the Najib government and became a government militia commander. This was partly because he was under such pressure from

Nasim Akhundzada. He stayed in the 'government' through the collapse of Hizb and then left when the 'Hizb-Khalq' coalition fell apart in Lashkar Gah. He then worked with Rasoul, his erstwhile enemy, to defeat the Akhwaendi-Khano coalition and became director of culture and information for Helmand. He was evicted by the Taliban in 1994 and spent the next seven years fighting them all over the country. In 2001, he managed to become the commander of the 93rd Division, Afghan Military Forces in Gereshk, with significant patronage from US Special Forces. The division was disarmed and Mir Wali became a member of parliament in 2005. He ran for re-election in 2010, was disqualified for fraud, but managed to retain his seat through the intervention of Karzai. He currently lives in Kabul.

### Sher Mohammad Akhundzada (Alizai/Hassanzai)—'SMA'

Sher Mohammad is forty and from Nachai village, Kajaki. He spent his childhood in northern Helmand and attended a madrasah in Zamindawar. Aside from his schooling in the madrasah he is not that well educated (he is literate, but not very numerate). His first battle was against the Taliban when they took over Kajaki in 1994–5. He was twenty-two. After various attempts to regain Helmand, the family fled to Quetta, where they befriended Hamid Karzai. He was appointed Helmand's provincial governor from 2001 to 2005, when he was removed at British insistence before their deployment. His governorship was characterised by a turf war between the other major commanders who made up the Helmandi government, and by predation on communities who had no way of defending themselves. Once removed by Karzai in 2005, he was appointed to the Senate in Kabul, where he has remained ever since. As well as being a senator he is a major supporter of the 'Taliban' in Helmand and he manipulates both government and Taliban actors to enhance his own drugs and power interests.

### Abdul Rahman Jan (Noorzai/Darzai/Parozai)—'ARJ'

Abdul Rahman is sixty. Born in Washir sub-district, he went to Shaepista school. When he was sixteen the family moved to Marjeh—they were one of the few families to move from within Helmand to the canal-zone. Upon completing school, he then served his conscription period during Daud's era in the police in Shah-e Now, Kabul.

Following the Saur Revolution he was imprisoned for four months before being freed and immediately began working under Mullah Baz Mohammad in 'Harakat'. According to Rahman, when the 'Hizb'–'Harakat' war began, he was disgusted and joined Etihad. Others comment that he spent the jihad swapping one party for another because he was able to get better supplies or more money. Two years later, he switched to Jamiat. At the time he was a petty commander with about fifteen men. He fought in several different alliances with other groups in the 'government' against Rasoul before switching to be on Rasoul's side against the 'government'. As that 'government' collapsed, he managed to take over some of its heavy weapons (from Khano) and established himself as the deputy chief of police for Helmand. He fled when the Taliban came and eventually settled in Iran, from where he came in 2001 to retake Marjeh. He then became the provincial chief of police. During this tenure he became (in)famous for fighting the other commanders in government and oppressing defenceless communities in Helmand. He was removed in 2005. Captain-General Abdul Rahman (as he is now) currently lives in Kabul.

### Hafizullah Khan (Barakzai/Omarkhanzai)—'Hafizullah'

Hafizullah is sixty and from Bolan. He went to school in Lashkar Gah and then went to study engineering at Kabul University, where he heard about Hekmatyar. Once the Saur Revolution occurred, he immediately went to Peshawar and met Hekmatyar. After training, he returned to Helmand as the Hizb-e Islami Amir. Most people comment that he did not fight much, but preferred to 'organise'. Once the communist state collapsed in 1992, Hafizullah went into partnership with Khano and became provincial governor. This soon collapsed and represents the highpoint in his 'career'; he has never managed to attain a 'government' position since. He left Helmand during the Taliban period and was one of the first to reoccupy Lashkar Gah once the Taliban left at the end of 2001. He was soon evicted by Sher Mohammad and Abdul Rahman. He currently lives in Bolan.

### Jabbar Qahraman (Noorzai/Daudzai)—'Jabbar'

Jabbar is fifty-two. He finished school in 1980 and joined Hizb-e Islami for a year. He then 'decided to join the government for the growth of

Afghanistan ... [he] could see that Pakistan just wanted to ruin Afghanistan'. He subsequently went through army officer training and was sent to Maiwand as a platoon commander. He spent the entire war in Maiwand and was made a Qahraman, or hero, of Afghanistan in 1986 for having the highest amount of government control in a district in the whole of Afghanistan. Many say that this was because he cut deals with all of his mujahidin opponents, and supported them with government patronage. As the Soviets left, he was then made a captain-general and given control of most of the south. A close ally of Najib, he joined Hizb when the government collapsed. Shortly after he went to Russia and worked in a market as a stallholder. During the Karzai era he worked for UNAMA for four years, during which time he allegedly smuggled weapons into Afghanistan from Russia. He was then elected to parliament where he remains. He currently lives in Kabul.

### Habibullah Khan (Noorzai/Ghorezai)—'Habibullah'

Habibullah is sixty-one and from Garmsir. He served in the army around the time of Daud's revolution (1973) and then returned to Garmsir to become a teacher. He claims that he never joined the PDPA, which others contest. Joining the police in 1988, he served as the Nawa district deputy chief of police. He then served as a battalion second-in-command in Lashkar Gah and as the district chief of police for Khan Eshin. During this period he visited Russia several times for training. Once the Soviets left in 1988/9, he served as chief of police in Nad-e Ali, which he describes as the worst period in his life. They were under constant attack. He was eventually forced to abandon his post and later reinvented himself as a militia commander. As the mujahidin progressively took control, he fled to Pakistan, returning only once the Karzai government was in power. He immediately joined the police and served as chief of police in Garmsir and Gereshk, before retiring. Called out of retirement, he was made district governor in Nad-e Ali in 2008. He currently lives in Lashkar Gah.

### Sir Sherard Cowper-Coles KCMG LVO (English)—'SCC'

Sherard is fifty-seven and was born in London. Educated in Classics at Oxford University, he was a career British diplomat. He speaks Arabic, Hebrew and French. He has served in Egypt, the United States, Hong

Kong, France, Israel and Saudi Arabia. He became UK ambassador to Afghanistan from May 2007 to April 2009 and served as UK special representative to Afghanistan and Pakistan from mid-2009 to mid-2010. He now works for BAE systems as international business development director. He currently lives in London.

1.2 Anonymous 'notable' interviews (conducted by the author either in Helmand, Kabul or London)

001 District governor, Nahr-e Saraj, Karzai era
002 Ex-Mahaz commander, Lashkar Gah
003 Barakzai ex-Mahaz commander, Lashkar Gah
004 Alizai Helmand government official, Karzai era
005 Ex-Jamiat commander, Nawa
006 Chief of police, Helmand Province, Karzai era
007 Kharoti ex-Hizb-e Islami commander, Nad-e Ali
008 Noorzai businessman, Nad-e Ali
009 Son of communist era Helmand Khad chief
010 ANP Lt Col., Helmand
011 Ex-Harakat commander
012 Chief of police, Nahr-Saraj, Karzai era
013 Alizai elder
014 Provincial council member, Karzai era
015 Ex-Harakat commander, Nad-e Ali
016 Ex-Jamiat commander, Marjeh
017 Ex-Hizb-e Islami commander, Nad-e Ali
018 Barakzai ex-militia leader, Babaji
019 ANP major, Karzai era
020 Member of Khad, communist era
021 Barakzai notable, Bolan
022 Barakzai ex-Hizb-e Islami commander, Lashkar Gah
023 Kharoti tribal leader
024 Ex-communist police officer, Nahr-e Saraj
025 Sayed from Now Zad
026 Jailor, Helmand
027 Barakzai tribesman, Nahr-e Saraj
028 Alizai shopkeeper from Now Zad
029 Noorzai ex-Khalqi, Nahr-e Saraj
030 Chief of police, Nahr-Saraj, Karzai era

031 Alakozai businessman, Gereshk
032 Kharoti ex-Hizb-e Islami commander
033 Noorzai tribesman
034 Ishaqzai village chief
035 Kharoti ex-Khalqi official
036 Chief of police, Nahr-e Saraj, Karzai era
037 NDS officer, Helmand
038 NDS officer, Helmand
039 Senior Noorzai tribal leader
040 ALP commander, Nahr-e Saraj
041 Noorzai ex-Etihad commander, central Helmand
042 Chief of police, Nad-e Ali, Karzai era
043 Ex-Khalqi militia commander
044 Head of HAVA, communist era
045 Parchami cadre
046 Achakzai shopkeeper, Lashkar Gah
047 NGO worker
048 Ex-Khalqi police commander
049 Ex-Khalqi police commander
050 Kharoti elder, Nad-e Ali
051 Nejad fighter, Nad-e Ali
052 Mahaz fighter, Nahr-e Saraj
053 Baluch elder, Garmsir
054 Provincial chief of police, Karzai era
055 Barakzai village elder, Nahr-e Saraj
056 Ex-Mahaz commander, Now Zad
057 Ex-professional army officer in 93rd Division
058 Schoolteacher, Nad-e Ali
059 Landowner, Marjeh
060 Hotak elder, Garmsir
061 Ishaqzai ex-Mahaz commander
062 Prominent USSOF militia leader, Nahr-e Saraj
063 Former engineer on the canal projects. Spoke good English
064 Ex-Etihad commander
065 Kharoti professional, Nad-e Ali
066 Former Taliban mullah (1996–2001 government)
067 ALP commander, Nad-e Ali
068 Ex-Hizb-e Islami commander, Nahr-e Saraj
069 Alakozai scribe, Sangin
070 Alizai ex-Harakat commander

071  Ex-Harakat commander, Nad-e Ali
072  Noorzai tribesman, Nad-e Ali
073  Former USSOF militia leader, Nahr-e Saraj
074  Scion of important Barakzai family
075  Barakzai mullah, Nahr-e Saraj
076  Chief of police, Helmand Province, Karzai era
077  Junior ANP officer, Helmand
078  ANA officer with five years' experience in Helmand
079  USSOF militia commander, Nahr-e Saraj
080  Member of Khad, communist era
081  Helmandi MP
082  Helmandi senator
083  Helmandi MP
084  Senior Noorzai tribal leader
085  Barakzai landowner, Nahr-e Saraj

1.3 Anonymous 'notable' interviews (conducted by Afghan researchers in Helmand)

086  Ex-jihadi commander (Nad-e Ali)
087  Alizai/Khalozai elder (Musa Qala)
088  Achakzai elder (Nahr-e Saraj)
089  Popalzai elder (Now Zad)
090  Elder (Now Zad)
091  Educated person (Garmsir)
092  Elder (Sangin)
093  Alizai elder (Musa Qala)
094  Elder (Nad-e Ali)
095  Alakozai elder (Sangin)
096  Hassanzai elder (Musa Qala)
097  Hassanzai elder (Musa Qala)
098  Suleimankhel elder (Nad-e Ali)
099  Madrassa teacher (Sangin)
100  Noorzai elder (Nahr-e Saraj)

1.4 Anonymous ISAF interviews (conducted by the author in Helmand or London)

101  ISAF civilian advisor
102  ISAF intelligence officer

103 ISAF officer
104 ISAF civilian advisor
105 ISAF intelligence officer
106 ISAF officer
107 ISAF infantry officer
108 ISAF intelligence officer
109 ISAF ISTAR officer
110 ISAF battle group officer
111 ISAF officer
112 ISAF intelligence officer


1.5 Anonymous 'Taliban' (TB) interviews (conducted by Afghan researchers in Helmand)

201 TB commander in Nad-e Ali
202 TB commander in Nad-e Ali
203 TB commander in Marjeh
204 Alakozai TB commander in Sangin
205 TB fighter in Garmsir
206 TB council member
207 Military trainer of TB in Garmsir
208 TB fighter in Garmsir
209 Alizai TB commander in Nad-e Ali
210 Barakzai TB fighter/facilitator in Marjeh
211 Ishaqzai TB commander in Marjeh
212 Barakzai TB commander in Marjeh
213 TB commander in Marjeh
214 TB commander in Sangin
215 Alizai TB commander in Musa Qala
216 TB commander in Sangin
217 Alizai TB commander in Musa Qala
218 Alizai TB commander in Kajaki
219 Noorzai TB sub-commander in Kajaki
220 Ishaqzai TB commander in Now Zad
221 Alizai TB commander in Musa Qala
222 Kharoti TB commander in Nad-e Ali
223 Alakozai TB commander in Nahr-e Saraj
224 Noorzai TB commander in Musa Qala
225 Alizai TB commander in Musa Qala

226 Ishaqzai TB commander in Sangin
227 Barakzai TB commander in Sangin
228 Kharoti TB commander in Nad-e Ali
229 Barakzai TB commander in Nahr-e Saraj
230 Noorzai TB commander in Nahr-e Saraj
231 Alizai TB commander in Now Zad
232 Alizai TB commander in Nahr-e Saraj
233 Alizai TB commander in Garmsir
234 Popalzai TB commander in Sangin
235 Popalzai TB commander in Now Zad
236 Ishaqzai TB commander in Garmsir
237 TB commander in Marjeh
238 Barakzai TB commander in Sangin
239 Alizai TB commander in Kajaki
240 Alizai TB commander in Garmsir
241 Alizai TB commander in Kajaki
242 TB commander in Kajaki
243 Noorzai TB commander in Marjeh
244 TB commander in Nad-e Ali
245 Ishaqzai TB commander in Marjeh
246 Alizai TB commander in Musa Qala
247 Ishaqzai TB commander in Now Zad
248 Popalzai TB commander in Now Zad
249 Noorzai TB commander in Nahr-e Saraj
250 Barakzai TB commander in Nahr-e Saraj

# APPENDIX 2

# GLOSSARY OF TERMS AND PEOPLE

*93rd Division* Afghan army division based in Gereshk during the Soviet period and headquartered on Artillery Hill. This then became a mujahidin organisation after the collapse of the government. The term fell into disuse during the Taliban era. The division was revived during the Karzai era, with the same designation, as part of the Afghan Militia Forces, before being disbanded again under DDR. See Appendix 5 for commanders.

*Abdul Agha (Haji)* Head of the slightly smaller Barakzai clan confederation in Malgir. This confederation consisted of the Shamezai, Nekazai, Yedarzai and Masezai. They were generally allied with Harakat during the jihad, with the Taliban during the Taliban government, but then with the government in the Karzai era.

*Abdul Ahad (Mullah)* Leader of the Ishaqzai in Now Zad during the jihad. They were allied with Harakat and then the Taliban. Helmand's chief of police under Rasoul (1993–4).

*Abdul Ahad Helmandwal* Noorzai/Gurg. From Loy Bagh. Shah Nazar Helmandwal's nephew. Fought under Etihad's label during the jihad, but the family was split across the government-mujahidin divide. First leader of Nad-e Ali District Council in 2009. See Appendix 4 for family tree.

*Abdul Khaleq* Leader of Ishaqzai/Mistereekhel. From Qala-e Gaz. Killed during the jihad, but his sons Qari Hazrat, Lala Jan and Mamouk then led the clan, fought ISAF and smuggled opium.

*Abdul Qayoum Zakir* Alizai/Khalozai/Arabzai. Rais Baghrani sub-commander when Baghrani was 93rd Division commander. Joined the Taliban with Baghrani and rose up the ranks. Eventually captured by the Americans and spent six years in Guantanamo (G008). At the time of writing, he is the head of the Taliban nezami system for the south of Afghanistan. See Appendix 6.

*Abdul Rahman Jan* Noorzai/Darzai/Parozai. Petty commander during the jihad. Originally in Harakat, he then worked under Jamiat, and possibly Hizb along the way. Born in Now Zad from a non-prestigious blood line; gained prominence through cutting a deal with Khano when he surrendered, accepting his heavy weapons. Helmand deputy chief of police under Rasoul/Abdul Ahad. Chief of police from 2001 to 2005, where he was rumoured to have stolen up to 20,000 jereebs of land in Marjeh. Not to be confused with Abdul Rahman Khan (Alizai). See Appendix 1.

*Abdul Rahman Khan* Alizai/Khalozai. Originally from Kajaki. Began allied to Mahaz then switched to Hizb for more funding. Forced out of Kajaki in 1987 by Nasim Akhundzada, and then from Malgir by Nasim's brother, Rasoul. Eventually settled in exile in Norway, where he was still living in 2012. Not to be confused with Abdul Rahman Jan (Noorzai).

*Abdul Razaq* Barakzai. Hizb commander during jihad. Was then a commander in the 93rd Division and became a militia commander. When the division was DDR'd, he managed to enter the police and, with American patronage, became the head of the District Response Team (a US Special Forces 'SWAT' team). This patronage allowed him, despite being only a sergeant, to become the de facto head of the Nahr-e Saraj police in the mid-2000s.

*Abdul Salam (Mullah)* Alizai/Khalozai. Brother of Zakir. Was responsible for the Taliban nezami system in northern Helmand until he was killed 3 June 2012. Not to be confused with Abdul Salam (Noorzai) or Mullah Salam (Alizai/Pirzai).

*Abdul Salam* Noorzai. From Now Zad. Hizb commander and the major Taliban commander. Rose to become commander of the Herat Corps during the Taliban era. Not to be confused with Abdul Salam (Alizai/Khalozai) or Mullah Salam (Alizai/Pirzai).

*Abdul Wali Koka* Alizai/Hassanzai. Musa Qala chief of police for most of the Karzai era. One of Sher Mohammad's commanders and hated by the non-Hassanzai community.

*Abdullah Jan (Haji)* Noorzai. From Now Zad. Major Hizb commander. Abdul Rahman Jan comes from his clan (Noorzai/Darzai/Parozai).

*Abu Bakr* Alizai. Leader of the 3,000–4,000 man Zamindawari/Alizai uprising against the British/Afghan (Barakzai) government in 1879. His forces almost certainly swung the Battle of Maiwand against the British.

*Achakzai* A tribe that is part of the Zirak branch of the Durrani tribal confederation. Said to have been split from the Barakzai (of which they were a sub-tribe) by Ahmad Shah Durrani (a Popalzai) as he feared the power of the Barakzai. In Afghanistan, they mainly live in Spin Boldak in Kandahar.

*Aghezai* Noorzai clan from Loy Bagh. Deliberately split itself across the government–mujahidin divide and the government–Taliban divide in the two eras. (In)famous members include Khano, Assadullah Sherzad, Abdul Sattar and Mullah Karim.

*Ahmad Shah Durrani* Popalzai. Reign: 1747–72. Seen as the founding father of the Afghan nation by the Pushtun. Forged and held a vast empire including Peshawar and Delhi. Direct descendants form the monarchical lineage of Afghanistan from 1747 to 1818: the Saddozais. Re-granted the Durrani tribes the land that they are (largely) still living on in Helmand in return for military service.

*Ahmad Wali Karzai* Half-brother of Hamid Karzai, the Afghan President at the time of writing. Extensive rumours circulated that he was involved in the narcotics business. Killed by one of his aides in July 2011.

*Akhtur Khan* Alizai. Leader of the 3,000-man Zamindawari-Alizai uprising against the British/Afghan government in 1841. At national level the government was Popalzai led, however, in the south it was still dominated by the Barakzai.

*Akhtur Mohammad Osmani* Ishaqzai/Chowkazai. From Sangin. Head of Kandahar Corps during the Taliban era. Taliban mahaz commander during the Karzai era. Killed by ISAF in 2006.

*Akhwaendi* Barakzai. Jamiat Amir for Helmand. Related to Allah Noor. Provincial governor in 1993.

*Akidawee* Used to describe ideological Taliban in the Karzai era.

*Alakozai* Tribe of the Zirak Branch of the Durrani tribal confederation. Related in ancestry to the Barakzai and Popalzai (Barak, Alak and Popal were bothers in antiquity). Mainly located in the

Arghandab River valley in Kandahar province. The indigenous Helmandi Alakozai are now in Sarwan Qala, north of Sangin.

*Alizai* Major tribe of the Panjpai branch of the Durrani tribal confederation. One of the three biggest tribes in Helmand (see Noorzai and Barakzai for others). Apart from the first Taliban government (1995–2001), they provided Helmand's provincial governors between 1993 and 2005. Live in the north of Helmand, in the ancient district of Zamindawar (modern districts of Baghran, Musa Qala, Kajaki and northern Sangin).

*Allah Noor* (Barakzai). Khalqi militia leader. Commander of the 93rd Division once Najib's government collapsed. Since 2001, he has been commander of the outer (militia) defence of Kandahar airfield and a highway policeman under USPI. At the time of writing he is the commander of the Afghan border police regiment in Helmand.

*Amir* lit. leader. The term used to designate the person in overall control of a mujahidin party's activities in a province. Effectively the head of the mujahidin patronage organisation.

*Amir Mohammad Akhundzada* Alizai. Sher Mohammad Akhundzada's younger brother. District governor of Musa Qala in the post-2001 period, and deputy provincial governor in 2005/6. Currently governor of Uruzgan.

*Andiwal/andiwali* lit. friend. The term used to denote the mujahidin style of government. The closest British equivalent would be sofa-government.

*Angrez* lit. English. Used as a derogatory term for people in Afghanistan (like 'the Hun' in British English). Still used to describe the British during the ISAF intervention.

*Arab* Noorzai. From Noorzo Kalay. A relative of Haji Lal Jan, the leader of the community. Allied himself with the 'Taliban' in order to attempt to take over leadership of the community from Haji Lal Jan.

*Arif Noorzai* Noorzai. Related to Hamid Karzai, Sher Mohammad and Israel (Mahmad Ashem's family). See family tree in Appendix 4.

*Artillery Hill (taapuh)* Soviet military HQ on the hill south of Gereshk.

*Aslee* The 'real' Taliban. Generally taken to be those who have a close link to the Quetta Shura (those above group commanders).

*Assadullah Karimi* The leader of the Hazara in Saidabad, southern Nad-e Ali. Also their head teacher. Had many feuds with the Popalzai and Ishaqzai over the water for his community.

*Assadullah Sherzad* Noorzai/Aghezai. Worked in Khano's militia. Involved in the ejection of 'Hizb' from Lashkar Gah in 1992. Chief of police in Helmand in 2008–9.

*Assadullah Wafa (Governor)* Achakzai. Provincial governor of Helmand from December 2006 to March 2008. Not considered effective by the British.

*Atta Mohammad* Ishaqzai/Chowkazai. Mujahidin commander in Sangin in the 1980s. Originally affiliated with Harakat, he later switched to Jamiat and then re-allied himself with Harakat again. Most of this was driven by fighting with Dad Mohammad and Abdul Khaleq. Died in Quetta in the late 1990s.

*Ayub (Khan)* Noorzai. From Now Zad. Deputy chief of police of Helmand during the early Karzai era. See Appendix 4 for family tree.

*Baghrani* Alizai. Known as Rais Baghrani—'King of Baghran'. From the Khalozai sub-tribe of the Alizai. Has fought under Hizb, Jamiat, Taliban and Harakat franchises, before reconciling with the Karzai government in 2005. There is no post-2001 government presence in Baghran, save for Baghrani.

*Barakzai* One of the three biggest tribes in Helmand (see Alizai and Noorzai). Mohammadzai branch provided the royal lineage from 1826 to 1973. Concentrated in central Helmand, they control Gereshk. Generally fought under the Hizb franchise during the jihad in central Helmand.

*Baz Mohammad (Mullah)* Taraki. From Marjeh. Most senior Harakat commander in Nad-e Ali and Marjeh during the jihad.

*Bismillah (Haji)* Alizai. G968. Arrested after Mir Wali and Kadus manipulated US Special Forces in Gereshk. See Appendix 6 for more details.

*Bughra* See Nahr-e Bughra.

*Burhanuddin Rabbani* Tajik leader of Jamiat. Also president of Afghanistan from 1992 to 1996 and briefly in 2001. Killed by a suicide bomber in 2011.

*Chaiboy* A man of even medium status will have a young boy to fetch tea and generally tend to his guests. Depending on their master, the boys are sometimes used for sex.

*Charwaki(an)* lit. (government) official. The rapacious nature of the government in Helmand over the past three decades has added other meanings to charwaki, including tax collector, policeman, bandit and robber.

*Communist* See PDPA.

*Cummerbund* lit. belt. Used to denote the Soviet defensive lines around Lashkar Gah and Gereshk. See Map 5.

*Daakhelee* Internal Taliban. Used to refer to those members of the post-2001 Taliban who are local, mostly resistance, fighters.

*Dad Mohammad* Alakozai. Jamiat Mujahidin commander in Sangin in the 1980s, fought Atta Mohammad for years, worked with the Akhundzadas, the Taliban and the Karzai government when he became head of the Afghan National Directorate of Security (NDS). Infamous for his continued mistreatment of the Ishaqzai. Eventually killed (probably by the Ishaqzai) in 2009. His brother, Juma Gul, was district governor of Sangin under the early Karzai administration.

*Dadullah* Kakar. Pre-2001 Taliban commander and post-2001 was the most iconic Taliban mahaz commander in the south. Killed in 2007 by ISAF.

*Daud (Governor)* Safi. Governor of Helmand from December 2005 to December 2006. A settler in Helmand during the canal projects, educated technocrat, spoke some English.

*Daud (Mullah)* Brother of Haji Kadus and Idris. Guarded Camp Price from 2007 to 2010. When removed, Camp Price came under attack every day. Was reinstated.

*Depaye* Zahir Shah-era militias raised in every district and usually led by the district head teacher. Their use continued sporadically into the communist era, alongside a plethora of other militias.

*Dostum* Major Najibullah militia commander based in Mazar-e Sharif. Declared independence from Najibullah, causing his administration's collapse. Supported Khano and the other 'communist' militia commanders post-Najib. Eventually arranged for their escape when their administration collapsed and Rasoul took over.

*Durrani* Eminent Pushtun tribal confederation in Afghanistan centred on Helmand, Uruzgan and Kandahar. Named after Ahmad Shah Durrani, who was titled Durr-e Durran (Pearl of Pearls) upon his enthronement in 1747.

*Etihad* Mujahidin party led by Sayaaf. Formed in 1981 as an alliance of all the parties. Split up immediately and became one of the seven mujahidin parties. Out of the seven parties, Etihad was the closest to Saudi Arabia and the UAE guaranteeing him the lion's share of their funding.

*Ezmarai* Barakzai. Former Khalqi police commander; his father (also a Khalqi policeman in Gereshk) was killed by Hizb. Squad commander during Taliban government. Made his money as a highway policeman under a USPI contract. Chief of police of Gereshk between 2009 and 2011.

*Fatah Mohammad* Ishaqzai/Chowkazai. Major drug smuggler originally from Sangin, but now living in Quetta. Funds various aspects of the Taliban resistance including a hospital in Quetta in which 'Taliban' fighters can receive treatment.

*Ghaffour Akhundzada* Alizai/Hassanzai. Brother of Nasim and Rasoul Akhundzada. Was provincial governor for less than a year after Rasoul's death in 1994 and before the Taliban chased the Akhundzadas out at the beginning of 1995. Eventually shot, supposedly by the Taliban, in Quetta in March 2000.

*Ghilzai* The second biggest Pushtun tribal confederation in Afghanistan after the Durrani. Lands between Kandahar and Kabul, but have fought against the Durrani for control of Kandahar over the ages, creating enmity. Not native to Helmand; however, thousands of families settled during the canal projects.

*Girdi Jangal* Refugee camp in Baluchistan province, Pakistan (opposite Helmand). Supposedly closed by the Pakistani government in 2007, it still has 40,000 people in it. Since its formation after the 1979 Soviet invasion, it has provided a safe area for Helmandis from the violence in the province, as well as a 'rear area' to equip, rest and relax.

*Gul Agha Shirzai* Barakzai. Leader of the Barakzai in Kandahar and son of famous mujahidin commander. Worked with US Special Forces in the 2001 attack on the Taliban in Kandahar and then closely with them in the early Karzai years when he was Kandahar's governor. Rival of Karzai, and posted to Nangahar province. Supported Malem Mir Wali.

*Gul Ehktiar (Haji)* Landowner in Western Malgir/Eastern Babaji. ISAF patrol base was on his land, for which he receives rent. His nephew Sur Gul is a Talib and was recently (at time of writing) the Taliban district governor for Washir.

*Gulbuddin Hekmatyar* Kharoti. The leader of Hizb-e Islami (Gulbuddin). One of the few mujahidin party leaders who is still alive and leading his party. Occasionally, rumours surface that he is holding talks with Karzai about reconciliation. He still 'leads' a major part of the post-2001 insurgency.

*Gurg* Noorzai clan in southern Afghanistan, but prominent in Loy Bagh. Important members include Shah Nazar Helmandwal, provincial governor during the Najib era, and Abdul Ahad Helmandwal, Etihad commander and first chairman of the Nad-e Ali community council in 2009.

*Habibullah (Khan)* Noorzai. Soviet-era police commander and Nad-e Ali district governor from 2008 to the present. See Appendix 1.

*Hafizullah Amin* Kharoti. Ruled for a few months in 1979. Extreme left-wing Khalqi president of Afghanistan. Killed by the Soviets when they invaded.

*Hafizullah Khan* Barakzai. Hizb-e Islami Amir for Helmand. See Appendix 1.

*Hamid Karzai* Popalzai. President of Afghanistan from 2001 to the present.

*Harakat-e Enqelab-e Islami (Harakat)* Traditionalist Afghan mujahi-din group fighting against Soviet forces. Mohammad Nabi Mohammedi was leader. Operated across southern Afghanistan. Was part of the 'Peshawar Seven' coalition of mujahidin parties. In Helmand, the most important commander was Nasim Akhundzada.

*Hassanzai*. Currently the preeminent sub-tribe of the Alizai in Helmand and led by Sher Mohammad Akhundzada. Notorious for feuding with the Pirzai and Khalozai sub-tribes.

*Hazara*. Ethnic group that populates the mountainous central area of Afghanistan. Said to be descended from Genghis Khan's men. Overwhelmingly Shia (as opposed to the mainly Sunni Pushtun). Small pockets of Hazara live in Helmand, a legacy of the canal project. Comprise around 10 per cent of the Afghan population.

*Hekmatullah* Barakzai. Malem Mir Wali's son and heir. Chief of police in Sangin in 2012.

*Hekmatyar* See Gulbuddin Hekmatyar.

*Hizb-e Islami (Hizb)* Two factions: Khales and Gulbuddin. Gulbuddin faction prominent in Helmand. Most well-funded mujahidin party, but was dropped by Pakistan upon the rise of the Taliban in 1994. One of the two major mujahidin parties represented in Helmand alongside Harakat. Prominent commanders include Malem Mir Wali, Abdul Rahman Khan and Hafizullah Khan.

*Hukomat* lit. government. Term used to describe the physical government buildings that comprise a district centre.

*Ibrahim (Mullah)* aka Shakir. Ibrahim. Local Taliban commander. Kharoti says he rejoined the Taliban due to police brutality. Killed by ISAF in 2009/10. His car was turned into a shrine by the Kharoti.

*Idris* Brother of Haji Kadus and Mullah Daud. Killed by Badr, the chief of police, when trying to take over Gereshk's security (supported by US Special Forces).

*Ikhwan* lit. brothers (Arabic). As in Muslim Brotherhood. Term (usually derogatory) used to describe members of Hizb and Jamiat.

*Ishaqzai.* The most marginalised of the Durrani tribes in Helmand. Important under the Taliban during 1995–2001, they provided senior commanders for the movement. Heavily persecuted by the Alakozai post-2001. Mainly live south of Sangin, Now Zad and Garmsir although there are some in Nad-e Ali, where they moved (illegally) during the jihad.

*ISI—Inter-Services Intelligence* Pakistan's premier intelligence agency. Responsible for channelling US and Saudi funding to the mujahidin during the jihad. Heavily financed the Taliban during 1995–2001; strong evidence that they are currently providing assistance to the Taliban Quetta Shura.

*Ismail Khan* Tajik. Originally an army officer who played a key role in the initial rebellion against the Soviets in Herat. Was a major Jamiat commander during the jihad becoming the ruler of western Afghanistan from 1992 to 1995. Became governor of Herat under Karzai and in 2005 was made a minister in Kabul. Despite differences in mujahidin franchise, was allied to the Akhundzadas in Helmand and helped them capture Lashkar Gah from the militias (who were also allied with Jamiat).

*Israel* Noorzai. Patriarch of Mahmad Ashem's important Now Zadi family. Important mediator during 'Hizb' and 'Harakat' war in the north of Helmand. Negotiated handover from Taliban when they fled in 2001. Respected by many. See Appendix 4 for family tree.

*Jabbar Qahraman.* Noorzai. Originally an army officer and then a commander of a very effective militia that was used by the government in other parts of the country as a mobile division. Jabbar Khan was appointed a hero, or 'Qahraman', of the communist government. Currently a Helmand MP. See Appendix 1 for description.

*Jailani (Dr) Kharoti.* Hizb commander from Shin Kalay. Supports Taliban narrative in the post-2001 era. Gave his 'clinic' over to the 'Taliban' during 2008 to enable them to keep the government out of Shin Kalay. Has a son in the 'Taliban'. Was on the security committee on the Nad-e Ali community council at the same time.

*Jamalzai (Haji) Kharoti.* Harakat commander from Noor Mohammad Khan Kalay. Haji Barakzai's uncle.

*Jamiat-e Islami (Jamiat)* Islamic political party in Afghanistan similar to the Muslim Brotherhood of Egypt. Oldest Islamic political party in Afghanistan. Communitarian ideology based on Islamic law but is also considered moderately progressive. From 1968 to 2011 the official leader of Jamiat was Burhanuddin Rabbani. Major commanders include Ahmad Shah Masoud and Ismail Khan. Akhwaendi was the Amir in Helmand.

*Jan Mohammad* Barakzai. US Special Forces militia commander. Currently ALP commander, runs militia defending Camp Price and is on the US-led district response team.

*Jereeb* Afghan unit of measure equivalent to 0.2 hectare or ½ acre. Approximately 40m x 40m.

*Jihad lit.* struggle (Arabic). Like the religious terms of any religion this is open to different interpretations. Appears in the Koran as 'striving in the way of God' [as in a mental struggle]; however, can be interpreted to mean physical fighting. Used as shorthand in Afghanistan to mean the period of resistance to the USSR (1979–89) and, depending upon your viewpoint, the current struggle against the Western-backed Karzai government.

*Jirga* See also Shura. Traditional Pushtun method of dispute resolution where male elders sit and discuss a problem until a solution is reached in a consensus manner as opposed to an adversarial manner. Younger children will sit and watch, but not participate. Male adults are all allowed to speak. Anyone may come. Sometimes used interchangeably with Shura.

*Kudos (Haji)* Barakzai. Militia leader who was Mir Wali's second in command. Controlled the Barakzai area from Gereshk westwards towards Nad-e Ali. Militia funded by Assadullah Wafa and US Special Forces; however, the funding stopped in 2007/8. The area previously occupied by his militia fell to the 'Taliban'. Now runs an aggregate mine near Camp Price.

*Kakar* A tribe from which families were settled during the canal projects, particularly in Garmsir and Nad-e Ali. Key member of this tribe was Mullah Dadullah—an infamous Taliban commander who was killed by ISAF in 2007. Predated upon by the provincial government during 2001–5.

*Karez* Underground water channel used for irrigation, particularly in northern Helmand.

*Karim (Mullah)* Noorzai/Aghezai. From Loy Bagh. Hizb commander and then worked with Taliban during 1994–2001. Continued to 'sit' on Taliban 'shura' in Nad-e Ali post-2001 as well as the district community council.

*Karmal, Babrak*. President 1979–86. Installed by the Soviets, and was never more than a client of theirs. Probably mixed ethnicity. Later seen by the Soviets as not able to achieve their aims and was moved to retirement in Moscow.

*Karzai* See Hamid Karzai.

*Khad* Later called Ministry of State Security (WAD) or the National Directorate of Security (NDS). Unsavoury organisation under the control of the KGB until the Soviets left Afghanistan in 1989. One of its major roles was to watch over the other security services to make sure that they remain loyal to the state. Helmandis still often call the NDS Khad.

*Khalifa Shirin Khan (Haji)* Barakzai. Leader of the stronger side of the Barakzai tribal coalitions in Malgir. This comprised the Akhundzadakhel, the Utmanzai, the Bayezai and the Sardarzai clans. They generally allied with Hizb and later with the Taliban.

*Khalozai* Khankhel of the Alizai tribe. Located mainly in Baghran. Important members include Rais Baghrani and Abdul Rahman Khan.

*Khalq/Khalqi* More extreme of the two factions of the PDPA. Was in power in Kabul in 1978/9; however, the army remained Khalqi-dominated throughout the 1980s. Ideologically defined the militias in Lashkar Gah at the end of the 1980s. Important leaders include Taraki and Amin.

*Khan* lit. Landowner. Also used as an honorific, like 'Esquire' in English.

*Khan Mohammad* Barakzai. Harakat commander. Fought with Rasoul against Mir Wali when he was in the government. First to occupy Gereshk in 2001 when the Taliban left. First chief of police in Gereshk in Karzai era. Prominent smuggler, now in jail for drug offences.

*Khano (Khan Mohammad)* Noorzai/Aghezai. Militia commander who controlled Lashkar Gah in the early 1990s. Real name Khan Mohammad, originally from Farah, he became a militia commander because his brother was a well-connected member of the Khalq faction. Settled back in Lashkar Gah post-2001 and became a businessman with a small militia, but was eventually disarmed by Abdul Rahman Jan.

*Kharoti* Important Ghilzai tribe. Very prominent in Nad-e Ali, where they compete with the Noorzai for district leadership. Important members include Gulbuddin Hekmatyar (leader of Hizb) and Hafizullah Amin (president in 1979). Closely allied to Taliban narrative in Nad-e Ali.

*Koka* See Abdul Wali Koka.

*Kuchi* lit. nomadic.

*Lal Jan (Haji)* Noorzai. Elder/militia leader of Noorzo Kalay in northern Nad-e Ali and he represents one of the communities of Noorzai who settled from Now Zad and Washir during the 1990s; during the post-2001 period he controlled the Nahr-e Bughra from Chah-e Mirza to Loy Mandah. By 2008, his militia had been rolled into the Nad-e Ali police.

*Lal Mohammad* Barakzai. From Torghai. Petty commander, who has worked for the Taliban, the 93rd Division, the Taliban again, ISAF (ALP) and finally the Taliban again. A 'Torghai nationalist', he will go with whoever will guarantee Torghai's security.

*Madrasah* lit. school (Arabic). Generally considered in the context of Afghanistan and Pakistan to mean a religious school with a focus on Quranic education. Many groups within the region also use them to train young men for battle.

*Mahaz* Mujahidin party led by Pir Gailani. Probably the most poorly funded party because they represented the old moderate (royal) order, which the ISI did not wish to re-empower. Many commanders in Helmand allied with Mahaz and then switched when it was unable to provide them with enough weapons and funding.

*Mahaz system* cf. nezami system. Channelled, patronage model of Taliban supply and organisation. Very similar to how the jihad was organised, with the different parties being analogous to the different mahazes.

*Maidan* lit. field. Used by Helmandis for the airfield to the south of Lashkar Gah that was the Soviet HQ in Helmand.

*Maiwand, Battle of* A serious defeat suffered by British forces at Khushk-e Nakhud in what is now Maiwand district, Kandahar province in 1880. The battle was won by Ayub Khan with support from Alizai tribesmen led by Abu Bakr Khan.

*Malem Mir Wali* See Mir Wali.

*Malem Yusof Barakzai* Hizb commander from Now Zad.

*Manan (Haji)* Noorzai. Nephew of Haji Lal Jan. Police commander who was seen as particularly cruel by the population of Nad-e Ali.

*Mangal (Governor)* Mangal. From Paktika. Appointed governor of Helmand in 2008 and moved on in 2012.

*Mir Wali* Barakzai. Previous Hizb commander during the jihad, then joined the government in 1987. Became the 93rd Division commander in the early Karzai era. Now MP. See Appendix 1 for more details.

*Miraw* Water manager. Sets out how much water each family can have from the canals and is the first person who arbitrates water disputes. Can either be selected by the community or appointed by the landowner, or a combination of the two. Usually paid in kind by the farmers. There are some government-employed miraws in the canal-zone areas.

*Mirwais (Khan)* Kharoti. Son of Wakil Safar.

*Mirza (Khan)* Barakzai. Hizb commander during the jihad who became a commander in the 93rd Division. Stole some land in Gereshk and set his militia up with housing in early 2000s. Area now called Mirza Khan Kalay.

*Mohammad Wali* Alizai. Brother of Bismillah (G968). Was close ally of Sher Mohammad Akhundzada, governor of Musa Qala when British first came, now an MP. No longer an ally of Sher Mohammad.

*Mohammadzai* Khankhel (chief lineage) of the Barakzai tribe and produced the lineage that ruled Afghanistan from 1826 to 1978. Concentrations of Mohammadzai around Gereshk, as it was a seat of the sub-tribe.

*Mujahidin* lit. holy warriors. In the context of Afghanistan it means those who fought in the anti-communist resistance, but the fighters currently fighting the government also call themselves mujahidin.

*Mullah* Prayer leader. Usually one per village, responsible for the mosque, life rites and some religious education of children.

*Murtaza* Kharoti. G361. See Appendix 6.

*Nahr-e Bughra* Canal. The original and most extensive of the canals from the canal project. Construction started in 1936. Provides water for at least 100,000 people in Marjeh, Nad-e Ali and parts of Nahr-e Saraj.

*Naim (Mullah)* Alizai. From Garmsir. District governor during Taliban era. Led 'Taliban' resurgence in 2005 in Garmsir.

*Najibullah, Mohammad* President 1987–92. Had previously been head of Khad. Instituted a reconciliation and national solidarity programme and expanded militias in preparation for the Soviet withdrawal. Made many concessions to the mujahidin that were not consistent with communism (for example, using Islam and its precepts more in governing), although this failed to bring an end to the conflict. Against all predictions, managed to remain in power for three years after the Soviet exit.

*Nasim Akhundzada (Mullah)* Alizai. Most (in)famous of the Helmandi jihadi commanders who led the Alizai and fought under the Harakat franchise. Accepted money from Khad throughout. Was so successful that many other commanders swore allegiance to him. He was killed by Hizb in 1990. His brothers (Rasoul and Ghaffour) succeeded him, becoming provincial governors of Helmand, as did his nephew, Sher Mohammad.

*NDS* See Khad. The Karzai-era Afghan internal security service.

*Nejad* Mujahidin party led by Mujaddidi. Not very prominent in Helmand.

*Nezami system* lit. organised or military. cf. mahaz system. A more institutional, centralised form of supply and organisation instituted in 2009 by the Taliban. Not fully implemented in Helmand.

*Noorzai.* One of the big three Helmandi tribes (see Alizai and Barakzai). Previously, they were marginalised from Helmandi politics due to their location in Now Zad, Washir and Garmsir; however, during the 1990s they occupied abandoned land in Nad-e Ali and Marjeh, as they were in control of the Helmandi police in the post-2001 era. Also significant in Kandahar province.

*Omar (Mullah)* Hotak. Leader of the Taliban movement. Ruled Afghanistan from 1996 to 2001. Probably currently living in Quetta.

*Osmani* See Akhtur Mohammad Osmani.

*Parcham/Parchami* Less extreme faction of the PDPA (see Khalq). Ruled from 1979 until 1992. Dominated Khad (and its successor organisations) during that time. Important leaders include Karmal and Najibullah.

*Paslow (Haji Mullah)* Popalzai leader and Harakat commander in the south of Nad-e Ali. Taliban commander. Prominent family with several links to the post-2001 Taliban movement.

*People's Democratic Party of Afghanistan (PDPA)* PDPA was split into two factions, Khalq and Parcham, roughly split along tribal and ethnic lines, rural Pushtun (particularly Ghilzai) and urban Pushtun/ Tajik respectively. The PDPA was formed in 1965 and split into its constituent factions in 1967, which were re-coalesced under Soviet pressure in 1977. The more extreme left-wing Khalq faction seized power in the 1978 coup, but was replaced by the more moderate

Parcham faction in 1979 upon the Soviet intervention. Due to Khalq purges during its time in power, the Afghan army was dominated by Khalq officers throughout the 1980s, yet the massive state internal security apparatus (Khad, or later, WAD) rapidly became Parcham dominated after 1979.

*Pir Mohammad Sadat* Kharoti. From Naqilabad. (In)famous Hizb commander. Was 93rd commander, then worked closely with the Taliban post-2005. Sat on the Nad-e Ali council 2009–10.

*Pirzai* One of the three main sub-tribes of the Alizai (see Hassanzai and Khalozai).

*Popalzai* Major Pushtun tribe in the Durrani confederation. President Karzai's tribe. Outside of Nawa, not very populous in Helmand.

*Pushtun* Ethnic group in the south of Afghanistan and the west of Pakistan. Split by the countries' borders (the Durand Line). Comprise around 40 per cent of the Afghan population.

*Qari Hazrat* Ishaqzai/Mistereekhel. Son of Abdul Khaleq. Major 'Taliban' commander post-2005. Killed by ISAF in 2010. Said to have been allied to Hizb and the Taliban at the same time in order to protect his clan's drug interests.

*Quetta Shura* The leadership shura of the Taliban in Baluchistan, Pakistan. Supported by the ISI. Allegedly surpassed in importance by the Peshawar Shura in 2011/2.

*Rahim* Ishaqzai. From Now Zad. Major Taliban commander during Taliban era. Taliban provincial governor 2001–8.

*Rahmattiar* Ishaqzai. Most prominent Hizb commander in the south of Nad-e Ali. From Jangal.

*Rais Baghrani* See Baghrani.

*Rasoul Akhundzada* Alizai. Brother of Nasim and Ghaffour. Helmand's governor briefly in 1993/4 when he captured it with Ismail Khan's help from the ex-communist militias led by Khano. Father of Sher Mohammad Akhundzada.

*Rauf Khadim (Mullah)* One of Baghrani's sub-commanders in the 93rd Division in 1993/4. Became commander Taliban in movement (was Zakir's boss), spent time in Guantanamo. Released and rejoined the Taliban movement. Now Taliban governor for Uruzgan.

*Rauf Khan* Ishaqzai. Mahaz Amir for Helmand. Joined government and became militia commander in 1987.

*Safar (Khan)* See Wakil Mohammad Safar.

*Salam (Mullah)* Alizai/Pirzai. Petty Taliban commander in post-2001 period. Had been Taliban governor of Kajaki during Taliban era.

Made government district governor of Musa Qala in 2007. Not to be confused with Abdul Salam (Noorzai) or Abdul Salam (Alizai/ Khalozai).

*Sardar Baghwani* Allegedly an Iranian intelligence officer. Appears on three occasions in the story: first, in 1993 talking to Khano and Abdul Rahman Jan; secondly, in 2002 inciting people to rise up against the Americans; and lastly in 2006 to incite people to rise up against the British.

*Shah Nazar Helmandwal* Also Shah Nazar. Noorzai/Gurg. Allied with Mahaz. Then provincial governor during Najib period. Murdered, probably by Hizb, in the early 1990s. Nephew, Abdul Ahad Helmandwal, was a prominent Noorzai leader in Nad-e Ali and was first community council chair in 2009.

*Shakir* See Mullah Ibrahim.

*Sher Mohammad Akhundzada (Alizai)* Son of Rasoul Mohammad Akhundzada. Helmand's governor from 2001 to 2005. Very close to Karzai with intermarriages between the clans. Sacked in 2005 at British insistence due to his links to the narcotics trade. Now a senator. See Appendix 1.

*Shirzai* See Gul Agha Shirzai.

*Shura.* See also Jirga. Meeting, less egalitarian/consensual than a jirga. In a strict sense, people should be invited to speak at a shura.

*Sur Gul* Barakzai. Nephew of Haji Gul Ehktiar. 93rd commander and then Taliban commander. Taliban district governor for Washir until 2012.

*Tajik* Ethnic group in the north-east of Afghanistan. Predominantly formed the Northern Alliance, which overthrew the Taliban with US support in 2001. Comprise around 30 per cent of the Afghan population. Significant leaders include Masoud and Rabbani.

*Tanai (General)* Khalqi general who led a coup against Najib in 1990. Then began working with Hizb and led a 'Hizb-Khalq' rapprochement in Helmand between Hafizullah and Khano.

*Taraki, Noor Mohammad.* Afghan president from 1978 to 1979. A member of the more extreme Khalq faction of the PDPA, he was ousted by Amin. Responsible for the reforms (especially land reforms) that caused so much damage and resentment in Helmandi society.

*Topak salaran* lit. warlords.

*Tor Jan* Noorzai. Cousin by marriage of Abdul Rahman Jan. Nad-e Ali chief of police 2006–8. Killed by a suicide bomber, which was described by some locals as a gift from the Taliban because he had been so cruel. Accused of being behind a spate of kidnappings for ransom of rich individuals in the district.

*Ushr* 10 per cent agricultural Islamic tithe.

*Wakil Mohammad Safar* Kharoti. Led the Kharoti into Nad-e Ali in 1954. Highly respected leader. Also MP during Soviet period. Died in March 2009.

*Yahya* Noorzai. Etihad commander from Marjeh. Fought Nasim for control of the Garmsir bridge in 1989.

*Zahir Shah* Barakzai. Reign: 1933–73. Was very young in 1933 and so only exerted influence towards the end of his reign. Keen to advance Afghanistan, he wrote the 1964 Constitution which enshrined hitherto unseen rights, but was deposed by his cousin Mohammad Daud in 1973. Lived in exile in Italy during the communist, mujahidin and Taliban eras before being invited back to an honorary position, *The Father of the Nation*, under Karzai. Died 2007.

*-zai (suffix)* Meaning sons of.

*Zakat* Annual Islamic tax on assets. Different rates, but for example, 2.5 per cent on money held over one lunar year. Redistributed to the poor and needy.

*Zakir* See Abdul Qayoum Zakir.

*Zamindawar* One of the four ancient districts of Pusht-e rud (ancient Helmand). Zamindawari is used interchangeably with Alizai.

# APPENDIX 3

# TIMELINE OF KEY EVENTS AFFECTING HELMAND

| | |
|---|---|
| 1978—April | Saur Revolution. |
| 1978—October | Baghran District falls. |
| 1979—January | Land redistribution begins; Musa Qala falls. |
| 1979—June | Now Zad, Sangin and Washir fall. |
| 1979—December | Soviets invade. |
| Mid-1980 | Remaining central districts of Helmand have fallen; rebels on outskirts of Lashkar Gah; Soviets deploy 500 men to stabilise Lashkar Gah. |
| 1981 | 'Mujahidin' start to fall out all over Helmand, particularly the north. Khad exacerbates this and offers them money to attack each other. |
| 1980–3 | Defensive cummerbund established around Lashkar Gah and Gereshk. District centres re-established in Nad-e Ali, Nawa, Garmsir and Kahn Eshin. |
| 1987 | Najibullah becomes president. Militia programme starts. Shah Nazar Khan becomes provincial governor; 'Hizb'–'Harakat' war in the north sponsored by Khad peaks. |
| 1988/9 | Soviets leave Helmand. District centres outside of Nad-e Ali, Nawa, Lashkar Gah and Gereshk abandoned. Final Soviet operation in Sangin. |
| 1991 | Nad-e Ali district centre falls. Tribes begin to have a series of tribal shuras to reconcile their members in the post-communist era. |

| | |
|---|---|
| 1992 | Najibullah falls, Hafizullah becomes provincial governor. Khano becomes chief of police; Allah Noor becomes 93rd commander; much fighting. |
| Late 1992 | Hafizullah ejected; Akhwaendi becomes provincial governor; much fighting. |
| 1993 | Rasoul takes over Lashkar Gah; Khano and others escape; some stability. |
| 1994 | Rasoul dies of natural causes; Ghaffour takes over. |
| Late 1994 | Taliban approach Helmand; Rais Baghrani switches sides; Ghaffour and other jihadis evicted. |
| 1995 | Several failed attempts to retake Helmand by the jihadis. Taliban establish control. Helmand stable. |
| 1997 | Conscription begins. |
| 2000 | Taliban opium ban. |
| Late 2001 | Taliban leave Helmand as other cities in the country fall from Taliban control; Hafizullah Khan takes over control of Lashkar Gah; Abdul Rahman and Sher Mohammad then take over and become chief of police and provincial governor, respectively. Dad Mohammad appointed NDS chief and Mir Wali 93rd Division commander. |
| 2002 | Tribes hold a series of tribal shuras to reconcile their members in the post-Taliban era; US Special Forces deploy to Helmand; raise militias and arrest people and send them to Guantanamo. |
| 2004 | Malem Mir Wali disarmed by UN-sponsored DDR process; many former 93rd groups ally themselves with the Taliban for protection; US PRT deploys to Lashkar Gah. |
| 2005 | Dad Mohammad and Sher Mohammad removed from posts (at British insistence). ISI-supported, Taliban-led series of assassinations to remove remaining government officials. |
| 2006 | Government continues to collapse; British deploy brigade to 'stabilise' the province; outbreaks of fierce fighting as they move to the north of the province; British in small numbers forced to use airpower to defend themselves; Sher Mohammad sends his men to work with the 'Taliban'. |

| | |
|---|---|
| 2006—April | Baghran falls/attacked. |
| 2006—Summer | Musa Qala, Now Zad and Sangin attacked. |
| 2006—Autumn | British pull out of Musa Qala; central Helmand still stable; Governor Daud removed and replaced by Assadullah Wafa. |
| 2007 | British conduct operations all over the north of the province particularly around Sangin. Described by some locals as like Soviet operations. |
| 2008 | US marines begin to deploy to bolster numbers of coalition troops; Governor Mangal appointed; British transport third turbine up to the Kajaki dam; Marjeh and Nad-e Ali 'fall' after Abdul Rahman's crops are eradicated; British launch operation to retake Nad-e Ali. |
| 2009 | Numbers of US troops continue to increase; British attempt to consolidate in Nad-e Ali; launch community shura to channel development and develop governance. |
| 2010 | US surge announced. US troop numbers increase and they expand into Khan Eshin and Now Zad; take over control of Musa Qala, Sangin and Kajaki from British. British consolidate in central Helmand; ISAF withdrawal announced for 2014. |
| 2011 | ISAF militia programme launched (ALP); Lashkar Gah handed over to Afghan control in July; British and Americans begin to close bases and hand them over to the Afghans; Nad-e Ali almost completely handed over by December. |
| 2012 | Problems with ALP programme causing it to be suspended; ISAF/Afghan operations continue into the desert, but generally stay away from the heavily populated areas; Governor Mangal sacked; tribes begin a series of tribal shuras to reconcile their members in the post-ISAF era. |
| 2014 | Afghan presidential election; ISAF full withdrawal date. |

# APPENDIX 4

## TRIBAL DIAGRAMS AND FAMILY TREES

Note: these are by no means fully authoritative. However, each one has been checked with two or more interviewees.

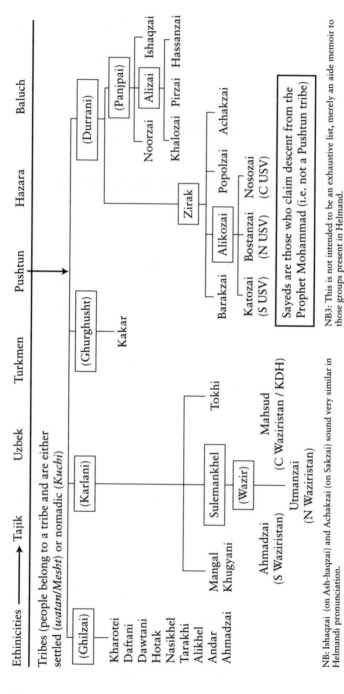

Figure 9: Diagram of the major tribes in Helmand

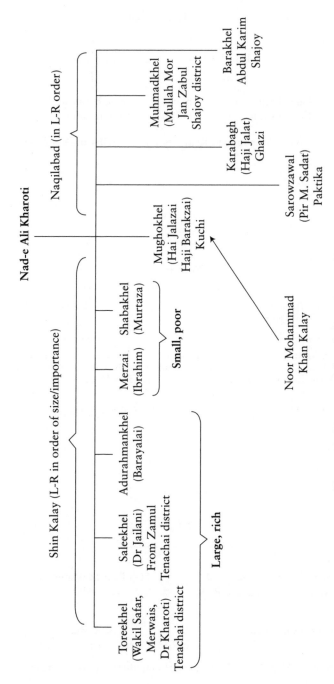

Figure 10: Diagram of the Kharoti sub-tribes in Nad-e Ali

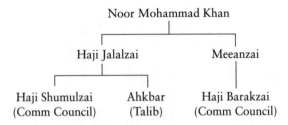

Figure 11: Noor Mohammad Khan's family tree (Kharoti/Mughokhel)

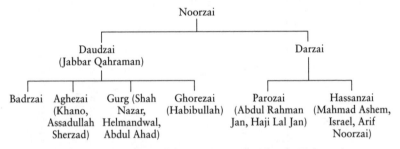

Figure 12: Diagram of the Noorzai sub-tribes in Helmand

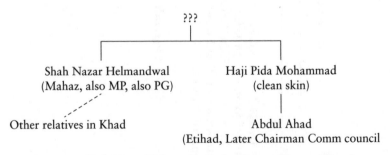

Figure 13: Shah Nazar Helmandwal's family tree (Noorzai/Gurg)

APPENDIX 4

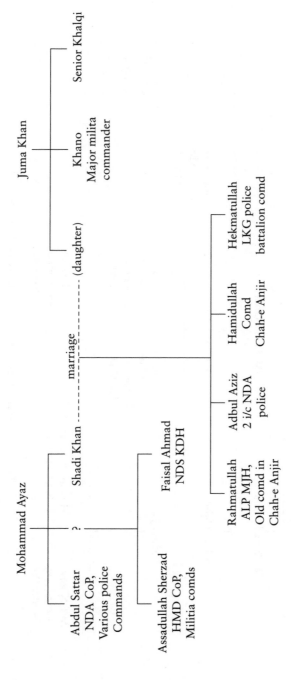

Figure 14: Khano's family tree (Noorzai/Aghezai)

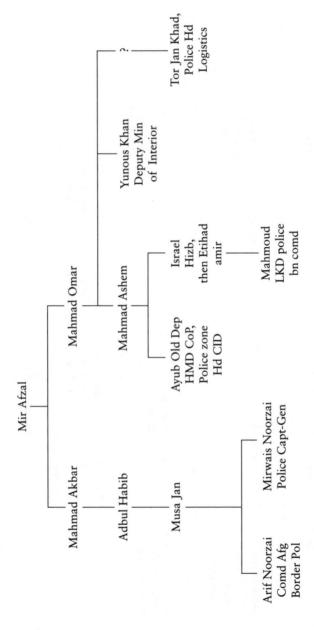

Figure 15: Israel's family tree (Noorzai/Darzai/Hassanzai)

APPENDIX 4

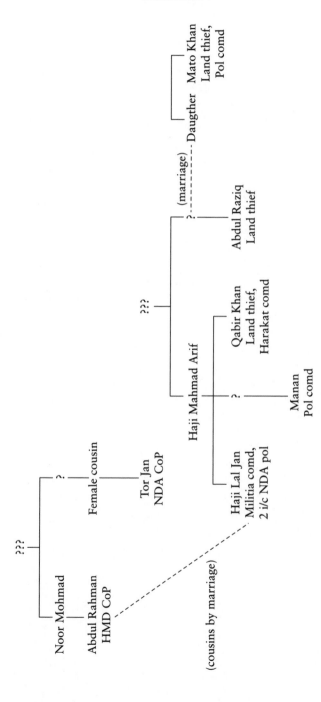

Figure 16: Abdul Rahman and Haji Lal Jan (Noorzai/Darzai/Parozai)

293

# APPENDIX 5

# LISTS OF HELMANDI PROVINCIAL, DISTRICT AND MILITARY OFFICIALS

*Provincial Governors*

| | |
|---|---|
| –1978 | Majid Serbilard (Barakzai, Parchami, from Kandahar) |
| –1979 | Fazal Jan Jahesh (Khalqi, from Paktia) |
| –1980 | Mama Rasoul (Shinwari, Khalqi, from Nangahar) |
| 1981–3 | Khan Jan (Alakozai, Khalqi, from Kunar) |
| 1984 (briefly) | Zeyarmal (Barakzai, Parchami, from Kandahar) |
| 1984/5–? | Gul Mahmad Khwashal (Noorzai, Khalqi, from Farah) |
| 1987–91/2? | Shah Nazar Helmandwal (Noorzai/Gurg, Mahaz, from Loy Bagh) |
| 1991/2? | Gul Mahmad Khwashal (Noorzai, Khalqi, from Farah) |
| 1992 (six months) | Hafizullah (Barakzai, Hizb, from Bolan) |
| 1992–3 | Akhwaendi (Barakzai, Jamiat, Nawa) |
| 1993–4 | Rasoul Akhundzada (Alizai, Harakat, Musa Qala) |
| 1994 | Ghaffour Akhundzada (Alizai, Harakat, Musa Qala) |
| 1994–5? | Mullah Mahmad Karim (Noorzai, Talib, from Kandahar) |

| 1995–2001 | Mullah Abdul Bari (Alakozai, Talib, from Uruzgan) |
| 2001–5 | Sher Mohammad Akhundzada (Alizai, Harakat, from Kajaki) |
| 2005–6 | Daud (Safi, technocrat, from Gereshk) |
| 2006–8 | Assadullah Wafa (Achakzai, from Kandahar) |
| 2008–12 | Gulabuddin Mangal (Mangal, Khalqi/Hizb, from Paktika) |
| 2012– | General Naim |

## Nad-e Ali District Governors

| 1978–89 | ? |
| 1989?–91? | Mahmad Razer (Barakzai, ?, from Chah-e Anjir) |
| ? | Rahman Jan? (Noorzai/Gurg, Etihad, from Now Zad) |
| 1992–? | Khalifa Khwashkea (Noorzai, Jamiat, from Loy Bagh) |
| 1993–4? | Mullah Said Gul (Alizai/Khalozai, Baghrani sub-commander, from?) |
| 1994–5 | Mullah Ibrahim (Laghmani, Talib, from Garmsir) |
| –1995 | Mullah Abdul Rahman (Noorzai, Talib, from Now Zad) |
| 1995–6 | Mawlana Sahib (?, Talib, from Uruzgan) |
| ? | Mullah Abdul Rahim (Ishaqzai, Talib, from Uruzgan) |
| ? | Mullah Sharwali (Daftani, Talib, from Nahr-e Saraj) |
| ? | Mullah Abdul Haq (Daftani, Talib, from Waziristan) |
| ?–2001 | Mullah Saifullah (Alizai, Talib, from Uruzgan) |
| 2002–4? | Mira Jan (Noorzai, Harakat, from Chah-e Anjir) |
| 2004–7? | Mullah Qasam (Noorzai, Jamiat, from Sangin) |
| 2007/8– | Habibullah (Noorzai, Khalqi, from Garmsir) |

## Nahr-e Saraj District Governors

| 1978–? | Zahir Khan (Barakzai, ?, Malgir) |
| ?–1981 | Malem Muskinyar (Barakzai, Khalqi, ?) |
| 1981–7 | Marg (Noorzai, Khalqi, from Uruzgan) |

| | |
|---|---|
| 1987–92 | Abdul Sangar (Barakzai, Parchami, ?) |
| 1992 (briefly) | Saran Sahab (Barakzai, Khalqi, from Farah) |
| 1992–4 | Khalifa Shirin Khan (Barakzai, Hizb, from Malgir) |
| 1994–2001 | Mullah Mir Hamza (Noorzai, Talib, Uruzgan) |
| 2001–? (briefly) | Khalifa Shirin Khan (Barakzai, Hizb, from Malgir) |
| 2002 | Mullah Qadoos (Alizai, Harakat, from Musa Qala) |
| 2002–3 | Mahmad Lal (Popalzai, Etihad, ?) |
| 2004–6 | Nabi Khan (Barakzai, Jamiat, from Nawa) |
| ?2006–8 | Manab Khan (Barakzai, Hizb, from Bolan) |
| ?2008–10 | Abdul Ahad Khan (Alizai, Khalqi, from Kajaki) |
| 2010 | Jan Gul (Barakzai, Khalqi, from Lashkar Gah) |
| 2010–11 | Mohayadin (Alizai, ?, from Kajaki) |
| 2011 | Amir Jan (Popalzai, Khalqi, ?) |
| 2011– | Salem Rodi (Alizai, Harakat, ?) |

*Provincial Chiefs of Police*

| | |
|---|---|
| 1978–80 | ? |
| 1980–? | Musa Ensanmal (?, Parchami, from Allahabad) |
| ?–1987 | Ayub Khan (Tajik, ?, ?) |
| 1987–9 | Karim Payekh (Alizai, ?, from Zamindawar) |
| 1989–91 | Mulakhel (Mulakhel, ?, from Ghazni) |
| 1991–2 | Hussein Khan Andiwal (Barakzai, Khalqi, from Babaji) |
| 1992–3 | Khano (Noorzai, ?, from Loy Bagh) |
| 1993–4 | Abdul Ahad (Ishaqzai, Harakat, from Now Zad) |
| 1995–2001 | ?Taliban era? |
| 2001–6 | Abdul Rahman Jan (Noorzai, various, from Marjeh) |
| 2006–7 | Hussein Khan Andiwal (Barakzai, Khalqi, from Babaji) |
| 2008 | Mulakhel (Mulakhel, ?, from Ghazni) |
| 2008–9 | Assadullah Sherzad (Noorzai/Aghezai, various, from Loy Bagh) |
| 2009–2012 | Angar (Alakozai, ?, from Kandahar) |
| 2012– | Nabi Elham (Tokhi, Khalqi, from Uruzgan) |

*Nad-e Ali Chiefs of Police*

| 1978–89 | ? |
|---|---|
| 1989–91 | Habibullah (Noorzai, Khalqi, from Garmsir) |
| 1991–5 | ?Andiwal government? |
| 1995–2001 | ?Taliban-era? |
| 2001–2 | Haji Jamalzai (Kharoti, Harakat, from Noor Mohammad Khan Kalay) |
| 2002–4 | Hakim Khan (Daftani, Jamiat, from Marjeh) |
| 2004–5 | Haji Twoyeb (Noorzai, ?, ?) |
| 2005–8 | Tor Jan (Noorzai/Darzai/Parozai, ?, ?) |
| 2008–9 | Abdul Sattar (Noorzai/Aghezai, ?, from Loy Bagh) |
| 2009 | Sheryar (Tajik, ?, ?) |
| 2009–11 | Shadi Khan (Popalzai, Khalqi, from Garmsir) |
| 2011– | Haji Omar Jan (Andar, ?, from Marjeh) |

*Nahr-e Saraj Chiefs of Police*

| 1978–92 | ? |
|---|---|
| 1992–3? | Wali Mohammad (Barakzai, ?, ?) |
| 1994–2001 | ?Taliban-era? |
| 2001–3 | Khan Mohammad (Barakzai, Harakat, from Deh Adam Khan) |
| 2004 | Badr (Popalzai, ?, from Uruzgan) |
| ?2004 | Amanullah (Noorzai, ?, ?) |
| ? | ?Khan Mohammad |
| ? | Haji Dil Jan (?, Hizb, from Kandahar) |
| 2005? | Haji Kadus (Barakzai, USSF, from Charkandaz) |
| 2006? | Habibullah (Noorzai, Khalqi, from Garmsir) |
| ? | Rafiq Sheryar (Noorzai, Khalqi, ?) |
| 2008–10 | Shuja (?, Khalqi, ?) |
| | Farouq (Barakzai, Khalqi, from Deh Adam Khan) |
| | Shuja (?, Khalqi, ?) |
| | Farouq (Barakzai, Khalqi, from Deh Adam Khan) |
| | NB Abdul Razaq (Barakzai, Hizb, from Malgir) de facto Chief of Police |
| 2010–11 | Ezmarai (Barakzai, various, from Gereshk) |
| 2011 | Saifullah (Alakozai, Khalqi, ?) |

| | |
|---|---|
| 2011–12 | Shadi Khan (Popalzai, Khalqi, ?) |
| 2012– | Gulie Khan (Baluch, Khalqi, from Garmsir) |

*Commanders of the 93rd Division*

| | |
|---|---|
| ?–1989 | Baba Tapa |
| 1989– | Jenat Gul |
| ? | Saber |
| ? | Wardak |
| 1992–3 | Allah Noor (Barakzai, ?, Nawa) |
| 1993–5/6? | Rais Baghrani (Alizai, various, from Baghran) |
| ?–2001 | ?Talib |
| 2001–4 | Malem Mir Wali (Barakzai, Hizb, from Malgir) |
| 2004 | *Disbanded* |

# APPENDIX 6

# SELECTED HELMANDI GUANTANAMO PRISONERS

The purpose of this appendix is to discuss some of the Helmandi Guantanamo prisoners' cases in the context of the information contained in this book. Reading the documents it is clear that the Guantanamo personnel believe in the unitary nature of organisations like the Taliban and believe the simplistic narratives surrounding them. The information contained in this appendix can be found in either deliberately released Guantanamo files (http://projects.nytimes.com/ guantanamo) or leaked Guantanamo files (http://wikileaks.org/ gitmo/—both accessed 21 November 2012). Also of great use was Andy Worthington's *The Guantánamo Files*. This appendix details the following prisoners (followed by prisoner number if available):

- Abdul Wahid (no prisoner number as died in Camp Price).
- Hamidullah/Janat gul—953.
- Abdullah Ghulam Rasoul (actually Abdul Qayoum Zakir)—008.
- Abdul Rauf Khadim—108.
- Abdul Rahman—118.
- Murtaza—361.
- Amanullah Alakozai—538.
- Qari Hassanullah Pirzai—562.
- Haji Bismillah—968.
- Abdul Razaq (Achakzai)—942.
- Haji Jalil—1117.
- Abdul Wahab—961.

- Rahmatullah—964.
- Hafizullah—965.
- Baridad—966.
- Nasirullah—967.
- Abdul Baghi—963.
- Kushky Yar—971.
- Akhtur Mohammad—969.
- Arif Mohammad—972.
- Abdul Kadus—929.
- Mohammad Ismail—930.
- Mohammad Nasim—958.

## Abdul Wahid

Very little is known about Abdul Wahid. It appears that he was tortured by the Afghan militia forces in Gereshk (that is, Mir Wali's men) before being handed over to US Special Forces in Camp Price, where he died (on 6 November 2003). His autopsy recognised 'multiple blunt force injuries to head, torso and extremities'.[1] Below is a US investigation report into his death. It can be concluded from this document that US Special Forces were aware of the use of torture by their Afghan allies but did nothing about it.

## Hamidullah/Janat Gul—953

Arrested 30 January 2003 in Lashkar Gah. Transferred to Afghan custody 18 April 2005. (Although the JTF–GITMO Assessment states that he was transferred to Guantanamo on 22 March 2002.) He was arrested because he was president of Ariana Airlines (Afghanistan's flag carrier) during the Taliban period. Evidence against him included the fact that the Ariana office was located in an area of Kabul near Taliban and al-Qaeda offices and that three previous employees of the airline had been located at an early 2002 Hizb-e Islami meeting: 'this indicates that the airline was not only supporting the Taliban, but also the [sic] Hizb-e Islami Gulbuddin'. Reading the transcripts it is clear that the tribunal members are not aware that there is a separate date system in operation in Afghanistan. An educated man, he claims that he joined Ariana to escape Taliban conscription. Assessed as having a high intelligence value.

## After Action Report (AAR)
### Preliminary Investigation into the death of a Detainee at
### Geresch Forward Operating Base, Helmand Province, Afghanistan

229
(1 of 4)

**MISSION:** Conduct a Preliminary investigation into the death of a detainee in custody at Geresch Forward Operating Base (FOB), Helmand Province, Afghanistan.

**SYSNOPSIS:**

b(7)(c)-5

On or about 4 Nov 03, USSF personnel took custody of Mr ████████ an Afghani male, 25-27 yrs of age, a self-confessed member of the Taliban. When processed by the USSF medical staff he was noted to having several bruises to his hips, groin and buttocks area (some severe to minor), and numerous burns to his chest (which is a known interview/interrogation "technique" used by the local Afghanistan Militia Forces (AMF)). Allegedly, during interrogation ████ admitted to being involved in ambushes of OGA, USSF personnel and other coalition forces. ████ admitted to being involved in intelligence collection in efforts to ambush or kill coalition members, or impede operations conducted by coalition members. On 6 Nov 03, ████ was guarded by the AMF security force at the Geresch FOB with one other detainee. The AMF security guard left the detainment area, and when he returned he discovered ████ laying in a supine position, wrapped in a wool blanket in the center of the detainee area. The guard immediately summoned USSF medical personnel, who determined ████ was deceased. No life-saving measures were attempted due to the presence of rigor mortis. USSF personnel at the FOB immediately notified their higher headquarters (3rd Bn, 3rd SFG, Kandahar Air Field, AF) of the death. During an examination of the areas and the remains, no apparent signs of foul play, or struggle were noted. b(7)(c)-5

An Autopsy of the remains is pending at the time of this report. The undetermined cause and manner of death is currently being investigated by the US Army Criminal investigation Command (████████████), Kandahar Branch Office, AF, APO AE 09355. b(6)

**SIGNIFICANT INTERVIEWS:** b(7)(c)-1      b(7)(c)-3      b(6)

b(6)
About 2130Z, 6 Nov 03, SA ████████ interviewed SFC ████████ (18D, SF Medic), ████ A Co, 3rd Bn, 3rd SFG, Geresch FOB, who stated he was the SF Medic notified that the detainee was found dead in the detainee area. SFC ████ stated he conducted a preliminary assessment and based on the onset of rigor mortis no lifesaving measures were attempted (see attached Sworn Statement of SFC ████ for details). b(7)(c)-3

b(7)(c)-3   b(6)      b(7)(c)-3   b(7)(c)-5   b(7)(c)-3   b(6)
About 2230Z, 6 Nov 03, SA ████████ interviewed SFC ████████, A Co, 3rd Bn, 3rd SFG, Geresch FOB, who stated he initially received ████ from the AMF. SFC ████ stated at the time of his release to USSF, he was photographed and medically assessed by USSF personnel (SFG ████ A Co, 3rd Bn, 3rd SFG, Geresch FOB, AF). SFC ████ stated he was the last USSF person to see ████ alive (See attached Sworn Statement for details). b(7)(c)-3

b(7)(c)-5      b(7)(c)-3
**AGENT'S COMMENT:** SFC ████ is a 18E; SF Military Intelligence NCO.

b(7)(c)-5                     b(7)(c)-3                              b(7)(c)-3
About 0030Z, 7 Nov 03, SA ████████ interviewed SSG ████ (18D SF Medic), who related he conducted an initial assessment of ████ when he was released to USSF personnel. SSG ████ stated ████ was observed to have burns to his chest and stomach areas, and bruising to his hips, groin and buttocks areas. SSG ████ it was not unusual to see detainees released to USSF with this injury. SSG ████ b(7)(c)-3 described these injuries as a normal interview/interrogation method used by the local AMF, that discovery was always determined by medical personnel and were reported by the detainee. SSG ████ stated this was due

b(7)(c)-3          b(7)(c)-5          b(7)(c)-3    6937C
For Official Use Only

000031      Exhibit 9

DOD-045198

303

APPENDIX 6

About 2100Z, 6 Nov 03, SA ▓▓▓ exposed photographs of injuries noted by MAJ (DR) ▓▓▓ who stated there was extensive bruising and swelling to the hips, buttocks and groin area. Further, there were burn marks (which were in various stages of healing) to the chest area. Further, there was a bruise to the left shoulder, and various abrasions to his lower extremities, in various stages of healing. There were no apparent injuries to the head or neck area, and the deceased did not have any injuries to his hands (palm or back of hand). DR ▓▓▓ noted the presence of rigor mortis, and lividity to the back and back of the legs of the deceased. At the time of the examination the deceased was unclothed and wrapped in a wool blanket. (See photographs for details).

NOTE: The clothes of the deceased were reported as removed by the family in preparation for burial.

Detainee injuries at time of processing of scene

*Physical Examination of the Remains:*

About 0830Z, 7 Nov 03, LTC (DR) ▓▓▓, General Surgeon, 911th Forward Surgical Team (FST), Task Force (TF) Warrior, KAF, conducted a physical examination of ▓▓▓ remains, in an effort to ascertain the cause and manner of death. LTC ▓▓▓ limited his examination to opening the chest cavity, obtaining tissue (heart and liver) and blood samples for toxicology. X-rays of the remains were exposed, and no remarkable injuries were noted. Photographs of the examination were exposed by SA ▓▓▓ (see the Medical Report, Evidence Form and Photographs for details).

"Pulmonary Trunk"   "Heart w/scale"

NOTE: LTC ▓▓▓ could not make an opinion of findings, and a medical legal autopsy was scheduled, to be performed at Bagram Air Field.

CRIME SCENE VERIFICATION:

About 2200Z, 6 Nov 03, SA ▓▓▓ conducted a crime scene examination of the detainee area, located 3' from the main entrance into Geresch FOB, Helmand Province, AF.

*CHARACTERISTICS OF THE SCENE*: The area identified, as the detainee area was a plywood structure shaped octagonal, with approximately 4' high, and 4' deep cubicles. The cubicle areas had a ceiling (about 3' x 4') and three walls (about 4' x 3'), and was open in the center of the structure. The area was free of debris and appeared clean. There was a folding metal chair, resting upright on the floor, and centered on the west wall, and a box, which contained drinking bottled water. The structure was unpainted and was constructed of treated plywood. There was an entrance and exit way, which was merely a 2" x 4" piece of wood, which made a person bend at the waist to enter the structure. There was no door, nor locks to keep a person from leaving. However, the structure was surrounded by concertina wire, and two Afghanistan Militia Forces soldiers, who was stationed inside the detainee area, guarded the area. The guard area consisted of merely a holding area within the structure, and the folding metal chair. The over watch consisted of US Special Forces (USSF)

For Official Use Only

LAW ENFORCEMENT SENSITIVE

000033 Exhibit 9

DOD-045200

305

soldier's on-duty in a guard tower within the FOB, which was 100 meters inside the base, and was about 50' high up.

**CONDITION OF THE SCENE**: The scene was clean of dirt, and there were several empty bottles of water laid on the floor of the detainee area at the time of the examination, and there was only one detainee sleeping in a cell of the structure. The detainee area was structurally sound, and appeared unsecured, besides the guards positioned inside the structure guarding the detainee. There was also a heat source in another of the cells, which was not operating at the time of the examination.

**ENVIRONMENTAL CONDITIONS:** At the time of the outdoor scene examination the outside temperature was about 35 degrees Fahrenheit, and there was a slight wind. No unusual odors were noted. There had not been any precipitation within the last twenty-four hours.

**SCENE DOCUMENTATION:** A Rough Crime Scene Sketch was completed by SA ███, and verified by SA ███. SA ███ also exposed digital photographs of the scene using a Nikon Coolpix, Model 995 (see sketch and photographs for details).

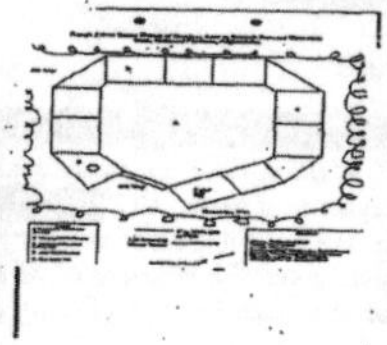

**IMPROVEMENTS:**
SA ███ coordinated with CPT ███ Trial Counsel, 3rd Bn, 3rd SFG, regarding future deaths of detainees at FOB's. SA ███ and CPT ███ agreed that medico legal autopsy's in the future be conducted by qualified Pathologist. Further, that CITF/CID could coordinate with our higher headquarters to ensure a Pathologist was available in a timely manner. CPT ███ stated this would become policy, to ensure future incidents were conducted properly.

**STATUS OF INVESTIGATION:** This investigation is currently being investigated by the local USACIDC element under Report of Investigation: ███. No further action is anticipated by this office.

**REPORT PREPARED BY:**

///S///

Special Agent
CITF-Kandahar, AF

**REPORT APPROVED BY:**

///S//

Resident Agent in Charge
CITF-A

6937F

Exhibit 9

DOD-045201

306

# APPENDIX 6

## *Abdullah Ghulam Rasoul (actually Abdul Qayoum Zakir)—008*

Arrested in the north at the end of 2001. Transferred to Afghan custody on 12 December 2007. Zakir gave his father's name during his detention and claimed that he was a foot soldier. The US interrogators thought that he might have been a bodyguard for a high-ranking Talib (he was actually a deputy corps commander under Rauf—see below). What is clear is that the Americans are not sure why Dostum, who originally captured him, included him in a group of prisoners given over to the Americans. He was accused of owning a Casio 'wrist watch', which could be used as a 'possible explosive device'. He admitted that it was 'fine to wage jihad against Americans, Jews or Israelis if they were in his country'. He was assessed as having a medium intelligence value. When released to Afghan custody, Zakir quickly rose to become the head of the Taliban military (nezami) commission.

## *Abdul Rauf Khadim—108*

Arrested in the north at the end of 2001. Transferred to Afghan custody on 12 December 2007. Claimed he was a bread deliverer (was actually a Taliban corps commander). Assessed as having a medium intelligence value. The tribunal president correctly identified him as Alizai and then asked if that tribe was associated with the Taliban. The next question made clear that the questioner thought that the Northern Alliance (NA) was a Pushtun organisation: he was confused that the detainee did not join the NA. Even though Rauf provides conflicting stories about when he lost his leg, the US released him. He quickly began working with the Taliban and is currently the Taliban governor for Uruzgan.

## *Abdul Rahman—118*

Abdul Rahman was arrested in the north at the end of 2001. Transferred to Afghan custody on 15 December 2006. He was severely mentally ill with schizoaffective disorder, depressive disorder and major depressive disorder with psychotic features. He was assessed as a medium risk to the United States and its allies. He claims he was conscripted in Sangin.

*Murtaza—361*

Arrested at the end of 2001 in the north. Transferred to Afghan custody on 23 March 2003. He claimed he was a Taliban driver and was assessed as a low intelligence value. Upon release he was harassed by Haji Manan, a Noorzai 'police' officer, based on the accusation that he had been in Guantanamo.[2] This continued for some time and included having his house raided several times and his opium stolen. He then went to Washir and formed links with the Taliban for his own protection from the police (see Chapter 4). The Kharoti claim that he fought to defend them from the police, but he also fought British forces in 2008/9 (who were unwittingly allied with the police). He was eventually arrested by ISAF in 2009.

*Amanullah Alakozai—538*

Arrested in early 2002 by Mohammad Jan, Karzai's appointee as governor of Uruzgan. Released to Afghan custody on 14 March 2004. Amanullah was the cousin of Abdul Bari, the Taliban governor of Helmand. Bari stayed in Amanullah's house briefly in January 2002, but not while Amanullah was there. The US assessed him as a low threat.

*Qari Hassanullah Pirzai—562*

Arrested on 24 February 2002. Transferred to Afghan custody on 25 August 2006. Hassanullah was actually working for Karzai's government in Kajaki as Sherafuddin's clerk (Sherafuddin was a relative of Sher Mohammad). It appears that he tried to turn in two former members of the Taliban who had been harassing him. It then appears that Sherafuddin turned him into the United States (that is, his arrest was the result of a feud and a counter-feud). His mental health problems meant that he was incorrectly assessed by US interrogators as using incoherence as a counter-interrogation technique. Accusations include that he spoke with an Iranian accent (he had spent nine years in an Iranian prison for smuggling drugs) and was an Iranian spy (he was captured with some 'code' books that were later shown to be religious talismans). Several accusations referred to incidents that occurred after he was arrested and in US custody. He was also accused of working with al-Qaeda, at the same time that he was an Iranian spy. He was assessed as a medium risk to the United States. Hassanullah told the US interrogators that their beliefs were 'too far from reality'.

*Haji Bismillah—968*

Arrested in Lashkar Gah on 12 February 2003. Transferred to Afghan authority on 17 January 2009. Bismillah was appointed director of transport in Gereshk by Sher Mohammad. Bismillah's brother, Mohammad Wali, was Sher Mohammad's driver and is now an MP for Helmand. During the course of his duties he had contact with both the Helmandi government and US forces. On the day of his arrest he was actually trying to help US forces and Amir Mohammad resolve an issue regarding weapons permits. Accused of being a member of the Taliban and of 'Fedayeen Islam' (not heard used in the context of Helmand, supposedly the 'combined effort of Hizb-e Islami and active Taliban'). Bismillah's US interrogators accuse him both of being with Sher Mohammad ('number two in the Taliban organisation in Helmand' and someone who '[alerted] his insurgent counterparts by satellite phone' about US troop movements) and Rais Baghrani ('leader of forty-man terrorist unit'), yet the most basic knowledge about Helmand would have shown that these two families have been feuding for decades. The United States rated him as a high threat to their interests.

Bismillah's brother claims that Bismillah was given to US Special Forces by Haji Kadus and brothers, because he ran the government transportation department road tolls in Gereshk, whose revenue Haji Kadus coveted (a point that Bismillah and his brother make independently in their respective testimonies). On the day of his arrest, Sher Mohammad, Dad Mohammad and Abdul Rahman all pointed out to the US that it was almost certainly a false denunciation. In 2006, his brother signed a sworn affidavit to this effect and took Donald Rumsfeld, the US secretary of defense, to court on behalf of Bismillah. Bismillah had previously requested his brother's testimony during his Combatant Status Review, as was his 'right'. Yet the US and Afghan government claimed they could not find his brother despite him making repeated representations to the US and Afghan authorities and actually working for the Afghan government. Mohammad Wali also confirmed in his affidavit that he had not been contacted. Meanwhile, Mohammad Wali had been appointed district governor of Musa Qala, a prospect that US officials found 'least appealing [among a series of corrupt appointments]'. One of the reasons given was that Mohammad Wali had a brother in Guantanamo.[3]

## Abdul Razaq—942

Arrested in Lashkar Gah on 21 January 2003. Died of cancer in Guantanamo on 30 December 2007. Was Rais Baghrani's driver during the jihad and was involved in freeing Ismail Khan from Taliban custody in Kandahar in March 2000 (for which the Taliban and al-Qaeda put a bounty on his head). He was assessed as a high threat to US interests. Much of the evidence against Abdul Razaq seems to come from another detainee.[4] This included being a member of al-Qaeda and the infamous forty-man Taliban and al-Qaeda unit, whose existence has not been discussed outside of Guantanamo files. The US also claimed that he had started as a driver for the Taliban in 1992 (before the movement was formed). The interrogator accused him of being a member of Jamiat Ulema-e Islam (a Pakistani political party with links to the Taliban), rather than Jamiat-e Islami (as he maintained), which was a group supplied by the United States during the jihad. He was kept in custody so that he could provide information on Rais Baghrani, who reconciled with the government (again) during his period of detention. He was also accused of things that happened after he was arrested. He claims he was arrested by a former Taliban commander who had reconciled with, and was working for, Sher Mohammad (this was because he was a Baghrani acolyte). Of him, Abdul Razaq said 'I'll put a horse's penis in his wife's vagina'.

## Haji Jalil—1117

Haji Jalil was handed over to US forces by Dad Mohammad in response to the deaths of two US soldiers in March 2003 (see Chapter 4). He was transferred to Afghan custody on 11 March 2005. There were multiple reports surrounding this incident as Sher Mohammad, Mir Wali and Dad Mohammad all gave names to the US of those they claimed were responsible. In this case the US realised and wrote 'it appears that his capture by AMF and subsequent handover to US forces was based on fraudulent claims given by AMF personnel themselves'. The US authorities then go on to state in the documents that they believe that Dad Mohammad may have been involved in the ambush and that Haji Jalil was offered as a way of escaping culpability. US forces on the ground in Helmand, however, continued to work with Dad Mohammad. This is one of the few Guantanamo reports where it can be shown that US personnel were aware of the fact that they were being manipulated.

*Abdul Wahab—961*

Abdul Wahab was one of the ten Helmandis rounded up after the Lajay incident in February 2003 (see Chapter 4). He was transferred to Afghan custody on 31 August 2008. He had voluntarily passed through a nearby US checkpoint after the incident to do some shopping. His crimes included wearing a green jacket (common in the area) that the ambushers had used. He was accused of hearing loss at the time of the incident but there is no evidence of the US testing his hearing. Abdul Wahab repeatedly pointed this out. The US Special Forces interpreters were Hazaras (who speak Dari) and it is possible that the miscommunication between the Special Forces and Abdul Wahab was misinterpreted as hearing loss. When it was pointed out that he had a watch that was used for making bombs, he pointed at the presiding officer, who was wearing the same watch. The tribunal also confused Bagram and Baghran, and Jamiat-e Islami and Jamiat Ulema-e Islami. This second confusion was further compounded when the US officer stated that because his brother had fought in 'Jamiat' that was valid grounds for Abdul Wahab's incarceration. Abdul Wahab described the accusations as 'nonsense'.

*Rahmatullah—964*

Rahmatullah was also arrested after the Lajay incident. He was transferred to Afghan custody on 15 December 2006. Many of the same accusations about hearing loss and jackets surface in his documentation as well. Unfortunately, one of the tribunal members did not know where Helmand was and so was unable to judge some of the evidence in front of him. He asks the detainee, who thinks it is a trick question, swears he does not know and that it is near to Kandahar. He was accused of having blood and powder burns on his clothes, but it appears that these items did not survive the detainee processing chain. Aged twenty-two, he was asked if he had ever fought the Russians.

'No, I was just a little boy', he replied. When asked what he thought of the United States, he replied 'I don't know. I don't understand.'

## Hafizullah—965

Arrested in the same incident and transferred on the same date as 964, above. Similar accusations. He asks to see the evidence against him, but this is refused because it is classified. He repeatedly points out that it is very important that the US makes efforts to find the witnesses that he nominated. There is some confusion over the name of an uncle who is allegedly a member of the Taliban. In the secret detainee assessment, Sher Mohammad and Rais Baghrani (they also got his tribe wrong) are both assessed as supporting the Taliban and al-Qaeda. There is no mention of Sher Mohammad being the provincial governor. These facts were both used as part of the justification for his imprisonment. The detainee claims to have never left his village and not to have known what Kabul was before he came to Guantanamo. He was assessed as a medium risk to the United States.

## Baridad—966

Same dates and same accusations as 964 and 965.

## Nasirullah—967

Arrested at the time of the Lajay incident but transferred to Afghan custody on 2 November 2007. He was accused of being a member of the forty-man unit that provided security for Osama Bin Laden. However, Nasirullah worked for Sher Mohammad at the Lashkar Gah airport—this information could have been easily checked.

## Abdul Baghi—963

Arrested at the time of the Lajay incident and transferred to Afghan custody on 8 February 2006. He was arrested with his uncle, 971, discussed below. Same accusations about green jackets. He was also accused of being a member of the forty-man group that Rais Baghrani led out of Musa Qala (which would have been difficult as it was Sher Mohammad's stronghold). His documents are littered with inconsistencies about whether he was arrested with a weapon, whether he had recently cached it (never recovered) or whether he did not have a weapon. 'It cannot be confirmed detainee was involved in insurgent operations ... his denial seems to be plausible.' He was in custody for just under three years.

## Kushky Yar—971

Uncle of 963, above, and has the same arrest and transfer dates. Same accusations. He attempted to hang himself in Guantanamo. He was accused of having a signalling mirror, but this was a snuff box carried by most males in Helmand. He pointed out that he was wearing a brown jacket rather than a green one, but their personal items do not seem to have made it to Guantanamo with them. An American officer alleges that the green jackets were the 'uniform' of the Taliban. A poor villager, he was asked what date he was captured. 'I don't know dates ... it was daytime when I was captured.' Much of the evidence against him is based on things that he 'said himself', yet in the review documents he denies ever saying them and there is no proof available that he ever did say them. Kushky Yar points out several times that there had been problems with the interpreters misinterpreting. The presiding officer admits that the only sources of evidence to their guilt that they have are Kushky Yar and his nephew, Abdul Baghi.

## Akhtur Mohammad—969

Arrested in the Lajay incident and transferred to Afghan custody on 14 March 2004. He was arrested because his name was similar to Rais Baghrani's driver (Akhtur Mohammad is a common name in Afghanistan, like Dave Jones in Wales).

## Arif Mohammad—972

Arif Mohammad was in his sixties at the time of his detention. He was captured on the day of the Lajay incident. He was transferred to Afghan custody on 15 December 2006. Same accusations about the green jackets. There is some confusion over his capture. He was either armed, in Baghrani's compound, washing himself in a stream outside (unarmed), or trying to escape with weapons and ammunition.

Guantanamo personnel are unable to resolve these inconsistencies, presumably because the evidence for one assertion or another (for example, statements) is not available. He was assessed as a medium risk to
the United States. The secret assessments make the deduction that the
residents of Baghran often defend the valley from 'invaders' and with
his mujahidin experience (he fought for Nasim Akhundzada) it is likely
that he would have picked up a weapon. This is a very poor standard
of evidence.

Arif claims that he has a blood feud with Baghrani, who the US
claims that he works for. He also claims that the Hazara interpreters
at the Lajay incident caused him to be arrested. Factual inaccuracies
include the fact that Nasim (who the US supported as a mujahed
almost until he died in 1990) was the Taliban director of transportation for Bamian province. Nasim had been dead for six years when the
Taliban took Bamian. Nasim was also linked to Hizb by Guantanamo
personnel, but he actually spent the 1980s fighting them (and they
eventually killed him). Baghrani is 'linked' in the evidence to Sher
Mohammad even though they have a decades-old family feud. Sher
Mohammad is also said to be part of the 'insurgent infrastructure'
(which was not true at that point). The most basic knowledge about
Helmand would have dismissed this evidence, irrespective of whether
it had any relevance to the detainee.

*Abdul Kadus—929*

Abdul Kadus was approximately fifteen when he was arrested in
Gereshk by (probably) Mir Wali's men in early January 2003 (the date
is not clear from his files, it could have been December 2002 due to his
detainee number). He was transferred to Afghan custody on 18 April
2005. He claims that he was travelling to Gereshk to visit his uncle and
spent the night in a military checkpoint ('soldiers in a tent'). The next
morning he tried to leave and they stopped him, told him that he had
to take a weapon and then fight the Americans. He said that he wanted
to go to his uncle's house. They took him to jail. In the secret assessment of Abdul Kadus, it is claimed that he went to the soldiers and
asked them for a weapon to fight the Americans. Reading the tran-
script, one gets the impression of a child who has no idea what is going
on. It appears that this could be a 'sting operation' to have him arrested
for the bounty money. See also 930.

*Mohammad Ismail—930*

Mohammad was approximately sixteen when he was arrested in December 2002. He was transferred to Afghan custody on 28 January 2004. He and a friend were travelling to Gereshk to look for work and found some 'soldiers in a tent'. They asked if they could work with them on a ditch-digging project they were engaged on, but they were offered the chance to fight the Americans. They agreed but were apprehensive. The next day they were turned over to American forces and his friend was released. The file paints a very similar picture to that of 929.

*Mohammad Nasim—958*

Mohammad was arrested on 11 February 2003. He was transferred to Afghan custody on 18 April 2005. He was arrested because he had the same 'last name' as a Taliban commander heard on an intercepted communication regarding US troop movements ('Mullah Nasim' was overheard, in a radio transmission in the north of Afghanistan). However, in Afghanistan people do not have last names. Everyone is given two 'first' names, and is identified by their father's name (and their tribe if they are Pushtun). Mohammad claimed he had never left Helmand, did not know where Lashkar Gah was (he was from Baghran) and did not know what 'north' or 'south' were.

# NOTES

## ACKNOWLEDGEMENTS

1. Benjamin Hopkins and Magnus Marsden, *Fragments of the Afghan Frontier*, London: Hurst, 2011, p. 44.

## INTRODUCTION

1. Carl von Clausewitz, *On War*, trans. Michael Howard and Peter Paret, 1984 edn, Princeton: Princeton University Press, 1976, pp. 88–9.
2. Seventeenth-century Pushtun poet.
3. Hereafter taken to mean the U.S. and European countries.
4. When I first went to Helmand, my 93-year-old grandmother wrote to me to wish me luck, while wondering how I would get on with the Afghans who were, she wrote, 'unrepentant individualists'.
5. House of Commons Defence Select Committee, 'Operations in Afghanistan: Fourth Report of Session 2010–12', London, 2011, p. 31.
6. Farrell and Giustozzi quoting 'COMISAF Initial Assessment' in 'The Taliban at War: Inside the Helmand Insurgency, 2004–2012', *International Affairs*, 89, 4 (2013) pp. 845–871.
7. 'Afghan Insurgency "Clearly on Back Foot"', *BBC News*, 1 Feb. 2012; 'Taliban Attacks Show Afghan Insurgents' Resilience', *The Guardian*, 21 Jan. 2013.
8. 'ISI Accused of Backing Taliban's [*sic*] Insurgency', *Pajhwok*, 13 Feb. 2012.
9. For example, Antonio Giustozzi, *Koran, Kalashnikov and Laptop*, London: Hurst, 2008; Thomas Johnson and Chris Mason, 'Understanding the Taliban and Insurgency in Afghanistan', *Orbis*, 51, 1 (2008); Farhana Schmidt, 'From Islamic Warriors to Drug Lords: The Evolution of the Taliban Insurgency', *Mediterranean Quarterly*, 21, 2 (2010).
10. 'Is Afghanistan a Narco-State?', *New York Times*, 27 July 2008; PersExp, Helmand, 2008–12.
11. Leon Poullada, 'The Pashtun Role in the Afghan Political System', *The Afghanistan Council of the Asian Society Occasional Paper*, 1 (1970), p. 12.

12. The highly idealised tribal code of the Pushtun focusing on reciprocity (including revenge), hospitality (including offering asylum), bravery, protection of women and protection of honour (Erinn Banting, *Afghanistan: The People*, New York: Crabtree, 2003, p. 14).

13. David Edwards, *Heroes of the Age: Moral Fault Lines on the Afghan Frontier*, Ewing: University of California Press, 1996.

14. Leon Poullada, 'Problems of Social Development in Afghanistan', *Journal of The Royal Central Asian Society*, 49, 1 (1962), p. 33.

15. Thomas Barfield, *Afghanistan: A Cultural and Political History*, Oxford: Princeton University Press, 2010, p. 348.

16. Richard Maconachie, 'Precis on Afghan Affairs, 1919–1927', Simla: Foreign and Political Department, Government of India, 1928, p. 335.

17. For example, Leon Poullada, 'Reform and Rebellion in Afghanistan, 1919–1929: King Amanullah's Failure to Modernize a Tribal Society', *The ANNALS of the American Academy of Political and Social Science*, 412, 1 (1973), p. 318.

18. Louis Dupree, *Afghanistan*, New Delhi: RAMA Publishers, 1980, p. 344.

19. Hugh Beattie, *Imperial Frontier Tribe and State in Waziristan*, London: Curzon Press, 2001, p. 120.

20. Louis Dupree, 'The Retreat of the British Army from Kabul to Jalalabad in 1842: History and Folklore', *Journal of the Folklore Institute*, 6 (1967), p. 59.

21. Poullada, Pashtun Role quoted in 'Pashtun Tribal Dynamics', Tribal Analysis Centre (2009).

22. Dupree, 'Retreat', cf. pp. 59 and 66.

23. David Edwards, *Before Taliban*, London: University of California Press, 2002, p. 259.

24. Gilles Dorronsoro, *Revolution Unending: Afghanistan, 1979 to the Present*, London: Hurst, 2005, pp. 1–6.

25. Afghans for Civil Society, 'Loya Jirga Focus Groups: Kandahar and Helmand Provinces', Kandahar, 2003.

26. Antonio Giustozzi, *Empires of Mud: Dynamics of Warlordism in Afghanistan, 1980–2007*, London: Hurst, 2009, pp. 2, 5–6.

27. Ana Pejcinova, 'Post-Modernizing Afghanistan', *CEU Political Science Journal*, 5 (2006), pp. 38–40; Seth Jones, 'The Rise of Afghanistan's Insurgency: State Failure and Jihad', *International Security*, 32, 4 (2008).

28. Mike Martin, *A Brief History of Helmand*, Warminster: Afghan COIN Centre, 2011, pp. 16 and 18.

29. See Chapter 1.

30. I speak fluid, if not fluent, Pushtu.

31. Jon Swaine, 'The British Soldier Reading Afghan Minds', *Sunday Times*, 29 May 2009.

32. Bruce Berg, *Qualitative Research Methods for the Social Sciences*, Boston: Allyn and Bacon, 2007, pp. 5–8.

33. Bjarte Folkestad, 'Analysing Interview Data: Possibilities and Challenges', *Eurosphere Working Paper Series*, 13 (2008), p. 1.

34. Ethics proposal submitted and approved by KCL Ethics Committee summer 2011; consent sheets explained to, and signed by, all interviewees; interviewees informed they could withdraw at any time; interview data kept securely.

35. Berg, *Methods*, p. 51.

36. For example, of the three main tribes in central Helmand, I interviewed fifteen Barakzai, twelve Noorzai and ten Kharoti. This broadly reflects their population densities in central Helmand. Similarly for jihadi parties. See Appendix 1 for interviewee breakdowns.

37. Alex Strick van Linschoten and Felix Kuehn, *An Enemy We Created*, London: Hurst, 2012, p. 141.

38. Antonio Giustozzi, 'The Great Fears of Afghanistan: How Wild Rumours Shape Politics', *Ideas Today*, 4 (2010), pp. 9–13.

39. There are 18.6 million GSM subscribers in Afghanistan as of June 2012—'Statistics', http://mcit.gov.af/en (accessed 12 Nov. 2012).

40. Edward Said, *Orientalism*, New York: Vintage, 1978, p. 11.

41. See Chapter 1.

42. Marvin Weinbaum, 'Pakistan and Afghanistan: The Strategic Relationship', *Asian Survey*, 31, 6 (1991), p. 498.

43. For example, Matt Waldman, 'The Sun in the Sky: The Relationship Between Pakistan's ISI and Afghan Insurgents', Crisis States Research Centre Discussion Papers, 18 (2010); a leaked ISAF report ('The State of the Taliban 2012') discussed here: 'Taliban Believe they will Take Over from US and NATO in Afghanistan—Report', http://www.guardian.co.uk/world/2012/feb/01/taliban-afghanistan-leaked-report-pakistan; assertions of US officials discussed here: 'ISI is Directing the Taliban', http://www.rediff.com/news/report/isi-is-directing-taliban-in-afghanistan/20121022.htm and here: 'Admiral Mullen: Pakistani ISI Sponsoring Haqqani Attacks', http://www.longwarjournal.org/archives/2011/09/admiral_mullen_pakis.php (all accessed 12 Nov. 2012).

44. G118.

45. Interviews 006, 013, 031, 037, 044, 047, 048, 050, 060, 063, 066, 067, 068, 084, 085, 086, 090, 096, 000, 201, 202, 203, 209, 213, 226, 237, 239, Hafizullah, SMA, ARJ, Habibullah, MMW.

46. Martin, *Brief History*.

## 1. PRE-1978 HELMANDI HISTORY

1. Olaf Caroe, *The Pathans: 550 B.C.—A.D. 1957*, Oxford: Oxford University Press, 1958, p. 97; Ludwig Adamec, ed. *Historical and Political Gazetteer of Afghanistan*, vol. 5, Graz: Akademische Druck und Verlagsanstalt, 1985, p. 262; Stephen Tanner, *Afghanistan: A Military History from Alexander the Great to the War Against the Taliban*, Philadelphia: Da Capo Press, 2009, p. 75.

2. Thomas Barfield, *Afghanistan: A Cultural and Political History*, Oxford: Princeton University Press, 2010, p. 42.

3. Bost means '20' after the number of forts in the area. It is probable that the fort occupied by British Forces in 2009 in Nad-e Ali (FOB Sawqat) is one of the orig-

inal 20 forts built by the Ghaznavids (Dr John Peaty, Defence Geographic Centre, *Pers comm.*, Jan 2011). Interestingly, local narratives emphasise that this is a British Fort from the first or second Anglo-Afghan wars, but this is unlikely (the British had no interest in this patch of desert—they were much more interested in Gereshk). According to local lore, however, it is obvious that the British would come back and re-occupy the same fort.

4. Adamec, *Gazetteer*, vol. 5, p. 262.
5. Ibid.
6. Barfield, *Afghanistan*, p. 50.
7. Adamec, *Gazetteer*, vol. 5, p. 262.
8. The Abdali became the Durrani when Ahmad Shah Khan was crowned *Durr-i durran* (Pearl of Pearls) in 1747.
9. And, also, Shah Shuja's British-supported second reign of 1838–42.
10. Caroe, *Pathans*, p. 223.
11. Ibid., p. 225.
12. Ibid., p. 222.
13. The leader of the Taliban movement (1994—ongoing in 2014).
14. Tribal Analysis Centre, 'The Panjpai Relationship with the Other Durranis' (2009), p. 7; Mountstuart Elphinstone, *An Account of the Kingdom of Caubul, and its Dependencies in Persia, Tartary and India: Comprising a View of the Afghaun Nation and a History of the Dooraunee Monarchy*, 2010 edn (Milton Keynes: Nabu Public Domain reprints, 1839, pp. 279–82.
15. Elphinstone, *Kingdom of Caubul*, pp. 280–1.
16. Mohammad Khan, *Afghanistan and its Inhabitants*, trans. H Priestley, Lahore: Sang-e Meel Publications, 1981, p. 33.
17. Lt Col CM MacGregor, *Central Asia: Part 2—A Contribution Towards the Better Knowledge of the Topography, Ethnology, Resources and History of Afghanistan*, Calcutta: Office of the Superintendent of Government Printing, 1871, p. 61.
18. Henry Rawlinson, *Report on the Dooranee Tribes*, 1841, paras 1–7.
19. MacGregor, *Central Asia*, p. 236; Elphinstone, *Kingdom of Caubul*, pp. 99–100.
20. MacGregor, *Central Asia*, pp. 99 and 170.
21. Rawlinson, *Dooranee Tribes*, paras 1–7.
22. Of the Saddozai sub-tribe.
23. MacGregor, *Central Asia*, p. 61.
24. Ibid., p. 254.
25. Ibid., p. 253.
26. Mohammad Khan, *Afghanistan and its Inhabitants*, 63.
27. Rawlinson, *Dooranee Tribes*, paras 8–10.
28. Antonio Giustozzi, 'Tribes and Warlords in Southern Afghanistan 1980–2005', *Crisis States Research Centre Working Paper*, Series 1, 7, 2006, p. 4.
29. Elphinstone, *Kingdom of Caubul*, p. 274.
30. Caroe, *The Pathans*, p. 253.
31. Ibid., p. 255.

32. In Pushtun folklore, Barak, Alak and Popol were brothers who went their separate ways to found tribes in their own namesake with the addition of the—zai (*son of*) suffix, for example, Barakzai.
33. Reign 1772–1793.
34. Barfield, *Afghanistan*, p. 105.
35. Rawlinson, *Dooranee Tribes*, para 15.
36. Ibid., paras 16–7.
37. Reign 1793–1800.
38. Barakzai tribe, Mohammadzai sub-tribe.
39. Barfield, *Afghanistan*, pp. 107–9.
40. Caroe, *The Pathans*, p. 269; Adamec, *Gazetteer*, vol. 2, p. 92.
41. Adamec, *Gazetteer*, vol. 2, p. 6.
42. Rawlinson, *Dooranee Tribes*, paras 21–3.
43. Ibid., para 24.
44. General Staff—India, *Military Report—Afghanistan: History, Topography, Ethnography, Resources, Armed Forces, Forts and Fortified Posts, Administration and Communications*, Dehli: Government of India Press, 1925, p. 8.
45. John Kaye, *History of the War in Afghanistan*, London: WH Allen and Co, 1878, p. 446.
46. Adamec, *Gazetteer*, vol. 2, p. 94.
47. Rawlinson, *Dooranee Tribes*, para 28.
48. Kaye, *War in Afghanistan*, p. 443.
49. Ibid., p. 101.
50. Adamec, *Gazetteer*, vol. 2, p. 234; Kaye, *War in Afghanistan*, p. 102.
51. Kaye, *War in Afghanistan*, pp. 394–8.
52. Ibid., p. 102.
53. Ibid., p. 117.
54. Ibid., p. 121.
55. Ibid., p. 128.
56. Adamec, *Gazetteer*, vol. 2, p. 94.
57. Afghan/Pushtun decision-making forum.
58. 1842–63.
59. Barfield, *Afghanistan*, p. 128.
60. Anatol Lieven, Speech given at his book launch—*Pakistan: A Hard Country*, (King's College London, 26 April 2011).
61. See Tony Heathcote, *The Afghan Wars, 1839–1919*, 2003 edn, Stroud: The History Press Ltd, 1980, p. 217 for a family tree.
62. Abdur Rahman, *The life of Abdur Rahman: Amir of Afghanistan*, trans. Mohammad Khan, Cambridge: J Murray, 1900, p. 80.
63. Waller Ashe, ed. *Personal Records of the Kandahar Campaign by Officers Engaged Therein*, London: D. Bogue, 1881, p. 3.
64. Kakar quoted in Barfield, *Afghanistan*, p. 138.
65. Ibid., pp. 171–4.
66. Henry LePoer Wynne, *Narrative of Recent Events in Afghanistan, from the*

*Recovery of Candahar to the Conclusion of the Rebellion of Yacoob Khan*, Calcutta: Govt of India Foreign Department, 1871, p. 84.

67. Adamec, *Gazetteer*, vol. 2, p. 232.
68. General Staff—India, *Military Report*, Dehli, p. 39; Adamec, *Gazetteer*, vol. 2, p. 94.
69. Barfield, *Afghanistan*, p. 144.
70. This was relearnt yet again in 2006.
71. Ashe, *Records of the Kandahar Campaign*, p. 42.
72. Adamec, *Gazetteer*, vol. 2, p. 235.
73. Maj Gen CM MacGregor, *Southern Afghanistan Field Force—Section 3*, Simla: Quarter Master General's Office, 1880, para 26; Ashe, *Records of the Kandahar Campaign*, p. 57.
74. Ashe, *Records of the Kandahar Campaign*, pp. 7–8 and 26.
75. General Staff—India, *Military Report*, Dehli, p. 55.
76. Ashe, *Records of the Kandahar Campaign*, p. 52.
77. Maiwand is in the present day province of Kandahar, just to the east of the province's border with Helmand.
78. See General Staff—India, *Military Report*, Dehli, pp. 58–61 for description.
79. Tanner, *A Military History*, p. 216.
80. Barfield, *Afghanistan*, pp. 53 and 149.
81. Adamec, *Gazetteer*, vol. 2, p. 237.
82. Nancy Tapper, 'The Advent of Pashtun "Maldars" in North-Western Afghanistan', *Bulletin of the School of Oriental and African Studies*, 36, 1, 1973, pp. 56–68.
83. General Staff—India, *Military Report*, Dehli, p. 381.
84. Richard Maconachie, *Precis on Afghan Affairs, 1919–1927*, Simla: Foreign and Political Department, Government of India, 1928, p. 335.
85. General Staff—India, *Military Report*, Dehli, p. 143.
86. Barfield, *Afghanistan*, p. 169.
87. Reigns 1929–33 and 1933–73, respectively.
88. General Staff—India, *Military Report—Afghanistan*, Simla: Government of India Press, 1940, p. 243.
89. Barfield, *Afghanistan*, p. 205.
90. Richard Scott, 'Tribal-Ethnic Groups in the Helmand Valley—Occasional Paper No. 21', *The Asia Society*, 1980, pp. 2–3.
91. Ghulam Farouq, 'The Effects of Local, Regional and Global Politics on the Development of the Helmand-Arghandab Valley of Afghanistan', *School of Oriental and African Studies*, 1999, p. 79.
92. Ibid., pp. 16 and 128.
93. General Staff—India, *Routes in Afghanistan, South West*, Lahore: North Western Railway Press, 1941, p. 277.
94. Helmand and Arghandab Valley Development Project, *Shamalan Unit, Draft Feasibility Report*, Bost: Helmand and Arghandab Valley Authority, 1967, p. 8.
95. Dupree, *Afghanistan*, p. 482.
96. Farouq, 'Development of the Helmand-Arghandab Valley', p. 25.

97. Nick Cullather, 'Damming Afghanistan: Modernization in a Buffer State', *The Journal of American History* 89, 2, 2002, pp. 522–3.
98. Dupree, *Afghanistan*, p. 483; Cullather, *Damming Afghanistan*, p. 523; Farouq, 'Development of the Helmand-Arghandab Valley', pp. 41 and 64.
99. Quoted in Cullather, *Damming Afghanistan*, p. 513.
100. Ibid., p. 524.
101. Ibid., p. 536, quoting Baron.
102. Later, the Helmand and Arghandab Valley Authority; both will be referred to as HVA.
103. Inaugurated in 1953.
104. Cullather, *Damming Afghanistan*, p. 525.
105. Dupree, *Afghanistan*, p. 484. This was a de jure recognition of his de facto power.
106. The Orkand Corporation, *Afghanistan: The Southern Provinces*, 1989, p. 36.
107. Dupree, *Afghanistan*, p. 502.
108. Scott, 'Tribal-Ethnic Groups', p. 3.
109. Dupree, *Afghanistan*, p. 502; Orkand, *The Southern Provinces*, p. 36.
110. Cullather, 'Damming Afghanistan', p. 527; Dupree, *Afghanistan*, p. 502.
111. Scott, 'Tribal-Ethnic Groups', p. 3.
112. Dupree, *Afghanistan*, p. 502.
113. *Op Cit.*
114. Ibid., p. 504.
115. Scott, 'Tribal-Ethnic Groups', p. 9; Dupree, *Afghanistan*, p. 502.
116. *Op Cit.*
117. Baron, quoted in Cullather, *Damming Afghanistan*, p. 529.
118. Farouq, 'Development of the Helmand-Arghandab Valley', p. 50.
119. Ibid., p. 167.
120. Ibid., p. 181.
121. The Commander of NATO forces in Afghanistan, Gen Stan McChrystal infamously described Marjeh as a 'bleeding ulcer' in mid-2010; he could have been parodying what the US thought of the canal projects fifty years earlier.
122. Dupree, *Afghanistan*, p. 505; Farouq, 'Development of the Helmand-Arghandab Valley', p. 51.
123. Farouq, 'Development of the Helmand-Arghandab Valley', p. 18; Dupree, *Afghanistan*, p. 484; Cullather, *Damming Afghanistan*, p. 52.
124. Adamec, *Gazetteer*, vol. 2, p. 1.
125. Ibid., p. 5.
126. Richard Scott, 'Email to USAID: Helmand Follow Up XXV—Need for an Integrated Reconstruction/Opium Poppy Reduction Program in Central Helmand', 18 June 2008.
127. Article 43 of the 1964 constitution of Afghanistan.
128. Adamec, *Gazetteer*, vol. 2, p. 108.
129. Orkand, *The Southern Provinces*, p. 68; Adamec, *Gazetteer*, vol. 2, p. 108.
130. Dupree, *Afghanistan*, p. 506.

131. Mildred Caudill, *Helmand-Arghandab Valley: Yesterday, Today, Tomorrow*, Lashkar Gah: HVA, 1969, pp. 38–9.
132. Farouq, 'Development of the Helmand-Arghandab Valley', p. 63.
133. USAID, *Assisted Development in the Helmand-Arghandab Valley, Notes on Program Successes and Problems*, Kabul: USAID, 1973, p. 2.
134. Orkand, *The Southern Provinces*, p. 37; Dupree, *Afghanistan*, p. 635.
135. Dupree, *Afghanistan*, p. 504.
136. Helmand and Arghandab Valley Development Project, *Shamalan Unit, Draft Feasibility Report*, p. 10.
137. Farouq, 'Development of the Helmand-Arghandab Valley', p. 167.
138. Richard Scott, *The North Shamalan: A Survey of Land and People*, 1971, p. 6.
139. Ibid., pp. 7–15.
140. Cullather, *Damming Afghanistan*, p. 534.
141. Scott, 'Tribal-Ethnic Groups', p. 24; Louis Dupree, Afghanistan, p. 505.
142. Orkand, *The Southern Provinces*, p. 58.
143. Cullather, *Damming Afghanistan*, p. 534; Ghulam Farouq, *Socio-Economic Aspects of Land Settlement in Helmand Valley, Afghanistan*, Beirut: American University, 1975, p. 79.
144. Scott, 'Tribal-Ethnic Groups', p. 16.
145. Farouq, 'Development of the Helmand-Arghandab Valley', p. 228; Dupree, *Afghanistan*, p. 499; Scott, 'Tribal-Ethnic Groups', p. 10.
146. Farouq, 'Development of the Helmand-Arghandab Valley', p. 63.
147. Scott, 'Tribal-Ethnic Groups', pp. 3, 24 and 33.
148. The number of tractors in Helmand rose from zero in 1950 to 1,300 in 1978 (Farouq, 'Development of the Helmand-Arghandab Valley', p. 229) and by 1991, 94 per cent of farmers in Nad-e Ali were using tractors (Professor Mohammad Omar Anwarzay, *Farming Systems of Nad-e Ali District, Helmand Province*, The Swedish Committee for Afghanistan, 1992, p. 25).
149. Orkand, *The Southern Provinces*, p. 57.
150. Farouq, *Land Settlement in Helmand Valley*, p. 81.
151. Scott, 'Tribal-Ethnic Groups', p. 32.
152. PersExp, Nad-e Ali, 2008–9.

## 2. FROM THE SAUR REVOLUTION TO THE SOVIET WITHDRAWAL, 1978–89

1. 031.
2. Gilles Dorronsoro, *Revolution Unending: Afghanistan, 1979 to the Present*, London: Hurst, p. 5.
3. Sandy Gall, *Afghanistan: Travels with the Mujahideen*, Sevenoaks: Hodder and Stoughton, 1988, p. xiii.
4. Arthur Bonner, *Among the Afghans*, Durham: Duke University Press, 1987, p. 281.
5. Jon Anderson, *Guerrillas*, London: Abacus, 2006, p. 244.

6. Artemy Kalinovsky, *A Long Goodbye*, Cambridge: Harvard University Press, 2011, p. 24.
7. Gregory Feifer, *The Great Gamble*, New York: HarperCollins, 2009, p. 17; Rodric Braithwaite, *Afgantsy*, London: Profile, 2011, pp. 87 and 106.
8. Artyom Borovik, *The Hidden War*, London: Faber and Faber, 1991, p. 19.
9. Olivier Roy, *Islam and Resistance in Afghanistan*, Cambridge: Cambridge University Press, 1985, p. 84.
10. Antonio Giustozzi, *War, Politics and Society in Afghanistan, 1978–1992*, London: Hurst, 2000, p. 67.
11. Gall, *Travels with the Mujahideen*, p. xiii.
12. Barnett Rubin, *The Fragmentation of Afghanistan*, New Haven: Yale University Press, 1995, pp. 84–5.
13. Dorronsoro, *Revolution Unending*, pp. 177–8.
14. David Edwards, *Before Taliban*, London: University of California Press, 2002, pp. 237–8.
15. Roy, *Islam*, p. 114.
16. Edwards, *Before Taliban*, p. 243.
17. Rubin, *Fragmentation*, pp. 205 and 243–4.
18. Ibid., p. 107.
19. Roy, *Islam*, p. 90.
20. 'Helmand and Samangan Provinces' Revolutionary Shuras Welcome the 6th Decree!', *Hewad*, 16 July 1978.
21. Roy, *Islam*, p. 84.
22. Ibid., p. 87.
23. Rubin, *Fragmentation*, pp. 115–19.
24. 006.
25. 032.
26. 084.
27. Mike Martin, *A Brief History of Helmand*, Warminster: Afghan COIN Centre, 2011, p. 31.
28. Giustozzi, *War, Politics and Society*, pp. 255 and 289.
29. 023.
30. Beverley Male, *Revolutionary Afghanistan: A Reappraisal*, London: Croom Helm, 1982, p. 69.
31. 060.
32. '7681 Farming Families are Distributed Free Land in Helmand and Nimruz', *Hewad*, 10 Feb. 1979; '6258 Jereebs in Helmand Redistributed to 600 Families', *Hewad*, 21 Feb. 1979.
33. 006, 058.
34. 018.
35. 031.
36. 057.
37. 043.
38. 048.
39. 043.

40. '363 Petitions Given to the Farmers' Problems' Internal Committee in Gereshk District, Helmand', *Hewad*, 17 Sep. 1978.
41. 031, 043.
42. 017.
43. 012.
44. For example, 015, 039, 023.
45. Edwards, *Before Taliban*, p. 127.
46. See Chapter 4.
47. Mohammad Kakar, *Afghanistan: The Soviet Invasion and the Afghan Response, 1979–1982*, London: University of California Press, 1995, p. 82.
48. Roy, *Islam*, p. 93.
49. 013, 049.
50. Edward Girardet, *Afghanistan: The Soviet War*, New York: St Martin's Press, 1985, pp. 112–13.
51. 'Are the Taliban Really Burning Schools?', *Sarak*, Sep. 2008, p. 6.
52. 'Shootings at Annual Graduation Ceremony in Lashkar Gah High School', *Hewad*, 11 June 1978.
53. 006.
54. 048.
55. 013. Akhundzada means 'son of a cleric'—Nasim's father, Akhundzada Sahib Mubarak, was a famous cleric in Helmand (Olivier Roy, 'Le Mouvement des Taleban en Afghanistan', *Afghanistan Info*, 36 (1995), p. 5).
56. 048. See Giustozzi, *War, Politics and Society*, p. 96 for confirmation of broad narrative.
57. 061.
58. For example, 017, 048, 034.
59. 063. Médecins Sans Frontières (MSF), 'Exploratory Mission in Helmand', Quetta: 1989, p. 7.
60. For example, 001, 007, 014.
61. 039, 064.
62. Antonio Giustozzi, '"Tribes" and Warlords in Southern Afghanistan, 1980–2005', Crisis States Research Centre Working Paper, 1, 7 (2006), p. 5.
63. Edwards, *Before Taliban*, pp. 235–76.
64. MMW.
65. SMA.
66. 018.
67. 044.
68. Kristian Harpviken, *Social Networks and Migration in Wartime Afghanistan*, London: Macmillan, 2009, p. 23.
69. 032, 047.
70. Hafizullah.
71. MMW.
72. SMA.
73. 003, 022.
74. 043.

75. 016, 039.
76. 023, 032.
77. 031.
78. 063.
79. 048.
80. 018.
81. Roy, *Islam*, p. 121.
82. Sherard Cowper-Coles, *Cables from Kabul*, London: Harper Press, 2011, p. 55.
83. 006.
84. 049. MSF, 'Mission', p. 38.
85. 054.
86. The Orkand Corporation, 'Afghanistan: The Southern Provinces', 1989, p. 164.
87. For example, 003, 008.
88. 049.
89. 063, 084.
90. Habibullah, 048.
91. 049, 063.
92. 049.
93. 044.
94. 040.
95. 012.
96. Jabbar.
97. Habibullah, 061.
98. 039, 045.
99. 049.
100. For example, 020, 045, 049, Jabbar.
101. Rubin, *Fragmentation*, pp. 205 and 243–4.
102. 025, 028.
103. 080.
104. 025, 048, 056, 064.
105. 028.
106. 025.
107. 025, 056.
108. For example, 020, 045, 049, MMW.
109. SMA.
110. Giustozzi, '"Tribes"', p. 9.
111. For example, 020, 045, 047, 048, 049, 070, 074, 081, 084 and 061 who claims eyewitness-status to Khad documents showing Nasim as a Khad beneficiary.
112. 006.
113. 047.
114. 048.
115. 012.

116. 020, including quote.
117. Edwards, *Before Taliban*, pp. 274–6.
118. 015.
119. 023.
120. 013.
121. 015.
122. 020.
123. 010.
124. 048.
125. ARJ.
126. 070. Orkand, 'The Southern Provinces', p. 203.
127. 020.
128. 048.
129. I am grateful to Kyle S for helping me elucidate these dynamics.
130. 048.
131. 061.
132. 020, 040.
133. 048, 061.
134. 020, 030, 031.
135. 069.
136. 020, 061, 064.
137. 025, 061.
138. Giustozzi, '"Tribes"', p. 10. Although the extent of this spread, or even its starting point, is unknown, as UNODC figures only run from 1994 (Pers. Comm. David Mansfield, 2012).
139. Orkand, 'The Southern Provinces', p. 165.
140. For example, Alain Labrousse, 'Les Drogues et les Conflicts en Afghanistan (1978–1995)', *Afghanistan Info*, 38 (1996), p. 16; Angelo Rasanayagam, *Afghanistan: A Modern History*, London: IB Tauris, 2005, pp. 136–7; Rubin, *Fragmentation*, p. 245.
141. I am grateful to David Mansfield for the email discussion that solidified this understanding.
142. Dorronsoro, *Revolution*, p. 135.
143. 'Afghan Rebel's Victory Garden: Opium', *New York Times*, 18 June 1986.
144. Pers. Comm. Mansfield, 2012. Some scholars imply that Nasim invented the Salaam system, but it has been in use in Helmand for centuries.
145. Rubin, *Fragmentation*, p. 245.
146. Afghan Embassy, 'News Bulletin', London, 13 Oct. 1989, p. 3.
147. Rubin, *Fragmentation*, p. 263.
148. Pers. Comm. Mansfield, 2012.
149. Eng. M. Rabi Amaj, 'Helmand Projects Monitor and Supervision Report', Quetta: Islamic Aid Health Center, 1991, p. 25.
150. Orkand, 'The Southern Provinces', p. 165.
151. Vanda Felbab-Brown, *Shooting Up: Counterinsurgency and the War on Drugs*, Washington: Brookings Institution Press, 2009, p. 118.

152. Neamatollah Nojumi, *The Rise of the Taliban in Afghanistan*, New York: St Martin's Press, 2002, p. 123.
153. Dorronsoro, *Revolution*, p. 126.
154. SMA.
155. 040.
156. 012, 075.
157. 075.
158. 012, 040, 075.
159. 040.
160. 031.
161. 074.
162. 052, 074.
163. 018.
164. 002.
165. 003.
166. Martin, *Brief History*, p. 23.
167. Richard Scott, 'Reconstruction and Opium Poppy Cultivation in Central Helmand', in Conference on Afghanistan Reconstruction, University of Nebraska: 2008, p. 6.
168. 023.
169. 023, 050.
170. 016, 032.
171. 023.
172. 065.
173. 047.
174. 039.
175. 032.
176. 016, 050.
177. 015.
178. 007.
179. 015.
180. 023.
181. 007, 015, 023.
182. 007.
183. 007, 015, 023.
184. 039.
185. 039.
186. 033, 071.
187. 033.
188. 016, 023, 067.
189. 033.
190. 008, 018.
191. 039, 071, 080.
192. 067, 071.
193. 023.

194. 039.
195. 033.
196. Pre-Saur revolution, Loy Bagh was a commuter village for government employees who worked in Lashkar Gah.
197. 016, 023, 072.
198. ARJ.
199. ARJ, 041.
200. 034.
201. 023, 034.
202. 067.
203. 038.
204. 016, 032, 038.
205. 082.
206. 005.
207. 029.
208. 043.
209. 015, 043.
210. 048.
211. 015.
212. 048.
213. 084.
214. 019, 084.
215. 049, 076.
216. 044.
217. 049.
218. 045. Artyom Borovik, *The Hidden War*, London: Faber and Faber, 1991, p. 248.
219. 049.
220. 045, 048, 049.
221. 043.
222. Giustozzi, *War, Politics and Society*, pp. 48–9.
223. 049.
224. 040.
225. 049.
226. 049. Giustozzi, *War, Politics and Society*, pp. 48–9.
227. 006.
228. 049.
229. 005, 043.
230. 020.
231. 023, 032, 049, 084.
232. 049.
233. Jabbar, 063.
234. For example, 002, 015, 040.
235. 032.
236. 015, 016.

237. For example, 008, 013.
238. 031.
239. 006.
240. 012.
241. 014.
242. 056, 064.
243. 063.
244. 006, 018.
245. 015.
246. 044 and 064 gave opposite views, for instance.
247. 015.
248. 007.
249. 008.
250. 015.
251. 007, 015, 017.
252. 008.
253. 015, 032.
254. 049.
255. 015.
256. Gregory Feifer, *The Great Gamble*, New York: HarperCollins, 2009, p. 189.
257. 023.
258. Orkand, 'The Southern Provinces', p. 78.
259. 044, 046.
260. 049.
261. 049.
262. 003.
263. Dorronsoro, *Revolution*, pp. 196–7.
264. 045, 080.
265. Rubin, *Fragmentation*, pp. 146–8.
266. 046.
267. Giustozzi, *War, Politics and Society*, p. 285.
268. 039, 070, 074.
269. Habibullah, 039.
270. 049, 057, 070.
271. 060.
272. MMW, 013. Giustozzi, '"Tribes"', p. 10.
273. 001, 048.
274. Gilles Dorronsoro, 'Helmand: Le Dernier Refuge des Khalqis', *Afghanistan Info*, 33 (1993), pp. 11–13.
275. 012, 061.
276. MMW, 013.
277. 061.
278. 031, 069.
279. 020.
280. Edwards, *Before Taliban*, p. 268.

281. 040.
282. 017, 019, 069.
283. 007.
284. 040, 070.
285. 025.
286. 012, 020.
287. 031.
288. 048, 064.
289. 080.
290. Azar Gat, *War in Human Civilisation*, New York: Oxford University Press, 2006, pp. 176–83.
291. Giustozzi, *War, Politics and Society*, p. 157.
292. Ibid., p. 266.
293. 048.
294. Jabbar, 041.
295. 003.
296. 012, 035.
297. 060.
298. 057.
299. 003.
300. Giustozzi, '"Tribes"', p. 15.
301. 033
302. 080.
303. 025.
304. 021.
305. 043.
306. 020.
307. 048, Jabbar.
308. AfghaNews, 'Provincial News', vol. 4, London, May 1988, p. 2.
309. 'Helmand—April and May', *Afghan Jehad*, Apr.–June 1988, pp. 279–80.
310. Ibid.
311. Mark Urban, *War in Afghanistan*, New York: St Martin's Press, 1990, pp. 240–1.
312. Martin, *Brief History*, p. 39.
313. For example, 018, 034, 040, 065.
314. 003, 031, 043, 074, MMW, Hafizullah.
315. Lester Grau, 'Breaking Contact Without Leaving Chaos: The Soviet Withdrawal from Afghanistan', Leavenworth: Foreign Military Studies Office (Army), 2007, p. 10.
316. 'Khan Eshin', *Afghan Jehad*, Apr.–June 1988, pp. 107–8.
317. MSF, 'Mission', p. 10.
318. Urban, *War in Afghanistan*, pp. 245 and 248.
319. Orkand, 'The Southern Provinces', p. 117.
320. Afghan Information Centre, 'Monthly Bulletin No 91', Oct. 1988.

## 3. FROM THE SOVIET WITHDRAWAL TO THE US INTERVENTION, 1989–2001

1. 061.
2. Gilles Dorronsoro, *Revolution Unending: Afghanistan, 1979 to the Present*, London: Hurst, p. 6.
3. Although see, for example, Afghan Information Centre's Monthly Bulletins.
4. Dorronsoro, *Revolution*, p. 6.
5. Victoria Schofield, *Afghan Frontier: Feuding and Fighting in Central Asia*, London: IB Tauris, 2003, pp. 336–9.
6. Ahmed Rashid, *Taliban*, London: Yale University Press, 2000, p. 65.
7. William Maley (ed.), *Fundamentalism Reborn?*, Lahore: Vanguard Books, 1998, p. 2.
8. Kamal Matinuddin, *The Taliban Phenomenon*, Karachi: Oxford University Press, 1999, p. 35.
9. John Simpson, *News From No Man's Land*, London: Macmillan, 2002, p. 300.
10. 061.
11. Eng. M. Rabi Amaj, 'Helmand Projects Monitor and Supervision Report', Quetta: Islamic Aid Health Center, 1991, p. 21.
12. Barnett Rubin, *The Fragmentation of Afghanistan*, New Haven: Yale University Press, 1995, p. 205.
13. Ibid., p. 263.
14. There were four crossing points at that time over which a car could cross during Feb.–Apr.: Kajaki (under Nasim), Gereshk and Lashkar Gah (under the militias) and Garmsir (contested, then captured by Nasim)—Médecins Sans Frontières, 'Exploratory Mission in Helmand', Quetta: 1989, p. 28.
15. Alain Labrousse, *Afghanistan: Opium de guerre, Opium de paix*, Paris: Fayard, 2005, p. 119.
16. Afghan Information Centre, 'Monthly Bulletin No 102', Peshawar, Sep. 1989.
17. 021.
18. Joel Hafvenstein, *Opium Season*, Guilford: The Lyons Press, 2007, p. 130; Afghan Embassy, 'News Bulletin', p. 3.
19. Afghan Information Centre, 'Monthly Bulletin No 123–4', Peshawar, June–July 1991.
20. For example, credit, economic stability, currency, portable wealth, agricultural hedging etc.
21. 022.
22. 031.
23. Dorronsoro, *Revolution*, pp. 204–5.
24. 006, 049.
25. For example, 048, Habibullah.
26. Told to me by many different people 2008–12, although he denied it to me, claiming that he was neutral in all conflicts.
27. All from Habibullah.
28. 008.

29. 043, 044.
30. 008, 033, 049.
31. Gilles Dorronsoro, 'Helmand: Le Dernier Refuge des Khalqis', *Afghanistan Info*, 33 (1993).
32. 007, MMW.
33. 048.
34. 007, 044.
35. Dorronsoro, *Revolution*, p. 205.
36. 068, 074.
37. AfghaNews, 'Provincial News', vol. 11, London, Apr. 1995; Afghan Information Centre, 'Monthly Bulletin No 109', Peshawar, Apr. 1990, p. 28. I cannot deduce from my interview-derived chronology when exactly the Tanai deal between Hafizullah and Khano occurred, particularly whether it was before or after Nasim was assassinated.
38. Labrousse, *Afghanistan*, p. 119; Rubin, *Fragmentation*, p. 263; Angelo Rasanayagam, *Afghanistan: A Modern History*, London: IB Tauris, 2005, p. 137.
39. Thirteen metric tons of opium taxed at 5 per cent in 1990 harvest (Amaj, 'Helmand Projects', p. 12); cf. US government figures which suggest a decrease from 3100ha to 195ha before rising again to over 3000ha in 1991 (Pers. Comm. David Mansfield, 2012).
40. 'Country Reports—Afghanistan', *The Economist*, 1990/Q3, p. 21.
41. Labrousse, *Afghanistan*, p. 119; Rubin, *Fragmentation*, p. 253.
42. Also probably murdered by Hizb in 1988 (David Edwards, *Before Taliban*, London: University of California Press, 2002, p. 285).
43. AIC, 'Monthly 109', p. 28.
44. AfghaNews, 'Provincial News,' vol. 8, London, Apr. 1990.
45. 003, 013, 020.
46. AIC, 'Monthly 109', p. 28.
47. MMW.
48. 040.
49. 020.
50. 070.
51. 007.
52. 039.
53. 007, 015, 071.
54. 034.
55. 051.
56. 061.
57. Afghan Information Centre, 'Monthly Bulletin No 113', Peshawar, Aug. 1990, p. 20.
58. Afghan Information Centre, 'Monthly Bulletin No 118', Peshawar, Jan. 1991, p. 16.
59. 014, 016.
60. ARJ, MMW.

61. 048.
62. 015, 043.
63. For example, 065, 081, 084.
64. Rubin, *Fragmentation*, p. 265.
65. Antonio Giustozzi *War, Politics and Society in Afghanistan, 1978–1992*, London: Hurst, 2000, pp. 232–5.
66. 031, 035. Amaj, 'Helmand Projects', pp. 11 and 16.
67. 008.
68. 029.
69. 063.
70. 038, 044.
71. 018, 074.
72. Afghan Information Centre, 'Monthly Bulletin No 121–2', Peshawar, Apr.–May 1991, p. 31.
73. Afghan Information Centre, 'Monthly Bulletin No 124–5', Peshawar, July–Aug. 1991, pp. 53–4.
74. Afghan Information Centre, 'Monthly Bulletin No 130–1', Peshawar, Jan.–Feb. 1992, p. 21.
75. Amaj, 'Helmand Projects', p. 12.
76. AfghaNews, 'Provincial News', vol. 15, Peshawar, Aug. 1991, p. 2.
77. 025.
78. 012, 060, Jabbar.
79. 001, 029.
80. 043, 048, 061.
81. Narrative taken from MMW except where indicated. Hafizullah. Overall details confirmed by Antonio Giustozzi, 'Tribes and Warlords in Southern Afghanistan 1980–2005', Crisis States Research Centre Working Paper Series 1, 7, 2006, p. 13; Dorronsoro, 'Helmand: Le Dernier', p. 13.
82. 084.
83. 007.
84. 029.
85. 023.
86. 005.
87. 084.
88. 007, MMW.
89. 007, 018, MMW, Hafizullah. Dorronsoro, 'Helmand: Le Dernier', p. 11.
90. 007, 043, 048.
91. 031, 048.
92. 012.
93. Hafizullah, ARJ.
94. 061.
95. Dorronsoro, 'Helmand: Le Dernier', p. 11.
96. Dorronsoro, *Revolution*, p. 239.
97. 023, 039, 041.
98. 038.

99. 041.
100. 071.
101. 023.
102. 034, 038.
103. 063.
104. 044, 049, 083, Habibullah.
105. 039, 049.
106. Redacted.
107. 006, 084.
108. Because of the Kajaki dam altering the Helmand's flow, Iran and Afghanistan negotiated a treaty in 1973 that spelt out minimum flow levels that should reach the Iranian Sistan region, where the water was essential for the local ecology. The treaty was never ratified and this issue is still causing problems today.
109. 'Iran Accused of Interfering in Afghan Affairs', *Dawn*, 9 Jan. 2002.
110. Tom Coghlan, 'The Taliban in Helmand: An Oral History', in Antonio Giustozzi (ed.), *Decoding the New Taliban: Insights from the Afghan Field*, London: Hurst, 2009, p. 147.
111. 'Hirmand [*sic*] River's Water to Flow into Iran Again Soon: Afghan Source', *Payvand*, 12 Dec. 2002.
112. Michelle Centlivres-Demont, 'Les Nouvelles d'Afghanistan', *Afghanistan Info*, 32 (1992), p. 12.
113. 060.
114. Assadullah Sherzad was a cousin of Khano who later became Helmand's chief of police during the Karzai era.
115. 007, ARJ.
116. 060. Dorronsoro, 'Helmand: Le Dernier', pp. 11–13; Giustozzi, '"Tribes"', p. 12.
117. Dorronsoro, 'Helmand: Le Dernier', p. 12.
118. 044.
119. 043, 057, 074, Hafizullah, MMW.
120. 046. Dorronsoro, 'Helmand: Le Dernier', pp. 11–13.
121. 047.
122. Redacted.
123. 007. Dostum was/is an ex-Khalqi militia commander in Mazar-e Sharif, then recently promoted to general by President Mujaddidi.
124. 013, 033, 035, 043, MMW.
125. 035.
126. 025, 074.
127. 013.
128. 043.
129. 007.
130. 035.
131. 007, 016, 035, 043.
132. 014.

133. 014, 016, 038, 060.

134. For example, 023, 033.

135. 084.

136. 006.

137. 080.

138. 035, 042.

139. 070.

140. Narrative by MMW, corroborated by 016, 074.

141. AfghaNews, 'Provincial News', vol. 9, London, July 1993, p. 2.

142. UN Drug Control Programme, 'Comparative Survey (Helmand Province)', Peshawar, 1995, p. ix.

143. Afghan Embassy, 'Press Release', London, 18 Jan. 1994.

144. 007.

145. 007, 023, 071.

146. 003, 012, 031.

147. 050.

148. AfghaNews, 'Provincial News', vol. 11, London, Nov. 1994, p. 2.

149. 013. AfghaNews, 'Provincial News', vol. 14, London, July 1992, p. 2.

150. 022.

151. 021. PersExp, Helmand, 2010.

152. For example, Rashid, *Taliban*, p. 23.

153. Ibid., pp. 26–7.

154. 013, 068, MMW.

155. Abdul Salam Zaeef, *My Life with the Taliban*, London: Hurst, 2010, p. 63; Anthony Davis, 'How the Taliban Became a Military Force', in W. Maley (ed.), *Fundamentalism Reborn? Afghanistan and the Taliban*, Lahore: Vanguard, 1998, pp. 47–8.

156. 074.

157. 013, 018, 074, MMW.

158. 070. Davis, 'How the Taliban', p. 51.

159. 013, 074.

160. For example, 021, 031.

161. 074. Neamatollah Nojumi, *The Rise of the Taliban in Afghanistan*, New York: St Martin's Press, 2002, p. 135.

162. 025, 070.

163. 010.

164. SMA.

165. 070.

166. 021.

167. 012, ARJ.

168. Gulbuddin Hekmatyar, *Secret Plans Open Faces: From the Withdrawal of Russians to the Fall of the Coalition Government*, ed. SF Yunas, trans. SZ Taizi, Peshawar: University of Peshawar, 2004, p. 156.

169. 018. William Maley, *The Afghanistan Wars*, New York: Palgrave Macmillan,

2002, pp. 51 and 61; 'Country Reports—Afghanistan Q1/1995', *The Economist*, p. 40.
170. ARJ, MMW.
171. Antonio Giustozzi, *Empires of Mud: Dynamics of Warlordism in Afghanistan, 1980–2007*, London: Hurst, 2009, pp. 256–7.
172. Ibid., p. 272.
173. ARJ.
174. Davis, 'How the Taliban', p. 61.
175. MMW, ARJ. Giustozzi, *Empires*, p. 257.
176. SMA.
177. ARJ.
178. 013.
179. 003, 018, 021.
180. 031.
181. 020, 070.
182. 012, 020.
183. 001.
184. 012.
185. 008.
186. 001, 012.
187. 003.
188. Note: not Abdul Rahman Jan, the jihadi commander from Marjeh, who had just been ejected by Ibrahim.
189. 023.
190. 007, 015, 023.
191. 015.
192. 005.
193. 053.
194. 056.
195. 040, 068, 074.
196. For example, 034.
197. 074.
198. 040, 074.
199. 074.
200. 075.
201. 001, 020.
202. 075.
203. 070, 075.
204. Zaeef, *My Life*, p. 265.
205. The same Zakir who went to madrasa with Sher Mohammad.
206. 070. Zaeef, *My Life*, pp. 264 and 270.
207. 019, 103.
208. 001.
209. 067.
210. 038, 067.

211. 039, 067.
212. 034.
213. 007.
214. 065.
215. 007.
216. 061, 069.
217. 'Taliban Leader Killed After RAF Plane Tracks Phone', *The Times*, 27 Dec. 2006.
218. Zaeef, *My Life*, p. 278.
219. 048.
220. 068.
221. 066.
222. 029, 041, 063, SMA.
223. Zaeef, *My Life*, p. 268.
224. 066.
225. 066.
226. 015, 023, 071, 083.
227. 021, 039.
228. 005, 050.
229. 008, 023.
230. 013, 021, 075.
231. 071.
232. 012, 013, 060.
233. For example, 013, 014, 019, 047, 080.
234. 046.
235. 001, 008.
236. 041, 067, 075.
237. 014, 015, 023.
238. Robert Crews and Amin Tarzi (eds), *The Taliban and the Crisis of Afghanistan*, Cambridge, MA: Harvard University Press, 2008, p. 262.
239. 015, 023.
240. 032.
241. 017.
242. 008, 046, 050.
243. 025.
244. 021.
245. 050.
246. 001.
247. 013.
248. Anna Pont, *Blind Chickens and Social Animals*, Portland: Mercy Corps, 2001, p. 13.
249. 050.
250. 007.
251. Pont, *Blind Chickens*, pp. 45–7.
252. 021.

253. 075.

254. 013, 021.

255. Dorronsoro, 'Helmand: Le Dernier', p. 12.

256. 013.

257. 007.

258. 020.

259. Pont, *Blind Chickens*, pp. 48 and 95.

260. UNDP, 'Helmand Planning Group—Baseline Survey of Helmand Province', Peshawar, 1999, p. ii.

261. Nojumi, *Rise of the Taliban*, p. 122.

262. 018, 027. Pont, *Blind Chickens*, pp. 58 and 97.

263. 008, 023, 075.

264. 013, 023.

265. Agency Coordinating Body for Afghan Relief, 'Helmand Profile', Quetta, 1999, p. 12.

266. 058.

267. ACBAR, 'Helmand Profile', p. 7.

268. Richard Scott, 'Letter to Counselor for Narcotics Affairs on Helmand, Islamabad, RE: Trip Report', 10 Feb. 1998.

269. Pont, *Blind Chickens*, p. 55.

270. UNDP, 'Baseline Survey', pp. 21–3.

271. Nojumi, *Rise of the Taliban*, p. 136.

272. AfghaNews, 'Provincial News', vol. 11, London, Nov. 1995, p. 7; Alain Labrousse, 'Les Drogues et les Conflicts en Afghanistan (1978–1995)', *Afghanistan Info*, 38 (1996), p. 19.

273. Labrousse, *Afghanistan*, p. 180.

274. Hafvenstein, *Opium Season*, p. 214.

275. 041.

276. 'Taliban's Ban on a Poppy a Success, US Aides Say', *New York Times*, 20 May 2001.

277. David Macdonald, *Drugs in Afghanistan*, London: Pluto Press, 2007, p. 83.

278. For example, 003, 008, 041.

279. Redacted.

280. 017, 023. Figures from David Mansfield, PERS COMM 2012.

281. 015, 031.

282. 'Southern Afghanistan: Drought Much Increased', *Hewad*, 1 June 2000.

283. Hassan Kamran and Sultan Ahmady, 'Drought Assessment in Southern Afghanistan', Quetta, 2000, p. 6.

284. 'Hirmand [*sic*] River's Water to Flow into Iran Again, Soon: Afghan Source', *Payvand*, 12 Dec. 2002.

4. FROM THE US INTERVENTION TO THE RETURN OF THE ANGREZ, 2001–6

1. For example, Antonio Giustozzi, *Koran, Kalashnikov and Laptop*, London: Hurst, 2008, pp. 1–8.

2. 003, 008, 014.
3. 012.
4. Richard Scott, 'Email to USAID: Helmand Follow Up XVII—9 May 2006—Poppies, Cash-for-Work and Cotton Again', 2006.
5. 051, 066, G118, G628.
6. 015.
7. 043, 057.
8. SMA, G968.
9. SMA, 064, G968.
10. 021.
11. 075.
12. 003.
13. ARJ.
14. 053.
15. 003, 015, 064.
16. 021, 064.
17. ARJ, 064.
18. Jon Anderson, *The Lion's Grave*, New York: Grove Press, 2002, p. 128.
19. 'Surrendered Chieftain Urges Taliban to Accept Amnesty', *New York Times*, 2 June 2005.
20. G008, G108.
21. G363.
22. 'Surrendered Chieftain Urges Taliban to Accept Amnesty', *New York Times*, 2 June 2005; 'Omar No Longer Believed to be in Baghran Area', Associated Press, 6 Jan. 2002.
23. 021, 064.
24. 069.
25. 017.
26. 012, 075.
27. MMW.
28. 025.
29. For example, 068, 079.
30. 074.
31. 012, 025.
32. 063.
33. 043.
34. 066. Michael Semple, *Reconciliation in Afghanistan*, Washington: US Institute of Peace, 2009, p. 14.
35. 016, 023, 071.
36. For example, 063.
37. 015.
38. For example, 041, 053, 060.
39. 015, 023, 031.
40. UNHCR, 'District Profile of Sangin', Dec. 2002.
41. UNHCR, 'District Profile of Musa Qala', Dec. 2002.

42. 009, 070.
43. PersExp, Helmand, 2008–12.
44. UNHCR, 'District Profile of Nawa', Dec. 2002.
45. SMA.
46. 034.
47. 032, 034.
48. 036, 068.
49. 034.
50. 032.
51. 068, 103.
52. See Chapter 1.
53. 062, 068, 075.
54. 062, 070.
55. Sarah Chayes, *The Punishment of Virtue*, New York: Penguin, 2006, p. 274.
56. MMW, Hafizullah.
57. This is a central theme in Chayes' book, *Punishment*.
58. 062, 079, MMW.
59. Personal observation of the SF compound's memorial, Camp Price, 2012.
60. MMW.
61. For example, 013, 029.
62. 013, 070.
63. 029.
64. 063.
65. Hafizullah was kind enough to provide me with these names, as he pointed out with a wide smile that they all later joined the Taliban and fought the British in 2006!
66. Drugs Enforcement Agency, 'Drug Investigations Lead to Treasury Designation of New Ansari Money Exchange', 18 Feb. 2011.
67. G942.
68. 016, 031.
69. International Crisis Group, 'Afghanistan: The Problem of Pushtun Alienation' Asia Report no. 62, 2003, p. 18.
70. 016, 029.
71. 084.
72. 016.
73. 016, 028, ARJ.
74. 033, 080.
75. Habibullah, 080.
76. 042, 060.
77. 10,000 acres.
78. Tom Coghlan, 'The Taliban in Helmand: An Oral History', in Antonio Giustozzi (ed.), *Decoding the New Taliban: Insights from the Afghan Field*, London: Hurst, 2009, p. 126; Anand Gopal, 'The Battle for Marjeh', Center for International Governance Innovation, 2010.
79. 071, 084.

80. See Appendix 4 for family trees.
81. 041.
82. 023. See Appendix 4.
83. 039.
84. UNHCR, 'District Profile of Nad-e Ali', Dec. 2002.
85. 017.
86. MMW. Ahmed Rashid, *Descent into Chaos*, London: Allen Lane, 2008, p. 322.
87. 025, 027.
88. 021, 041.
89. 217, 246.
90. UNHCR, 'Sangin', Dec. 2002.
91. 069.
92. 057.
93. Giustozzi, *Koran*, p. 60.
94. G1117.
95. Edwina Thompson, *Trust is the Coin of the Realm*, Karachi: Oxford University Press, 2011, p. 230.
96. 'Loya Jirga sees Wheeling-Dealing and Pressure from US', e-ariana, 14 June 2002.
97. 047, 083.
98. For example, 068, 082.
99. All taken from ACS, 'Focus Groups', except where shown by interview numbers.
100. The Pushtun find it difficult to distinguish the sound of the letter 'f' from the letter 'p' hence 'specialporce'.
101. 105. 'Surrendered Chieftain …' *New York Times*, 2 June 2005.
102. 027, 063, 096.
103. G929.
104. G850. For a detailed discussion of torture in Guantanamo see Andy Worthington, *The Guantanamo Files*, London: Pluto Press, 2007.
105. G942.
106. G942, G963.
107. G850.
108. G958.
109. G960, G961, G963–7, G969, G971–2.
110. 'Surrendered Chieftain …' *New York Times*, 2 June 2005.
111. G968.
112. For example, 068, 084.
113. PersExp, Memorial SF Compound, Price, 2012.
114. Chayes, *Punishment*, pp. 272–4.
115. G1117.
116. MMW.
117. 068.

118. Worthington, *Guantanamo*, p. 245. 'US Detainees "Murdered" during Interrogations', Associated Press, 25 Oct. 2005. See also Appendix 6.
119. 061.
120. 029, 057.
121. 073.
122. 062.
123. 047, 073.
124. 062.
125. 070.
126. 069.
127. 034.
128. 000, 218, 219, 221, G942.
129. 047, 069, 073.
130. 057, 062.
131. G968; eventually released in 2009.
132. 215, 217, 246.
133. Semple, *Reconciliation*, p. 85.
134. 019, 079. 'Fierce Fighting and a Kidnapping in Afghanistan', *New York Times*, 2 Nov. 2003.
135. 001, 026.
136. MMW.
137. 068.
138. 069.
139. 068.
140. 073.
141. 062.
142. For example, 062, 073, 079.
143. 057.
144. 063.
145. 057.
146. 063.
147. 079.
148. 026, 030.
149. PersExp liaising with US detachment in 2011/2.
150. 029.
151. PersExp, Kabul, 2012.
152. 015, 084.
153. MMW.
154. 029, SMA, ARJ. 'Provincial Security Chief among 20 Killed in Helmand Clash', *Pajhwok*, 11 Oct. 2005.
155. 006, MMW.
156. 013.
157. 'Dozens of Insurgents Killed, 60 Rounded up in Helmand', *Pajhwok*, 11 Sep. 2005.

158. 'One Cop Killed, Three Wounded in Clash with Smugglers', *Pajhwok*, 19 Sep. 2005.
159. Seth Jones, 'The Rise of Afghanistan's Insurgency: State Failure and Jihad', *International Security*, 32, 4 (2008), p. 14.
160. 001, 013.
161. 024, MMW, ARJ.
162. 012, 019, 075.
163. Richard Scott, 'Opium Poppy Cultivation in Central Helmand, Afghanistan: A Case Study in Bad Program Management' (paper presented at the 67th Annual Meeting of the Society for Applied Anthropology, Tampa, 2007), pp. 10–11.
164. Richard Scott, 'Cotton & Alternative Crops Pilot Project, 7 Apr–20 May 02', Lashkar Gah, 2002, pp. 1, 5 and 18.
165. Rashid, *Descent*, p. 326; Jonathan Goodhand and David Mansfield, 'Drugs and (Dis)order: A Study of the Opium Trade, Political Settlements and State-Making in Afghanistan', Crisis States Research Centre Working Papers, Series 2, 83 (2010), p. 20.
166. G363.
167. 007.
168. 065.
169. 017.
170. 007, 065.
171. 015.
172. 038, 098.
173. Redacted.
174. 065.
175. 038.
176. 038, 065.
177. 007, 065.
178. 050.
179. 023.
180. Redacted.
181. Redacted.
182. Coghlan, 'The Taliban in Helmand', p. 120.
183. 087, 215, 217, 230.
184. Gopal, 'The Battle for Marjeh'.
185. Patrick Bishop, *3 PARA*, London: Harper Press, 2007, p. 153.
186. Stuart Gordon, 'Aid and Stabilization: Helmand Case Study', Chatham House: 2010, pp. 51–3.
187. PersExp, Helmand, 2008–10.
188. Rashid, *Descent*, p. 323.
189. Established in 2004, initially manned (150–300 men) by the Iowa National Guard and then the Texan National Guard (Joel Hafvenstein, *Opium Season*, Guilford: The Lyons Press, 2007, pp. 94 and 249).
190. Ibid., p. 207.

191. 039, 058.
192. 050.
193. PersExp, Helmand, 2008–12.
194. Detailed in Hafvenstein, *Opium Season*.
195. 076.
196. Sequence from 001, 012, 029 unless otherwise referenced.
197. 018, 036.
198. 029.
199. 001, 036, 061.
200. 024, 025.
201. 027.
202. 024.
203. 040.
204. 024, 040, 057.
205. 036.
206. Hafvenstein, *Opium Season*, pp. 68–70 and 76.
207. MMW.
208. 057. Hafvenstein, *Opium Season*, pp. 165 and 211.
209. 057.
210. 036.
211. For example, 'Drivers Rail against Herat–Kabul Highway Officials', *Pajhwok*, 23 Oct. 2005.
212. Crisis Group Asia, 'Afghanistan: Getting Disarmament Back on Track—Briefing No 35' (2005), p. 7.
213. 'The Gunmen of Kabul', http://www.corpwatch.org/article.php?id=14863 (accessed 4 Apr. 2011).
214. 036. Gordon, 'Aid and Stabilization', 21.
215. 'Disarmament being Completed in Afghan Kandahar Province', Independent Radio Kelid (Kabul), BBC Summary of World Broadcasts, 22 Oct. 2004.
216. 020.
217. 'Six Jihadi Commanders Surrender Weapons', *Pajhwok*, 22 June 2005.
218. Hafvenstein, *Opium Season*, pp. 243–4.
219. 060.
220. 'Helmand Gets New Governor, Deputy', *Pajhwok*, 12 Dec. 2005.
221. ARJ.
222. 'Protesters Demand Seat for Disqualified Candidate', *Pajhwok*, 30 Oct. 2005.
223. 033. PersExp, Helmand, 2010. Data from http://afghanistanelectiondata.org/election/2005 (accessed 14 Nov. 2012).
224. For example, 024, 026, 036, 037.
225. 'Helmand Governor Injured in Assassination Attempt; Taliban Blamed', *Mashhad*, 11 May 2003.
226. 062.
227. 'Religious Scholar Wounded in Helmand Attack', *Pajhwok*, 4 Apr. 2005.
228. 'Seventh Aspirant Killed as Electioneering Ends', *Pajhwok*, 16 Sep. 2005.
229. 'Judge Gunned Down in Helmand', *Pajhwok*, 20 Dec. 2005.

230. 'Helmand Governor Escapes Life Attempt', *Pajhwok*, 11 July 2005.
231. 'Attendance in Helmand Schools Thin after Attacks', *Pajhwok*, 25 Dec. 2005; 'Night Letters Scare Helmand Teachers, Residents', *Pajhwok*, 3 Jan. 2006.
232. For example, 047, 050, 053.
233. 'Feature: Where Government Job is a Life Risk', *Pajhwok*, 17 Mar. 2006.
234. Giustozzi, *Koran*, pp. 60–1 and 103.
235. 007, 074.
236. For example, 204, 211, 213, 237.
237. 006, 104. Coghlan, 'The Taliban in Helmand', p. 143.
238. 047.
239. For example, 247 who contacted his father's friend and was introduced to Mansour.
240. Coghlan, 'The Taliban in Helmand', p. 143.
241. 072, 211, 233.
242. 017, 034, 063, 069.
243. 202, 215, 216.
244. 088, 089, 235.
245. UN Sanctions list, http://www.un.org/News/Press/docs/2012/sc10542.doc.htm (accessed 14 Nov. 2012).
246. 201.
247. David Loyn, *Butcher and Bolt*, London: Hutchinson, 2008, p. 292.
248. Rashid, *Descent*, p. 359.
249. 'Al Samood Biography of Taliban Military Commander Mullah Dadullah', NEFA Foundation, July 2007.
250. 017, 038, 105.
251. 202.
252. 007, 050, 083.
253. 086, 088, 089.
254. 039.
255. For example, 213
256. 065, 067, 201, 202.
257. 065.
258. 067.
259. For example, 201, 202.
260. 038.
261. 034, 067.
262. 067.
263. 067, 072.
264. 072.
265. 244.
266. 201.
267. For example, 201, 202, 209.
268. 062, 068.
269. PersExp, Helmand, 2012.
270. MMW.

271. G968.
272. 011, 018.
273. 017, 062.
274. 'Six Jihadi Commanders Surrender Weapons', *Pajhwok*, 22 June 2005.
275. Leo Docherty, *Desert of Death*, London: Faber and Faber, 2007, pp. 136–7.
276. 075.
277. 017.
278. For example, 037, 060, 061, 062.
279. 069.
280. 062.
281. 073.
282. 062.
283. 068.
284. 062.
285. 060, 223.
286. 062.
287. 074.
288. 061.
289. 062. He was eventually killed in Aug. 2010 by ISAF Special Operations forces (Toby Harnden, *Dead Men Risen*, London: Quercus, 2011, p. 490).
290. 068.
291. 062, 068.
292. 017.
293. 'MP's Brother, Six Taliban Killed in Helmand', *Pajhwok*, 18 June 2006; '32 Killed in Taliban Ambush in South', *Pajhwok*, 19 June 2006.
294. Giustozzi, *Decoding*, pp. 119–20.
295. 010, 013, 093, 215.
296. 087.
297. 215, 217, 218.
298. Kim Barker, *The Taliban Shuffle*, New York: Doubleday, 2011, p. 111.
299. SMA.
300. For example, 000, 001, 013, 219, 241.
301. 'Afghan Governor Turned 3000 Men Over to the Taliban', *The Telegraph*, 20 Nov. 2009.
302. 221.
303. 219.
304. 212, 221, 222, 223, 225, 228, 230, 231. This is such a critical point that I have listed all the interviews in which this was covered. Note: these interviewees cover three separate interviewers, who did not have any contact with each other.
305. 001, 013, 070.
306. Hafizullah, 029.
307. WikiLeaks, 'HELMAND GOVERNOR ON TRIBAL WARFARE, SECURITY, NEED FOR ADDITIONAL ASSISTANCE' (3 Sep. 2006).
308. Antonio Giustozzi, 'Tribes and Warlords in Southern Afghanistan 1980–

2005', Crisis States Research Centre Working Paper Series 1, 7, 2006, p. 14; WikiLeaks, 'HELMAND GOVERNOR SENT TO PARLIAMENT; REPLACED BY SENIOR NSC ADVISOR' (14 Dec. 2005).

309. WikiLeaks, 'HELMAND GOVERNOR PROMISED COOPERATION ON ERADICATION' (27 Jan. 2006).

310. Giustozzi, *Koran*, p. 87.

311. WikiLeaks, 'PRT/LASHKAR GAH—POPPY ERADICATION MOVING FORWARD; ATTACKS EXPECTED' (8 Mar. 2006).

312. 069.

313. 069. WikiLeaks, 'PRT/HELMAND—HELMAND ERADICATION WRAP UP' (3 May 2006).

## 5. FROM THE RETURN OF THE ANGREZ TO US RE-ENGAGEMENT, 2006–9

1. 082.

2. To be completely fair, this would not have meshed with the political context set for the British military by the British government and by the US, the senior partner in the NATO coalition. I would like to reiterate here the point I made in the Introduction: I take as much blame as anyone else for the problems encountered by the British military in Helmand. I was involved in many of the decisions and actions discussed here. It is far too easy to criticise with hindsight: many of the decisions that we had to make on a daily basis were on a 'least-worse-case' basis.

3. House of Commons Defence Select Committee, 'The UK Deployment to Afghanistan', London, 2006, p. 7.

4. Michael Clarke (ed.), *The Afghan Papers*, London: RUSI, 2011, p. 16.

5. Ibid., p. 15.

6. Ibid., p. 20.

7. Ibid., p. 21.

8. Mike Martin, *A Brief History of Helmand*, Warminster: Afghan COIN Centre, 2011.

9. 082.

10. Redacted.

11. WikiLeaks, 'UK OFFICIALS DISCUSS TRANSITION WITH PROVINCIAL COUNCIL AND MULLAHS' COUNCIL' (24 Mar. 2006).

12. WikiLeaks, 'MOUSA QALA DISTRICT CHIEF AND ELDERS WELCOME UK DEPLOYMENT' (28 Mar. 2006).

13. WikiLeaks, 'FROM THE STARS AND STRIPES TO THE UNION JACK THE UK ASSUMES CONTROL OF LASKAR GAH PRT' (1 May 2006).

14. Patrick Bishop, *3 PARA*, London: Harper Press, 2007, p. 149; Leo Docherty, *Desert of Death*, London: Faber and Faber, 2007, p. 65.

15. Stuart Tootal, *Danger Close*, London: John Murray Publishers, 2009, p. 41.

16. Ibid., p. 45.

17. Hew Pike, *From the Frontline*, Barnsley: Pen and Sword, 2008, pp. 173 and 176.

18. Clarke, *Afghan Papers*, p. 19.

19. 013. Resonates with PersExp Helmand, 2008–12.

20. James Fergusson, *A Million Bullets*, London: Transworld Publishers, 2008, p. 159.

21. Bishop, *3 PARA*, p. 154.

22. For example, 217

23. Bishop, *3 PARA*, pp. 52–3.

24. WikiLeaks, 'POPPY ERADICATION MOVING FORWARD; ATTACKS EXPECTED' (8 Mar. 2006).

25. 028.

26. 066.

27. Bishop, *3 PARA*, p. 55.

28. Fergusson, *Million Bullets*, p. 57.

29. Docherty, *Desert*, p. 119.

30. 069.

31. Docherty, *Desert*, p. 136.

32. Tootal, *Danger*, p. 84.

33. Bishop, *3 PARA*, p. 49.

34. Ibid., p. 108.

35. Tootal, *Danger*, p. 84.

36. 069. Pike, *From the Frontline*, pp. 194–9. The British base was in Haji Lal Jan, a local drug dealer's compound. He funded successive attacks in these early days on the British because they had occupied his home.

37. Bishop, *3 PARA*, p. 155.

38. 000, 060. 'Taliban Capture Garmsir District', *Pajhwok*, 17 July 2006.

39. 'Taliban Capture Another District in South', *Pajhwok*, 18 July 2006.

40. 'Defence Ministry Claims Recapturing [*sic*] Garmsir from Taliban', *Pajhwok*, 19 July 2006.

41. 023. Tootal, *Danger*, p. 329.

42. ARJ.

43. 013, 069.

44. 069. Docherty, *Desert*, p. 138.

45. 032.

46. Docherty, *Desert*, p. 127.

47. 006. Ibid., p. 160.

48. 013. Ibid., p. 188; Pike, *From the Frontline*, p. 182.

49. 028. Fergusson, *Million Bullets*, p. 128; 'British Commander Rejects Civilian Casualties in Now Zad', *Pajhwok*, 15 July 2006.

50. 056.

51. 006, SMA. Fergusson, *Million Bullets*, pp. 68 and 71.

52. WikiLeaks, 'HELMAND GOVERNOR ON TRIBAL WARFARE, SECURITY, NEED FOR ADDITIONAL ASSISTANCE' (3 Sep. 2006).

53. Tootal, *Danger*, p. 49.

54. Docherty, *Desert*, p. 145.
55. Bishop, *3 PARA*, pp. 52–3.
56. 'Retreat in Musa Qala', *Sarak*, Oct. 2006, p. 10.
57. For example, 217.
58. David Loyn, *Butcher and Bolt*, London: Hutchinson, 2008, p. 259.
59. See Martin, *Brief History*, pp. 16–19.
60. Fergusson, *Million Bullets*, p. 266.
61. Syed Saleem Shahzad, *Inside Al-Qaeda and the Taliban*, London: Pluto Press, 2011, pp. 22–35.
62. Tootal, *Danger*, p. 144; Bishop, *3 PARA*, p. 157.
63. Shahzad, *Inside Al-Qaeda*, p. 21.
64. 047.
65. Fergusson, *Million Bullets*, p. 267.
66. WikiLeaks, 'MUSA QALA? AN INSIDER VIEW' (30 Nov. 2006); WikiLeaks, 'MUSA QALA AGREEMENT: OPPOSING INTERESTS AND OPPOSING VIEWS, BUT ONE WAY FORWARD' (27 Nov. 2006).
67. Fergusson, *Million Bullets*, p. 268.
68. WikiLeaks, 'MUSA QALA? AN INSIDER VIEW' (30 Nov. 2006).
69. WikiLeaks, 'NORTH QUIET AFTER ISAF WITHDRAWAL' (7 Nov. 2006).
70. WikiLeaks, 'GOVERNOR DEFENDS DEAL WITH MUSA QALA SHURA' (14 Nov. 2006).
71. 'Retreat in Musa Qala', *Sarak*, Oct. 2006, p. 10.
72. Ewen Southby-Tailyour, *3 Commando Brigade*, London: Ebury Press, 2008, pp. 35 and 72; WikiLeaks, 'GOVERNOR DEFENDS DEAL ...' (14 Nov. 2006).
73. WikiLeaks, 'MUSA QALA AGREEMENT: OPPOSING INTERESTS AND OPPOSING VIEWS ...' (27 Nov. 2006).
74. Southby-Tailyour, *3 Commando*, p. 35.
75. 013, 070.
76. Bishop, *3 PARA*, p. 267.
77. Southby-Tailyour, *3 Commando*, pp. 247 and 252.
78. WikiLeaks, 'SEMI-ANNUAL HELMAND REVIEW' (1 Apr. 2007).
79. 107.
80. 015.
81. 032, 080.
82. Stephen Grey, *Operation Snakebite*, London: Penguin, 2010, p. 62; James Cartwright, *Sniper in Helmand*, Barnsley: Pen and Sword, 2011, pp. 64–5.
83. 107.
84. 013, 025, 038.
85. 029.
86. 036.
87. 018, 026, 057.
88. PersExp, Nahr-e Saraj, 2009–12.
89. 062.
90. 017, 065. PersExp in village, 2009.

91. For example, 015, 017, 023, 065.

92. 065.

93. 017.

94. 065.

95. For example, 'UK Forces Take Key Taliban Bases', *BBC News*, 4 Jan. 2009.

96. WikiLeaks, 'SPECIAL MEDIA REACTION: AMIDST MUSA QALA FIGHTING, AFGHANS BLAME BRITISH TROOPS FOR ITS TAKEOVER BY TALIBAN' (10 Dec. 2007).

97. 105.

98. Grey, *Operation Snakebite*, p. 70.

99. SMA.

100. 108. Grey, *Operation Snakebite*, p. 318.

101. G008, G108. Rajiv Chandrasekaran, *Little America*, London: Bloomsbury, 2012, p. 288.

102. Grey, *Operation Snakebite*, pp. 275–6.

103. Ibid., p. 122.

104. Grey, *Operation Snakebite*, pp. 122 and 130.

105. 013, 105.

106. Chandrasekaran, *Little America*, p. 289.

107. WikiLeaks, 'MUSA QALA POLITICAL UPDATE: MULLAH SALAM'S LEADERSHIP WAVERING' (26 May 2008).

108. PersExp, Helmand, 2009.

109. 004.

110. WikiLeaks, '... MULLAH SALAM'S LEADERSHIP WAVERING' (26 May 2008).

111. For example, 225, 231.

112. For example, 225, 230.

113. 013.

114. 221, 228.

115. 023, 039.

116. 102.

117. 081, Jabbar. 'Great Game or Just Misunderstanding?' *BBC News*, 5 Jan. 2008.

118. PersExp, Nahr-e Saraj, 2010.

119. I have drawn heavily on Claudio Franco's and Antonio Giustozzi's forthcoming Afghan Analyst Network's paper 'Introducing the Nezami System Within the Taliban Discourse' in this section.

120. Theo Farrell and Antonio Giustozzi, 'The Taliban at War: Inside the Helmand Insurgency, 2004–2012', *International Affairs*, 89, 4, 2013, pp. 845–871

121. 202, 204, 243.

122. 204, 213.

123. 224, 225, 230, 239.

124. 202.

125. 201, 204, 209.

126. 209.

127. 204.
128. 201, 210.
129. 006.
130. 235.
131. 237.
132. For example, 218, 228, 231.
133. 215, 216.
134. PersExp, Helmand, 2009–12.
135. 'Musa Qala and the English', *Sarak*, Jan. 2008, p. 32; 'First, Do Not Accept the Judgement of Widowhood', *Elham*, July 2009, p. 2.
136. 105.
137. Shahzad, *Inside Al-Qaeda*, pp. 22–35.
138. 'Al Samood Biography of Taliban Military Commander Mullah Dadullah', *NEFA Foundation*, July 2007.
139. 038, 105.
140. Discussion recounted by 105.
141. 201, 202, 203, 204, 232.
142. Naval Postgraduate School (NPS), 'Analyzing the Taliban Code of Conduct', Monterey, 2009, pp. 2–5.
143. Franco and Giustozzi 'Introducing the Nezami System' (forthcoming).
144. cf. 'A New Layeha for the Mujahideen', http://www.signandsight.com/features/1071.html (accessed 14 Nov. 2012).
145. NPS, 'Analyzing the Taliban Code of Conduct', pp. 7, 15–19, 21 and 22.
146. Franco and Giustozzi 'Introducing the Nezami System' (forthcoming).
147. Rudra Chaudhuri and Theo Farrell, 'Campaign Disconnect: Operational Progress and Strategic Obstacles in Afghanistan, 2009–2011', *International Affairs*, 87, 2 (2011), p. 273.
148. Theo Farrell, 'Improving in War: Military Adaptation and the British in Helmand, 2006–2009', *Journal of Strategic Studies*, 33, 4 (2010), p. 23.
149. Sam Kiley, *Desperate Glory*, London: Bloomsbury, 2009, p. 14; Chandrasekaran, *Little America*, p. 66.
150. Peter Viggo Jakobsen and Peter Dahl Thruelsen, 'Clear, Hold, Train: Denmark's Military Operations in Helmand 2006–2010', *Danish Foreign Policy Yearbook* (2011), pp. 78–80.
151. WikiLeaks, 'HELMAND PROVINCE: GOVERNOR MANGAL TAKES CHARGE' (26 May 2008).
152. 036, 047, 081.
153. Habibullah, 035, 064.
154. 047, 048, 050, 053.
155. 047.
156. Kiley, *Desperate Glory*, p. 32; Docherty, *Desert*, p. 104.
157. WikiLeaks, 'READOUT OF NORTH ATLANTIC COUNCIL MEETING' (9 Apr. 2008).
158. 013, 047, 060, 105, Habibullah.
159. Ewen Southby-Tailyour, *Helmand Assault*, London: Ebury Press, 2010, p. 37.

160. Docherty, *Desert*, pp. 127–30.
161. Kiley, *Desperate Glory*, pp. 227–9.
162. 050. Docherty, *Desert*, pp. 127–8.
163. 050.
164. Habibullah.
165. See Chapter 4.
166. 007, 023, 050.
167. 039.
168. Habibullah.
169. 102, 109. Theo Farrell, Frans Osinga, and James A. Russell (eds), *Military Adaptation in Afghanistan*, Palo Alto: Stanford University Press, 2013, pp. 5–11.
170. Farrell, Osinga and Russell, *Military Adaptation*, pp. 5–11.
171. 'Taliban Killed in Afghan Battles', *BBC News*, 12 Oct. 2008.
172. Habibullah, 038, 048.
173. 'Newsletter', Green Village Schools, Oct. 2008.
174. 048, 050, 051, 058.
175. 051. See below and Chapter 6 for discussion about Mullah Karim.
176. 023, 047, 048, 050, 051, 058. http://www.greenvillageschools.org/ (accessed 15 Nov. 2012). Following testimonies from same sources, though detailed attribution redacted for personal security reasons.
177. 023, 050.
178. 'Are the Taliban Really Burning Schools?' *Sarak*, Sep. 2008, p. 6.
179. 'Taliban Bases Fall after Major Offensive', *The Times*, 4 Jan. 2009.
180. 007, 209, 212, 222.
181. 038, 047, 048.
182. 007.
183. 065.
184. PersExp, Shin Kalay, Dec. 2008.
185. 007, 023, 237.
186. 222, 237, 245.
187. Southby-Tailyour, *Helmand Assault*, pp. 136–9. PersExp, Zhargoun Kalay, Dec. 2008.
188. 237. 'Soldier "Showed Great Potential"', BBC News, 18 Dec. 2008.
189. 'NATO Secretary General Praises Estonia's Commitment to Smart Defence', http://www.nato.int/cps/en/natolive/news_83519.htm; (accessed 15 Nov. 2012).
190. PersExp serving with Estonian troops in Nad-e Ali, 2009.
191. 039, 051, 067, 071.
192. PersExp, Chah-e Mirza, Dec. 2008.
193. 'The Deadly Consequences of Cultural Insensitivity in Afghanistan', *Radio Free Europe*, 15 Nov. 2012.
194. 017.
195. PersExp, Nad-e Ali, 2008–9.
196. 004, 006, 007, 021, 023, 038, 047.

197. 047.
198. 015, 023.
199. 023, 050.
200. 015.
201. 067.
202. PersExp, Nad-e Ali, 2009.
203. 015, 023, 039.
204. Theo Farrell and Stuart Gordon, 'COIN Machine: The British Military in Afghanistan', *Orbis*, 53, 4 (2009), p. 12.
205. Andrew Wilder and Stuart Gordon, 'Money Can't Buy America Love', *Foreign Policy* (2009).
206. 023, 038.
207. 038. PersExp, Nad-e Ali, 2009.
208. PersExp, Nad-e Ali, 2009.
209. 015.
210. 034, 038. I was originally informed of these dynamics by Anne SS, to whom I am grateful.
211. 073.
212. 002, 014, 018.
213. 060, 061, 062, 073, 074, 075.
214. Toby Harnden, *Dead Men Risen*, London: Quercus, 2011, p. 98.
215. Ibid., p. 298.
216. Ibid., p. 446.
217. 062. WikiLeaks, 'BUILDING A POLICE FORCES [*sic*] IN BABAJI, HELMAND PROVINCE' (27 Sep. 2009).
218. 229, 230.
219. PersExp, Helmand, 2009.
220. 016, 068.
221. 085.
222. PersExp, Helmand, 2009. Chandrasekaran, *Little America*, p. 208.
223. To understand these tensions better see Chandrasekaran, *Little America*, Chapter 11.
224. Discussions with American colleagues, Helmand, 2009–10.

6. FROM THE US RE-ENGAGEMENT—'COUNTERINSURGENCY', 2009–12

1. 086.
2. SCC.
3. Tony Blair, *A Journey*, London: Hutchinson, 2010, p. 611.
4. Rajiv Chandrasekaran, *Little America*, London: Bloomsbury, 2012, p. 248.
5. Bob Woodward, *Obama's Wars*, London: Simon & Schuster, 2010, p. 127.
6. Matt Pottinger, Paul Batchelor and Michael Flynn, 'Fixing Intel: A Blueprint for Making Intelligence Relevant in Afghanistan', Washington, DC: Center for a New American Security, 2010, pp. 14 and 23.

7. This neatly matches the responsibilities of the three British government departments charged with executing this strategy: the military, the Department for International Development and the Foreign and Commonwealth Office.
8. Theo Farrell and Stuart Gordon, 'COIN Machine: The British Military in Afghanistan', Orbis, 53, 4 (2009), pp. 12–13.
9. For example, 001, 015, 039.
10. 'Afghan Offensive is New War Model', New York Times, 12 Feb. 2010.
11. PersExp, Helmand, 2010.
12. 244.
13. 014, 018.
14. 019.
15. PersExp, Helmand, 2010.
16. 112.
17. British Army, 'Countering Insurgency', pp. 4–9.
18. PersExp, Helmand, 2010–12.
19. 035, 038.
20. PersExp, Helmand, 2011.
21. 007, 023.
22. 059.
23. David Mansfield, 'Between a Rock and a Hard Place', AREU (2012), p. 33.
24. David Mansfield, 'All Bets Are Off!', AREU (2012).
25. 004.
26. 006.
27. 105.
28. 'Taliban Leader Surrenders', The Sun, 22 July 2008.
29. 105.
30. Rudra Chaudhuri and Theo Farrell, 'Campaign Disconnect: Operational Progress and Strategic Obstacles in Afghanistan, 2009–2011', International Affairs, 87, 2 (2011), p. 272.
31. 105. PersExp, Helmand 2009–12.
32. For example, 015, 034, 050. Alex Strick van Linschoten and Felix Kuehn, An Enemy We Created, London: Hurst, 2012, pp. 293 and 346.
33. 047, 051. PersExp, Helmand, 2010.
34. 015, 038.
35. 'Karzai Lashes Out at NATO Over Deaths', New York Times, 16 Mar. 2012.
36. WikiLeaks, 'CENTCOM COMMANDER PETRAEUS JAN 20 MEETING WITH PRESIDENT KARZAI' (23 Jan. 2009).
37. PersExp, Helmand 2009–12. I was lucky in this event: many other times I was manipulated without realising until it was too late.
38. See Introduction.
39. 007, 047, 068.
40. 062, 066.
41. For example, 007, 020, 034, 047.
42. 047.
43. I have drawn heavily on Claudio Franco's and Antonio Giustozzi's forthcom-

ing Afghan Analyst Network's paper 'Introducing the Nezami System Within the Taliban Discourse' in this section.

44. 047. Tom Coghlan, 'The Taliban in Helmand: An Oral History', in Antonio Giustozzi (ed.), *Decoding the New Taliban: Insights from the Afghan Field*, London: Hurst, 2009, p. 143.

45. 018, 040, 220, 231.

46. 047, 050, 201.

47. 202.

48. 201.

49. 047.

50. For example, 231, 239, 254.

51. 201, 202.

52. Franco and Giustozzi 'Introducing the Nezami System' (forthcoming).

53. Pers. Comm. Franco, 2012.

54. Kate Clark, 'The Layha: Calling the Taliban to Account', AAN (2011), pp. 15–16.

55. 201, 202, 209. 'Funds for Taliban Largely Come from Abroad: Holbrooke', *Dawn*, 28 July 2010.

56. See Introduction.

57. 047.

58. 047, 203.

59. Franco and Giustozzi, 'Introducing the Nezami System' (forthcoming).

60. For example, 204, 233, 236

61. 013, 223, 225.

62. 209, 218, 222, 230.

63. Mike Martin, *A Brief History of Helmand*, Warminster: Afghan COIN Centre, 2011, p. 13.

64. Franco and Giustozzi 'Introducing the Nezami System' (forthcoming).

65. 202, 234, 246.

66. Drawn from Franco and Giustozzi, 'Introducing the Nezami System' (forthcoming).

67. 105. Chandrasekaran, *Little America*, p. 289.

68. 215, 234, 246.

69. 204, 216, 234, 238.

70. 215, 217, 221, 246.

71. 239, 241, 242.

72. Until he died on the 3 June 2012 (SMA).

73. For example, 215, 234, 242.

74. 212, 234.

75. 201, 202, 210, 212. Although many of the mahaz commanders are dead, their organisations still take their names.

76. 209.

77. 202, 211, 212, 243, 245.

78. 202, 213.

79. 223, 229, 230.

80. 223, 230.
81. 232, 250.
82. 232.
83. Chandrasekaran, *Little America*, p. 287.
84. 'Taliban Opening Qatar Office, and Maybe Door to Talks', *New York Times*, 3 Jan. 2012.
85. Pers. Comm., Giustozzi and Franco, 2012.
86. Franco and Giustozzi, 'Introducing the Nezami System' (forthcoming).
87. For example, 201, 202, 203, 211, 213, 224.
88. 201, 202, 203.
89. 209.
90. Pers. Comm. Giustozzi, 2012.
91. 201. Franco and Giustozzi, 'Introducing the Nezami System' (forthcoming).
92. 'Afghanistan War Logs: Iran's Covert Operations in Afghanistan', *The Guardian*, 25 July 2010.
93. 038, 058.
94. 209, 218.
95. SMA.
96. 013, 070.
97. Franco and Giustozzi, 'Introducing the Nezami System' (forthcoming).
98. PersExp, Helmand, 2008–12.
99. Martin, *Brief History*, p. 36.
100. 'Is Afghanistan a Narco-State?', *New York Times*, 27 July 2008.
101. 081.
102. 009.
103. 001, 008, 023, 025.
104. 009, 047, 081.
105. 063.
106. For example, 008, 039.
107. PersExp, Nad-e Ali, 2009.
108. 054.
109. Hafizullah.
110. 'NATO in Afghanistan: Helping and Empowering the Locals', NATO TV, 24 July 2009.
111. 015, 016, 023, 039, 067.
112. 039, 050.
113. Stuart Gordon, 'Exploring the Civil–Military Interface and its Impact on European Strategic and Operational Personalities', *European Security*, 15, 3 (2006), pp. 345–7.
114. Stuart Gordon, 'Aid and Stabilization: Helmand Case Study', Chatham House: 2010, p. 37.
115. 050.
116. PersExp, Nad-e Ali, 2010–11.
117. 067, 071.

118. 'Watershed of Waste: Afghanistan's Kajaki Dam and USAID', *Global Post*, 11 Oct. 2011.
119. Chandrasekaran, *Little America*, p. 305.
120. 004, 070.
121. 011, 013.
122. 020.
123. 004.
124. 'Letter from Islamic Republic of Iran to United Nations, Addressed to the Secretary-General A/55/855-S/2001/273', 26 Mar. 2001; J. Etaat and I. Varzesh, 'Hyropolitic of Hirmand: Reasons, Results and Outcomes', *Human Geography Reseach Quarterly*, 80 (2012).
125. 'Corps of Engineers to Improve Access to Water, Power in Southern Afghanistan', www.army.mil, 25 June 2012 (accessed 10 Dec. 2012).
126. 'Iran Seeks its Share of Hirmand [*sic*] Water', PressTV, 15 Apr. 2011.
127. 020, 209, 218. Pers. Comm. Antonio Giustozzi and Claudio Franco, 2012.
128. 063, 068.
129. 'Watershed of Waste: Afghanistan's Kajaki Dam and USAID', *Global Post*, 11 Oct. 2011.
130. Chandrasekaran, *Little America*, p. 81.
131. The sheer volume of such opinions, and the frequency with which they came up in my interviews and interactions, reflect a strong Helmandi perception and hence are worthy of discussion here. The other option, that there exists an extraordinary and widespread campaign against Mangal, I consider to be less likely. This is because of the wide political spread of interviewees who attest to his method of governance (including British and American officials). For balance, in 2011 I asked Mangal for an interview but he declined my offer. See also David Mansfield, 'All Bets Are Off!', AREU (2012).
132. For example, 006, 008, 023, 047, 054, 081, 082, 085.
133. PersExp, Helmand, 2008–12. WikiLeaks, 'HELMAND UPDATE: NEW GOVERNOR BRINGS IMPROVEMENTS, MARINES ENGAGE TALIBAN' (21 July 2008).
134. Helmand Plan Annual Review 2010, 'Helmand PRT/RC(SW)/Regional Platform SW' (2010), p. 2.
135. WikiLeaks, 'HELMAND UPDATE: FOOD ZONE ALLEGATIONS ARE BUILDING AGAINST GOVERNOR MANGAL' (27 Oct. 2009).
136. 'President Hamid Karzai Sacks Helmand Governor in Blow to British Influence', *The Telegraph*, 20 Sep. 2012.
137. 'Todai Khbrai [lit. Hot Talk]', Lemar TV, 2 June 2012.
138. PersExp, Kabul, 31 May 2012.
139. 'Protestors Want Helmand, Logar Governors Fired', *Afghanistan Times*, 24 May 2012.
140. 084.
141. 054.
142. The Gereshk model is based on a large number of author interviews—001, 008, 009, 012, 020, 029, 030, 031, 054, 070, 079—conversations, rumours

and participant-observations conducted in the autumn of 2011 in Nahr-e Saraj in order to understand 'corruption' in Gereshk. Money flow was modelled using i2 analyst notebook. This more informal approach (that is, using conversations, observations and rumours) was required because of the sensitivity and (particularly) the currency of the issue. The model's concepts were verbally tested with 020, 031 and 070, who offered (already incorporated) comments. See Figure 8.

143. Martin, *Brief History*, pp. 47–51.
144. 'How the US Funds the Taliban', *The Nation*, 11 Nov. 2009. I also argue this based on my experiences staying regularly in the Gereshk police station (2010–12): 'the big money in the ISAF trucking' was the enduring theme.
145. For example, House of Commons Public Accounts Committee, 'The Use of Information to Manage the Defence Logistics Supply Chain', 18 July 2011: paragraph 3; UNODC, 'Afghanistan Opium Survey', Oct. 2011, p. 1.
146. 'How the US Funds the Taliban', *The Nation*, 11 Nov. 2009.
147. PersExp, Helmand, 2010–12.
148. 029, 036.
149. PersExp, Lashkar Gah, Nov. 2011.
150. 020, 029.
151. 'New Evidence of Widespread Fraud in Afghanistan Election Uncovered', *The Guardian*, 19 Sep. 2009.
152. PersExp, Helmand, 2010–12.
153. For example, 039, 059, 076.
154. For example, 'Blooming Financial Support', FOX News, 4 Sep. 2009. SCC.
155. WikiLeaks, 'HELMAND GOVERNOR MANGAL UPBEAT, HOPEFUL IN MEETING WITH AMBASSADOR' (27 June 2009).
156. SCC.
157. 'Brown Rejects Criticism from Afghan Leader', *Financial Times*, 26 Jan. 2008.
158. 006 (claimed to have been told this by Karzai), SMA, ARJ; WikiLeaks, 'BROWN URGES KARZAI TO KEEP HELMAND GOVERNOR; PRAISES UNSYG REP' (22 Aug. 2008).
159. WikiLeaks, 'PLANNING FOR GOVERNANCE CHANGES IN HELMAND' (2 July 2009).
160. 'Karzai in his Labyrinth', *New York Times*, 4 Aug. 2009.
161. WikiLeaks, 'HELMAND GOVERNOR SEES SOME PROGRESS BUT BLAMES PRESIDENT,S GOVERNING STYLE FOR PROVINCE,S OVERALL WOES [*sic*]' (26 Feb. 2009).
162. 081.
163. PersExp, Helmand, 2010. I am grateful to Anne SS for tracking these events at the time.
164. 'Exclusive: Official—Troops out of Afghanistan by 2014', *The Independent*, 18 July 2010.
165. Human Rights Watch, 'Just Don't Call it a Militia', New York, 2011, p. 55.
166. Ibid., p. 15.

167. PersExp, Helmand, 2011–12.
168. 035, 039.
169. Habibullah, 040, 057, 075.
170. PersExp, Helmand, 2011–12.
171. 017.
172. 023.
173. 011, 023.
174. 017, 034.
175. 039.
176. 015, 017, 034.
177. 058.
178. 007, 017, 033, 067.
179. 103, 228.
180. 007, 032.
181. 017, 033.
182. 081.
183. 065.
184. 061, 077.
185. 012, 057.
186. PersExp, Helmand, 2011–12.
187. 018, 068, 103.
188. 085.
189. 007.
190. 017.
191. 015, 081.
192. 007, 023, 067, 073, 078.
193. ARJ, MMW.
194. For example, 032, 054.
195. PersExp, Helmand, 2012.
196. 103.
197. 'Eleven Afghan Police Defect to Taliban in Helmand Province', BBC News, 6 Aug. 2012.
198. 'Afghan Police Recruits' Training Halted after Attacks on NATO', BBC News, 2 Sep. 2012.
199. 'Lashkar Gah Transition Should Send "Powerful Signal to Insurgents"', *The Guardian*, 19 July 2011.
200. PersExp, Helmand, 2011–12.
201. 068, 074.
202. 031, 032, 078.
203. 084.
204. 020.
205. SMA.
206. 054.
207. 'Afghanistan's Battle to Re-Integrate Reformed Taliban Fighters', *The Independent*, 22 May 2012.

208. SMA.
209. 069. PersExp, Gereshk, 2012.
210. 007, 023, 039, 081, 084.
211. 'Afghan Believe US is Funding Taliban', *The Guardian*, 25 May 2010; 'CIA Pays for Support in Pakistan: It has Spent Millions Funding the ISI Spy Agency, Despite Fears of Corruption. But Some Say it is Worth it', *LA Times*, 15 Nov. 2009; 'How the US Funds the Taliban', *The Nation*, 11 Nov. 2009.
212. 082.
213. 023.
214. 006.
215. For example, 001, 003, 004, 005, 006, 007, 011, 013, 014, 015, 020, 021, 023, 024, 027, 029, 034, 041, 051, 059, 065, 066, 068, 070, 071, 072, 074, 077, 082, 083, 085, Hafizullah.
216. Redacted.
217. 068, 070.
218. 068, 069.
219. For example, 220, 221, 234, 235, 244.
220. Chandrasekaran, *Little America*, pp. 208–11.
221. PersExp, Helmand, 2010–12.
222. See Introduction.
223. Jean Mackenzie, 'The Battle for Afghanistan: Militancy and Conflict in Helmand', New America Foundation (2010), p. 6.
224. 006, 047, 068, ARJ.
225. 007.
226. 093.
227. Andrew McGregor, 'Karzai Claims Mystery Helicopters Ferrying Taliban to North Afghanistan', *Terrorism Monitor*, 7, 33 (2010). 'Helicopter Rumour Refuses to Die', *IWPR*, 2 Nov. 2009.
228. 'UK Army "Providing" Taliban with Air Transport', Press TV, 17 Oct. 2009.
229. 047, 072, 085, Hafizullah.
230. Unknown, 'FORMER TALIBAN COMMANDER ALLEGES UK SUPPORTS TALIBAN, REGRETS JOINING GOVERNMENT', *Terrorism Monitor*, 8, 26 (2010).
231. 085.
232. 072. He showed me the video, but I could see nothing that linked it to the British.
233. 047.
234. 082.
235. 000.
236. For example, 005, SMA, Jabbar.
237. 004, 066, 068.
238. SCC.
239. 005.
240. 066.
241. 068.

242. 068, 072.
243. 230.
244. 047.
245. 244. PersExp, Helmand, 2009–10.
246. 047.
247. 086.


CONCLUSION

1. Quoted in Peter Tomsen, *The Wars of Afghanistan*, New York: PublicAffairs, 2011, p. 391.
2. William Thomas and D. Thomas, *The Child in America: Behavior Problems and Programs*, New York: Knopf, 1928, p. 571.
3. Although see Emile Simpson, *War from the Ground Up: Twenty-First-Century Combat as Politics*, London: Hurst, 2012, for an excellent analysis of the conflict in Helmand.
4. So described Afghanistan, the UK Defence Secretary Dr Liam Fox MP in May 2010.
5. Edward Said, *Orientalism*, New York: Vintage, 1978, p. 290.
6. Human Terrain Teams are the US method for understanding the Human Terrain. Comprised of social scientists and analysts (some in quite diverse fields such as education), their interface with Helmandis habitually derives through diasporic Afghans that are members of their teams.
7. 048.
8. This was brought home vividly to me when, in Kabul, I would walk about in flip flops visiting Helmandis in their homes and would be passed by British military armoured vehicles, with machine guns mounted. I had been in their position shortly before.
9. Artemy Kalinovsky, *The Blind Leading the Blind: Soviet Advisors, Counter-Insurgency and Nation-Building in Afghanistan*, Wilson Center, 2010, p. 21.
10. Woodward, *Obama's Wars*, London: Simon & Schuster Ltd, 2010, p. 120.
11. Theo Farrell, 'Improving in War: Military Adaptation and the British in Helmand, 2006–2009', *Journal of Strategic Studies*, 33, 4 (2010).
12. Michael Clarke (ed.), *The Afghan Papers*, London: RUSI, 2011, p. 15.
13. 'Rajiv Chandrasekaran on the MAGTF in Afghanistan', *Marine Corps Gazette* (2 July 2012).
14. Kjetil Anders Hatlebrekke and M. Smith, 'Towards a New Theory of Intelligence Failure? The Impact of Cognitive Closure and Discourse Failure', *Intelligence and National Security*, 25, 2 (2010).
15. Artyom Borovik, *The Hidden War*, London: Faber and Faber, 1991, p. 14.
16. Of course, whether solving the Alizai's water issues would resolve the conflict is another matter, but that was expressed narrative.
17. Simpson, *Ground Up*, p. 75.
18. Borovik, *Hidden*, p. 248.
19. Stuart Gordon, 'Aid and Stabilization: Helmand Case Study', Chatham House:

2010, Andrew Wilder and Stuart Gordon, 'Money Can't Buy America Love', *Foreign Policy* (2009), p. 1.

20. Abdulkader Sinno, *Organisations at War in Afghanistan and Beyond*, New York: Cornell University Press, 2009, p. 15.

21. 'Analysis: The Taliban's "momentum" has not been broken', *The Long War Journal* (6 Sep. 2012).

22. 'UK and Afghan Soldiers launch Operation COURAGEOUS MOUNTAIN', *MOD News* (24 Nov. 2011).

23. This emerged when talking with US intelligence personnel in 2012. Apparently, US Special Forces (not based in Helmand) had been talking to Sher Mohammad for years, without being aware of any of the politics in Helmand. This was only discovered when they began to link him up to other branches in the US government because 'he was a really useful guy, and seemed to know loads of people'.

24. Chandrasekaran, *Little America*, London: Bloomsbury, 2012 p. 247.

25. I also wish to point out that the alternative livelihoods programme, in place to support farmers' transition from the opium trade, does not support them adequately, and is often pilfered away before it reaches the farmer.

26. See David Mansfield, 'Between a Rock and a Hard Place', AREU (2012) for a collection of comments from farmers in Helmand about eradication and the government.

27. What is hard to understand is that (even conceptually) eradicating people's poppy is clearly going to drive them away from you: the opposite of what counterinsurgency is meant to do. So even using ISAF's own theoretical constructs their policies make no sense, let alone picking apart their assumptions. I assume eradication was used in a counterinsurgency construct because they were implemented by different bits of the ISAF governments' structures and so were not deconflicted.

28. For example, Woodward, *Obama's Wars*, pp. 258–60.

29. Rudra Chaudhuri and Theo Farrell, 'Campaign Disconnect: Operational Progress and Strategic Obstacles in Afghanistan, 2009–2011', *International Affairs*, 87, 2 (2011).

30. British Army, *Countering Insurgency*; US Army, *Field Manual 3–24: Counterinsurgency*, Washington DC: Department of the Army, 2006.

31. John Mackinlay, 'Is UK Doctrine Relevant to Global Insurgency?', *The RUSI Journal*, 152, 2 (2007), p. 35.

32. British Army, *Countering Insurgency*, para 1–10.

33. Sun Tzu, *The Art of War*, Minneapolis: Filiquarian Publishing, 2006, p. 15.

34. The social-political make-up of the societies in which militaries operate.

35. British Army, *Countering Insurgency*, pp. 3–4.

36. PersExp, Helmand, 2011–2.

37. 'Analysis: The Taliban's "momentum" …', *The Long War Journal* (6 Sep. 2012).

38. 'Beyond US withdrawal: India's Afghan options', Observer Research Foundation (24 May 2012).

APPENDIX 6: SELECTED HELMANDI GUANTANAMO PRISONERS

1. Andy Worthington, *The Guantanamo Files*, London: Pluto Press, 2007, p. 245.
2. 007, 015.
3. WikiLeaks, 'PRT/LASHKAR GAH—POPPY ERADICATION MOVING FORWARD' (8 Mar. 2006).
4. G850.

# SELECT BIBLIOGRAPHY

Adamec, Ludwig (ed.), *Historical and Political Gazetteer of Afghanistan*, vols. 2 and 5, Graz: Akademische Druck und Verlagsanstalt, 1985.

Afghan Embassy, 'News Bulletin', London, 13 Oct. 1989.

———— 'Press Release', London, 18 Jan. 1994.

AfghaNews, 'Provincial News', London: Press Information Committee Afghanistan (Jamiat-e islami), May 1988.

———— 'Provincial News', London: Press Information Centre (Jamiat-e Islami), Apr. 1990.

———— 'Provincial News', Peshawar: Press Information Committee Afghanistan (Jamiat-e Islami), Aug. 1991.

———— 'Provincial News', London: Press Information Centre (Jamiat-e Islami), July 1992.

———— 'Provincial News', London: Press Information Committee Afghanistan (Jamiat-e islami), July 1993.

———— 'Provincial News', London: Press Information Committee Afghanistan (Jamit-e Islami), Nov. 1994.

———— 'Provincial News', London: Press Information Committee Afghanistan (Jamiat-e islami), Apr. 1995.

———— 'Provincial News', London Press Information Committee Afghanistan (Jamiat-e islami), Nov. 1995.

Afghan Information Centre, 'Monthly Bulletin No 91', Oct. 1988.

———— 'Monthly Bulletin No 102', Peshawar, Sep. 1989.

———— 'Monthly Bulletin No 109', Peshawar, Apr. 1990.

———— 'Monthly Bulletin No 113', Peshawar, Aug. 1990.

———— 'Monthly Bulletin No 118', Peshawar, Jan. 1991.

———— 'Monthly Bulletin No 121–2', Peshawar, Apr.–May 1991.

———— 'Monthly Bulletin No 123–4', Peshawar, June–July 1991.

———— 'Monthly Bulletin No 124–5', Peshawar, July–Aug. 1991.

———— 'Monthly Bulletin No 130–1', Peshawar, Jan.–Feb. 1992.

Afghans for Civil Society, 'Loya Jirga Focus Groups: Kandahar and Helmand Provinces', Kandahar, 2003.

Agency Coordinating Body for Afghan Relief, 'Helmand Profile', Quetta: UN Centre for Human Settlements, 1999.

Ahmed-Ghosh, Huma, 'History of Women in Afghanistan: Lessons Learnt for the Future or Yesterdays and Tomorrow: Women in Afghanistan', *Journal of International Women's Studies*, 4 (2003).

Allen, Charles, *Soldier Sahibs: The Men Who Made the North-West Frontier*, London: Abacus, 2001.

Amaj, Eng M. Rabi, 'Helmand Projects Monitor and Supervision Report', Quetta: Islamic Aid Health Center, 1991.

Ashe, Waller (ed.), *Persomal Records of the Kandahar Campaign by Officers Engaged Therein*, London: D. Bogue, 1881.

Barfield, Thomas, *Afghanistan: A Cultural and Political History*, Oxford: Princeton University Press, 2010.

Barker, Kim, *The Taliban Shuffle*, New York: Doubleday, 2011.

Beattie, Hugh, *Imperial Frontier: Tribe and State in Waziristan*, London: Curzon Press, 2001.

Berg, Bruce, *Qualitative Research Methods for the Social Sciences*, Boston: Allyn and Bacon, 2007.

Bishop, Patrick, *3 PARA*, London: Harper Press, 2007.

Blair, Tony, *A Journey*, London: Hutchinson, 2010.

Bonner, Arthur, *Among the Afghans*, Durham: Duke University Press, 1987.

Borovik, Artyom, *The Hidden War*, London: Faber and Faber, 1991.

Braithwaite, Rodric, *Afgantsy*, London: Profile, 2011.

British Army, 'Field Manual Vol 1: Part 10 Countering Insurgency', London: The Stationery Office, 2009.

Caroe, Olaf, *The Pathans*, Oxford: Oxford University Press, 1958.

Cartwright, James, *Sniper in Helmand*, Barnsley: Pen and Sword, 2011.

Caudril, Mildred, 'Helmand-Arghandab Valley: Yesterday, Today, Tomorrow', Lashkar Gah: USAID, 1969.

Centlivres-Demont, Michelle, 'Les Nouvelles d'Afghanistan', *Afghanistan Info*, 32 (1992).

Chandrasekaran, Rajiv, *Little America*, London: Bloomsbury, 2012.

Chaudhuri, Rudra, and Theo Farrell, 'Campaign Disconnect: Operational Progress and Strategic Obstacles in Afghanistan, 2009–2011', *International Affairs*, 87, 2 (2011), pp. 271–96.

Chayes, Sarah, *The Punishment of Virtue*. New York: Penguin, 2006.

Clark, Kate, 'The Layha: Calling the Taliban to Account', AAN, 2011.

Clarke, Michael (ed.), *The Afghan Papers*, London: RUSI, 2011.

Clausewitz, Carl von, *On War*, trans. Michael Howard and Peter Paret, 1984 edn, Princeton: Princeton University Press, 1976.

Coghlan, Tom, 'The Taliban in Helmand: An Oral History', in Antonio Giustozzi (ed.), *Decoding the New Taliban: Insights from the Afghan Field*, London: Hurst, 2009.

Cowper-Coles, Sherard, *Cables from Kabul*, London: Harper Press, 2011.

Crews, Robert, and Amin Tarzi (eds), *The Taliban and the Crisis of Afghanistan*, Cambridge, MA: Harvard University Press, 2008.

Crisis Group Asia, 'Afghanistan: Getting Disarmament Back on Track—Briefing N°35', 2005.

Cullather, Nick, 'Damming Afghanistan: Modernization in a Buffer State', *The Journal of American History*, 89, 2 (2002), pp. 512–37.

Davis, Anthony, 'How the Taliban Became a Military Force', in W. Maley (ed.), *Fundamentalism Reborn? Afghanistan and the Taliban*, Lahore: Vanguard, 1998.

Docherty, Leo, *Desert of Death*, London: Faber and Faber, 2007.

Dorronsoro, Gilles, 'Helmand: Le Dernier Refuge des Khalqis', *Afghanistan Info*, 33 (1993).

——— *Revolution Unending: Afghanistan, 1979 to the Present*, London: Hurst, 2005.

Dupree, Louis, 'The Retreat of the British Army from Kabul to Jalalabad in 1842: History and Folklore', *Journal of the Folklore Institute* (1967), pp. 50–74.

——— *Afghanistan*, New Delhi: RAMA publishers, 1980.

*The Economist*, 'Country Reports—Afghanistan Q1/1995', London, 1995.

Edwards, David, *Heroes of the Age: Moral Fault Lines on the Afghan Frontier*, Ewing: University of California Press, 1996.

——— *Before Taliban*, London: University of California Press, 2002.

Elphinstone, Mountstuart, *An Account of the Kingdom of Caubul, and its Dependencies in Persia, Tartary and India*, 2010 edn, Milton Keynes: Nabu Public Domain reprints, 1839.

Etaat, J., and I. Varzesh, 'Hyropolitic of Hirmand: Reasons, Results and Outcomes', *Human Geography Reseach Quarterly*, 80 (2012).

Farouq, Ghulam, 'Socio-Economic Aspects of Land Settlment in Helmand Valley', Beirut: American University, 1975.

——— 'The Effects of Local, Regional and Global Politics on the Development of the Helmand-Arghandab Valley of Afghanistan', London: School of Oriental and African Studies, 1999.

Farrell, Theo, 'Improving in War: Military Adaptation and the British in Helmand, 2006–2009', *Journal of Strategic Studies*, 33, 4 (2010).

Farrell, Theo, and Stuart Gordon, 'COIN Machine: The British Military in Afghanistan', *Orbis*, 53, 4 (2009), pp. 665–83.

Farrell, Theo, Frans Osinga and James A. Russell (eds), *Military Adaptation in Afghanistan*, Palo Alto: Stanford University Press, 2013.

Feifer, Gregory, *The Great Gamble*, New York: HarperCollins, 2009.

Felbab-Brown, Vanda, *Shooting Up: Counterinsurgency and the War on Drugs*, Washington: Brookings Institution Press, 2009.

Fergusson, James, *A Million Bullets*, London: Transworld Publishers, 2008.

Flynn, Michael, Matt Pottinger and Paul D. Batchelor, 'Fixing Intel: A Blueprint for Making Intelligence Relevant in Afghanistan', Center for a New American Security, 2010.

Folkestad, Bjarte, 'Analysing Interview Data: Possibilities and Challenges', Eurosphere Working Paper Series, 13 (2008).

Gall, Sandy, *Afghanistan: Travels with the Mujahideen*, Sevenoaks: Hodder and Stoughton, 1988.

—— *War against the Taliban*, London: Bloomsbury Publishing, 2012.

Ganguly, Šumit, *Conflict Unending: India–Pakistan Tensions since 1947*, New York: Columbia University Press, 2001.

Gat, Azar, *War in Human Civilisation*, New York: Oxford University Press, 2006.

General Staff India, 'Military Report—Afghanistan: History, Topography, Ethnography, Resources, Armed Forces, Forts and Fortified Posts, Administration and Communications', Delhi: Government of India Press, 1925.

—— 'Military Report—Afghanistan', Simla: Government of India Press, 1940.

—— 'Routes in Afghanistan, South West', Lahore: North Western Railway Press, 1941.

Girardet, Edward, *Afghanistan: The Soviet War*, New York: St Martin's, 1985.

—— *Killing the Cranes*, White River Junction: Chelsea Green, 2011.

Giustozzi, Antonio (ed.), *War, Politics and Society in Afghanistan, 1978–1992*, London: Hurst, 2000.

—— '"Tribes" and Warlords in Southern Afghanistan, 1980–2005', Crisis States Research Centre Working Paper Series, 1, 7 (2006).

—— *Koran, Kalashnikov and Laptop*, London: Hurst, 2008.

—— *Decoding the New Taliban: Insights from the Afghan Field*, London: Hurst, 2009.

—— *Empires of Mud: Dynamics of Warlordism in Afghanistan, 1980–2007*, London: Hurst, 2009.

—— 'The Great Fears of Afghanistan: How Wild Rumours Shape Politics', *Ideas Today*, 4 (2010).

Goodhand, Jonathan, and David Mansfield, 'Drugs and (Dis)order: A Study of the Opium Trade, Political Settlements and State-Making in Afghanistan', Crisis States Research Centre Working Papers Series 2, 83 (2010).

Gopal, Anand, 'The Battle for Marjeh', Center for International Governance Innovation, 2010.

Gordon, Stuart, 'Exploring the Civil–Military Interface and its Impact on European Strategic and Operational Personalities', *European Security*, 15, 3 (2006).

—— 'Aid and Stabilization: Helmand Case Study', Chatham House, 2010.

Grau, Lester, 'Breaking Contact Without Leaving Chaos: The Soviet Withdrawal from Afghanistan', Leavenworth: Foreign Military Studies Office (Army), 2007.

Grey, Stephen, *Operation Snakebite*, London: Penguin, 2010.

Hafvenstein, Joel, *Opium Season*, Guilford: The Lyons Press, 2007.

Harnden, Toby, *Dead Men Risen*, London: Quercus, 2011.

Harpviken, Kristian, *Social Networks and Migration in Wartime Afghanistan*, Macmillan: London, 2009.

Heathcote, Tony, *The Afghan Wars, 1839–1919*, 2003 edn, Stroud: The History Press Ltd, 1980.

Hekmatyar, Gulbuddin, *Secret Plans Open Faces: From the Withdrawal of Russians to the Fall of the Coalition Government*, trans. S.Z. Taizi, edited by S.F. Yunas, Peshawar: University of Peshawar, 2004.

House of Commons, 'The UK Deployment to Afghanistan', London: The Stationary Office Ltd, 2006.

——— 'Operations in Afghanistan: Fourth Report of Session 2010–12', London, 2011.

Human Rights Watch, 'Just Don't Call it a Militia', New York: Human Rights Watch, 2011.

International Crisis Group, 'Afghanistan: The Problem of Pushtun Alienation (Asia Report No 62)', 2003.

Jakobsen, Peter Viggo, and Peter Dahl Thruelsen, 'Clear, Hold, Train: Denmark's Military Operations in Helmand 2006–2010', *Danish Foreign Policy Yearbook* (2011).

Johnson, Rob, *The Afghan Way of War*, London: Hurst, 2011.

Johnson, Thomas, and Chris Mason, 'Understanding the Taliban and Insurgency in Afghanistan', *Orbis*, 51, 1 (2008), pp. 71–89.

Jones, Seth, 'The Rise of Afghanistan's Insurgency: State Failure and Jihad', *International Security*, 32, 4 (2008), pp. 7–40.

Kakar, Mohammad, *Afghanistan: The Soviet Invasion and the Afghan Response, 1979–1982*, London: University of California Press, 1995.

Kalinovsky, Artemy, *A Long Goodbye*, Cambridge: Harvard University Press, 2011.

Kalyvas, Stathis, *The Logic of Violence in Civil War*, Cambridge: Cambridge University Press, 2006.

Kaye, John, *History of the War in Afghanistan*, London: WH Allen and Co., 1878.

Kiley, Sam, *Desperate Glory*, London: Bloomsbury, 2009.

Kvale, Steinar, and Svend Brinkmann, *Interviews: Learning the Craft of Qualitative Research Interviewing*, Thousand Oaks: Sage, 2008.

Labrousse, Alain, 'Les Drogues et les Conflicts en Afghanistan (1978–1995)', *Afghanistan Info*, 38 (1996).

——— *Afghanistan: Opium de guerre, Opium de paix*, Paris: Fayard, 2005.

Linschoten, Alex Strick van, and Felix Kuehn, *An Enemy We Created*, London: Hurst, 2012.

Loyn, David, *Butcher and Bolt*, London: Hutchinson, 2008.

Macdonald, David, *Drugs in Afghanistan*, London: Pluto Press, 2007.

MacGregor, Lt Col. C.M., 'Central Asia: Part 2—A Contribution Towards the Better Knowledge of the Topography, Ethnology, Resources and History of Afghanistan', Calcutta: Office of the Superintendent of Government Printing, 1871.

——— 'Southern Afghanistan Field Force—Section 3', Simla: Quartermaster General's Office, 1880.

Mackenzie, Jean, 'The Battle for Afghanistan: Militancy and Conflict in Helmand', New America Foundation, 2010.

Maconachie, Richard, 'Precis on Afghan Affairs, 1919–1927', Simla: Foreign and Political Department, Government of India, 1928.

Male, Beverley, *Revolutionary Afghanistan: A Reappraisal*, London: Croom Helm, 1982.

Maley, William, (ed.), *Fundamentalism Reborn?* Lahore: Vanguard Books, 1998.

—— *The Afghanistan Wars*, New York: Palgrave Macmillan, 2002.

Mansfield, David, 'All Bets Are Off!', AREU, 2012.

—— 'Between a Rock and a Hard Place', AREU, 2012.

Marsden, Magnus, and Benjamin Hopkins, *Fragments of the Afghan Frontier*, London: Hurst, 2011.

Marston, Daniel, and Carter Malkasian, *Counterinsurgency in Modern Warfare*, Oxford: Osprey Publishing, 2008.

Martin, Mike, *A Brief History of Helmand*, Warminster: Afghan COIN Centre, 2011.

Matinuddin, Kamal, *The Taliban Phenomenon*, Karachi: Oxford University Press, 1999.

McGregor, Andrew, 'Karzai Claims Mystery Helicopters Ferrying Taliban to North Afghanistan', *Terrorism Monitor*, 7, 33 (2010).

Médecins Sans Frontières, 'Exploratory Mission in Helmand', Quetta, 1989.

Misdaq, Nabi, *Afghanistan: Political Frailty and External Interference*, Florence: Routledge, 2006.

Naval Postgraduate School, 'Analyzing the Taliban Code of Conduct', Monterey, 2009.

Nojumi, Neamatollah, *The Rise of the Taliban in Afghanistan*, New York: St Martin's Press, 2002.

The Orkand Corporation, 'Afghanistan: The Southern Provinces', 1989.

Pejcinova, Ana, 'Post-Modernizing Afghanistan', *CEU Political Science Journal*, 5 (2006), p. 32.

Pike, Hew, *From the Frontline*, Barnsley: Pen and Sword, 2008.

Pont, Anna, *Blind Chickens and Social Animals*, Portland: Mercy Corps, 2001.

Poullada, Leon, 'Problems of Social Development in Afghanistan', *Journal of the Royal Central Asian Society*, 49, 1 (1962).

—— 'The Pashtun Role in the Afghan Political System', The Afghanistan Council of the Asian Society Occasional Paper, 1 (1970).

—— 'Reform and Rebellion in Afghanistan, 1919–1929: King Amanullah's Failure to Modernize a Tribal Society', *The ANNALS of the American Academy of Political and Social Science*, 412, 1 (1973).

Rahman, Abdur, *The Life of Abdur Rahman: Amir of Afghanistan*, trans. Mohammad Khan, Cambridge: J. Murray, 1900.

Rasanayagam, Angelo, *Afghanistan: A Modern History*, London: IB Tauris, 2005.

Rashid, Ahmed, *Taliban*, London: Yale University Press, 2000.

—— *Descent into Chaos*, London: Allen Lane, 2008.

Rawlinson, Henry, 'Report on the Dooranee Tribes', 1841.

Roy, Olivier, *Islam and Resistance in Afghanistan*, Cambridge: Cambridge University Press, 1985.

—— 'Le Mouvement des Taleban en Afghanistan', *Afghanistan Info*, 36 (1995).

Rubin, Barnett, *The Fragmentation of Afghanistan*, New Haven: Yale University Press, 1995.

Said, Edward, *Orientalism*, New York: Vintage, 1978.

Schmidt, Farhana, 'From Islamic Warriors to Drug Lords: The Evolution of the Taliban Insurgency', *Mediterranean Quarterly*, 21, 2 (2010), p. 61.

Schofield, Victoria, *Afghan Frontier: Feuding and Fighting in Central Asia*, London: IB Tauris, 2003.

Scott, Richard, 'Letter to Counselor for Narcotics Affairs on Helmand, Islamabad, RE: Trip Report', 10 Feb. 1998.

—— 'Cotton & Alternative Crops Pilot Project, 7 Apr–20 May 02', Lashkar Gah: Central Asian Development Group, 2002.

—— 'Email to USAID: Helmand Follow Up XVII—9 May 2006—Poppies, Cash-for-Work and Cotton Again', 2006.

—— 'Opium Poppy Cultivation in Central Helmand, Afghanistan: A Case Study in Bad Program Management', Paper presented at the 67th Annual Meeting of the Society for Applied Anthropology, Tampa, 2007.

—— 'Reconstruction and Opium Poppy Cultivation in Central Helmand', Paper presented at the Conference on Afghanistan Reconstruction, University of Nebraska, 2008.

Semple, Michael, *Reconciliation in Afghanistan*, Washington: US Institute of Peace, 2009.

Shahzad, Syed Saleem, *Inside Al-Qaeda and the Taliban*, London: Pluto Press, 2011.

Simpson, John, *News from No Man's Land*, London: Macmillan, 2002.

Southby-Tailyour, Ewen, *3 Commando Brigade*, London: Ebury Press, 2008.

—— *Helmand Assault*, London: Ebury Press, 2010.

Tanner, Stephen, *Afghanistan: A Military History from Alexander the Great to the War Against the Taliban*, Philadelphia: Da Capo Press, 2009.

Tapper, Nancy, 'The Advent of Pashtun "Maldars" in North-Western Afghanistan', *Bulletin of the School of Oriental and African Studies*, 36, 1 (1973).

Thomas, William, and D. Thomas, *The Child in America: Behavior Problems and Programs*, New York: Knopf, 1928.

Thompson, Edwina, *Trust is the Coin of the Realm*, Karachi: Oxford University Press, 2011.

Thompson, Paul, *The Voice of the Past: Oral History*, Oxford: Oxford University Press, 2000.

Tomsen, Peter, *The Wars of Afghanistan*, New York: PublicAffairs, 2011.

Tootal, Stuart, *Danger Close*, London: John Murray Publishers, 2009.

Tzu, Sun, *The Art of War*, Minneapolis: Filiquarian Publishing, 2006.

Ucko, David, *The New Counterinsrugency Era: Transforming the US Military for Modern Wars*, Washington, DC: Georgetown University Press, 2009.

UN Drug Control Programme, 'Comparative Survey (Helmand Province)', Peshawar: ADCRP, 1995.

—————— 'Helmand Planning Group—Baseline Survey of Helmand Province', Peshawar: Afghan Relief Survey Unit, 1999.

—————— 'Drought Assessment in Southern Afghanistan', Quetta: UN, 2000.

Unknown, 'FORMER TALIBAN COMMANDER ALLEGES UK SUPPORTS TALIBAN, REGRETS JOINING GOVERNMENT', *Terrorism Monitor*, 8, 26 (2010).

Upreti, Bishnu, *The Price of Neglect: From Resource Conflict to Maoist Insurgency in the Himalayan Kingdom*, Kathmandu: Bhrikuti Academic Publications, 2004.

Urban, Mark, *War in Afghanistan*, New York: St Martin's, 1990.

US Army, 'Field Manual 3–24: Counterinsurgency', Washington, DC: Department of the Army, 2006.

Waldman, Matt, 'The Sun in the Sky: The Relationship between Pakistan's ISI and Afghan Insurgents', Crisis States Research Centre Discussion Papers, 18 (2010).

Weinbaum, Marvin, 'Pakistan and Afghanistan: The Strategic Relationship', *Asian Survey*, 31, 6 (1991).

Wilder, Andrew, and Stuart Gordon, 'Money Can't Buy America Love', *Foreign Policy* (2009).

Woodward, Bob, *Obama's Wars*, London: Simon & Schuster Ltd, 2010.

Worthington, Andy, *The Guantanamo Files*, London: Pluto Press, 2007.

Wynne, Henry LePoer, 'Narrative of Recent Events in Afghanistan, from the Recovery of Candahar to the Conclusion of the Rebellion of Yacoob Khan', Calcutta: Govt of India Foreign Department, 1871.

Zaeef, Abdul Salam, *My Life with the Taliban*, London: Hurst, 2010.

# INDEX

Abdalis 18
Abdul Agha, Haji (Barakzai/
  Shamezai) 57, 116, 150
Abdul Ahad Helmandwal (Noorzai,
  Etihad) 60, 81, 84, 187, 220
Abdul Ahad, Mullah (Ishaqzai,
  Harakat) 52, 94, 100, 103
Abdul Baghi 312–13
Abdul Bari (Alizai/Hassanzai) 120,
  154
Abdul Bari (Alakozai) 99, 190, 308
Abdul Ghaffour, Mullah 102
Abdul Hakim 44
Abdul Haq, Mullah 99, 100
Abdul Kadus 125, 314
Abdul Karim 185, 187
Abdul Khaleq 46, 55, 71, 84, 118,
  128, 140, 168
Abdul Malik 187, 201
Abdul Qader 126
Abdul Qayoum Zakir 57, 101,
  169–70, 191, 204–9, 307
Abdul Rahim, Mullah 100
Abdul Rahman 307
Abdul Rahman Jan 61, 84, 87, 89,
  93–4, 97–9, 102, 113–15, 117,
  120–2, 130, 132–4, 137–8, 142,
  147, 154, 163, 176–8, 192, 221,
  229, 256–7, 309
Abdul Rahman Khan 54, 55, 70,
  83, 84, 118

Abdul Rahman, Mullah (Noorzai)
  99
Abdul Rauf Khadim 224, 307
Abdul Razaq 90, 310
Abdul Raziq 115, 118, 122, 125,
  127, 140, 167, 216
Abdul Salam (Noorzai) 103, 148,
  161, 169
Abdul Sangar 88
Abdul Sattar (Barakzai) 214, 216
Abdul Sattar (Noorzai/Aghezai)
  127, 183, 184, 207
Abdul Wahab 311
Abdul Wahid 127, 302
Abdul Wali Koka (Alizai/Hassanzai)
  161, 166, 170, 224
Abdullah 136
Abdullah Akhund, Mullah 183
Abdullah Ghulam Rasoul (Abdul
  Qayoum Zakir) 307
Abdullah Jan (Barakzai) 89, 94,
  118
Abdullah Jan, Haji (Noorzai) 52,
  133
Abdullah, Mullah 183
Abdur Rahman Khan, emir of
  Afghanistan 24, 25, 26
Abhashak Wadi 51, 75, 97, 123
Abhazan, Helmand 51
Abu Bakr (Alizai) 24, 25
Abu Bakr Khan 8, 165

Achakzai tribe 55, 62, 220
Afghan Military Forces 310
  3rd Commando 125
  93rd Division 88, 89, 94, 96, 97,
    115, 118, 123, 127, 140, 149,
    150, 151, 172, 256
Afghan Information Centre (AIC)
  83
Afghan Local Police (ALP) programme 219–23, 249
Afghan National Army (ANA) 155,
  159, 162, 163, 176–7, 185
*Afghan News* 83, 94
Afghanistan
  963–1187 Ghaznavid Empire 17
  1149–1215 Ghorid Empire 17
  1501–1738 Moghul Empire 18
  1510–1709 Safavid Empire 17,
    18
  1747–1826 Durrani Empire
    19–20
  1826–1919 Emirate of Afghani-
    stan 20–6
  1839–1842 Anglo-Afghan War
    21–2
  1878–1880 Anglo-Afghan War
    24–6
  1919–1973 Kingdom of Afghani-
    stan 26–34, 65
  1973–1978 Republic of Afghani-
    stan 34–6
  1978 Saur revolution 41–2, 255,
    257
  1978–1992 Democratic Republic
    of Afghanistan 41–76, 79–90
  1979–1989 Soviet War 39–41,
    50–76, 235, 240
  1989–1992 Najibullah era 54,
    68–9, 74, 81, 250, 251, 255
  1992–2001 Islamic State of Af-
    ghanistan 78–9, 90–6
  1992–1996 Rabbani era 90,
    92–109
  1996–2001 Islamic Emirate of
    Afghanistan 96–109

  2001–2004 Interim/Transitional
    Administration 111–138
  2001–present Karzai era 65, 87,
    98, 101, 106, 111–56, 157–93,
    195–231
  2001–present US-led War
    111–56, 157–93, 195–231
  2004–present Islamic Republic of
    Afghanistan 138–56, 157–93,
    195–231
  2005 parliamentary elections
    142–3, 150
Agha Mohammad 140
Aghezai clan 60, 73, 102, 147–8,
  184
Ahmad Shah Durrani, emir of
  Afghanistan 19, 20, 23, 26, 43
Ahmad Shah Masoud 78
Ahmad Shah, Mullah 101
Aka, Haji 118, 128
Akhtur Khan 8, 22, 165
Akhtur Mohammad (Guantanamo)
  313
Akhtur Mohammad (Popalzai) 102,
  147, 201
Akhtur Mohammad Mansour
  (Ishaqzai) 145, 152
Akhtur Mohammad Osmani 102
Akhund, Mohammad 183
Akhundzada, Amir Mohammad
  117, 143, 153, 154–5, 161, 224,
  251
Akhundzada, Ghaffour 96–9, 104,
  106, 107
Akhundzada, Nasim 8, 45–6, 49,
  52, 53, 54, 55–6, 63, 69, 70, 71,
  72–3, 75, 76, 79–80, 83, 145,
  256, 314
Akhundzada, Rasoul 53, 56, 71,
  80, 83–9, 91–6, 104, 106, 107,
  109, 257
Akhundzada, Sher Mohammad 8,
  49, 53, 57, 111–13, 115–21, *121*,
  123, 125–9, 132–4, 138, 142,
  143, 145, 150–5, 166, 171, 176,